# HOUSE ON WHEELS
Chapter 1
September, 1950

"What do you mean, your mother won't like it?" Eddie barked pushing his chair away from the dining table. I sensed his frustration but avoided his eyes and continued to clear the dishes from the table.

"Mama says a trip around the country is absurd." I started toward the pantry with the plates when he suddenly stood before me.

"Now wait! You know I love your mother, and she's very practical, but..."
I felt the strength in his hands as he took the dishes from me and placed them back on the table. "This has nothing to do with your mother. Try to understand."

"But..."

"Ssh, listen, Sweetheart." His fingers touched my mouth.

I sat down again and he drew a chair next to me. I watched his face become reflective as he told me about his brother Del.

"He was only 23 when he was killed on Guam in World War II." he said. He shifted in his chair, picked up a spoon and began to trace circles on the tablecloth. "When we received news about his death, I wanted to enlist so badly I ran away and lied about my age."

"But you were still in school."

"That's what my mother told the police when they brought me back from up-state New York."

"I know about your brother; he was a Seabee, right? Your mom told me you were very close." I looked at him for a long moment. "Why are you bringing this up now?"

His eyes focused on an imaginary spot on the table appearing to be lost in a memory. Finally, he looked at me. "I registered for the draft just before graduation. The war ended that summer and I figured this war business was over." He got up to pour himself another cup of coffee. "Now I see there's another war brewing in Korea." He took a sip of his coffee and sat down. "My name is still in the pool; I could still be called up."

"But we're married!" I placed my hand over his. "They'll call the single guys first, won't they?"

"I don't think it'll make a difference," he said quietly. "We have no kids and if my number comes up, I'll have to go."

I reached over and touched his cheek. "Is that why this trip is so important?"

He took my hand and held it in both of his. "When we were kids, Del and I used to talk about visiting the National Parks someday. He called them the seven wonders of the United States." He ran his fingers through his short blond hair. "I guess I'm thinking I kind of owe it to Del." His gaze met mine. "By taking this trip, even if I should get called up, you and I would've lived out both mine and Del's dream, too." He hesitated.

1

"If anything should happen…"

"Stop talking like that!" I bolted up. "Nothing's going to happen!"

It was time to get done with the task at hand. I picked up the dishes and headed for the tiny pantry adjacent to the small paneled dining room.

He followed close behind me. "We can do this, sweetheart."

"I don't see how!" I turned to look at him. "The little money we have in the bank isn't enough for hotels and restaurant meals and whatever else we'll need on the way."

"I'm a journeyman ironworker. I can work anywhere in the country if we run out of cash," he said. "We can sleep in the car and eat baloney sandwiches."

"Baloney sandwiches! Yeah, right, my favorite!" I pushed past him to retrieve the salt and pepper shakers and the butter dish.

"Aw, come on, sweetheart, can't you at least try to think about this?" He bent down to take containers out from the lower pantry cabinet.

I picked up a spoon and began to fill the containers. "I know this is important to you, and it sounds like it could be exciting, but I just don't see how we can afford to do it."

"We've talked about this before," he said, his chocolate eyes pleading. "You know how much this means to me."

I filled the kettle and put it on the gas stove to heat water for the dishes. I turned on the jet and lingered with my hand on the handle, facing the stove. "Do you think I'm ever going to be a mother?"

A moment passed before he answered, "I don't know, kid." He gently lifted my hand from the kettle and turned me around to face him. "I want a family too, but, it just isn't happening." He put his arm around my waist. "We both want a baby and someday it'll happen, but don't you see?" He stroked my short, dark, wavy hair. "If we're ever going to make this trip, now is the time, before I'm called up and before we have kids."

"What about my mother?"

"Your mother?" The kettle began to whistle. He picked it up and turned off the jet. "She'll warm up to the idea when we tell her we'll be visiting her relatives in Canada and Montana." He poured the water into the dishpan.

"Do you really think we'd be able to do that?"

"We can do anything we want to." He picked up the dish towel and swatted her backside. "Now, let's get these dishes done."
***

Eddie had left for work. There was still time before I had to get dressed to catch the bus. I poured myself a second cup of coffee and pondered over the events of the night before. Was Eddie's dream so farfetched? Traveling around the country, seeing places we'd never seen did sound exciting. But how? Sleeping in the car was not my idea of practical travel arrangements. And baloney sandwiches were not appealing to me, not even on picnics. There was a lot to think about. Eddie wanted to leave on the trip in late spring so we'd have the whole summer to travel. There'd be a lot of planning to do before that could happen. I sipped the last of my coffee. A busy workday lay ahead for both of us.

I got dressed in a gray skirt and pale green blouse, then pulled on my gray buttoned jacket, adjusted the lapels and headed for the bus stop. It was a bright sunny fall day. The foliage on the maple tree in the front yard gleamed in warm reds and gold. It wouldn't be long before the cold of winter would be setting in. I thought about how much Eddie wanted this trip. We'd visited Canada and the New England states but Wyoming and Montana were on the other side of the world as far as I was concerned. I was scared and unsure. Part of me said, "let's do this," and another part said, "there's no way we can." What would I say when the subject came up again?

***

"I've been thinking," Eddie said as he carried a bucket of water and a sponge for his Saturday ritual of washing our tan 1948 Studebaker Commander. It was unusually warm for early November. He was barefoot, wearing overalls and a skivvy's shirt.

I frowned. "Are you going to talk about that trip again?" I had my own Saturday morning chores. With my hair wrapped in a red bandana, wearing a red shirt and bib overalls rolled up to just below my knees, I held a mop in my hand as I prepared to tackle the housecleaning chores.

"Hear me out." He put down the bucket and grabbed the mop. "How about if we buy a tent?"

"A tent!"

"It would solve the 'where are we going to sleep' problem."

I rolled my eyes and tried to pull the mop from his grip. "You really think a tent will solve the problem?" I yanked at the mop again. "I don't think so." I adjusted my bandana. "Can you imagine what it's going to be like when it rains?"

"Lots of people go camping in the rain,"

"Well, good for them," I whisked around toward the kitchen, leaving him and the mop and bucket standing in the hallway. Suddenly I turned back to face him. "Honey? What about a trailer?"

"A trailer?" He put the mop in the corner. "That's a thought!" He came toward me. "But trailers can be expensive and we don't want to go into debt."

"If we got one, second hand, maybe we could have it paid off in a couple of months."

Eddie looked hopeful. "That's a great idea. Do you think we can do it?"

I picked up the mop. "Tomorrow's Sunday, maybe we could take a ride to some trailer sales places and see."

He picked me up, mop and all, and swung me around. I giggled. "Okay, that's enough of that. We've still got lots of stuff to do today."

***

At first glance, it wasn't impressive. "This is exactly what you need," Jack, at Stanley's Trailer Sales assured them. "It's right in your price range, five hundred bucks, cash. I can hold it until you get a tow bar hooked up to your car."

The structure was sixteen feet long and home built in masonite. There were two windows in the front, one on either side of the angled central point above the hitch. One long window stretched across the back and two smaller ones graced both sides at the rear. It was dull gray with a faded black dome with the single door next to the driver side window.

"It's not much to look at." I shook my head opening the narrow door to look inside.

"I don't know." Eddie checked under the trailer to examine the axle supporting the

two large wheels. "Five hundred? That's pretty high when you think of all the work

we'll have to do."

Jack kicked a tire. "This is a solid piece of work, and worth every cent."

"I'll give you four hundred."

The dickering continued while I checked the inside. A small, narrow kerosene space heater sat immediately to the left of the door. The faded upholstery and tattered curtains had seen better days. The sickly green breakfast nook below the front windows needed painting and fixing. I finally walked to the doorway and listened for a while. "It's really a mess in here," I said.

"Well..." Jack lifted his brown cap and scratched his head. "I said it needs a little work." He adjusted his green and yellow-striped tie and brushed off imaginary dust from his beige shirt. "Four seventy-five."

I stepped out and watched as Eddie took one last look inside. "It has possibilities, but I won't be able to rig up my car with a hitch for another couple of weeks," he said. "Four hundred and you store it. That's my offer."

"Tell ya what!" Jack pointed a bony finger at Eddie. "Gimme me a down payment today, and we'll deliver it for ya." He scratched his ear. "Four fifty."

I looked at Eddie, shrugged and nodded my assent.

Eddie beamed. "Looks like we've got a deal."

\*\*\*

Because our apartment yard was too small to store the trailer, Eddie's parents had agreed to accept delivery. During the winter months, Eddie and his dad, Leo, spent weekends making repairs on the inside walls and cabinets, transforming the drab green into bright white. My mother, Aura, and I made blue and red naughahide covers for the cushions in the breakfast nook and white organdy curtains for the front windows. We sewed a new green, blue and red-striped slipcover for the sofa and matching curtains for the rear and side windows. The space heater and chimney were refurbished with heat-resistant black paint. On a warm day in early spring, the dull gray on the outside was painted bright fire-engine red and the dome gleamed in silver. We stocked the cabinets and drawers with dishes and utensils as well as non perishable food. Linens and extra blankets fit well in the storage area under the sofa. All seemed to be going well for an early May departure. Both Eddie and I worked as much overtime as we could to increase our nest-egg which Aura saved for us. She agreed to wire the funds, as needed, via Western Union, should we run out of money during the trip.

"I've written to Aunt Marie and Uncle Louis to tell them about your visit," Aura said admiring the little kitchen. "They've written back and they can't wait to see you."

"We're excited too," I said. "This will be our house on wheels for the next few months."

\*\*\*

Everything was going according to plan when suddenly, in mid-April, Eddie got up one morning feeling nauseated. A severe pain gripped his right side. Unable to walk, he collapsed on the bedroom floor of our apartment. I called my father and we rushed him to Saint Anne hospital where he underwent an emergency appendectomy.

"The appendix burst as I was removing it," Doctor Bludd told me in the waiting area. "We almost lost him in the operating room."

"Will he be all right?" I twisted my moist handkerchief. "How long will he have to stay in the hospital?'

"It's hard to say," the doctor looked at me intensely. "He's a pretty strong guy; we'll just have to keep an eye on him."

I sat at his bedside every day, leaving him only when the nurse sent me away at the end of visiting hours. On the third day after surgery, Eddie developed a high fever.

"I'm going to have to go in again," the doctor said. "The incision is infected."

"But...! What happened?" I fought back the tears.

"There's no need to panic," said Dr. Bludd. "Just let me get a look inside and we'll take it from there."

Eddie's body was motionless, his face ashen. Please, Lord, help him, I prayed silently as the nurses in their starched white uniforms and stiff caps pushed the gurney down the corridor to the operating room.

CHAPTER 2

"Come on, kid, it's three o'clock," Eddie said, shaking me awake. "We've got to get moving if we're going to beat the morning traffic through Boston." He was already dressed in his gray slacks and his maroon and gray sweater. "Are you ready to drive?"

"Not really," I groaned. "How can you be so wide awake at this hour?"

I could hear him whistling "California Here I Come" as he clanked the cereal bowls in the pantry.

"This is the big day, sweetheart," he said.

I rolled out of bed, pulled on a pair of dark blue slacks and slipped into a red checkered blouse. "I know," I said, sounding a bit sleepy as I slipped on my penny-loafers.

"Come on, let's eat." He pulled out a chair and motioned me to sit down. We gulped down our corn flakes and did a quick tidying up. One last look around the house and we were on our way.

The pale moon and bright stars lit up the dark blue sky in the early morning hours. Everything was quiet in the neighborhood.

We had hitched the trailer to the car the night before, so we could slip out of Fall River, Massachusetts long before dawn. Doctor Bludd had agreed to the June 1st departure for our trip, provided Eddie would not drive or do anything strenuous until mid-June.

I got settled behind the wheel. I double-checked the electric hand-brake on the steering wheel, which controlled the trailer. South Main street was clear of traffic as I pulled away from the curb. An occasional car passed us as we headed down to Davol Street and crossed the Taunton River over the Brightman Street Bridge. "I can't believe we're really on our way," I said.

"Yeah." Eddie smiled broadly. "A week or so ago I didn't think the doctor would give his okay."

I kept an eye on the side view mirrors to make sure the trailer followed behind. BANG! I stiffened and flinched.

Eddie looked back. "What the hell was that?"

"I don't know." My hands gripped the wheel in panic. I yanked on the hand brake and pumped the foot brake. "I'm pulling over."

Eddie bounded out of the car. "Geez, it's a blowout on the trailer tire! We'll have to unhitch the trailer to get the tire fixed."

He knocked on the trunk of the car. "Open it up and get the jack."

I pulled out a carefully wrapped package. "Here, is this the right one?"

"There's only one jack," he snapped. "Pull it out of the cloth."

"What's this rod for?"

"Don't worry about the rod until you make sure that flat surface is lined up with the axle, close to the wheel."

My patience grew thin as my lack of experience in tire changing made the project more difficult. Eddie's limited ability to help was even more frustrating because of his unlimited ability to bark directions.

6

"Now, stick the rod into that hole and start pumping," he ordered. "Are you sure the jack is lined up?"

"For crying out loud, do you wanna do this?" I shouted. "I'm doing the best I can here."

"Okay, okay. Just keep pumping. I think the wheel is almost off the ground. Now take out the lug wrench."

"I can't move these bolts or whatever they are!"

"Lugs!" His voice became louder. "Keep trying. Stand on the wrench, your weight will give you leverage." He leaned closer to me.

"Oh, fine, now we're going to talk about my weight!"

"Oh, brother!" He rolled his eyes.

As I leaned on the trailer and jumped on the lug wrench, the first lug gave way. I landed on one knee on the gravelly shoulder of the road. With renewed determination I finally removed the wheel, unhitched the trailer, loaded the wheel into the car and headed back to Fall River. It was just past 4:00 a.m. when I saw the Esso station open on Davol Street.

With a new tire in tow, I headed back. The first rays of dawn appeared in the sky as I crossed the bridge. Yellow, orange, purple and red streaks of sunlight painted the horizon. The reflection of the swamp maples in the smooth water along the riverbank had a calming effect on me. As I approached South Street in Somerset, I saw Eddie leaning against the disabled trailer. He approached the car as I backed into the space ahead of the trailer.

"We'd better get busy," he said. "We don't want to be in the middle of that Boston traffic."

Just as I was rolling the tire out of the car, a trucker pulled up ahead of us.

"Need help?" He asked.

"Sure do," I said gratefully.

He extended his hand to Eddie. "Name's Jerry"

"Hi. I'm Eddie and this is the wife." As they shook hands Eddie said, "I just had surgery…"

"Not to worry," Jerry said. "Where are the tools?"

Eddie pointed to the jack on the ground. Jerry got to work and in no time replaced the tire and re-hitched the trailer. Jerry refused Eddie's offer to pay him. The two men shook hands, "Glad I could be of help for the lady," Jerry said looking at me.

Within minutes, Jerry was back in his truck and on his way.

Confident our problems were over; I resumed my place behind the wheel. I looked at my watch. "It's six o'clock, and we were still an hour and a half from Boston."

"We'll be there right in the middle of traffic," Eddie said.

"I know." I kept up with the pace of traffic and watched the trailer in the rearview mirror for any signs of trouble. "Maybe we'll be lucky."

Barely fifteen miles further, as we passed through Taunton, the trailer began to wobble again. I spotted a Shell service station ahead and pulled in.

"What now?" Eddie muttered.

The service attendant came over to examine the vehicle. "Looks like you've got a flat."

"We just bought that tire," I exclaimed to Eddie.

"Might have picked up a nail or something," said the tall young man in a blue uniform. He set his equipment under the axle to remove the tire as Eddie supervised the

7

procedure.

I watched. Could this be an omen? We were barely 30 miles from home and it had taken us more than four hours to get this far.

This dream trip was becoming a nightmare. Less than an hour later the service attendant had finished the job and we were on our way. Traffic began to pick up around Brockton, and by the time we reached Boston, it was stop and go with drivers in a hurry to get to work. Horns honked. Brakes squealed. Cars advanced at a snail's pace. I edged my way north onto the Mystic River Bridge as a taxicab tried to pass on the right. CRUNCH!

"What was that?" I screamed.

"It's a cab." Eddie bellowed. "It looks like he hit the side of the trailer."

We got out of the car to assess the damage and found a small piece of wood had been pulled from the rear corner of the trailer.

"Do you know how much time I'm losing here?" the cabbie yelled.

"What were you doing passing on the right?" I shouted.

Raging commuters stuck their heads out of their cars.

"Move that heap out of the way!"

"Can't you see you're tying up traffic?"

"Geez, I'm going to be late for work!"

With both thumbs in his belt, the cabbie calmly hiked his dark grey work pants over his plump belly. He tugged at the collar of his red plaid shirt, then removed his leather cap and raked his fingers through his thinning hair. He shrugged and turned his head, first looking to one side then the other. Then with an outstretched palm he leaned toward Eddie and said: "Hey, if you give me ten bucks I could forget the whole thing!"

"Forget what?" We chimed in disbelief.

"I don't see any damage to your cab," Eddie yelled.

A police officer arrived on the scene. "What's going on here?"

"This cab was passing us on the right and a piece of wood broke off from our trailer," I wailed.

"They don't have any sign saying 'Wide Load'," said the cabbie.

The officer calmly walked around the vehicles. He raised his cap, scratched his head and said, "I don't see much damage here. Is anybody injured?"

"No, but this guy banged into us and he's complaining about losing money," I said.

The officer rolled his eyes. The halted commuter line was getting longer and the cacophony of angry voices and horns and engines grew louder. He put his fists on his hips. "Get back in your cars and move." The officer barked. "You're holding up traffic."

"That's it?" I grumbled. "That cab hit us; he was wrong."

"It's okay, kid," Eddie said.

He nodded to the officer and grabbed my elbow leading me to the car.

"Let's go." He said settling me in the driver's seat.

That was the third mishap, and according to the old saying 'things come in threes', I reasoned our problems should be over.

\*\*\*

It was noon by the time we reached the New Hampshire border. We made good time as we traveled northward.

"I'm getting hungry," I said.

"Yeah, me too." Eddie said. "There's a wide shoulder up ahead. Why don't you pull over?

I eased the trailer to the side of the road. The air was crisp. It felt good to stretch. The coffee was still warm in the thermos and I pulled out the sandwiches from the picnic basket in the back seat.

"Do you think we'll get to the Canadian border tonight?" I bit into my peanut butter sandwich.

"I doubt it." He took a sip of coffee. "New Hampshire is a pretty long state and the mountains will slow us down."

"Yeah, those delays really hurt us." I drank the last of my coffee.

Eddie looked around the car and the trailer "Everything looks all right." He turned to me. "Are you still okay to drive?"

"Sure, why not?" I sat behind the wheel. "What else can happen?"

"Yeah. Three's the magic number!" He smiled. "Hey! You did good. I'm sorry I yelled at you back there."

"Thanks." I eased my way back onto the road. "I guess we won't get to Tante Marie's until late tomorrow."
***

Soon the majestic White Mountains loomed before us. The Old Man of the Mountain, whose profile is forever etched in stone, appeared to beckon us on. The calm reflection in Mirror Lake seemed to have swallowed the surrounding mountains and trees in its crystal water. The quiet tramways on Twin Mountains were evidence of a ski season succumbing to spring.

The car lumbered up the winding steep road. On the downward slopes I found myself using the electric trailer brake almost constantly as we made our way to the base of the mountain.

The first long shadows of evening appeared as we entered Colebrook.

" I think it's time to call it a day, kid." Eddie said. "Let's see if we can find a trailer
park."

A few miles down the highway we saw the neon sign of Cozy Nook, just past Cole-brook: Trailers welcome

$1.00.

Eddie waved directions as I backed into our assigned spot. I had no

problem going forward but parking this small monstrosity was another thing.

"How many times do I have to tell you?" Eddie waved his arms in

desperation. "When you're backing up you need to turn the wheels to

the left for the trailer to go right." His arms flailed as though he was fighting

off a swarm of bees. "A little more to the left...no, no, no turn right!"

"Okay, okay, I'm doing the best I can!" Finally the trailer edged into the parking

space and I breathed a sigh of relief.

9

We unhitched the trailer and connected the electricity and water. Supper was easy, thanks to Campbell's and our little electric hot plate. It was a glorious evening. The last pink rays of sunset over the lake had given way to the first star and the rising moon. We sat at the picnic table beneath the maple trees enjoying our soup and salad.

"It was quite a day wasn't it?" Eddie said.

"Yeah, but we got through it."

"You did okay with the trailer, Kid," he said. "The way you backed in here, I bet you'd be able to apply for a truck driver's job."

I glared at him. "Not in your life."

We sat quietly in the cool night air, giddily recounting the events of the day. A cricket sang in the nearby trees.

"How about pouring us a glass of wine?" I said.

From our "wine cellar" beneath the couch, cushioned between the linens, he pulled out a bottle of Merlot and filled our glasses.        He kissed me gently. "Here's to our first night in our house on wheels,"

Chapter 3

Eddie was up and dressed by the time I opened my eyes. I felt a chill and reached for my blue satin robe. As I wrapped it around myself, I peeked out the window. The sun reflected a golden path across the blue waters of the lake. I glanced at the Big Ben alarm clock perched on the counter. "It's only five-thirty! What time did you get up?"

"I guess it was about four," he said, pulling a frying pan out from under the counter. "I'll get breakfast ready while you hit the shower."

I grunted as I folded the bed linens, tucked them under the folding couch, and gathered my clothes from the tiny closet.

"We still have to hitch up the trailer." He reached for the bacon and eggs in the ice box. "We should get going as soon as we can."

I nodded sleepily, and proceeded to the shower house where three empty stalls awaited. I stepped into the center one, adjusted the water temperature and pulled the lever, allowing the stream of hot water to relax my body. Yesterday had been a trying day; I hoped this day would go more smoothly. I got dressed in a navy and white striped dress and penny loafers, combed my short hair and headed back to the trailer.

Bacon, eggs and toast were already on the table. "Come and get it!" Eddie said, motioning for me to sit down.

The smell of bacon and coffee permeated the air as we sat together for our first breakfast in our trailer.

"Shall I put some of this hot coffee in the thermos?" I asked, picking up the pot from the hot plate.

"Sounds like a good idea." He gathered the dishes while I filled the large thermos.

Working together, the tiny kitchen was cleaned up in no time.

"I think I saw a gas station up the street as we pulled in last night," Eddie said, putting the last of the dishes in the cupboard.

"Maybe we should wait until we get closer to the border before we gas up."

"You're probably right." He took one last look around. "There's no telling how much gas will cost in Canada. "

It was close to seven-thirty when we entered Hereford, Vermont. Driving through the center of town, I pointed to a sign with the flying red horse.

"Hey, there's a Socony station," I said. "Look!"

Last chance to fill up before entering Canada.

"17.7 cents a gallon!" Eddie said. "Geez, you can tell we're close to the border. It's gonna cost us at least two bucks to gas up! "

I edged the car close to the glass topped pump, keeping an eye on the trailer in the side view mirror.

An attendant wearing a blue uniform leaned to the open window. "What'll it

11

be?"

"Fill 'er up." Eddie got out of the car and looked around. "Are we close to the border?"

"Yeah, just keep going straight, about a mile or so." He adjusted his blue cap. "How far are you going?"

"Rimouski."

"That's pretty far up." He disconnected the hose. "I hear they're doing a lot of work on the roads up there." He walked toward Eddie. "That'll be $1.75. You'll want to watch it with this load you're carrying."

"We've got a good driver." Eddie nodded toward me.

The attendant pumped the large handle on the side of the pump to refill the 10 gallon glass storage top.

"Hey, drive slow!" The attendant smiled and tapped the window as I started the car.

When we crossed into Canada, it was as though we'd entered another world. Vast farmlands and small cottages dotted the countryside. The trailer danced behind us, pitching and swaying over the stones on the narrow unpaved roads. Here and there a farmer leaned on his hoe to watch and wave as we drove along. The time passed quickly as we sang along with Arthur Godfrey who wailed on the radio about looking for 'Florence' among the Thousand Islands on the Saint Lawrence iver.

"We must be getting close to Quebec city," Eddie said. "The roads are oiled and smoother."

Farmlands disappeared as we came closer to the city and houses were closer to each other as well.

"We should be seeing Chateau Frontenac pretty soon."

"No sooner said!" Eddie pointed his finger straight ahead. "There it is. Slow down a little."

The street just past Chateau Frontenac led to the ferry, in old Quebec, which crossed the St. Lawrence River to Levis and the road leading to Rimouski in Northern Quebec.

"I think we have to go down that cobblestone road to get to the ferry." I said.

"Look at that line of trucks and cars. It's bumper to bumper, all the way down."

"I hope we can get on."

"I don't think that'll be a problem." Eddie said. "That's a pretty big ship."

" Par ici (this way)," the ferry guide shouted in French.

I kept my eyes focused on the guide as I gripped the wheel and edged the car and trailer onto the ferry.

"Cars on this side, trucks over there." He waved a large green flag. "Hey, you!" He pointed at me. "Get with the trucks on the lower level. All passengers topside."

Once the car was safely parked in its spot for the crossing, we made our way to the top level with the other passengers, happy we didn't have to unhitch the trailer.

"This has to be one of the narrower spots on the Saint Lawrence River." Eddie said. "It shouldn't take us too long to get across."

" I don't care how long it takes." I said. "What an incredible view!"

From topside we observed Quebec's skyline dominated by the green towers of the chateau. Perched on a cliff, the hotel looked like an ancient fortress overlooking the old city and harbor below, where stone buildings stood, reminiscent of structures built in 16th century France. As we approached Levis, we could see boat houses and cargo ships and their shimmering reflections which lined the shore.

"According to Mama's directions," I said, "if we head north on the road along the river, it'll take us about five hours to get to Bic."

"That's if the roads are good."

A loud whistle shrieked as we approached the dock in Levis. "All passengers and drivers, please return to your vehicles," the guide announced on the loudspeaker. He waved his flag directing the orderly disembarkation. Once off the ferry, vehicles turned in varied directions. Some turned south toward La Beauce and others turned north toward Rivière du Loup and Rimouski. Drivers were forced to leave wide spaces between their cars to allow the blinding clouds of dust to settle. The road was narrow and unpaved but well-maintained.

"See if you can get something on the radio." I said.

"I don't know." Eddie fiddled with the dial. "There's a lot of static. We're pretty far away from any U.S. stations."

"What about Canadian stations?"

"They keep fading in and out." He sat back and began to whistle On Top of Old Smokey.

I began to sing along. "...all covered with snow. I lost my true lover, from courting so slow."

Small fishing villages appeared and disappeared along the river bank, as we moved between rolling hills and the sea. Traffic thinned out as cars made right and left turns into their respective villages.

It was late afternoon by the time we reached Bic on the shore of the Saint Lawrence in Rimouski county.

Entering the village, we passed a small railroad station. Hotel Laval, once owned by my uncle Joseph Morin, stood a few feet away. The only gas station in town occupied the small block across the street from the hotel. The tall stone tower of Saint Cecile's Catholic Church dominated the center of the village and the grey stone rectory stood next to it. An apothecary and a country store, which also served as a Post Office, faced the church, completing the commercial picture. Well kept, small country houses dotted the landscape within walking distance of the church.

"I guess the church parking lot is as good a place as any to park this thing," I said.

"I don't see anywhere better." Eddie got out of the car.

"Let's go up to Matante's before we unhitch." I looked around.

"Yeah, just in case we have to move it."

"Right." I picked up my purse from the back seat. "It's only a short walk up her street."

Tante Marie's small white house stood at the base of Mount Saint Louis, in the cul-de-sac of a short street facing the church. Perched behind the house on the 500 foot hill stood a twenty-seven foot iron cross, set on top of a sixteen foot granite base, to which was attached a wooden crucifix. The cross was visible from anywhere in the village. When lit up at night, the glow filled the sky for miles around. Access to the cross was from a set of stone steps about twenty feet from Tante Marie's house.

Two wide windows, trimmed in blue on either side of the matching front door, peeked onto the latticed porch, which extended across the full length of the cottage. A small wooden structure, carefully constructed over a large fissure behind the house, eliminated the need for interior plumbing. Before ascending the steps to the front door, we passed between rows of neatly planted vegetables in Tante Marie's garden. The house seemed to hover on the fringes of the past. Although there were electric wires and street lamps in the village, none reached this house.

Before we could knock, the door flew open. "I've been watching for you!" Tante Marie reached out and gathered us both in a warm embrace. "I received your mother's letter a few days ago and she told me you'd be coming."

Her lively brown eyes sparkled through round wire-rimmed glasses. She was a tall angular woman with wavy gray hair tucked neatly into a chignon at the nape of her neck and held together with a fine hairnet. She wore a blue and white cotton, flowered print dress, lisle stockings, black Enna Jettick shoes and a white bib apron. Her large hands, no longer graceful, bore evidence of many years of hard work, yet her touch was soft and gentle. "Come in, come in." She said, not giving us a chance to respond. "Where did you leave your car?"

"In the church parking lot," Eddie said. "I hope that's okay."

"We'll go down later and talk to Monsieur le Cure (the pastor)." She immediately began to fix dinner for us.

"You must be hungry!" She drew water from the big green pump, fastened to a large white porcelain sink, which stood against the far wall close to the side entrance of the house.

"This is a new water pump." She said filling the copper kettle. "I've only had it a few months. It draws water from the well on the other side of the house"

Turning to Eddie she said, "Will you get some wood to stoke up the stove?"

She placed the kettle on the black surface of her large Franklin stove, which dominated the back wall of the kitchen, facing the front door."You know what to do."

In an instant she pulled the kitchen table aside and removed a hand-woven multi-colored scatter rug which revealed the trap door leading to a root cellar. She yanked it up and disappeared down the narrow wooden steps. She re-emerged a few seconds later, her head and shoulders visible above the opening in the floor.

"What would you like?" She plopped down three mason jars, containing beef, pork and chicken then rested her elbows on the floor.

I shrugged. "I guess chicken would be nice."

"Good." She disappeared under the floor and a moment later reappeared. "Here, grab these." She handed me some fresh potatoes, carrots, a jar of home-canned green beans and a jar of blueberries. She climbed up, closed the trap door and replaced the rug.

Eddie stoked the stove with quick-burning kindling. While Auntie fixed the cobbler, I prepared the vegetables. Within an hour, we all sat down to a dinner of creamed chicken, mashed potatoes, carrots, green beans and blueberry cobbler for dessert.

During the summer months, the sun doesn't set until past ten o'clock in northern Canada. It was still light by the time the dishes were done. It was a balmy evening as we walked back to the church. From the parking lot we had a clear view of the river. The orange sun cast purple shadows in the western sky as the last rays of light shimmered on the water..

"I don't know if Monsieur le Cure is still up," Matante (my aunt) said. "Even if he's not, I'd like to see the little house your mother wrote me about."

As we got closer to the church, we saw a group of nearby residents gathered around the trailer. There were a few quick introductions and handshakes before Matante noticed the lights in the pastor's house and went over to knock on the door. It wasn't long before they emerged from the rectory. The priest was wore his black cassock and biretta.

"You'll have to park that thing way over in the corner," Monsieur le Cure said, walking around the trailer and car. "I don't want it in the way in case we have a funeral." He adjusted his biretta and stood next to Tante Marie, supervising as Eddie directed while I moved the trailer to the designated area. When the maneuver was over, he bowed graciously to Matante, "Mademoiselle", and returned to the rectory. She walked toward the trailer.

"You plan to live in this thing?" Tante Marie asked, bending her head to step through the door.

"We have everything we need in here," I said, showing her around.

"Well, you won't be staying in here tonight, or any night while you're here. I've got your room all set up in the attic." She reached in and grabbed a piece of luggage. "I'll help you bring up your suitcases."

It was settled. The trailer would stay in the churchyard and the car would be used to visit relatives. Eddie and I would sleep in the attic. Tante Marie had spoken.

"Here, put the suitcases in the dining room for now." She opened the door on the back wall, which extended from behind the stove up to the sink. Besides the dining room, there were two bedrooms. All the rooms were accessed from the kitchen. On the back wall, to the right of the sink, was an L-shaped stairway leading to the attic. Through the door, left of the sink, there was a hallway leading to a storage area under the stairs for wood, snow shoveling equipment, gardening tools, along with special cubby-holes for overshoes. The door to the out-house was at the end of this hallway. We received our instructions:

"When you finish your business," Matante demonstrated, "take a full scoop of powdered lime from the box and sprinkle it in the hole. If you don't think it's enough, use another scoop and that should do it."

Potty chambers were strategically placed in little wooden seats in every bedroom, each of which was decorated with a print skirt to match the bedroom decor. Each room was also equipped with a washbowl and pitcher, placed neatly on a small table with a towel and a wash cloth.

"Now, at night," she warned. "Never go outside, use the potty." She never told us why. We never asked. We picked up our luggage before going upstairs for a tour of our bedroom. Here was a large single room where two weaving looms sat next to each other with a spinning wheel behind them. One loom was for fine wool and the other for heavy blankets or rugs made from narrow strips of cotton fabric. On both sides of the room, crisp white curtains hung at the double windows, giving the room a homey look. Facing the far window stood a double bed with a hand carved headboard. Under the eaves there was an army-style cot on one side and several trunks and boxes stacked neatly according to their contents.

"Good night, you two, make yourselves at home." Matante pointed to the wind-up clock on the side table next to the bed. "No need to set the alarm., I'll let you sleep in the morning." She hugged us "It's been a wonderful day, but I'm ready to turn in." She handed me the kerosene lamp and we walked to the stairs. The light from the kitchen cast an eerie glow. I followed Matante half way down the steps and watched her disappear into her room on the other side of the kitchen.

Eddie rummaged through the luggage. "Where are my pajamas?"

"Pajamas?" I turned to look at him in the dim light of the kerosene lamp. "How come all of a sudden you need pajamas? You haven't needed them before."

"I don't know." He peeked out the screened open window into the darkness. A few stars had already made an appearance. "I just thought maybe I should have pajamas on in case Matante comes up here for something."

"If you're that worried, you can throw on my peignoir."

"Don't be silly."

I pulled out the blue satin robe. "I don't know if it'll fit, but it's here at the foot of the bed."

"Of course it'll fit. Are you kidding?" He pulled the narrow-sleeved garment over his broad shoulders. "I'll just prove to you what a dumb idea this is." He struggled to force his arms in.

"Hey, you're the one who suddenly feels the need to be covered."

His brawny shoulders did not compliment the dainty beige lace edging the narrow collar and the V neckline which didn't quite close over his slightly hairy chest. I snickered. He was a unique sight in the pale light of the lamp.

"I can't close it and my arms are stuck!" He yanked at the silky creation. "You should've packed my pajamas."

"I should've...?"

"Help me get this thing off."

He sat down on the edge of the bed to enlist my help. At that moment the bedboards collapsed and we both landed on the floor and began to laugh hysterically. In a matter of seconds, Matante appeared at the top of the stairs. Eddie and I stiffened. Her kerosene lamp cast long, eerie shadows on the walls and slanted ceiling. Appearing like a phantom in her long flowing white nightgown and nightcap, she held the lamp in one hand and lifted the skirt of her nightgown with the other. Her gray hair hung down her back in one long braid.

"Are you both all right?" She froze when she spied Eddie in the blue robe. For a long moment, everyone appeared to be in suspended animation, just staring at one another.

Tante Marie broke the silence. "Humph, what happened here?" She did not wait for an answer, her eyes tactfully avoiding both of us. "Lift up the mattress on your side." She nodded to Eddie as he tried to tie the blue sash around his waist.

He dropped the sash and obeyed.

"Now line up the boards so they are straight and parallel with each other."

I did what I was told.

"Now be careful when you put the mattress down. One, two, three."

The task was complete.

"Good night, sleep well." She turned away, walked past the looms and disappeared down the stairs. The shadows followed in the glow of her lamp.

"I'm sure glad the light was dim so she couldn't see our red faces," I admitted.

"Me, too. Now help me get this thing off."

I tugged at the collar and the sleeves until he was finally free.

"Okay, I guess the first thing we shop for will be pajamas," Eddie said.

"Good idea."     .

A soft breeze wafted in to cool the summer night. Somewhere a cricket chirped as we slid beneath the counterpane and drifted off to sleep.

Chapter 4

Eddie came in from the back porch with an armful of wood as Matante and I were coming in from morning mass at Ste. Cecile's. I walked over to kiss his cheek "Hey, you look like a ray of sunshine in that yellow dress," he said, placing the wood in the box next to the stove.

Tante Marie removed her black coat and straw hat, hung them up on the clothes tree in the corner of the kitchen and quickly donned her white print apron over her navy-blue polka dotted dress. She reached for the gray enamelware coffee pot on the shelf. "Today we're going fishing," she said pumping water into the pot. "I saw Cousin Lionel at mass this morning and we'll meet him at his house after breakfast."

"Where does he live?" Eddie asked, adding kindling to the stove.

"He lives on the other side of the railroad tracks, near the river." Matante added coffee to the pot and placed it on the stove.

"Tante Marie says Lionel has a boat." I took the plates down from the cupboard.

"Yes, and he invited us to go salmon fishing," she adjusted the bib on her apron. "We'll have breakfast first then we can get changed."

I continued to set the table while she mixed the batter for biscuits. With lightning speed they were ready for the oven. Scrambled eggs and ham in her iron skillet were next.

Matante and I worked well as a team. Hardly a word between us, yet we moved from one task to another. I retrieved the jelly and applesauce from the cache beneath the floor and continued to set the table.

"Come on let's sit down, everything is ready. Lionel will be waiting for us." She set the biscuits on the table in a napkin-lined basket followed by a tray of ham and eggs.

"Now this is a real feast," Eddie said. "I think you two must have set a record in getting this put together."

"Never mind the chatter, just eat up," Matante said. "We still have to change into our fishing clothes. We don't want to keep Lionel waiting."

"I don't have to change," Eddie said. "I'll clean up while you two get ready."

Eddie wore navy slacks, a red, green and blue multi-striped sweater and sneakers. I wore a matching outfit. Auntie changed into a black pinstriped midi skirt, black lisle stockings and black Cuban-heeled shoes. She had on a white long-sleeved cotton blouse with a small flower pin at her neck. Her black, three quarter length jacket and her wide brimmed black straw hat completed her fishing attire. She carried a black leather pocketbook in her right hand, and handed the wicker picnic basket to Eddie with the other.

"Here, you carry this. I don't know how long we'll be out on the water. This will tide us over until we get back." She led the way down the short, narrow street toward the parking lot of Ste. Cécile's church where our car was parked.

"You'd better sit up front with the wife, Matante." Eddie unlocked the door and placed the basket on the floor behind the driver's seat. "You can direct us to Lionel's house." She settled herself down next to me and he climbed into the back seat.

The tall, stone tower of the church dominated the village scene. Rue Sainte Cécile was the main road and small wooden frame houses crowded both sides of the street near the church. We turned off the paved section of the road and found ourselves on a dusty lane, then crossed the railroad tracks and left the mountainous terrain behind as we headed toward the sea. There were small farmhouses with metal roofs, wooden barns and silos. A few shade trees dotted the countryside where sheep and cows were grazing. Long rambling log fences separated the properties where newly planted fields of grain were barely tall enough to identify. "See that sawmill over there?" Matante pointed her bony finger toward the sea. "Loggers bring their trees down from the mountains on trucks to be cut and loaded on barges right from here."

"Is it much farther to Lionel's house?" Eddie asked.

"No, his house is just past the sawmill." Tante Marie adjusted herself to get a better look through the windshield. "There, that's it see it? It's the one with the red roof."

Lionel was waiting. He was anxious to get going. The men shook hands. Lionel politely kissed Matante and me on both cheeks.

She brushed off her skirt. "Do you have the bait ready?" She asked.

"Yes." Lionel led the way to the dock. "My wife had me kill two chickens for supper last night and I saved the livers." He held up a can to display more than a handful of coarsely chopped bait. "Salmon really like chicken livers."

Suddenly I felt a wave of nausea and looked away.

"Hey, those are some pretty fancy fishing poles you got there." Eddie examined the Bamboo rods.

"Yes, I sent away for them from a catalogue," Lionel tugged at the line. "You can't get stuff like this around here."

"Well, if everything's ready let's get going." Tante Marie bent over, reached for the back hem of her skirt, pulled it up between her legs, and tucked it into the belt at her waist. "I don't want this thing to fly up in the air when the fishing gets exciting." Everyone chuckled. She looked like a genie out of Arabian Nights.

"All right, let's go." Lionel grinned as he took charge. "The boat is at the end of the dock." He led the way carrying the bait and the poles. Matante carried her purse, Eddie had the picnic basket and I pulled the red coaster wagon containing a galvanized bucket and burlap bags. The 18 foot white dinghy was tied to the end of the dock. "You ladies can sit in the center," Lionel directed as he stored his equipment in the bow of the boat. Eddie sat in the bow and Lionel made sure everything was in its proper place before he sat down in the stern, then started the engine and we were on our way. We sped over the calm water and could barely see the shoreline when Lionel turned off the engine and nodded toward Eddie, "Throw out the anchor!"

Eddie obliged. Lionel walked to the bow like a drunken sailor. Although the water was calm, the swells in the Saint Lawrence River caused the boat to rock. The horizon was moving up and down and I began to feel queasy again. Lionel gathered a fishing pole to teach us how to attach the liver to the hook. At the sight of the red chunks of liver I hung my head over the side and began to heave violently. Tante Marie's wonderful breakfast was floating in the river.

18

"Don't worry about it, Kid," Eddie volunteered, "It'll make good chum for the fish."

"Ach!"

"Lie down in the stern, dear." Matante took my arm gently. "If you don't look at the water you'll be all right." I took her advice.

She baited her hook with a piece of liver and threw her line in the water. Lionel and Eddie did the same. Her line had barely touched the water when she cried, "I think I've got one!"

"So soon?" Lionel looked shocked. "I usually have to wait at least a half-hour before I get a hit. Maybe you're snagged on a rock."

"Rocks don't wiggle." She said, adamantly, as she pulled at the line.

"We'd better pull our lines in or they might get tangled." Eddie said winding in his line.

"Here it comes." The fish jumped out of the water and dove down again before she could reel it up to the surface.

"Where's the net, Lionel?" Eddie grabbed the fish as he asked the question. In one motion he swung the handle of the net and swooped up the foot-long salmon.

"Wow, that's quite a beauty." Lionel said examining the catch. "It's gotta weigh about five pounds. I didn't think you could do it."

Looking very smug, she adjusted her hat and reached for more bait, "Shall we try this again?"

All three re-baited their hooks and threw in their lines. After about two hours, Eddie and Lionel had caught one fish each. She had caught two more.

"Let's head back to shore," Matante ordered as she secured her line. "There seems to be a breeze picking up."

Back to shore; those were the words I wanted to hear. The men pulled in their lines. Lionel secured the poles to the side of the boat and I took my place in the center. The engine was music to my ears and I could hardly wait to plant my feet on Terra Firma.

"Here, Lionel," Matante said. "You take these two fish for your family. We'll have enough with Eddie's and mine."

We said our goodbyes and headed back to Tante Marie's. The tires made a crunching sound on the unpaved street.

The mountains rose up ahead of us. Now and then we could see puffs of dust as cars ahead of us climbed the narrow dirt roads. Horizontal rows of houses called 'rangs' formed clear boundaries for small, numbered rank farming communities. The tin roofs on the village houses shone like stripes of silver dots under the bright sun, ascending the mountain. When we reached the pavement of the town, Eddie parked the car in the churchyard and we walked up the short cul-de-sac to Matante's house. As we reached the steps to her house, she turned to Eddie and said, "Help me take out my cutting table." She opened the white lattice door next to the stairs, revealing a storage area under the porch.

Eddie pulled out a small well-worn butcher-block table. "It looks like you've used this thing a lot."

"Oh yes," she pulled out a bottle of eau de javelle and a brush. "This is what I use to butcher my meat and clean fish. This bleach will kill the microbes so we can clean and filet the fish."

"I can do that," Eddie volunteered.

She disappeared into the house and returned with a narrow-bladed thick handled knife. "Here, this should do it. I'll get the fire going while you prepare the fish." I fol-

19

lowed Matante back into the house.

She hung up her coat and hat then donned an apron. The routine of food preparation began again. First, the clean-up at the water pump. Next, she gathered potatoes, carrots and peas from her underground cache. She pulled a bottle of milk from her wooden icebox and cornstarch from the cupboard. "I think I have everything." She turned to me, "If you like you may peel the potatoes and carrots."

"Sure," I said. "I think I'm beginning to feel human again."

She smiled as she lifted the round lids on her stove to check the fire. "The fire's just about ready." She prepared the baking dish for the salmon then reached into the cupboard under the sink to pull out three pots. "Here, after you rinse and slice the potatoes you can put them in the biggest pot, and the sliced carrots in the smaller one, " she said.

The screen door slammed as Eddie placed the plate of bright pink salmon filets on the round pedestal table. She examined the fish. "A little corn starch, a little milk, a little butter, and these should be ready in no time at all."

Eddie turned to me and asked, "How do you feel, Kid?"

"Like the room is still rocking." I set the plates and silverware on the white tablecloth. "But, now that I'm on firm ground and the salmon smells so good, I'm beginning to feel hungry."

***

Sunlight shone through the outer edges of the attic window. We could hear Tante Marie moving about the kitchen downstairs, preparing to attend the daily 7 o'clock Mass at Sainte Cécile's as was her usual routine. The smell of coffee perking on the stove floated up to our attic room. Eddie was already awake and was using the ewer next to the bed for his morning shave.

"Good morning," I said sleepily. "You're up early,"

"Not really, I just wanted to get cleaned up and dressed before I go downstairs."

"Smells like coffee is brewing," I said as I pulled up the blankets to make the bed.

"Yeah, I'll get a fresh pitcher of water for you to get cleaned up before we leave for church."

"Thanks." I raised the window shades. The sun's blinding light promised it was going to be a beautiful warm day. A robin, perched at the tip of a branch, sang in the nearby maple tree, its red breast contrasting the green leaves. "It's going to be a great day."

Eddie was dressed in gray slacks and a blue, long-sleeved buttoned down shirt. I reached into the suitcase and pulled out a tan and brown plaid dress with a wide white V-necked collar. I laid it on the bed and prepared for my morning ablutions. I could hear Matante and Eddie chatting as I got washed and dressed before heading downstairs.

"Well, it's about time, sleepyhead," Eddie and I are ready for church are you coming with us?"

How could I say no? This was to be the routine for the next few days. "There are lots of cousins for you to meet," She wore a dark blue flowered dress and was adjusting her prim navy blue, narrow-brimmed, straw hat. "We'll have to get an early start every day."

***

Marie Gagnon was my maternal grandmother's sister. She had returned to the

20

place of her birth after having worked for many years in the cotton mills of Fall River, Massachusetts. She had saved enough money to purchase her cherished little cottage. She was determined to remain in touch with her roots. Her greatest pleasure was to visit her relatives. Our Studebaker was the magic coach she needed to see cousins she had not seen for a long time.

Oncle (uncle) Pierre Morin was my maternal grand-father's younger brother. He, his wife Anna, and their daughters, lived in the village close to the church. When we dropped in on them after Mass, Rita and Bernadette were in the midst of painting alternate black and white squares on the kitchen linoleum to freshen the worn out floor. Matante, stood in the doorway and introduced us. "I see the girls are busy," she pointed to the floor. She put an arm around my shoulders, "this is Aura's daughter, Jeanne, and her husband, Eddie. We thought you'd like to go with us see Sister Joseph Hervé at the Rimouski Hospital today."

"Oncle Pierre looked at his wife. She nodded. "It'll take us about an hour to get changed." He turned to his two daughters, "I'm sure you can finish this floor without us."

"You're leaving us?" "Why can't we go?" I could hear the fussy protests as we left.

When we returned Tante Anna and Oncle Pierre were waiting. She had on a brown midi a-line skirt, a tan, long-sleeved blouse and a brown straw hat with a long yellow feather perched next to the crown above the narrow brim. He wore a navy blue vested suit, a blue tie and a gray fedora.

The trip north to Rimouski took less than two hours. Our car bounced over the dirt road as I followed Matante's directions. Tante Marie sat up front with me and the others sat in the back. I was amazed at how a woman who never drove a car had such knowledge about the country roads and knew exactly how to get everywhere.

Sister Joseph Hervé was my mother's sister, Josephine, a Gray Sister of Charity, who was a pharmacist at the hospital in Rimouski. Since our visit was unexpected, we were pleased when she was given time off to show us around the hospital. We had lunch in a private dining room and chatted happily through the courses of soup, meat loaf and mashed potatoes, and vanilla pudding for dessert. I had not seen my aunt since I was about five years old and it was a time for great reminiscing for all of us. Matante Anna laughed and nodded a lot but otherwise did not engage in the conversation. I was mesmerized by her yellow feather which moved gracefully each time she bobbed her head with her cackled laughter.

During the two weeks we spent in Bic, Tante Anna and Oncle Pierre accompanied us on many of our visits to relatives in the surrounding area. We visited third cousins and second cousins. It was wonderful to see how everyone was so delighted to see her. And us!

There was a maple sugar cabin at our cousin's farm in Saint Jean de Dieu. Although the sugar season was over, we got the grand tour of how maple sugar is made. We visited other Rioux cousins in Trois Pistoles where two cows on the same farm gave birth to twin calves on the same day, only an hour before we arrived. At Trois Rivières, our second cousins, the Belisles, had a smoke-house for curing herring and meat.

In Saint Fabien Tante Marie announced, "This was your great-grandfather's farm where your mother's father was born."

A gray-haired man of medium height and build, dressed in bib-overalls greeted us. "This is your grandfather's brother, Elzéar Morin, named after your great-grandfather."

I had seen pictures of my grandfather I and saw a resemblance. "Come on let me show you around the farm." He put an arm around my shoulder, "Aura's daughter,eh?"

There were neat rows of vegetables and various produce on the land, including short stalks of newly planted corn. There was a special section where he planted flax to make into linen for use in their home. Every home had a spinning wheel and at least one loom to make home spun kitchen towels and blankets.

***

Toward the end of our first week in Bic, we heard a loud rap on the front door.

"Pardon, Mademoiselle Gagnon, they tell me your guests are the owners of that red cabin," said the tall, young dark haired curate robed in a black cassock and wearing a black biretta.

"Yes, mon Père, is there a problem?"

"Monsieur le Curé has died suddenly, and we need to have the parking lot cleared completely," the curate said. "We can't have anything that big and red in the way."

Matante stepped out on the front porch with the curate. I could hear them talking as they walked toward the church. A few minutes later she came back and announced, "My neighbor, Mr. Chénard, offered space in his yard to park your little house until after the funeral."

Eddie and I went out, under Matante's supervision, hitched the trailer, moved it, secured it then unhitched the car and drove it to the front of her house.

She was upset for the next few days as she mourned her pastor. This was the same pastor who had given us permission to park the trailer only a few days before. Wasn't he the one who had been concerned about a possible funeral? Who could have guessed it would be his own?

The funeral day was rainy, dark and dreary. We were the last car in the procession when we drove Matante to the funeral. All the dark colored cars went first. The procession was long and the cemetery was in the next village of Saint Fabien.

Our visiting took a back seat for a day or two, so we caught up with housework and laundry. It was a bit tricky to iron without electricity. Matante had two heavy flat irons which she heated on her stove. One would be heating while she attached the snap-on handle to the other alternating the irons as needed.

Our first day back to visiting was another opportunity to visit with Lionel. When he met our car in his driveway, he asked, "Where do you want to go clamming?"

Matante was decked out in her fishing clothes, straw hat and all. "I thought we'd go to Baie Rose first, then to Cap à l'Orignal."

"The tide should be low for a couple of hours," he said. " I think we can get a couple of buckets full."

" Are the clams as good from the Saint Laurence as they are from New England?" Eddie asked.

"They're not as salty, I think," she said. "But, they're good."

"Let's get going," Lionel said as he placed the buckets into the trunk and got in the car.

When we arrived at Baie, Rose Matante was the first to exit. She hurried out of the car, found a flat rock to sit on and removed her shoes and lisle stockings. The skirt was again pulled from the back hem and tucked in her belt. She had already checked the tide and was first to get to the water line. She immediately dug her toes into the wet sand, squishing to find buried clams, collected them and placed them one by one into her bucket. We all did the same for about an hour. Lionel had brought a large screen container. Matante reached for it, poured the clams into it and gave instructions to Eddie. "Here, rinse these clams in the river to get the sand out. It's time to move up further up the other beach."

We piled into the car and drove up the coastline. She carried her shoes and stockings to the next destination. This time she went directly to the shoreline and got to work digging clams with her toes. We collected two buckets full, one at Baie Rose and one at Cap à l'Orignal. "Lionel, you and your wife come over tonight, we are going to make clam fritters."

Matante and I were busy for the rest of the afternoon, cooking and chopping clams, onions and potatoes for chowder and clam cakes. The Rioux's came over early in the evening. We ate fully of Tante Marie's feast and spent the rest of the evening playing cards. We had just barely turned on the kerosene lamp when Lionel decided it was time to leave. It was still light when we walked down the street to our car. Lionel's wife, Laurette, and I sat in the back seat on the ride to their house. Lasting memories had been created that day and the crescent moon and first star were witnesses on that evening.

CHAPTER 5

On the morning we said our goodbyes, our hearts were heavy. Two weeks had gone by all too quickly. We set our alarm for 4:00 a.m., then Eddie walked down to the churchyard and drove our car to the front of Matante's house.

Tante Marie was already dressed in a brown print dress and white apron with her hair wound neatly around her head. "I'll make breakfast while you two get your things together and loaded into your car," she said, as she proceeded to set the table and make coffee with her usual flair. "Don't bother with the bedding; I'll take care of that after you're gone."

It was still dark out and the stars were bright in the sky. Eddie wore gray trousers and a red and gray pin-striped short sleeved shirt. I wore a navy blue skirt and a pink blouse with a ruffle at the neck. The aroma of Matante's pancakes and slab bacon teased us as we finished loading the car. She placed the platters of pancakes and bacon on the table, reached for the coffee pot, poured our steaming hot coffee, and joined us.

"Will you be able to visit with my sisters at Saint Sulpice?" She reached for the maple syrup.

"I promised my mother we would," I said, taking an extra pancake. "She reminded me in her last letter."

"That sounds like your mother," she said. "Your aunts will be glad to see you again."

"We won't be able to stay long," Eddie took the last two pancakes and reached for the butter.

"Don't worry about that," Matante was already gathering up the dishes from the table. "I'm sure you'll get the grand tour of the facility anyway."

Tante Marie waved us off from any kitchen clean-up. "Maybe you should make one more trip to the back house," she pointed to the side door. "I'll take care of the table. I'm going to need something to do before going to Mass." We took one last look around. She opened the front door and we walked down the stairs together. When we reached the car, she immediately put her hand on the front passenger side door, pulled it open and sat down.

"It's my last chance to ride with you. " She brushed a tear from her eye. It was strange to see her outdoors without her hat. She sat next to Eddie for the bumpy ride to the church. Once in the parking lot she quietly watched as we hitched our trailer to the car. "I'll miss you," she said and held us both in a warm embrace. Eddie kissed her cheek then took his place behind the steering wheel. I held on to her a little longer. I felt her teary face as we kissed, then climbed into the car. She reached into the open window, gently patted my shoulder, and waved as we turned toward the road. She was still standing in the churchyard as we turned onto the highway.

The fishing villages were more familiar now, since we had fished along the shores and met some of the people. We took with us a new sense of our existence along with the realization that our lives had been rooted in this beautiful place.

One of our cousins told us of a ferry to Québec which left regularly from Rivière du Loup. This was about fifty miles south of Bic and would shorten our road time by several hours if we could board. We drove down the familiar road and reached the pier in about an hour and a half. Unlike the dock at Lévis, there were no cars or trucks waiting in line. "This place looks deserted compared to the ferry landing in Québec. All the cars are parked," I observed. "I don't see any vehicles getting on the ferry."

"I'll wait here," Eddie said. "Just check to see if we're in the right place."

I hadn't gone very far when a uniformed attendant came toward us at a quickened pace, rushing past me as he headed towards Eddie with his hand uplifted in a STOP gesture and said in French. "What are you doing here?"

"Isn't this the ferry to Québec?" Eddie inquired.

"Mais oui," he replied. "But it is for passengers only. If you wish to cross with your 'roulotte' you will have to drive down to Lévis." He frantically waved his arms, "Allez-vous-en!" He pointed to the road and rambled while directing us to move the trailer as though we were contaminating the crushed clamshell parking area. Eddie finally got the car turned around to face the exit and I returned to my seat next to him. We could hear the crunching sound of the wheels as we climbed toward the highway. "It would have been great to sail down the river instead of driving along the coast," Eddie said.

"Yeah, I wonder if it would have taken the same amount of time."

"I don't know," he said. "But I'm sure it would have been a lot smoother."

It was a beautiful day. The sky was blue and the sun was bright. By now it was around nine and we still had another hundred and fifty miles to go before we would reach the ferry landing.

"It took longer at that ferry dock than I expected," I said. "What do you think about me riding in the trailer and preparing lunch to save a little bit of time?"

"I don't know, Kid, the roads aren't that smooth," he said. "It could get a little bumpy."

"Hey, bumpy in the car, bumpy in the trailer, what's the difference?"

"Well, okay, if you're sure you want to. I'll stop at the next wide strip on the road."

We passed wooden farmhouses with shingled roofs and wide wooden steps leading to the front door. Every family had a vegetable garden instead of a front lawn. Most of the houses were painted white but were trimmed in a variety of colors. Some windows, shutters and door frames were painted bright red, or royal blue, or yellow, or even black, giving each one its own personality. Puffs of smoke coming up through the narrow chimneys gave evidence of life within the homes. Now and then we saw a house made of red brick with white wood trim. Tall silos with shiny metal domes and animal pens attached to large tin roofed wooden barns were part of nearly every property.

The trailer danced behind us as it pitched and swayed over stones on the rocky highway.

"Look ahead," Eddie said. "If you're serious about riding in the trailer, I think I can pull over to the side of the road at the entrance of that farm."

"Seems like as good a place as any," I answered. "It should only take a few minutes to get settled in."

We stopped on the flat stretch of road. Traffic wasn't heavy. We had passed only a few cars during the last several miles and the dirt road was well maintained. I got out of the car and opened the door to the trailer.

"I'll stop in about an hour when I see a nice place for a picnic," he said. "That should give you enough time to get set up for lunch."

"Sounds good to me."

He closed and latched the door, returned to the car and I felt the movement of the trailer as he drove back to the road. The trailer rocked from side to side. It took me a few minutes to steady myself in my new surroundings. As I opened the ice-box door, I barely caught the box of tomatoes before they hit the floor. I wasn't so lucky with the ham or the bread, nor the salad fixings. The head of lettuce rolled out and went back and forth on the floor from under the table to the sofa. I slammed the door of the icebox shut. I tried to pick up the food from the floor. I landed on my knees and banged my shoulder into the lower cabinets. I pulled myself up to try to sit at the table, missed the seat and slid down to the floor on top of the cukes and green peppers. I got dizzy crawling on my hands and knees trying to pick up the smashed food from the slippery floor. I found a brown paper bag, stuffed as much as I could find into it and pushed the whole thing back into the ice box. By now nausea was setting in. I pulled myself up, stretched across the cushions in the breakfast nook and started to pound on the window in the hope of getting Eddie's attention. Forget it!! He couldn't see me. The rear-view mirror and the side mirrors did not reflect the front windows of the trailer. I was doomed! Our little house pitched with every stone, every pot-hole and every turn in the road. I could only hope to hang on to the table and not fall again.

"Ooooh Please, God. Let him stop!" I prayed.

I sat on the floor with my back against the ice-box and my arms wrapped around a large bowl which I had planned to be the recipient of a succulent salad. Now it was set a-ready in case the nausea materialized into something more unpleasant. Finally, I felt the vehicle slowing down. I couldn't see out the window. I hope we're at a gas station, I thought. I rolled onto my knees, pushed the bowl under the table and burst out the door as soon as he stopped and before he could take off again. "Couldn't you hear me banging on the window?" I exploded. "I was dying in there."

"No I couldn't." Without looking at me, he calmly checked the map. "I think we may have gone about 40 miles." He looked up and smiled. "You look a little frazzled. Is lunch ready?"

"Lunch? Lunch? Are you kidding? I tell you I'm dying and all you can think about is lunch? Lunch will have to wait until my stomach is ready to handle it," I huffed. "And not until WE can clean up the mess in there."

"Calm down, Sweetheart," he reminded me. "It was your idea to ride in the trailer. We made good time. The way I figure it, we only have a little more than 50 miles to go to the Levis crossover."

"Humph!" I plopped into the car and crossed my arms.

He gently held my elbow. "Look, Kid," he consoled. "You can change in the rest-room over there and we can watch for a small restaurant along the way. We'll worry about cleaning up later."

I went back into the trailer and tried not to focus on the messy floor as I reached into the tiny closet for a clean dress. Eddie chatted with the attendant while he gassed up the car. I felt more presentable when I emerged from the restroom in my red and white polka dot dress and we were finally on our way again. Traveling on the east shore of the Saint Lawrence River we felt the peace and serenity of the sea and countryside. By late morning the small fishing boats were returning from their early morning fishing and some lay quietly at anchor while the fishermen washed their nets. On the other side of the road, Guernsey cows, grazing in the fields, were oblivious to the din we created as we drove past. As we neared Berthier sur Mer, a large red sign with a picture of a torpedo sandwich appeared before us: "Croque Monsieur à la Française". Several pairs of curious eyes watched as we pulled into the parking lot of the small wooden sandwich stand. Three ladies in bright cotton dresses and matching straw hats were sitting at one of the picnic tables with three men wearing light summer suits with bow ties and Maurice Chevalier style straw hats. They were all speaking French. The lady with the pink dress and hat cocked her head in our direction. "Where do you think they're from?"

The man with the mustache raised his bushy dark eyebrows, "I think they're Americans."

The lady in yellow sat up straight and nodded toward the trailer, "I wonder what they've got in that big red thing."

Eddie and I pretended not to understand. I found a seat at a small round picnic table while Eddie ordered the food. I had no idea what we were about to eat and was delighted to find a wonderful toasted ham and cheese creation on a home baked roll. I took my first bite as we sat at our table under a maple tree. "This is mood altering food!"

"You feel better, now, Kid?"

"It's so peaceful here." I looked around. Time was standing still.

Our croque monsieur satisfied our stomachs and the warm sun lifted our spirits. The lovely blue cloudless sky touched the dark blue-gray river on one side of the horizon, and the deep green meadows on the other. I began to feel we might reach the Lévis ferry pier in time for the noon crossing. We smiled and waved to the patrons as we slid into our car. The gentlemen tipped their hats and the ladies nodded. We drove away. Somehow, though the roads were still bumpy, the ride became smoother as we sat side by side.

The pier at Lévis was busy. We took our place in line with the trucks, as we did before in Québec, and then climbed to the top level for the crossing. The river was calm and the ride was smooth as we observed the skyline of the city appear before us. Chateau Frontenac dominated the upper cliff, like a massive stone sentinel, keeping watch over the cobblestone roads and European style houses and shops at sea level. The Saint Lawrence River stretched for miles to the north and south with barges and boats heading in both directions.

"All passengers please return to your vehicles, please," the announcement came over the loudspeaker. "Prepare for debarkation from the vessel."

"It seems like the trip back took less time," Eddie said as we headed to our car on the lower level.

We followed in line behind the trucks, drove off the ferry ramp and onto the steep cobblestone road headed for upper Québec and our next adventure toward Montréal.

     \*\*\*

Saint Sulpice was a large facility for the mentally challenged, set back on a tree-lined entrance on the main road to Montréal. It was staffed by the Grey Sisters of Charity where my grandmother's two sisters were serving. We drove up the quarter-mile driveway and parked just past the main portal with the tall white columns.

"I guess we'll be out of the way over here," Eddie said.

"Yeah, I guess we're okay," I stepped out of the car. "We won't be here for that long a time."

We walked up the stone steps to the large wooden doors and pushed the doorbell. A small nun dressed in a tan and black habit answered. "May I help you," she asked in a soft voice.

"We'd like to see Sister Saint Illuminat and Sister Saint Nicodème," I held on to Eddie's hand. "They're my aunts and we'd like to visit."

"Please come into the parlor while I ring for them." She disappeared behind a mesh door and soon we heard two distinct sets of bell codes.

We waited. The room was simple with one heavy wooden rectangular table in the center and four large high-back chairs. Along two of the walls there were two small tables with lace doilies and white lamp on each one. The large table had a matching lace tablecloth and a bowl of imitation fruit in the center.

Sister Saint Illuminat was tall and slender. "Jeanne," she hugged me. "Your mother wrote and told me you would be coming."

Sister Saint Nicodème was shorter and chubby. "Here you are at last."

"Sister Saint Patrice will be preparing a collation for you both but first you have to come see where we work and meet our helpers," Sister Saint Illuminat said.

My aunts worked in the laundry room and kitchen respectively. We proceeded out of the parlor and followed Sister Saint Illuminat down the long corridor to the laundry room where Pierre-Paul, one of the residents, was folding sheets. We exchanged greetings and Sister encouraged him to get on with his work. We then went on to the kitchen where Reina-Louise and Francine were peeling potatoes for the evening meal. My aunt introduced us to them and they smiled as they continued to work among the large bags of tubers, chatting and giggling as they filled a huge pot. Sister Saint Patrice met us at the entrance of a small dining room. A square table with a blue flowered tablecloth and a vase of daisies, surrounded by four chairs, was in the center of the room. Sister Saint Nicodème poured tea into the China cups from a gracious flowered teapot and served hot biscuits on small plates. They wanted to hear all about our recent visit with their sister Marie in Bic and all of the cousins we had visited while we were there. The afternoon passed very quickly and soon we were back on the road to Montréal.

"I'll have a lot to tell my mother when I write tonight," I said. "I never knew my grandmother but it sure is nice to have a connection to her through these aunts."

"It looks like some gray clouds are moving in," Eddie observed. "We might get some rain before long."

"You can tell we are further south," I said. "It's getting dark earlier than it did up at Tante Marie's."

"I think I'll look for a place for the night," Eddie said. "We don't want to be driving in the rain in the dark."

We drove along a little while longer and came upon a gas station with a large parking area and a sign that read 'Open all night'. Eddie pulled up to the pump. "Fill it up," he said.

"That's some rig you've got there," the attendant said.

"Yeah," Eddie answered. "It looks like rain, would you mind if we parked here overnight?"

"Hey," he lifted his cap and scratched his head. "I'll have to charge you a dollar."

"That's fair enough," Eddie reached for his wallet. "We'll be out of here first thing in the morning."

What more could we ask for? We had a place to sleep, a place to freshen up and a quiet dry place to listen to the rain, and even time to write letters to my mother and tante Marie. Both would want news of our visit with our aunts.

Tante Marie had written to her brother, Elzéar, in Lavaltrie to apprise him and his wife Emilienne of our visit. Their home was a small country house on the way to Montréal. It was a natural wood shingled house with blue shutters and matching trim on the front porch. When we arrived about mid-morning, they were sitting in large cane rockers on the porch which stretched the entire length of the house. As we pulled up in front of the house, Oncle Elzéar popped up from his chair to come and greet us. He wore black horn-rimmed glasses and a crown of gray hair covered the balding head above his ears. He was dressed in gray trousers, a green plaid shirt and work boots. Tante Emilienne's feet didn't quite reach the floor as she sat in her chair. She was short and round and wore a brown plaid skirt and yellow long-sleeved blouse with small pearl buttons. Her gray hair was neatly braided and wrapped around her head. Her bright blue eyes and smile greeted us warmly. Oncle Elzéar led us to two straight wooden chairs and invited us to sit down. We chatted about the relatives we had visited with Tante Marie and they had a million questions about my mother. Tante Emilienne excused herself to prepare lunch and I followed her into the kitchen to help. She was already well prepared with home-made chicken and rice soup and roast chicken in the oven. I mashed the potatoes while she prepared the gravy. Fresh green beans from their backyard garden were already cooked in the pot. The feast was ready. The men came in from the porch and took their places at the round dining room table set with a blue table cloth and white dishes. Tante Emilienne and I brought in the platters of food and took our places next to the men.

"The last time I saw your mother," Oncle said, "was two summers ago when she brought your brother here to visit."

"We'll be seeing him tomorrow," Eddie replied.

"He talked a lot about the boys at the orphanage." Oncle reached for the platter of chicken.

"Yes, my mother says he really likes being chaplain over there." I looked over at my aunt. "This meal is really good."

"Just wait," Oncle said. "She made blueberry pie. It's the best in the world."

"Did you say blueberry pie?" I asked. "That just happens to be Eddie's favorite."

We finished the meal with gusto. Oncle was right, this pie was the best. Tante and I shooed the men back out to the porch while she and I cleaned up the kitchen. She told me about her grown children who had since moved away to other areas in Canada. The day had gone by too quickly and soon it was time for us to be on our way.

We left Lavaltrie around 3:30 and headed south toward Montréal. It was a bright afternoon and the traffic was light. We tuned in an American radio station originating in New York and sang along with the music. "They tried to tell us we're too young…" Nat King Cole sang in his golden voice. The one and a half-hour drive to

Montréal went by fast as we listened to our favorite singers and familiar songs. When we reached the city we stopped at a gas station to inquire about a trailer park for the time of our stay in Montréal. The attendant directed us to a little town called Dorion which is about 20 miles southwest of Montréal. We drove less than an hour when we saw the large orange sign with black letters: CAMP DORION. "Hey, there it is, " I said.

Eddie pulled on the trailer hand brake and prepared to make the turn into the driveway. The camp was situated on the Ottawa River. He drove into the circular drive-way and stopped. He looked around as he got out of the car then walked to the office below the neon sign. I looked around and saw the shower house, the laundry room and restrooms in a long building behind the office. The camp director, wearing khaki pants and a short-sleeved orange shirt came out and led us to our parking spot where we un-hitched our trailer. Once settled in, we walked around the park, checked the facilities, and then strolled down to the river's edge where we saw some boats for hire. We decided to take a ride on the picturesque river. A man with a wide-brimmed hat, trimmed with a blue plaid ribbon, escorted us to the center seat and started the motor of the small boat. It was a perfect night. The moon was high in the sky and stars shone brightly. We could see the lights in the houses along the shore. Our driver pointed out several places of interest as we went along. Every once in awhile he sang an old Canadian song in his pleasant tenor voice. "A la Claire fontaine, m'en allant promener…"

"My mother used to sing that song," I said to Eddie.

"Yeah, I've heard her sing it and some of the other songs he sang are familiar too."

It was nostalgic and rapt— we were in the beauty of the moment— then our little boat returned to shore. "I'm beginning to get hungry," I said.

"Me too," Eddie reached over and held my hand to help me out of the boat.

As we walked toward the Camp we saw a small restaurant called 'Chez-Nous'. The menu was posted in the window. Soupe du jour: Soupe aux Pois à la famille. "Can you believe this?" Eddie said. "Pea soup. Is your mother around here somewhere?"

"It's as though someone had planned this whole adventure." I slipped my hand into his and we walked slowly up the path to the eatery. It was a perfect ending to a perfect day.

   ***

Eddie was up before dawn. "Come on, sleepyhead," he pulled the blankets off me. "It's a beautiful morning." He had already made his trip to the shower house before coming to wake me up. A lovely breeze wafted through the open window and the morning sun reflected a golden path across the river.

I stood up and folded the blankets. "Let's have an easy breakfast this morning," I said.

"That's a good idea," he closed the couch, "It's a good thing the milk didn't spill out during your 'ride-in trailer' experiment."

"Don't remind me." I slipped on my robe and picked up my clothes to bring to the shower. "Cereal will be fine with me."

"I guess your brother will be at the orphanage early." He reached for the bowls in the cupboard. "Doesn't he say an early Mass at the orphanage chapel?"

"I guess so," I headed out the door. "If not for the kids, I guess he would do it for the sisters who live there."

My brother René was a Dominican Priest assigned as chaplain to the Catholic Orphanage in Montréal. This was a perfect assignment for him. He loved children and seemed to know just how to please them. We arrived there around 11:30 and Father met us in the foyer just inside the front door, wearing his white robe and a large wooden rosary attached to the black belt around his waist. After warm greetings, he introduced us to the sisters. Sister Marie Antoine gave us the grand tour of the parlors and dining room before we were ushered into a large study hall where there were about a hundred boys. "Here comes Father Paré," the chorus resounded as soon as they saw him. He seemed to know each one personally. The older students led us upstairs we visited classrooms, each one equipped with its own tank of tropical fish. The boys acted as guides, pointing out different species and in general explaining the wonders of tropical fish.

"Who feeds these fish?" I asked.

"We do," said one tall boy with red hair. "We have our assignments and are responsible for cleaning the tanks and caring for them."

"Sounds like a big job," Eddie said.

"It is," my brother said. "Each classroom has its own responsible students who take turns caring for the fish."

We proceeded down to the second floor where the younger children were assembled. Within minutes he was surrounded by boys with extended hands. He reached in his seemingly bottomless pocket and pulled out a handful of colored balloons and distributed them to the kids. From his other pocket he drew out a fistful of lollipops. A chorus of 'Merci, mon père' and 'Moi aussi' filled the room as the confections disappeared into plump little hands.

"Don't forget," he warned, "no papers, no sticks and no popped balloons are to be thrown on the floor or on the ground!"

"Oui, mon père (yes, father)," they answered in one voice.

"Venez, venez les enfants (come, come children)!" the ever-vigilant sisters appeared in the doorway to round up the children for summer activities. They followed two by two and disappeared down the long corridor. My brother, René, excused himself to change into his black suit and white Roman collar.

32

"We'll meet you at the car," Eddie said as we left and walked out to the parking lot. It was a beautiful campus with well manicured lawns and one large cement area which was flooded during the winter for skating. It wasn't long before my brother was back; he opened the door to sit next to Eddie. "There's some interesting stuff to see around here," he opened the back door and motioned with his head for me to get in the back seat. "But, first let me see where you're staying."

From Montréal we drove west along the Saint Lawrence River. "I know it doesn't look it," René said. "But right here in Montréal, the Ottawa River drains into the Saint Lawrence and it's nearly impossible to determine where one body of water ends and the other begins."

"It's a beautiful scenic road." Eddie said.

"The Ottawa River flows along the border between Québec and Ontario," René said as we approached the trailer park.

"That's a pretty long river," I said as Eddie turned into the driveway toward our little house.

My brother was first to exit the car and look around.

"This is a pretty good set-up." He said after his short tour. "You have everything you need."

"That's true," I replied. "But there's not much room for entertaining guests."

"Let's go to "Chez-Nous" for lunch," Eddie said. "We were there last night and the food was very good.

\*\*\*

"Kateri Tekakwitha will probably be canonized one day," René said.

"Who is she?" I asked.

"She was a Mohawk girl who grew up around here," my brother said. "She became a Catholic convert when she was a teenager."

"Is her tomb around here?" Eddie looked around.

"Actually, it's a sort of shrine, René answered. "Her body was turned to ashes so there is no actual burying place." He pointed to a sign, "There it is," he said. "You'll be taking a left turn in about a half mile."

"How old was she when she died?" I asked.

"Twenty-three. She contracted smallpox when she was only two and survived but was left terribly scarred and disfigured," he continued. "It is said that one half hour after she died, her scars disappeared and she appeared to be a beautiful young woman."

"When was this?" My curiosity was peaked.

"Around 1677," he said. "There have been many healings reported of people who have prayed to her."

"There it is!" Eddie said.

We stopped to look around the grounds. There was a small parking lot and about 10 cars. Pilgrims to the small shrine walked about in silence or spoke in whispers. It was a holy place; one could sense an aura of divine presence. Beautiful icons and paintings of the young Indian maiden were displayed in and around the small rustic chapel. Devoted visitors, men, women and children alike, prayed fervently with apparent devotion. Quietly we knelt in the chapel, each of us with our own personal petitions. Mine was that I would one day become a mother.

Silently we returned to the car. As he reached for the driver's side door, Eddie asked, "How far is it to Longueil?"

"Probably around 10 more miles," my brother answered. "I'd like to go to the City Hall. I heard there is an exhibit of tropical fish over there."

I closed the back door. "That should be interesting. I'm sure the boys would be happy to see an increase in the population of the aquariums."

"You're right," he looked toward the back seat. "You'd be amazed at the questions they ask as they observe the behavior of the fish."

"I'm sure. Kids are always full of a lot of questions," I said.

The ride wasn't long and we were not disappointed. There were nearly fifty tanks of tropical fish. The most popular were the Guppies, the Neons, Tetras and Black Mollies. "Hey look at these!" I said. "I've never seen such a beautiful fish." Each fish was kept in its own separate bowl. There were two varieties in amazing shades of red and blue each proudly displaying a graceful fringe of both colors from their tails to their under-belly.

"Those are Bettas," the docent said. "Some people call them the fighting fish," He picked up one of the bowls. "You want to keep these fish separate from regular tropical fish," he said. "They tend to be a little belligerent."

"My boys would get a kick out of these fish," René said. "They're not like any of the ones in the fish tanks at the orphanage." He walked back and forth among the tanks. Finally he stopped by the Bettas. He couldn't resist the urge to buy two, a red one and a blue one, with a separate bowl for each of them. He picked up some brochures regarding the care of his new beauties and managed to acquire some free fish food from the salesperson. He picked up the partitioned cardboard box and set it on the floor of the car, between his feet. "I have to be careful with these guys," he said. "I know there'll be a lot of oohs and aahs when the kids see these new fish." Fortunately each fish was in its own section of the partitioned box with a lid to prevent the water from sloshing out of the bowls. "I'll be able to get them set up tonight," he kept peering in the box. "That should be a lot of fun for them."

I wondered who would be having the most fun.

On Sunday, we attended Mass at Saint Anastasia's church in Dorion before meeting with my brother. We were invited to have lunch with him at the Orphanage. The sisters were gracious and full of questions as we feasted on chicken rice soup, roast chicken, mashed potatoes, carrots and peas. "Is this your first visit to Canada?" "How long have you been married?" "Is your mother well?" "Will your parents be coming again this summer?" "How long will you be staying in Montréal?" "Have you been to the Oratoire Saint Joseph yet?"…

After the dessert of apple pie and ice cream we thanked the good sisters and left for a quick tour of the places of interest in town. We then visited more cousins who lived in Montréal. I never knew I had so many cousins, but my brother knew them all and also, how to get to their homes. Most importantly, he knew how to make a visit short. We were back at the Orphanage in time for another delicious meal and a movie afterwards: 'Boy's Town' with Spencer Tracy and Mickey Rooney, complete with French captions.

"Tomorrow I won't be able to see you until around 5:00 p.m." René said. "I have a meeting I can't get out of and it will last most of the day."

"I'm sure we'll find something to do," Eddie said.

"We'll probably go into town and do a little shopping," I chimed in.

Eddie rolled his eyes at my brother, "We'll see about that," he said. "We'll pick you up around suppertime."

***

Eddie was up and dressed when I got back from the shower room. He was wearing a pale blue short-sleeved shirt and dark blue trousers. I wore a white dress with red polka-dots and a white bolero and sandals. Bacon was already sizzling in the frying pan and coffee was perking on the other electric burner. I put the towels away on the drying rack near the couch before I started to make toast. "Where do you think we should go first?" I said.

"I would like to see the downtown district," he said. "Someone told me there are a lot of little places where they feature foods from different countries."

"That sounds interesting," I buttered the toast. "We can leave the shrines and cathedrals for when we are with my brother."

"Good thinking," he poured the last of the coffee in his cup. "We'll get these dishes done and we can be on our way."

It was a short half hour ride into Montréal. We drove around small side streets and on the longer avenues in the heart of the city until we found a parking spot in the center of downtown. "Who'd expect FW Woolworth in Canada?" I asked.

**35**

"Well there it is," Eddie said. "I wonder if the prices are as cheap as they are in the U.S.?"

As we stepped inside we were amazed to find the merchandise and lunch counters very similar to what we were accustomed to in the states. One major difference was that all signs and sale items were printed in French. Our vocabulary for personal items improved somewhat as we walked through the aisles. We left without buying anything.

We walked through the downtown and found a small Italian restaurant which featured antipasto, veal parmesan and pasta. "I didn't expect to find Italian food in Canada," Eddie told our server.

"My father came to Canada after the first war," Giuseppe said. "Papa started this little place, people seemed to like our food and we've been here ever since." He pointed to the paper menu. "What would you like?"

"Spaghetti and meatballs," Eddie said.

"I'll have the same."

The red and white checkered tablecloths and the empty Chianti bottle stuffed with a lit, dripping multi-colored wax candle in the center of each table, created a perfect atmosphere.

"You speak French very well," I remarked when Giuseppe returned.

"I was born here. We speak Italian at home, but when we go out we speak French," he said as he put the family style platters on the table.

"Are there many other Italians in this city?" I asked.

"Oh, yes, there is a section of town called Little Italy," he said. "Over in that neighborhood, everybody speaks Italian. When they meet on the street you'd think you were in the old country." He poured fresh coffee into our cups. "Bon appétit!"

We ate with gusto, left the restaurant, then resumed our tour of downtown. There was the Capitol Theater. The Marquée announced a movie: 'Le Retour de Monte Christo' avec Vaudeville. "Hey, that looks interesting," Eddie said.

"I wonder what kinds of acts they have in the vaudeville?" I asked.

"I don't know," Eddie examined the large posters. "They must be the same kinds of acts we have back home."

"You mean like dog acts and singers and dancers and crazy comedians?"

"I would think so." He headed for the box office. "We won't know until we go in."

The matinee started at 1:00 p.m. The movie was dubbed in French with English captions. It seemed funny to see Louis Hayward and Barbara Britton speaking French and moving their lips out of sync with the dialogue. The English captions were more than a little off from what was actually being said, causing us to chuckle more than once.

When the movie was over, the screen disappeared into the ceiling, and the band appeared in the orchestra pit. The Master of Ceremonies came out and told a few risqué jokes and introduced a couple who danced à la Fred Astaire. Next came a team of jugglers who tossed balls and rings in the air, while others stood on each other's shoulders and threw juggling clubs to one another across the stage. This was followed by a group of little dogs dressed in tutus that ran around on two legs jumping through hoops at the trainer's command.

"Let's hear it for these wonderful talented puppies," the EmCee said, waving his arms then telling more jokes. "And now...our feature presentation!" Wild applause..."La Belle Isabelle!"

The orchestra started to play a provocative rhythm to George Gershwin's 'Summertime'...Boom-ba-da-boom sounds came from the pit, and loud whistling came from the audience. Isabelle strutted on to the stage in an elaborate sequined gown of chartreuse and deep rose, flowing scarves draped about her neck and shoulders, and dragging a huge pale pink fan behind her. Boom-ba-da-boom. Isabelle wiggled from one side of the stage to the other. Boom-ba-da-boom... and one scarf went flying across the stage. Eddie sat up straighter in his seat. "Hey, I didn't expect this."

"Didn't expect what?" I said, sinking lower into my seat.

"It looks like Isabelle is going to strip," his eyes get brighter.

Boom-ba-da-boom...one or two more scarves went flying. "I think you're right," I can feel my face getting red. "Come on let's get out of here."

"Wait...wait," he sat up a little higher and leaned forward to get a better view.

"Are you crazy?" I was almost under the seat. "Her dress is coming apart!"

"Yeah...yeah!"

I peeked over the seat in front of us, "Why is she waving that big fan?"

"Ssh! Be quiet!" Boom-ba-da-boom...another part of the shiny dress fell off. The fan was waving strategically in front of her and behind her, as she swirled gracefully about the stage. She peeked over it, smiling broadly. The whistling and applause got louder.

"Can we leave now?" I sank down a little more. "I thought Isabelle was a singer."

"Yeah, yeah," Eddie said. "Be quiet!"

"Oh, my God, what are we going to tell my brother?"

"Don't worry about him." Eddie's eyes were fixed on the onstage action.

**37**

Boom-ba-da-boom-ba-da-boom. Isabelle threw kisses with one hand while holding the fan with the other, then she slithered off stage to thunderous applause and more whistles. The lights came on and we finally could 321 leave. "Wow, that was something," Eddie said, grinning from ear to ear.

"Right," I couldn't get out of the theater fast enough. "What are we going to tell René when he asks where we went?"

"We'll say we went to a movie," he took my elbow and we walked back to our car.

Sister Marie Antoine met us at the door when we returned. Father Paré wasn't back yet. She said he'd be back for supper and that we should wait.

"He should be here shortly," she said as she led us to the parlor. "Supper will be ready in about fifteen minutes. He's usually on time." She invited us to sit down, "Did you have a nice afternoon?"

"Yes," Eddie said. "There are some very interesting things to see in Montréal."

I chose to allow Eddie to carry on the conversation about the Italian restaurant and the remarkable similarity of the department stores. Sister excused herself when my brother entered the room wearing his white Dominican habit, "I hope I didn't hold up supper," he said.

"Not at all," she smiled. "Everything is ready."

The aroma of pot roast wafted through the corridor as we approached the dining room. "Something sure smells good," I said.

"Oh yes," René said. "The good sisters know how to cook very well." We took our places around the dining room table. "By the way," he looked at Eddie. "I hope you don't have any great plans for tomorrow."

"Why?" He looked puzzled, "what's going on?"

"I think you'd enjoy going to the Montréal Botanical Garden in the afternoon."

"What's over there?" Eddie asked.

"There are wonderful exhibits of plants and flowers from all over the world."

"That sounds interesting," he turned to me. "What do you think, Kid?"

"You know me, Hon, I'm game for anything."

"We'll be back in time for supper and after that the boys are having a baseball game."

"I'd like to watch that,"

"Well, actually," my brother said. "We need an umpire and I was hoping you'd be available."

"That sounds like fun," I took a bite of roasted carrot.

"Don't get too excited," my brother looked at me. "You won't be there."

"Why not?"

"The sisters asked me if you'd take them to Notre Dame Cathedral."

"We've already been there."

"I know," his face grew serious. "There's been a fire at the Saint Cunégonde facility for the elderly. Twenty-three residents and two sisters have died and Sister Marie Antoine and Sister Caron, our refectory attendant, want to pay their respects to the bodies laid out at Notre Dame. "

"How can I refuse?" We finished our meal almost in silence. "I guess we should call it an early night," I said. Somehow, the apple pie had lost its appeal.

"Mass is at 11:00 a.m. tomorrow and we can leave after that," my brother said. "We can grab a hot dog at the park."

"No such thing," Sister Caron said. "You'll have dinner with us, here, before you go."

My brother shrugged, "Never argue with sister."

***

By 6:00 a.m. I had my wash in the dryer. We were preparing for our departure on the next day. Eddie picked up a Montréal Gazette at the main desk of the trailer park. "There's quite an article in here about that fire at Sainte Cunégonde," Eddie said. "There were orphans housed there on the first floor and the elderly were on the upper floors. The place has been staffed by the same sisters as your aunts since it was established in 1889."

"My aunts probably knew some of them," I said. "Did the kids get out all right?"

"Yes, the fire started on one of the upper floors and spread quickly up there, the death toll is up to 38," Eddie pointed to a picture of the structure in flames and firefighters lowering residents to the ground in long body baskets. "Mother Superior and another nun lost their lives trying to save others."

"I sure don't look forward to going to Notre Dame tonight and seeing all those coffins."

"I know," he said. "But it's the least we can do for the sisters who have been so good to us on this visit."

39

Eddie was wearing gray trousers and a pale green, short-sleeved plaid cotton shirt. I had on a navy blue skirt, a white blouse and a blue and white striped short-sleeved jacket. I wore white sandals. We ate a simple breakfast of toast, fruit and coffee. I folded the laundry while Ed read the paper. By 10:30 the clothes were ironed and put away in the closet, the kitchen was cleaned up and we were ready to go.

Sister Caron was true to her word. After Mass we went to the refectory where there was a lovely table prepared with soup and ham and cheese sandwiches, tea and cookies. We sat down, and René blessed the food. "Bon appétit!" sister said. "Enjoy your meal and we'll see you when you get back from your busy afternoon."

"We'll have to stop at a gas station before we go to the Gardens," Eddie said.

"There's one not far from here," René replied. "The Gardens are close to the center of town so it won't take us long to get there."

"Do you go there often?" I asked.

"I've gone with some of the older boys," he answered. "They enjoyed it a lot."

"How long has this place been there?" Eddie got into the driver's seat.

"It was built during the depression, in 1931," my brother said as I closed our doors at the same time.

Eddie backed slowly out of his parking space— "that was twenty years ago!"

"Actually," my brother said, "it didn't start out to be a Botanical Garden. Brother Marie Victorin wanted a place where he could display flowers and plants to show the world the wonders of God's creation."

"How did it go about that?" I asked.

"By making a pest of himself and praying a lot," he said. "He went to the mayor of Montréal over a period of years to plead his case, and finally the mayor gave in and decided it would be a good opportunity to put some people to work and make use of the land at Maisonneuve Park". "Here, turn left just ahead," René said. "The entrance should be on the right."

We proceeded as directed and entered a new world of exotic plants and flowers. "Oh, my God!" was all I could say.

Eddie drove slowly by the beds of red and white Geraniums, sculptures of nymphs in various poses and past orange Tiger Lilies in large round cement borders. Each display was more colorful than the one before. Potted date palms and tall coconut palms lined the pathways of tropical plants and colorful orchids. "Did Brother Victorin plan all this?" I asked.

"Oh no," René answered. "A horticulturalist named Henry Teuscher drew up the plans back in 1936." He pointed to some buildings in the distance. "There are lots of tall

40

greenhouses where the tropical plants are stored in temperature-controlled rooms during the winter and brought outside as the weather gets warmer."

Eddie parked the car near a pond where a large shiny brownish, dotted, sculpture of a frog overlooked floating lily pads and white flowers. We walked along the pathways of multi-colored phlox and gladiola and black-eyed-susans. It seemed every flower bed was more beautiful than the one before. Camellias and Gardenias, violets: domestic and African varieties, Hyacinths and Hollyhocks, all were displayed in bright profusion, capturing our gaze as we walked from one pathway to the next. The afternoon passed all too quickly.

By the time we returned to the orphanage, the boys were in the schoolyard waiting for Father to remind him of the baseball game planned for after supper. Eddie had already been assigned as the umpire and was looking forward to it. The ever-watchful sisters were not long in coming with a hand bell to announce clean-up time in preparation for their meal. The bell was like magic, the schoolyard was empty in less than five minutes and the boys were on their way to the refectory.

"It looks like the boys are really anxious for this game," Eddie remarked.

"Oh yes," my brother said. "They play a couple of times a week."

"How many teams are there?" Eddie asked.

"Four: Red, Green, Blue and Yellow and the boys range in age from 16 to 10 on each team. Tonight the Red and Yellow teams are playing."

"So you have a real competition going here?" I asked. "Who usually umpires?"

"One of the La Salle brothers who teaches here," he answered. "They usually come to watch the game anyway."

Sister Marie-Antoine appeared in the hallway. "Will you be taking Sister Caron and me to the wake at Notre Dame tonight, Jeanne?"

"Yes," I answered. "I'll just need some directions on how to get there."

They assured me it would not be a problem, and they would be ready as soon as supper was over. I was not looking forward to this visitation and did not contribute much to the conversation during the meal. The men were enthusiastically discussing the game but I only half listened. We ate chicken vegetable soup, meat loaf, mashed potatoes and peas. As always it was delicious. I passed up the chocolate layer cake and excused myself to go meet the sisters. They met me in the foyer at the entrance and we walked together to the car. Sister Marie-Antoine sat up front with me and except for an occasional directive to turn left or right, the trip was quiet. The parking lot was full so I drove around the block a few times until I found an empty parking space. We followed a long line of mourners, entered the front door of the Cathedral where the caskets of the sisters were set in the sanctuary in front of the large golden altar. The rest of the caskets formed a semi-circle around the two coffins and filled the inner sanctuary. An honor guard of sisters from various religious orders knelt between the nuns and the other victims praying the Rosary aloud. The mourners were a teary procession of men in dark suits and ties, and women in black dresses and hats or veils, many with a handkerchief in one hand and a rosary in the other. Some took seats in the pews but most moved slowly down the long aisle of the church and left through the side entrance. We took seats in the side pews long enough to pray the rosary then proceeded in silence to the car. "Thank God the children made it out of the building safely," Sister Caron said as she closed the back door.

"That's definitely true," said Sister Marie-Antoine. "It's sad enough when old people die; it's disastrous when children lose their lives."

\*\*\*\*\*\*\*\*\*\*\*\*\*\*

The Yellow team won 22 to 21 and the boys were celebrating with cookies and milk when we returned. Children, blessed children, I thought, I hope someday children will be part of my life.

Chapter 6

The subtle changes of red, yellow, and orange began to appear in the early morning sky. A path of golden ripples sparkled on the river as the red sun peeked over the horizon. "It's going to be a beautiful day," I said to Eddie as he secured the trailer hitch and electric hand brake to the car.

"It sure looks that way," he answered. "I'm glad we decided to leave early." He gave one last tug on the security chain. "We should make it to the U.S border ahead of the early morning traffic."

"It was hard to say good-bye to my brother last night," I took one last look inside the trailer before closing the door and walked toward the car. "Who knows when we'll see him again?"

"Maybe next summer when he comes to visit your parents," he checked around once more then took his place behind the wheel and started the engine.

"It was a great visit and those sisters were certainly very gracious to us."

"You'll get no argument from me about that," he drove slowly toward the business office. "You want to settle up our account?"

I shrugged, got out of the car, went into the office and paid the bill. "Thanks for everything," I told the manager and left.

"We'll stop for gas," Eddie said as I settled in the passenger seat, "and New York State, USA here we come."

We were dressed in our traveling clothes. Eddie wore gray trousers and a gray, red and green argyle sweater. I wore a brown plaid A-line skirted dress with a wide white collar, a white long sleeved buttoned down sweater and penny loafers.

He picked up a map at the gas station. "It looks like we have to go west toward Ontario before heading south to the New York border," he said.

"My brother said it should take us about three hours to get to customs."

"According to this map it looks like another couple of hours to Alexandria Bay," he said as he turned on to the highway.

As we had encountered on our way to Québec, we found the roads closer to the big cities were well paved while the country roads were gravel, although well kept. We drove for miles between farm houses and encountered little activity other than on the farms where we saw farmers tending their neatly planted fields. Tall silos dominated the fields like sentinels overlooking the grazing horses, cows, and pig enclosures. Children waved at us energetically from their perch on the fences as our silver domed house danced behind the car.

"There's not a lot of music on this radio," I said as I turned the dial from one station to the other.

"We'll probably be able to get a New York station before too long," he nodded toward the radio. "Just move the dial very slowly."

Slowly! That was the trick. I caught the golden tones of Mario Lanza singing 'Loveliest Night Of The Year'. We both chimed in. The transmission was a bit scratchy but it was good enough for us to sing along and our vocal renditions helped the time pass more quickly.

We were never far away from the Saint Lawrence River and we crossed the border at the bridge at Cornwall, Ontario. We went through customs without incident. The inspector examined our birth certificates, looked through our trailer and car, asked where we had been in Canada, and then gave us 'carte-blanche' to re-enter the States. We continued on our way to the Thousand Islands.

It was about 11:30 a.m. when we reached Alexandria Bay. We looked for a trailer park and found one just outside of the city. Once we were unhitched, we walked into town. Most of the activity was going on at the river's edge. It was almost a carnival atmosphere with little snack stands here and there and large signs advertising short or long cruises between the islands. We stopped for a hot dog and root beer and inquired about the different ships available.

"You've got to take Uncle Sam's Cruise Ship," said a man sitting on a stool at the wood paneled counter. He was wearing bib overalls, a red plaid shirt and a navy blue cap said. "That's the best one."

"Have you taken it before?" Eddie asked.

"A couple of times," he answered. "But I live here and I've heard other people say it's great because the captain talks about the Islands and there's even a stop on Heart Island."

"Heart Island?" Eddie was interested.

"That's where the castle is; Boldt Castle."

"Is the pier far?" I took a sip of root beer.

"Nah!" he pointed his finger at the line of docks along the river. "Just a little ways down. There's a big sign, you can't miss it." He slid off the stool. "You'll enjoy visiting the castle." He tipped his cap and was gone.

It was cool by the riverside. The sun was bright and there was hardly a ripple on the water. We found Uncle Sam's dock, bought our tickets and boarded the double decked cruise ship. We sat on the benches near the bow to have a better view of the islands. The scenery was spectacular. Some islands were as small as our trailer with nothing but trees and large rocks. Some were large enough to accommodate two or three Cape Cod style houses in semblance of a mini-village, accessible only by boat. One small island had a grounded fishing boat about thirty feet long, with a high cabin and a long flat stern which covered most of the island. It appeared to have been re-vamped into a home.

"How many of you remember Arthur Godfrey, the red-headed ukulele player? ",
the tour director asked. Most of the tourists raised their hands. "I'm sure you also remember he had a hit song 'Florence' a couple of years ago. I still hear it once in a while." He had everyone's attention and we nodded to one another in agreement. "The lyrics still bemoan the loss of his girlfriend, Florence, on one of the Thousand Islands." Our tour director pointed to a tiny island about twenty feet in circumference, covered with vegetation and surrounded by a sandy shore. "There is Florence," he said. "She's not much to look at but she's the island which was given to Mr. Godfrey by the Alexandria Bay Chamber of Commerce," he shrugged. "It seems Florence has increased tourism to the Thousand Islands," he looked at each of us. "Maybe even some of you decided to check out the islands because of Florence." The passengers responded with loud laughter and applause.

We saw large mansions on a few of the larger islands with sturdy docks and boats. The tour director told us that at the turn of the twentieth century this area was a favorite vacation spot for the rich and powerful. "One such man," he said, "was George Boldt, the General Manager of the Waldorf Astoria Hotel in New York." He pointed to a large island in the distance. "Mr. Boldt had a wife Louisa and two children," he continued. "In 1900 he decided to build a Rhineland Castle on Heart Island for his wife."

The upper level of the six-story, one hundred-twenty room castle became more visible. "He spared no expense," the guide went on. "In 1904, when it was nearly finished, Boldt sent a message to the workers to stop all work and abandon the area."

The boat slowed down as we approached the pier. The passengers waited for the guide to continue. "Louise died unexpectedly only three months before her husband was to present the castle to her as a birthday gift." The passengers began to line up for debarkation. "George Boldt never returned to this island and what you are about to see is an unfinished castle that has stood the ravages of time and the elements for more than forty years."

The passengers filed off the boat in whispers. Eddie took my hand as I stepped down to the sand of the island. We were guided through room after room of exquisite architecture. Never-lit stone fireplaces dominated many of the rooms, bare ceilings where one could only imagine graceful chandeliers, unfinished counters and empty spaces where cabinets and shelves with elegant china should be. All of these reminders of a dream ending in tragedy. We stepped outside and walked to the tiny cottage playhouse intended for the Boldt children, Louisa and George, Jr. Built of wood to resemble the 'house that Jack built' of storybook fame, the floors were slanted and the walls uneven. Even the staircase to the roof had crooked steps. I climbed out an attic window to the roof and sat next to the chimney. I looked back at the castle, "Crazy as it seems," I observed, "this is the only place on this whole island that turned out right, and those kids never had a chance to play here."

"Now don't go getting all teary-eyed," Eddie said as he offered me his handkerchief and his hand. "It looks like the passengers are heading back to the boat."

We walked hand in hand in silence, and boarded the vessel for the return trip to the pier. The tour guide pointed out a lighthouse and other picturesque islands. The sun was warm and the breeze was cool, making the return trip to the dock seem shorter. We returned to our trailer, tuned in our small radio to a local station and listened to quiet music. "What's the matter?" Eddie asked.

"I don't know," I shrugged. "I can't help thinking about that Mr. Boldt."

"What about him?" He opened the newspaper we bought on the way home.

"He must have loved his wife a whole lot to build her that kind of a castle"

"Well, when you have money you can do anything."

"I suppose so," I reached for the frying pan under the counter. "What about those two kids?"

"Yeah?" he looked up from the paper.

"Whatever happened to them?" I reached in the ice-box for the bread and cheese. "It seems like he should have finished the place for them."

"Now, don't start getting sentimental." He returned to his paper. "How long before the grilled cheese will be ready?

"In a few." I put the kettle of water on the hot plate for tea, sliced the pickles and listened to the music.

***

Eddie had the map of New York spread out on the table. "It looks like Niagara Falls is more than 250 miles south of here," he said as he traced the route with his finger.

I leaned over his shoulder. "How long do you think it'll take us to get there?"

"I'd say a good part of the day". He folded the map with northern New York displayed on top. "If we leave around nine we should get there by late afternoon."

**45**

"Of course that depends on traffic." I poured two cups of coffee.

"Right," he took a sip. "We have to go through Syracuse and Buffalo before we get there."

"Sounds like another long ride." I placed the plates of scrambled eggs and bacon on the table along with toast and butter.

"There are a lot of clouds up there," he said pulling the drapes aside. "I hope the rain holds off while we're driving."

"That would be nice."

We finished breakfast. I cleaned up the dishes and closed the sofa-bed while Eddie went out to hitch the trailer to the car. Trailer living was becoming a new normal: up early in the morning, shower and dress, breakfast, tidy up and go. This day was no different; we were hitched up, checked out and on our way by 9:00a.m. Eddie was at the wheel and I had the map; driver and navigator with the first destination Syracuse.

It was a pleasant ride. We passed beautiful dairy farms where hundreds of black and white Guernsey cows fed on the green grass. Also, lovely farmhouses, mostly white in color with various colored trim. Most of the homes had a large garden not far from the house. Now and then we saw farms with corn and other vegetables which the families sold in small roadside stands. The traffic was light and the road was good. We reached Syracuse by noon. We stopped for gas at a Socony station. This is a good sized city," Eddie said while the attendant filled the tank.

I walked over closer to the street. "Maybe one day we can come back here and stay a little longer."

"I don't know about that," he said as he turned to check on the attendant. "I'll ask if we can use those picnic tables over there to have lunch."

There was room enough to back the trailer into the space under the sign of the Flying Red Horse. I went in the trailer and made ham sandwiches while Eddie bought cokes from the coke machine.

"Where are you guys headed?" the attendant, dressed in a green uniform with the flying red horse logo, asked.

"Niagara Falls," Eddie answered.

"That'll take you another couple of hours," he said. "You should get there around 4:30p.m. It's a nice drive." He waved as he went to serve another customer.

"We should get going," I said as I picked up the paper plates to throw in the trash.

We took our places in the car and were on our way. Once back on the highway we were looking for signs for Buffalo. The sky was overcast for most of the day but it had not rained. The sun peeked out now and then but only for minutes at a time. The winding roads and scenery were similar to what we had seen on the way to Syracuse. There was a small town now and then and usually a small white church close to the center.

"Uh, Honey," I remarked. "I think we're going the wrong way."

"What are you talking about?" he stretched his neck to look at the road. "What makes you say that?"

"We just passed a sign that pointed to Utica," I pointed to the map. "Utica is east of Syracuse, Buffalo is west."

"Are you sure?" He slowed down a little. "How did that happen?"

"Maybe we should stop someplace and ask."

"We'll wait till we see another sign."

46

"But if we're going the wrong way we'll be wasting a lot of time."

"I can't see where we made a wrong turn, you must be mistaken."

"I'm sure if you stop at a gas station they'll tell you if we're headed for Niagara Falls."

We drove on for a few more miles before we came to another small town. "There's a gas station ahead, let's stop there to ask someone if we're going the right way."

""There's no need to stop," he said as we drove past the Gulf station. "We'll know soon enough when we see another sign."

We drove another twenty miles before we passed another station. "Honey, I really think we should stop."

"No, no we're all right." The words were barely out of his mouth when we came to an intersection with signs pointing to Utica. He pulled up on the wide shoulder of the road and stopped. He got out of the car and walked closer to the corner to examine the signs in all directions. He came back to the car, looked at the map and said, "I think we should turn around," he shook his head. "That sign says Buffalo is in the other direction."

"No kidding! Humph!"

We drove along in silence while we listened to news and music on the radio. A few 'I told you so's' ran through my mind. The time passed quickly enough and we arrived in Buffalo around 5:30p.m. We found a trailer park close to Niagara Falls, had a quick supper and decided to walk to see the falls at night. We followed a queue of other sightseers until the falls came into view. It was a breathtaking sight. We stood on a platform to see the wide semi-circle of falls tumbling to a depth of what seemed like hundreds of feet. The many strategically placed lights in the area reflected on the thundering water creating a prism of rainbows. We stood hand in hand, in awe of the magnificence before us and were mesmerized by the incredible beauty and powerful sound of the falling water. The clouds had parted in the evening sky and the stars began to fill the night. "Move along," someone said, and we shuffled along the wooden path until the falls were no longer in view. Eddie put his arm around me and we walked quietly back to our house. "We'll come back in the daytime," he said softly.

A bright flash of lightning and a loud clap of thunder awakened us. Eddie pushed the striped drape over our bed aside. Large drops of rain were pounding in the window. "I don't think we'll be going to the falls today," he sat on the edge of the bed.

I yawned and looked at the Big Ben alarm clock on the counter. "It's only 6:00a.m. Maybe it'll clear up later on."

"Maybe; in the meanwhile I'll take the umbrella and go down to the washroom while you make the coffee."

I put on my robe, made coffee, and gathered clothes for the laundry. When Eddie returned I took the umbrella, "I'll be a little while," I said. "I'll do a load of wash while I'm showering, and then put it in the drier." I pushed the door with my shoulder, "we'll have breakfast when I get back."

When I returned Eddie had the Niagara Falls newspaper spread out on the table in the breakfast nook. "How long before breakfast is ready?"

"Not long," I pulled out the frying pan from under the counter and took four eggs out of the ice box. "Toast and eggs okay?"

"Sure," he folded the paper and began to set the table. "When do you have to go back for the clothes?"

"About an hour." I put the eggs in the sizzling butter and turned the bread in the toaster to toast the second side of the slices. "It looks like this rain is good for the day."

"I think you're right," he looked in the ice box. "How about frying up some of this bologna?"

"Sure." I slid the sunny-side eggs on the plates and browned the meat. "What do you want to do today?"

"I thought we'd play cards this afternoon and go to the movies tonight."

"What's playing?" I handed him the toast to butter.

"There's a double feature tonight," he looked up at me. "'Man in the Saddle' with Randolph Scott and 'Bells of San Angelo' with Roy Rogers."

I served the bologna then sat across from him "Sounds like your kind of movies."

"I didn't think you'd want to go to the falls in this kind of rain."

"You're right." I took a sip of coffee. "When we go to the falls I don't want to be carrying an umbrella."

We finished our breakfast then I picked up the umbrella to go back to the laundry room. The day went as planned and although the sky was still overcast on the next day, it wasn't raining so we walked down to see to the falls. Now and then it was misty but we realized that some of the mist was generated from the falls. We were provided with Nor'easter raincoats and were guided to Luna Island. The view from that point was incredible. We saw the rough water of the rapids tumbling down the river to the shear drop of the falls. Our tour guide pointed out several areas where persons had attempted to ride over the falls in barrels. Few survived. The memory of this phenomenal spectacle is forever engrained in my mind.

The next day was Sunday. We wanted to get an early start so we attended 7:00a.m. Mass at Saint John de la Salle Church about 10 minutes away from the falls. It was a large stone church with three tall stained glass windows above the main wooden portal of the church. The tallest was in the center and one a little shorter on either side over which a large cross stood atop the peak of the facade. We entered the stone foyer and found an empty pew in the center. The priest processed down the center aisle wearing a green chasuble. Ahead of him were 2 acolytes carrying tall candles. They wore black robes with white surplices. The priest said the opening prayers at the foot of the altar then climbed the few steps, then faced the altar with his back to the assembly to say the Mass in Latin. There was no choir, which shortened the Mass considerably and we were home 45 minutes after we had arrived at the church.

We returned to the trailer, had a quick bowl of corn flakes with milk then began our, now familiar, ritual of hitching up, paying up and moving on. Our next destination was Northeast Pennsylvania. My grandmother's brother, Antoine Gagnon, lived there and Tante Marie had made us promise we'd try to visit with him. "He's my most adventurous brother," she had said. "He has a mink farm over there and sometimes he has to wrestle with bears to keep his animals safe."

I don't know how true that is but my mother had said he was a fun uncle and she enjoyed visiting with him. Mom and Tante Marie had both written to him and he told them he was looking forward to meeting us. Although we had an address we didn't find him. We drove around for more than an hour and a half and couldn't locate his farm. Maybe if we had stopped to ask for directions???

We continued on our journey west until we reached Ashtabula, Ohio, where we decided to spend the night. I began to write letters to Mom and Tante Marie to let them know we didn't locate Uncle Antoine and tell them about our recent experiences at the

Thousand Islands and Niagara Falls. Eddie sat across from me at the breakfast nook reading the Ashtabula Star Beacon. All of a sudden we heard the sound of rain; we closed the windows of the trailer then heard 'rat-a-tat' on the roof as though rocks were falling on us. Eddie opened the door and we saw hail, the size of ice cubes beginning to cover the grass. "Hey, Sweetheart," he said. "Come look at this!"

I had seen hail before, but, never this big. The ice was piling up. Eddie, the ever practical one, said, "Get a couple of bowls that will fit in the ice box."

"What for?" I wanted to know.

"Didn't you say we were running low on ice?"

"Yes, but?"

"If we fill up the bowls with the hail it'll keep the icebox cold until we can find a place to buy a block of ice tomorrow."

No more questions. I gave him a bowl, kept one, and we collected enough hail-stones to fill the bowls. Our neighbors probably thought we were nuts. I saw the man two trailers away peeking at us out of his door but no one else was out gathering ice during the twenty minute storm. "Hey!" Rain was dripping down my face. "This has to be our lucky day!"

"If you mean we got ice for the ice box," he answered. "I guess it is."

"Yeah, that was lucky. But look at this." I held up my treasure. "I just found a four-leaf clover; June 24, 1951, I'm going to remember this date forever."

I held out my hand for him to see. "It's so small," he said. "How did you ever find it?"

"I just looked and it was there." I grinned at him. "I'm going to save it." I pressed it my diary. We changed out of our wet clothes, I finished my letters and we called it a day.

We awoke to a bright sunny day. I checked our bowls in the ice box. The hail-stones had stuck together and melted enough to fit into one bowl after I poured out the water. I made sunny-side eggs, toast and bacon while Eddie went for his shower.

"Is the coffee ready?" he was wearing khaki trousers and a short sleeved green cotton shirt.

I poured coffee for both of us and set the filled plates on the table. "How far do you think we'll get today?"

"I'm hoping we can get to Chicago," he took a sip of coffee.

"We can get a map at the gas station," I took a bite of toast.

"That's a good idea," he dunked his toast in the egg yolk. "The maps we have don't go as far as Illinois."

We finished breakfast, cleaned up the dishes, and I went for my shower while Eddie hitched up for an early start. I came back from the washroom wearing a short sleeved yellow and white polka dot dress and white sandals. Our clothes were still damp from the night before so we spread them on the breakfast nook table to finish drying. We were on our way.

We drove through Cleveland at the peak of the morning traffic. Eddie was a good driver and maneuvered very well between cars as he hauled our little house behind us. Once we were out of the city we continued on through Ohio and into Indiana. The scenery was beautiful; the music on the radio kept us entertained and we stopped only for ice, gas and lunch as we headed for Illinois. In South Bend, Indiana we saw the Bendix Plant where new front-loading washing machines had just been introduced. "Maybe one day we'll own one of those," I said as we passed the large photo.

"Maybe," Eddie smiled. "And maybe we'll have kids and a house too."

"You never know." I moved closer to him on the seat and he patted my hand.

It was about 4:30p.m. when we reached Roby, Indiana and found a trailer park. The sign outside the park told us we were only 5 blocks from Chicago. It made sense to stop here for the next few days. It was a great place to begin another adventure.

The trailer park was on the main highway to Chicago. The front office looked like a small brown cottage with green shutters and trim. There was a registration desk in the foyer and large paned glass doors that led to a small coffee shop with four round tables. "You can get coffee in there in the morning," the bald concierge in the brown trousers and white short sleeved shirt had told us when we checked in. "My wife will have muffins." We thanked him and went out with him to the parking lot. Eddie got in the car and the concierge waved him on to our assigned spot.

The trailers were lined up along the side closest to the road. Each trailer had its own parking space for the car and enough distance from the neighbor to afford privacy. While the men were maneuvering the trailer, I walked to the long wooden, brown and green, one story building housing the showers and laundry facilities which stood on the far side of the site. Small yews and alternate pansy and petunia beds along the low fences separated the trailer spaces creating a homey atmosphere. I watched as the concierge directed Eddie into our space and supervised our connections to the electricity and water.

"Okay, Sweetheart," Eddie said as he opened the trailer door. "We're all set and I'm getting hungry."

"So am I," I stepped inside and looked around. "We're getting pretty good," I observed. "Nothing fell on the floor today."

I reached in the ice-box and pulled out some eggs and cheese. "We're running low on groceries." I reached for a bowl in the cabinet. "Maybe before we come home tomorrow we could find a food store."

"We'll probably need ice too." He placed our hot plate on the counter, filled the tea kettle with water and opened the windows.

I proceeded to prepare a cheese omelet, pulled out the bread for toast and put two teabags in the teapot. "Tomorrow's going to be an exciting day." I set two plates, teacups, forks and napkins on the table.

"Yeah, I picked up brochures in the office," he fixed the toast. "I'll look them over after we eat."

A soft breeze came in through the windows as we ate and chatted about our day. I poured the boiling water into the teapot, cleared the dishes and Eddie spread the brochures on the table. I poured the rest of the hot water from the tea kettle into the sink to soak the dishes. "Do you see anything interesting?"

"Look at this," he showed me a picture of the Museum of Science and Industry. "This is the only building still standing from the 1893 World's Fair. They called it The White City."

"Why did they call the building White City?" I was curious.

"The building is all white," he turned the picture to show me. "See? It looks like a Greek palace with all those white columns in the front."

"Is that where you want to go first?"

"No. I think Grant Park will be our first stop," he picked up another brochure. "According to this brochure there's a lot to see over there."

"From these descriptions, both places appear to be close," I wiped my hands and placed the towel to dry on the rack next to the ice-box and sat next to him.

"I guess we'll find that out when we get to Chicago." he gathered the brochures. "The park is near the center of town and it's right on Lake Michigan," he folded the brochures of both places and lay them on top of the pile. "In the meanwhile, let's call it a day." He gathered the papers and laid them on the table. "We can look at these again tomorrow."

We opened the sofa together, listened to the radio for awhile, then settled in for the night. We were so tired that even the rumble of traffic on the busy highway didn't prevent us from sleeping. We didn't bother setting old Big Ben since we had already decided to spend a few days in the city to take in all there was to see.

We didn't need the alarm. The bright sunlight came through the open windows and we were up before seven. I made coffee while Eddie went for his shower. We ate Kellogg's Corn Flakes with milk when he returned. He was wearing tan slacks and a short-sleeved green plaid shirt and loafers. "I'll look over the city map of Chicago while you go to the washroom."

By the time I returned he had planned out our day. I was wearing a yellow sundress and white sandals. "I wish my uncle Désiré still lived here," I said. "He knew everything there was to know about Chicago."

"I remember him," Eddie looked up from the map. "He was your mother's brother who drove a taxi here in Chicago."

"He came to visit Mama the summer before we were married," I reminded him. "He told us how much he loved this city."

"He invited us to visit," he folded the map. "It's too bad he died before we had the chance to take him up on his invitation." He looked up at me," I really liked him."

"Me too."

It was 9:00 a.m. The sky was clear and blue. "It looks like we're going to have a beautiful day," Eddie said.

"It sure looks that way," we gathered up the night clothes and blankets and tucked them into the sofa as we tidied up. "What time do you want to leave?"

"What do you think about shopping now instead of waiting until tonight?" Eddie asked.

52

"Why not?" I put the last of the dishes away. "That way we can have lunch at home and I can pack a sandwich for later on this afternoon."

The store was in Roby, not far from the trailer park. We picked up groceries and ice and stopped to fill the gas tank. We allowed ourselves the luxury of Campbell's chicken noodle soup and crackers for lunch, then I packed a small bag with peanut butter and jelly sandwiches and we were on our way. We drove the few city blocks from Roby to Chicago shortly after noon.

Midday traffic was heavy but without the additional weight of the trailer we drove to the city without incident. It wasn't long before we saw Grant Park. As we drove toward Michigan Avenue we saw several streets which formed bridges that crossed over railroad tracks below. Now and then we saw trains traveling beneath the bridges. The city was on one side of the bridges and the park on the other. On the city side of the bridges we could see tall buildings and on the other side we saw the gardens, paths and trees and the quiet waters of Lake Michigan in the distance. It was a lovely summer day. The sun was high in the cloudless blue sky. We drove up to the Michigan Bridge which crosses the Chicago River and continued driving toward Lake Michigan. "I don't know where we are," Eddie said. "None of these street names sound familiar."

It seemed like we were driving nowhere until we came upon Lake Shore Drive. "This is the street the Museum is on, according to the brochure," Eddie remembered. "The only problem is that I don't know if we're going in the right direction." He drove a little farther.

"That must be it over there!" I pointed to a large white building with tall white columns in the front.

"That has to be it," Eddie agreed. "I'll find a parking place."

As we walked toward the entrance we could see a white dome connected to the building behind the entrance. Once in the foyer we read through the lists of exhibits to be found in this museum. There was an exhibit of a Santa Fe train, the Wright brothers' airplane, a coal mine, science displays and more. We decided to visit the giant heart. We were amazed to observe the complexities of the human heart displayed in a 16 foot heart, made of plaster and chicken wire. We stepped inside and saw how the arteries and valves functioned to keep us alive. It was a new world of modern science and medicine where new things were being discovered every day. When we came upon the display in glass containers depicting the development of life from conception to birth we stood in silence. Eddie held my hand. We looked at each other and read one another's unspoken thoughts. Could it be that one day this miracle of life would become a reality for us? "I think we're going to need more than one afternoon to really see this place," Eddie said.

"I agree." We walked out of the museum hand in hand, returned to our car in silence and drove to find the entrance of Grant Park.

It was the largest park I had ever seen. It was divided into sections with flower lined pathways, lawns, large enough for a carnival, and trees.... trees of all kinds everywhere. There were monuments and statues and fountains throughout the park. One particularly intriguing statue was of a sitting Abraham Lincoln. His bearded face reflected kindness and wisdom. The statue stood on a semi-circular platform with a tall Greek column on either side. It wasn't far from Buckingham Fountain, a large tiered fountain modeled after one in Versailles, France. The brochure told us the fountain is more spectacular at night so we agreed to return after dark. As we walked around we saw signs directing us to the underground theater. The door was slightly ajar. We entered the theater and sat in the back row. The opera star, Eugene Conley, was rehearsing for a concert to be held that evening. We marveled at the voice of this remarkable tenor who, we learned later, had recently appeared as Alfred in Chicago's operatic presentation of "Der Fledermaus ". No one noticed us as we sat mesmerized, listening to the magnificent music. We slipped out unseen and walked back to our car. "Shall we eat our sandwiches before we go into the city?" Eddie unlocked the door.

"That's a good idea," I reached in the back seat for the sack with the lunch. Eddie pointed to a bench facing the lake and we walked toward the shore. There was still some ice in our towel wrapped jelly jars full of lemonade. I handed him a wax-paper wrapped peanut butter and jelly sandwich. "This is the life," I said.

The late afternoon sun warmed our faces. We watched as a boat with a tall white sail danced across the rippling water of the lake in the summer breeze. Two smaller boats with billowing sails, floated near each other at a much slower pace. "One day I'll own a boat. " Eddie took a sip from his jar of lemonade.

"And someday a man will walk on the moon," I lifted my arm in a mock toast with my jar of lemonade. "In the meanwhile, how would you like a few vanilla Nabisco wafers for dessert?" We clinked our jars. "Where to next?"

"We'll head for State Street in the city," Eddie took a bite of his cookie. "That's where the theaters are."

"I'm sure we'll find a good movie to see." I put the empty jars and wax paper back into the bag. Eddie walked ahead of me to the car.

We crossed one of the bridges over the railroad tracks and headed for State Street. "The streets are well laid out and well marked in this town," Eddie said. "We shouldn't have a problem finding the theater district."

He was right. We were no sooner on State Street than we saw the vertical Marquee of the Chicago Theater with CHICAGO printed in huge letters on a field of red, glowing brighter than a tree on Christmas. "Oh my gosh, look at those lights," I exclaimed. "That Marquee has to be about six stories high!"

"Yeah, it's almost as tall as the building itself," Eddie slowed down and looked for a parking space. "This theater takes up half of the city block."

We were impressed by the whiteness of the building, the bright lights and the size of the horizontal Marquee emblazoned with CHICAGO in oversized letters on a red background similar to the vertical one. This one was on the street side and extended over the sidewalk, nearly to the street at the entrance. We got out of the car to get a closer look. The box office was open. Large posters advertised two performances by the Nat

King Cole Trio for that evening. I grabbed Eddie's elbow. "Oh, Honey, do you think we could?"

Without a word, he smiled at me and headed for the box office. I held my breath. He came back holding up two tickets. "The show starts at 7:00p.m."

"Are you sure we can afford it?"

"The tickets cost $2.75 each," he shrugged. "This is a night to splurge."

We entered the theater around 6:30 p.m. As we approached the main lobby we saw huge crystal and brass chandeliers hanging from the domed ceiling. Large murals depicting a Greek and Roman theme covered the underside of the dome on the incredibly high ceiling. There were paintings of horses pulling chariots and charioteers and others with soldiers on horseback, armored and helmeted, holding their spears aloft, as though ready for battle. The theme carried throughout the theater from its ornate walls to the proscenium arch of the stage. It was a breathtaking experience. An usher in a gold and red uniform led us to our seats in the center of the side aisle. It was the side closest to the piano. When the curtain opened at exactly 7:00p.m., I felt Goosebumps all over my body as I heard the thunderous applause. Mr. Cole stepped to center stage, wearing a dark gray narrow lapeled two button suit and a dark narrow tie. He smiled broadly and raised his hand, bowed slightly, said a few welcoming words to the audience and placed his hand over his heart as he made his way to stage left where a guitar player and a bass player, also dressed in gray suits and ties, were standing beside a white piano. He nodded to the two men and took his seat on the white piano bench. I moved closer to Eddie and he reached for my hand as the music began.

Mr. Cole's hands glided over the piano keys and his golden voice filled the theater: "There was a boy, a very strange enchanted boy..." The familiar lyrics of 'Nature Boy' created an atmosphere of joy and awe as he began to fill every moment with music. An accomplished pianist, he played interludes of classical and contemporary pieces and spoke easily to the audience in between his vocal renditions. He sang song after song: 'Autumn,' 'Portrait of Jennie' 'Unforgettable'... enhanced by the two string instruments completing the Nat King Cole Trio. We were captivated completely. Finally, when he sang his latest hit song: "They tried to tell us we're too young, too young to really be in love..." we knew we were in the presence of one of the great singers of the century. "Encore! Encore!" the standing audience cried out. After several minutes of continuous applause, this gracious entertainer obliged us with a classical piano solo and one final song: "Mona Lisa." The audience stood up again and shouted loudly in appreciation of this great talent. Resounding applause filled the auditorium as Mr. Cole acknowledged his two musicians, bowed to the audience, raised both hands and the curtain closed. "What a gentleman!" I said to Eddie.

"He is great, no doubt about it." Eddie stood up and faced the back of the theater. "I think we should take our time to leave, it's pretty crowded in the lobby." He put his arm around my waist and slowly guided us both toward the exit.

Traffic had picked up by the time we left the theater. For Chicagoans, the night was just beginning. The streets were more congested than when we had arrived. We drove back to find Buckingham Fountain in Grant Park and found fewer available parking spots. It was a clear night and the moon was low in the early evening sky. Eddie looked up at the stars. "Funny isn't it?" He pointed upwards, "no matter where we are we can always find the North Star and the Big Dipper up there."

"Yeah, here we are two small people, here in Chicago and we know that other people in Florida and Massachusetts and other places on earth also see that same enormous sky covering the whole world." I looked around. "But can we find that huge fountain again in the dark?"

Eddie laughed. "Don't worry about that." He pointed to a reflection of colored lights in the distance. "I think it's over there." We followed the spectrum of red, green, blue, purple, orange and yellow lights until we reached the fountain. It was a large, wide, circular, two tiered fountain. The water shot up from the center to what seemed like a hundred feet in the air and the colored spotlights made the spectacle all the more beautiful; almost like seeing a rainbow in a darkened sky. We stood there in awe while crowds milled around on every side. "I'm glad we came back," I said.

"It's really something." Eddie put his arm around me. "We'd better move on, though, it looks like a lot of other people want to see this too."

"Just a couple of minutes more" I said nodding reluctantly. We walked to our car and headed for home. "What's on the agenda for tomorrow?" I wanted to know.

"What do you think about going to Lincoln Park Zoo?" he asked.

"That sounds interesting." I turned on the radio. 'On top of ole Smokey, all covered with snow...' we heard and sang along, "I lost my true lover, from courting too slow..."

The trip back to Roby was short. The trailer park was quiet. We sat at the table and snacked on graham crackers and milk before preparing the sofa for the night.

We awoke early and decided to go to the showers at the same time. I brought a pale green shirtwaist dress and sandals and Eddie brought gray trousers and a blue short-sleeved shirt to wear for the day. I made coffee and we ate scrambled eggs, bologna and toast for breakfast. Eddie had stopped by the office to collect a newspaper. "Have to keep up with what's going on in the world," he said. "The news about the war in Korea isn't good."

"I heard President Truman has extended the draft until 1955," I said.

"That's true," he looked up from the newspaper. "I was too young to go into the service for World War II but I could be called up for this one."

"I don't even want to think about that." I heated water in the kettle to do the dishes.

"Neither do I," he folded the paper so he could do the crossword puzzle. "But, it could happen. I could be drafted."

I tried to drive the thought away. I busied myself making lunches to bring with us to the zoo. I filled the jelly jars with ice and lemonade, closed the lunch sack and said, "Okay, I'm ready."

"Come on," he picked up the bag with the lunches. "Don't look so sad," he kissed me on the lips. "It's going to be a good day."

We arrived at Lincoln Park around eleven o'clock. It was a cloudy day but it was a pleasant walk around the zoo. We were impressed with a large red brick building which housed tigers and lions. There were terra cotta figures of lions above the entrance. Inside, the walls were ornate with mosaics of lions and tigers and about a dozen dens with skylights allowing fresh air in for the comfort of the animals. The enclosed area was easily viewed by visitors and safely separated from the public by high iron bars. When we left this building we went to an outdoor area where we saw elephants, zebras and rhinos. "Look over there," Eddie said. "There's a big area inside the fence with dead-looking trees."

"Let's get closer," I walked a little faster. "Monkeys! Look at them all."

"I'll be darned!" Eddie observed. "Look at them jumping from limb to limb like they're playing tag." He grinned. "It kind of makes you expect to see Tarzan popping up at any minute."

Our visit was shortened by a huge downpour. We didn't have umbrellas so we hurried to our car, turned on the heater to dry off, and then drove around the city of Chicago. We drove by the stockyards and the Navy pier. It was still raining. "Why don't we go back to the Museum?" Eddie said. "At least we'll be out of the rain."

"I'm game for that." I ran my hand over my dress. "Our clothes are almost dry."

We ate our lunch in the car before entering the museum. This time we knew what we wanted to see. Our first stop was the coal mine. We entered an open car on the upper level and simulated a descent of 600 feet down the mine shaft in the dark which brought us into the mine. There, a guide wearing a hard hat, directed us on a walking tour through the mine and explained how coal is mined and brought up to the surface. We learned about the hazards of mining and that mine workers got paid by the amount of coal they mined, not by the number of hours they worked. An experienced miner could earn about $17.00 a day back in the 1930's. "I'm glad I'm an ironworker," Eddie said. "I don't think I could stand working in the dark like these guys."

The tour lasted about a half-hour. We made our way to the Santa Fe model train exhibit. This was an incredible display of scale model cities, plains, farms and mountains with model trains traveling throughout; over bridges and through tunnels, showing how our country grew commercially and economically by the construction of the railroad. "Gosh," I observed, "you can almost picture real people and merchandise being transported all over the country on these trains."

"During the war, this was the chief means of travel," Eddie remarked. "Especially for servicemen; that's how the Navy shipped my brother Benny from Boston to California. It took five days to go from coast to coast."

"I remember seeing pictures of those trains on Movietone News in the movie theater," I said. "It was hard for civilians to travel because of the overcrowded troop trains." We were fascinated by the details in the small train stations, especially houses and buildings which made the display even more realistic.

In the automobile exhibit we saw cars from the earliest Ford models to the more modern ones. We saw the first airplane and wondered how it ever got off the ground. We saw experiments on how glass and aluminum are tested for strength in the labs. We went from one display to another. There was so much to see. There was so much to learn. "The museum will be closing in thirty minutes," a voice came over the loudspeaker. "Please proceed to the exits."

The afternoon had flown by. "I wish we could spend at least another day here," Eddie said.

"I know." I took Eddie's hand as we followed the other visitors to the exit. "Maybe one day we can come back."

The rain had stopped by the time we left the Museum. The drive home was short. I needed to get some laundry done in preparation for leaving the next day. We listened to the radio while I ironed and put our clothes away. "Beans and hot dogs okay for supper?" I asked.

"Sure," he said as he looked up from the morning paper he had been reading. "I'm going to set the alarm tonight." He folded the paper and threw it in the rubbish. "I want to get through Chicago before the heavy traffic."

"Right," I put the plates on the table. "And we still have to hitch up before we go."

"I'll put on a little dinner music while we eat." Eddie turned on our small Philco radio.

'Come On-a My House My House' Rosemary Clooney was singing. We had settled into a daily routine: up early in the morning, sightseeing or driving during the day and a quiet dinner with music and conversation. I washed the dishes while Eddie prepared the sofa-bed.

\*\*\*

We hitched up in the dark and were on our way before dawn. When the sun rose it cast a golden glow on the farmlands. The sky was blue and the roads were good but very winding through the mountains. Straight patches of highway were few and far between. We crossed the Illinois state line into Iowa by mid-morning. The scenery was beautiful. We saw our first herds of cattle grazing on huge ranches. Cowboys, wearing ten-gallon hats, rode on horseback here and there. It was like watching a western movie come to life. "I wonder if we'll get to see Hopalong Cassidy?" Eddie joked.

"I don't think so," I replied. "We're not even close to Texas."

We passed wheat fields and corn fields growing in neat rows on large farms and occasional farmers tending the crops.

I pointed to the clock on the dashboard. "It's one o'clock, do you think we should stop for lunch?"

"We've got to stop for gas too," he glanced at the gauge. "I'll stop at the next station I see."

It wasn't long before we saw an Esso station. As we pulled in we saw a picnic table just beyond the gas pumps. "Hey, Sweetheart, this looks like the perfect place to have lunch," he got out of the car and spoke to the attendant dressed in a gray, blue pin-striped uniform and matching round, brimless cap, who motioned toward the table and nodded his head. Once we were gassed up and parked next to the table, I entered the trailer, made sandwiches and poured lemonade in glasses. "You're a long way from home," the attendant said as he pointed to our Massachusetts license plate. "How far are you going?" the young man approached the table.

"I'm not sure," Eddie sat down. "We're headed for Yellowstone."

"You can't make it there today," he raised his cap and scratched his head. "But you should be able to get to Minnesota by late this afternoon."

"Would you like a glass of lemonade?" I asked.

'There's another customer driving in." He walked toward the pumps, "but after they've gone, I'll take you up on that."

I went into the trailer for an extra glass. Eddie was eating his baloney sandwich when the attendant returned. "How are the roads between here and South Dakota?" Eddie inquired.

"They're pretty curvy but well paved," the attendant took a sip of his lemonade. "It might take you a little longer because of the load you're hauling."

"We haven't had many problems so far," Eddie reached for his glass of lemonade. "And if you think we can make it to Minnesota this afternoon, that'll be good."

The attendant gulped the last of his drink. "You should be okay." Another car was approaching the pumps. "Thanks for the lemonade, and good luck," he waved as he walked away.

It was about 5:00p.m. when we crossed into Minnesota. We were lucky to find a trailer park a few miles from the state line. We unhitched and settled in to our new routine: Dinner, dishes, newspaper, radio, conversation and our comfy sofa for the night. We planned an early departure for the next morning.

The sky was overcast when we got up. The park manager helped us unhook the water hose and wires before we hitched up the trailer. "It looks like we might get a little rain before the day is out."

"I think you're right," Eddie agreed. "It's only 7:30, maybe it'll clear up before we get to  South Dakota."

"You never know," he said as he closed the door of the car and waved as I took my place in the passenger seat. "Have a good trip!"

The roads were as the attendant in Iowa had said: well paved but very curvy. We had traveled about twenty five miles when Eddie exclaimed, "What's that funny noise?"

"I don't know," I looked toward the back of the car. "But it seems to be getting louder."

"When I see a straight stretch of road, I'll pull over."

We drove on for another ten miles before we came upon a flat, straight section of the road. The noise kept getting louder and louder. Eddie parked on the shoulder, got out and looked under the car. "We need to find a repair station, the muffler's hanging," he shook his head. "I can't fix this on my own."

"I don't understand it," Eddie had a firm grip on the wheel. "The car is shaking. I looked at the car tires when we were stopped and they were okay."

"I hope we find a garage soon," I grabbed on to the edge of the seat. "This is getting kind of scary."

Several more miles down the road we came to a garage and Eddie pulled in. The loud noise of the muffler announced our arrival and a repairman in navy blue coveralls walked over to the car. "Sounds like you've got big problems," he said.

"The muffler's hanging down," Eddie said.

"Unhitch the trailer over there," the repairman pointed to the far corner of the lot, "and we'll put the car on the lift."

He watched as Eddie freed the car. The attendant shook his head. "You've got more than a muffler problem." He was standing next to the trailer. "You've got a flat on this right tire."

Eddie walked over to examine the tire. It was like a bright light went on in his head, "No wonder the car was shaking!" He got back in the car and drove it onto the lift.

"Well, let's take a look at the muffler first." The repairman pushed a button and the car rose from the floor. "I'm afraid I don't have the part to fix this thing properly," he said. "I'll tie a wire around it and it will hold until you get to another station." He walked to the workbench, took out a spool of wire and began to wrap it around the muffler. He lowered the car and went over to the trailer. "I have one of these tires in stock." He disappeared to the back of the garage and returned, rolling a large tire. He jacked up the trailer and removed the damaged tire. We saw the huge gash with a piece of glass wedged in it. "Here's your problem," he pointed to the glass. "There's no way we can fix that, I'll have to sell you this new one."

60

Eddie and I looked at each other, "Double trouble," he said. "And, we still have to get the muffler fixed."

The repairman was busy fixing the tire, "Don't worry," he glanced over at us. "There's a garage in Austin and he's right on the highway." He nodded to the car. "That wire will hold till you get there, and I'm sure that guy will have the parts to fix it."

It started to rain before we left the service station. The sky was really dark now and it looked like the rain wouldn't let up for a while. We got back on the highway and headed toward Austin. The car was still noisy but the wire seemed to hold the muffler in place and the ride was smoother. Fortunately, we didn't have to cross the entire state of Minnesota before finding the garage in Austin. It was just as the first repairman had told us. It was right on the highway and Eddie pulled in the wide driveway. The repairman wearing a tan coverall and matching military style cap walked over to meet us. "Hi, my name is Jim." He extended his hand to Eddie who stood next to the car.

Eddie shook his hand, "Eddie here. I guess you already know we've got a muffler problem."

Jim nodded, "Let's get out of the rain." He pointed to a spot where Eddie could unhitch the trailer. "When you're ready, drive the car over to the lift and I'll take a look at it." He opened the passenger side door for me and said, "you, little lady, can go into the office over there to get out of the rain."

There was a young girl sitting at a large metal green desk. A cash register sat on the left front corner of the desk facing me and two large stacked incoming and outgoing boxes were on the other front corner. A black Smith-Corona typewriter was in the middle. The girl was busy typing when I came in. She looked up. "Hi, pretty wet out there, eh?"

"I'll say." I looked around the room. The walls were covered with photographs of what looked like washed out houses and strewn about debris. There were people standing in some of the photos who looked despaired as they appeared to hold on to salvaged treasures. "What are these pictures?" I asked.

She got up from her green desk chair to stand next to me. She wore a flower print 'broomstick' skirt and a pale blue cotton sweater. "These are pictures from the flood we had a couple of months ago. Some of these people are friends of ours."

"It looks like they lost their homes," I looked at her. "How did it happen?"

"Sometimes, in early spring when it rains a lot, the Cedar River and Dobbins Creek get blocked up by ice-jams," she continued. "That's what happened this past April; the water rose fifteen feet and overflowed the riverbanks. It was sad. Some people lost everything." She turned to look at the pictures. "People are still trying to recover."

"I guess it will be a while before they can rebuild," I said. "Did you lose any property?"

"No, the water didn't come up this high." She went back to her seat at the desk. "Most of the ones rebuilding will probably not settle so close to the river."

"That makes sense." I took a seat on a wooden chair next to the wall and waited for the car repairs to be finished. The repairman came in about a half hour later and made out the bill for the muffler. The girl tallied the cost and rang it up on the cash register. Eddie came in about 20 minutes later. He had taken the time to settle the trailer on to the car. He handed her ten dollars saying," does this cover it?"

The girl nodded and gave him the receipt and said, "thank you, have a nice trip." She waved to us as we left the office.

"Drive safely," Jim shook hands with Eddie.

"Thanks," Eddie opened the office door.

We ran to the car and took our seats. "I'll be glad when we pass the Minnesota border," it was still raining and Eddie's clothes were soaking wet. "We'll stop when I see a flat spot so we can have something to eat and I can change into dry clothes."

"It shouldn't be too far and, I'm sure you'll be more comfortable." I turned on the heater and the radio. 'California Here I Come' Al Jolson was belting out. We both laughed. "Now that sounds more like it!" I said.

HOUSE ON WHEELS

Chapter 8

When we crossed the state line into South Dakota it was nearly 6 o'clock. We looked for a place to spend the night and finally found a trailer park on the outskirts of Sioux Falls. It's smaller than the ones we've stayed at before but it has all the amenities we need. By the time we settled in, it was beginning to get dark. We ate, I wrote letters to my mother and Tante Marie while Eddie read The Argus Leader he had picked up at the registration desk. "It's been quite a day." Eddie stood up and folded up the paper. "I'm going to bed."

"As soon as I finish this letter I'll join you." By the time I slid under the covers, he was already asleep.

***

"Come on, sleepyhead," Eddie prodded gently. "It's 6:00 0'clock, if you want to get a look at this town before we head toward Rapid City, we have to make the move."

I rolled out of bed reluctantly. He had already showered and was dressed in his gray trousers and blue shirt. "The coffee smells good," I said sleepily.

"We'll have toast when you get back from the shower room." He handed me my blue robe.

"Don't rush me." I ran my fingers through my hair. "This is a good day for my brown plaid dress with the wide white collar," I said half to myself as I pulled it out of the closet and slipped into my sandals on my way out the door carrying soap and a towel.

He was true to his word. When I got back he not only had toast but also scrambled eggs and fried baloney on two plates.

"What a feast!" I said as I put the clothes and towel away. "I didn't expect all this."

"Nothing to it," he said and poured the coffee. "I'd like to see some of the city too while we're driving through. The park owner said there were some Lakota Indian reservations around here."

"Won't it be a little tough to get on a reservation while we're hauling the trailer?" I asked.

"I don't think we'd be allowed on Indian territory anyway, but we might be able to get a glimpse of their location and whatever else is around here."

"Let me heat up some water for the dishes before you disconnect," I cleared the table. "Then you can get the hitch ready while I finish up in here."

We were ready to leave around 7:30. Everything was secure in the icebox and on the shelves. One last check to make sure the windows were closed and locked, "Let's go," he said.

We turned on to the main road and saw the signs guiding us to the Big Sioux River. As we got closer to the river, the sound of the falls grew louder and louder until it became deafening. We parked by the side of the road, got out of the car and watched the wide river race downhill over large, smooth rocks. Some of the rocks, farther downriver, were like wide columns, high and alone, stacked with what appeared to be broken pieces of shale-like slabs. Others, not quite as tall and flat on top, seemed to rise up from a deep hole. Water from the upper river rushed over them and fell all around to the lower river like giant fountains. The sound was created by the rapid flow of water over the large uneven stones cascading into narrow falls in some areas, and taller wider falls in other places as the water tumbled into the cracks between the boulders…always gushing…

63

always thundering…always spectacular as it sloped and flowed fiercely for what looked to be more than a mile. "I'm glad we didn't miss this," I said as we stood watching the awesome river.

"It's quite a spectacle, all right," Eddie pointed to a small calm pool sheltered among smooth rocks. "Look at the ducks! They're swimming around like they're in a mill pond!"

"What about those guys close to the cracks?" I nodded toward some people walking close to the edge of the crashing water. "I'd sure hate to be the one to fall into one of those crevices."

"I know what you mean," Eddie said and took my hand. "Let's get back to the car."

"According to this brochure you picked up there's a stockyard here and a Morrell's Meat Packing Plant too."

"We'll probably see them from the highway. I really want to get going."

We never did find any evidence of Indian Reservations, nor of any Indians, for that matter. I guess we expected the Indians would look like the ones we had seen portrayed in the movies and we didn't see anyone wearing beaded headbands or hats with feathers. The main road and the downtown areas were well paved but we could see, from the clouds of dust produced by traveling vehicles, the side roads leading to the farms and cornfields were dirt. We didn't see the stockyards but we did pass a complex of large buildings, mostly brick, with the name Morrell set perpendicularly in large letters on the front which we assumed to be the meat packing plant. We didn't stop. We drove on and soon crossed the city line. The terrain was flat and we could see for miles in the distance. Now and then we saw evidence of cars on the farm roads.

"Hey," I sat up higher on the seat. "There's another set of Burma Shave signs." These were small signs, each one about 12 inches by 14 inches, mounted on narrow poles at driver's eye level about 300 feet apart on the shoulder of the road. Each little sign contained only a few words from a limerick to advertise Burma Shave Cream.

I read: "Every day…We do…our part…To make your face…a work of art… Burma Shave"

"I'll have to try some of that stuff," Eddie commented. "There's another sign," he pointed, "Mitchell, straight ahead."

"We made good time," I looked at the clock on the dash. "It's not even noon."

"This a small town compared to Sioux Falls," Eddie said as he slowed down. "According to the advertisements, the main attraction here is the Corn Palace. Whatever that is."

It wasn't hard to find. It was on the corner of Sixth and Main Streets. The structure was tall and large. The roof looked like a design from 'Arabian Nights': an onion-like tower on both ends and a large minaret in the center. The palace was made of reinforced concrete but the entire façade consisted of dried corn cobs and organic materials. It was the most amazing building I had ever seen. Two large framed pictures adorned the front of the palace. One, about 15 feet by 30 feet, depicted scenes of Indian figures by an open campfire with the sea and a tall sailing ship in the background. The other one on the left front was smaller and featured Indians with teepees and settlers. Three more framed pictures about 15 feet high and 3 feet wide were shaped like windows, each with its own red and white rounded canopy, featuring Indian folklore such as arrows, bows, eagles and buffalos. Beneath the 'windows' a marquee extended to the edge of the sidewalk. The edge was decorated with horses in various positions. These were all in keeping with the theme for 1951 which was 'South Dakota: Indians to Modern Times'. Three double-door entrances were located below the marquee. All the designs were made from three species of different colored corn which were used to create colorful mosaics covering the entire outer walls. The spaces between the pictures were filled with grain less cobs, corn husks, multicolored dried kernels and grasses from the region.

Eddie pointed to some birds perched on the largest frame and said, "That wall is like a big bird feeder."

"I wonder how much corn is left by the time winter sets in." I was curious.

"Didn't the guide say they used more than 300,000 ears of corn to cover this palace?" He took my hand to lead me toward the entrance doors. "I would guess that's a good enough food supply for the birds even when the snow starts to fall. Come on, let's go in"

Inside the building, the space was large and contained folding chairs. The walls were decorated according to the same theme as the outside walls with settlers and Indians depicted in smaller framed mosaics made from the same corn materials. There wasn't an event going on while we were there, but the caretakers told us they were setting up for a Saturday night dance that evening.

"Let's get back to the car." Eddie reached for my hand and we headed back toward the entrance. "We've still got a ways to go before we get to Rapid City."

"One last look around," I pleaded. "This is an incredible place."

"Okay," he said, "Since we're already stopped, we may as well have lunch here before we head out."

I was in full agreement with that. I made sandwiches, poured lemonade in our glasses and we ate in the trailer. I wrapped the dirty glasses in a towel and placed them in the sink to wash later. "There, all safe for travel." I said.

The road was straight as far as the eye could see. There were miles and miles of farms and cornfields. We had learned in Mitchell that all the corn used at the Corn Palace was grown and dried locally. The evidence of this fact was before our eyes. It was really a community project.

We passed neatly tended farms, simple farm houses, silos and enclosed farm animals like pigs and chickens. Now and then we saw a cattle ranch and cowboys. After a couple of hours the scenery began to change. We saw odd-looking hills of sandstone in different shapes, heights and widths. Some were cone shaped, like skinny rough-sided pyramids. The ground between the formations was a lovely green with occasional yellow wildflowers and tall grasses gracefully bending in the breeze.

A few miles into this phenomenal area, Eddie slowed down. He parked by the side of the road and we got out of the car. "Check the brochures," he said, "let's see where we are."

"This must be the Badlands." I looked at the picture on the face of the brochure.

""That's what I thought" he said as he spread it out on the hood of the car. "It says here this place is over 230,000 acres and once was home to the Lakota Indians."

"I don't know how anyone could ever live here." I observed.

"I guess there'd be room for a teepee on the grass here and there," he looked around, "but not much else. Let's get back in the car."

The road snaked around the thousands of formations consisting of layers of different kinds of sediment. The lower layers appeared yellow in some places and in others we saw layers of orange and purple. Most of the pointed formations were of sandstone and gray in color. No two mounds were alike. Some peaks had spaces we could see through; others were formed in the shape of huge rough mushrooms. We saw one with a snail-like ball on top.

"This place is totally incredible," Eddie said as we drove the winding road through the Badlands.

It didn't matter the radio reception wasn't good; we were completely fascinated by the amazing scenery. Soon we saw a sign: Rapid City 45 miles. "We'll make that by 6 o'clock easy," Eddie calculated.

We found a trailer park within the city limit and settled in. After supper we drove into town to pick up some ice and groceries. We gassed up for the next day and asked the station attendant for directions to a Catholic Church. "It's not far," he said. "You'll find the Cathedral down there to your left on Fifth St."

Immaculate Conception Cathedral was smaller than we expected. It was built of sandstone in the Romanesque Revival style with a tall square entrance rising up into a bell tower. The stone formed a pointed peak with a cross on each side of the square and a metallic pointed tower rose from the center. The body of the church was rectangular with the longer sides extending from a wall with a stained glass window, and stretching from the red entrance doors which stood beneath the tower. There were narrow stained glass windows with rounded tops on all sides. We checked the times for Mass on Sunday morning and headed back to our trailer.

Mass was at 8 o'clock. Eddie wore gray trousers, a teal sports jacket, a white shirt and red and gray striped tie. I wore a navy blue dress, a red close fitting hat, and red high heels, and carried a red purse. Inside the Cathedral, a wide center aisle between two rows of white pews led to an ornate white altar. The Mass was short and in Latin with no music.

On our return home we saw the entrance to Dinosaur Park and drove in. To our amazement, we saw life sized concrete sculptures of all species of dinosaurs throughout the park. We went from one sculpture to the other; I sat on the tail of one, then walked over and grabbed what looked like large ears of another. Eddie took pictures here and there, but we didn't stay long. Our 'Sunday, goin' to church' attire was not conducive to walking around the park. We went home, had breakfast and changed to appropriate dress for sightseeing around Rapid City. I changed into a blue A-line waffle pique dress with a peter pan collar, a narrow belt and penny-loafers. Eddie had removed his jacket and tie at the park so he simply changed his shirt to a short-sleeved blue one.

"There are lots of things to see around here," Eddie said as he pulled out the map of the area.

"Did you decide where you want to go first?" I asked as I finished up the dishes.

"It looks like we can make a circle around the city up to the Petrified Forest of the Black Hills on one side, catch the Reptile Gardens and come around to Mount Rushmore before coming back here". He drew an imaginary line on the map as he spoke.

"That seems like a lot of territory to cover in one afternoon," I said.

"I guess it is," he said as he got up from the table. "So we'd better get going."

I grabbed my black purse, handed our lunch bag to Eddie and we were on our way. Our first stop was the Petrified Forest. "I thought the Petrified Forest was in Arizona," I said.

"Yes," he answered, "there is one in Arizona and it's supposed to be much bigger than this one." He pulled in the parking area of the forest. "From what I've read, though, they were both formed the same way."

The gravel path from the parking area led to a small log cabin where a park ranger was waiting. We joined a group of about 12 visitors and followed along a narrow trail. We heard how, millions of years ago, this once fertile area was flooded and the trees became saturated in waters that contained minerals which slowly turned the wood to stone and eventually were buried under volcanic sediment where they remained for eons. The trees absorbed the colors of the minerals and remained buried until severe earthquakes shifted the volcanic deposits and the sediment and returned the trees to the surface. There is no denying these were trees; we could actually count the growth rings on the broken trunks. The colors were incredible: amethyst, emerald, ruby, topaz, sapphire, all looking like genuine gemstones. Some of the logs were long while others were broken into three or four-foot lengths haphazardly strewn throughout the park. "Where

67

you're standing right now," the ranger said, "it is likely that a dinosaur stood and ate from trees that grew alongside these stone trees."

"That's hard to imagine," I said.

"Yes and no," Eddie remarked. "We know for sure dinosaur fossils have been found around here; I'd say it's logical the trees and the dinosaurs were here at the same time."

When we returned to the cabin, another group was waiting to accompany the ranger on a tour of the forest. We returned to our car and continued through The Black Hills heading for Reptile Gardens. We stopped at a small picnic area on the way. The sky was beginning to cloud over and the mountain air was cool so we didn't linger. We drove the winding road back toward Rapid City until we came to signs guiding us to the entrance of Reptile Gardens. This was an interesting place with all kinds of specimens on display, not so much in caged enclosures but in easily viewed, controlled areas safely apart from the visitors. We saw different varieties of snakes, including rattlesnakes, large and small; and not so small turtles, and alligators. There were beautiful flower gardens and now and then the guide stopped to give informative lectures about the habitats of the animals featured in the gardens. The time went by quickly and the sky was getting darker. According to the road signs we were only a few miles from Rapid City and Mount Rushmore was on our way there. We hadn't traveled far when we got our first glimpse of the huge sculptures of Washington, Jefferson, Lincoln and Teddy Roosevelt ahead of us.

"There they are!" Eddie said. He slowed down as we entered the parking area.

We stepped out of the car and walked toward the viewing area of the gigantic monument and gathered with other tourists around the Park Ranger who was carrying an umbrella. "It took 14 years to construct these monuments," he said, using his umbrella as a pointer. "It was a massive undertaking during the Great Depression," he continued. "There were 400 workers who earned $8.00 a day, and not one life was lost."

"That's amazing," Eddie whispered, "with all that blasting and sanding so high up in the air, it's hard to believe."

"The final sculpture was completed in 1941," the ranger said. "Unfortunately the original sculptor, Gutzon Borglum, died in March of that year and never saw the dream of his life completed. His son, Lincoln, finished it in late October, barely 6 weeks before the start of World War II."

We heard whisperings among the visitors like;"What a marvel this is!" "Too bad he didn't get to see it finished," and "What a legacy he's left our country!" The sky was getting darker and the visibility began to lessen as a light rain began to fall. The ranger opened his umbrella and some of the visitors began to walk back toward the parking area.

"I wish we could get up closer," I said, "we're too far away to get a decent picture."

"We should probably think about leaving anyway," Eddie said. "It's starting to rain harder and it doesn't look like it's going to stop any time soon."

By the time we reached the trailer park, it was lightning and thundering. We took turns using our umbrella to get to and from the showers. We were glad to get into dry clothes and have a warm spaghetti supper. The rain continued through most of the night.

We were up before sunrise, "I'm glad the weather cleared up," I said as I took out the frying pan. "It's not so much fun, driving in the rain."

"I agree," he poured coffee into our cups.

"How far do you think we can travel today?" I placed the plates with sunny-side eggs and toast on the table.

"With an early start, we should be able to get to Wyoming by mid-morning," Eddie said. "I'll hitch up while you clean up in here and we should be able to get to Yellowstone Park late this afternoon."

The pale red rays of the pre-dawn sky began to appear as we turned out of the trailer park and headed west. The air smelled fresh after the rain, and the moisture on the grass and trees reflected the purples, pinks and orange colors of early morning until the bright sun gradually transformed the western horizon to hills bathed in gold. We continued through the Black Hills for about 100 miles enjoying valleys and hills and waterfalls. We saw green pastures and grazing cattle, and fields of colorful wildflowers.

"This sure is pretty country," I said.

"It sure is." Eddie answered." "According to the map, the Black Hills extend into the eastern part of Wyoming."

"I didn't know that." I hesitated. "I thought the Big Horn Mountains were in Wyoming."

"They are, but it's not the same range," he pointed to the folded map. "Look it up, I think there may be some flatland in between, but I'm not sure."

"Interesting!" I unfolded the map. "I don't even have to look," I pointed ahead. "There's another set of Burma Shave signs. "They wouldn't have those in the mountains. Would they?" I read: 'I'd heard...It praised...By drug store clerks...I tried the stuff... Hot Dog... It works! Burma Shave.

"Check the map," Eddie directed.

I didn't see any names of towns which would indicate the Big Horns were close by, but it did seem like we were climbing. It was hard to tell where one mountain range ended and the other began. There were rocks and hills and patches of green and more wildflowers, and then the road began to narrow. The shoulders did not allow much space between the road and the edge of the cliff. We were definitely climbing and the road up the mountain was barely wide enough for two cars. In some places the road was gravelly because of fallen rocks and at times it looked like we might easily be propelled down into the canyon, far below. I was more than a little nervous as we continued our constant upward climb to the top of the 13,000 foot mountain. The engine labored as it pulled the heavy trailer and at times we were barely crawling. "I don't like the way the car is acting," Eddie said. "This isn't a good place to have car trouble."

"This is a good time to start praying," I said. "A few Hail Mary's couldn't hurt."

"In the name of the Father…" After, what seemed like hours we finally reached the summit where there was snow on the distant peaks and in the level areas near the rest-stop. Eddie pulled out the lunch bag. "We might as well eat now and let the car cool off a little."

I set out the jars of cold lemonade, "We'll still have to take it slow going down won't we?"

"Yes," he bit into his cheese sandwich. "I'll have to use the electric hand brake to slow down the trailer; otherwise the weight of it, going downhill, could cause serious problems."

"Well," I observed, "the roads are just as narrow and winding going down as they were going up," I shrugged. "But, at least the car won't have to work so hard."

"I don't think we'll make it to Yellowstone today," he said. "If we see a town on our way down, we should probably stop for the night."

"We don't know what kind of facilities there are in the park, either, and I would really like to get the laundry done." I said.

"That's good thinking," we gathered our things. "Let's get going."

We saw spectacular scenery as valleys or snow covered mountains or waterfalls appeared around each curve of the road during our slow descent. We stopped in Powell, Wyoming, a town at the 4,365 foot elevation, where we found a trailer park near a gas station. We filled up the tank then replenished our food supply at a grocery store. When we assessed our total treasure we found we had dwindled down to twenty dollars. An assessment on the map showed Yellowstone to be 75 miles away. I made corned beef hash for supper. It was a beautiful, cool, starry evening and we sat close to each other on the step of the trailer.

"The air smells so clean up here," Eddie had his arm around me.

"I never dreamed it could be this peaceful anywhere on earth." I put my head on his shoulder.

We sat in the quiet of the night, enjoying the stillness, enjoying the warmth of each other until he said, "Okay, kid, let's call it a day!"

It was around 8:30 a.m. by the time we got underway. We didn't realize we had crossed into a different mountain range as we headed towards Shoshone National Park on our way to Yellowstone. We were in the Absaroka Range, the eastern part of the Rocky

Mountains. As we neared the Buffalo Bill Dam, the hill was so steep we had to be towed to the top by a tractor. The dam was 375 feet high and 200 feet wide. It provided water for human consumption and irrigation for the grain and sugar beet farms in the area. It also provided spectacular scenery. From the dam to the entrance to Yellowstone we had no problems. It was around 11:45 a.m. when we entered the park. The road was clear but there were piles of snow hugging the base of the mountain. The car in front of us was stopped and a huge black bear was on all fours, next to it. Suddenly something that looked like bread came out of the open window of the car and the bear stood up and lunged to grab at it. We stayed well behind with our windows closed.

"There are a couple of more mooching bears up ahead," Eddie said. "I think those people are not too smart."

"Yeah, one swipe of his paw and that cute looking bear could cause some serious damage."

"We've got to be careful," Eddie warned. "We can't pass the car, the road is too narrow. We'll just have to wait until they stop playing with the bear and move forward."

"In the meanwhile, we'll keep the windows closed." I sat stiffly.

The bears sniffed around the side of our car and trailer then ambled back to the snow piles on the side of the road and we proceeded forward. We made our way to a camping area where we unhitched the trailer and connected to the water. We drove to Canyon Lodge where we inquired how we could send and receive mail, and then we sat in the lounge so we could write home. My letter to my mother included instructions on how and where to send us money via Western Union. We mailed our letters at the front desk and were given a map of the park and a list of the events going on. It was mid afternoon when we returned to the campsite. We parked the car and decided to take a walk to Upper Falls where we saw part of the Grand Canyon of Yellowstone. The light wasn't good enough for us to take pictures so we headed back to the campsite.

"Don't move," Eddie said. "Look over there at the garbage barrels."

"Oh, my God," my eyes widened. "It's another bear!"

"We'd better not attract his attention," he held my hand. "We don't want be his dessert."

We stood frozen in that one spot. The bear didn't seem to notice us. He left the overturned barrel and headed in another direction. We looked around cautiously as we made our way back to the trailer. There were no fireworks that night even though it was the eve of the 4th of July. It was a quiet cold evening and Eddie started our small kerosene heater in the trailer for the first time. "This is a good night to stay in," he said. He set up the Coleman gasoline burner for cooking outside and we heated water for hot tea. "It looks like another couple is setting up a pup-tent two sites down from us."

"I don't envy them sleeping out in a tent on such a cold night," I said.

"It's warm enough in here," he said and opened the sofa. "I'm going to turn off the heater for the night; we should be okay under the blankets."

When we awoke in the morning, we were surprised to see the ground covered with snow. We left our footprints when we crossed the campground to the shower house wearing heavy sweaters over our bathrobes. "This is not exactly 4th of July weather," Eddie remarked as he entered the trailer. "I'll hold off lighting the heater, though, I think the sun will warm the air soon enough."

He lit the Coleman burner and I made coffee and cooked eggs. It was still warm inside as we ate and by 10 o'clock the snow began to melt. "Have you got your camera?" Eddie asked.    "I'm all set." I slipped on my sweater over my long-sleeved striped blouse. "It looks like it's going to be a nice day."

We walked down to Lower Falls hoping to take pictures with our Brownie camera. The Falls were spectacular.  Here the Yellowstone River tumbles down more than 300 feet between cliffs of yellow rocks on each side which form the deep canyon below. In some places the rocks appeared to be a blinding white.  Next we walked up to Artist Point and we could see the entire Canyon in all its colorful beauty and the Yellowstone River cascading from the very top.  Everywhere we looked there was a different perspective of the landscape:  snow covered mountains, the deep creviced canyon, tree-laden forests, and rich green fields.  It was a paradise for as far as we could see.  We walked everywhere.  In the early evening we gathered around the campfire with a Park Ranger and other visitors.  The ranger told us some of the history of Yellowstone: how important it was to the Indians, and how it was the first designated National Park in the world.

"That's pretty interesting," the man next to Eddie observed.

Eddie turned to him and said, "I knew it was the first in the U.S. but not the whole world."

"Neither did I." He extended his hand. "Don here, and this is my wife, Edna. We're from Ohio."

"Name's Eddie," they shook hands. "The wife, we're from Massachusetts."

"It was pretty cold last night," he looked at his wife. "We had to sleep in our car."

"We tried to rent a cabin but, because of the holiday, all the cabins were already rented," Edna said.

"And it was too cold in our pup-tent," Don added.

Eddie and I looked at each other, "We have a trailer, and it was plenty warm enough," Eddie said.

Don looked at Edna and said, "I know you don't know us at all, but could you rent us a space for the night?"

Eddie shrugged. "There is space for another couple if we lower the table of the breakfast nook and spread the cushions." He looked at me quizzically. "What do you think?"

"We'll pay you," Don said. "It's only for one night."

"Nah, it's okay," Eddie shrugged. "I don't think I'd want to sleep in our car either."

"Is $5.00 enough?" Don asked.

"We don't want your money," Eddie said. "Do you play Hi-Lo-Jack?"

We were all up by 6:30 a.m. Don had gone back to his tent to get his camp stove and supplies and was cooking pancakes and bacon by the time I came back from the shower house. It was still cold enough for warm sweaters, but the blanket of snow from the day before was gone. Edna and I reset the breakfast nook for breakfast, cleaned up after we ate and our guests were gone before 8:30.

"Let's take a walk toward those trees. " Eddie pointed to a grove beyond the field where we had gone the day before.

"I don't know," I hesitated. "I'm not looking forward to meeting up with any stray bears."

"I don't think we have to worry about that," he tried to reassure me. "As long as we don't have any visible food I don't think they'll bother us."

"I don't know. It seems risky."

"Well, what would you rather do?" he pressed on. "Sit in the trailer and not see anything?" He reached for my hand. "Come on, it'll be fun." He grinned.

We walked across the field hand in hand.

We stopped now and then to admire the delicate yellow and blue wildflowers growing in great profusion. "Whee-oo-whee," I heard a sound like a whistle.

"What was that?" I stopped to look around, and saw nothing.

"I don't know," he turned and looked puzzled too. "It sounded like someone was whistling at us." After a few minutes of silence, we resumed our walk.

"Whee-oo-whee!" we heard it again.

"It came from behind us," Eddie whispered. "Turn around and stand still."

We stood perfectly quiet and suddenly a tiny gray animal, standing about 10 inches high, popped out of a hole in the ground whistling loud and clear, "whee- oo-whee!"

73

"There it is! " I pointed. "What is that little animal?" I asked.

"I think it's a prairie dog," we didn't move.

"It's sort of cute isn't it?" I said softly. "It sure sounded like someone was whistling for our attention, didn't it?"

We watched it disappear and waited. "Whee-oo-whee" it popped up again.

"I'll be danged," Eddie said and shook his head. "I don't think we need to be afraid of that little fella."

"Do you think there's more than one?"

"Maybe," he shrugged. "Does it matter?"

We laughed and continued our walk toward the trees. We didn't venture more than twenty or thirty feet into the forest of evergreens. The ground was covered with soft branches and pine needles from the trees and our footsteps made no sound. "Maybe we should turn back," I said. "I don't think it would be a good idea for us to get lost in here."

"I was hoping to see elk, Eddie looked all around. "But I guess they're hiding deeper in the trees." He reached for my hand. "We might as well head back."

After lunch we drove to Norris Junction, the geyser area of the park. We were following the signs directing us to Old Faithful when we saw a large crowd of people standing around in a large semi-circle. We parked the car and made our way to the viewing site about 300 feet from the geyser. At first we only saw a greenish pool of quietly bubbling water, then, all at once a plume of steam escaped from the pool rising a few feet. Another column of steam rose higher from the pool and swayed in the gentle breeze. A few seconds later, water and steam blew out from the ground in a spectacular eruption to a height of about eighty feet or more and kept up the display for at least three minutes. The afternoon sun created small colorful prisms in the steamy droplets of water. The experience was over almost as soon as it began and it would be at least another 90 minutes before Old Faithful would erupt again.

There were many other pools in that area of the park; some were a deep sapphire blue, others were muddy some yellowish-green. All were bubbly. There was a strong odor of sulphur everywhere. Some geysers spewed forth steam and erupted but they were not as tall as Old Faithful and some were much smaller. Every geyser was beautiful, but none was as impressive or consistent as Old Faithful.

In the evening, we attended another campfire chat given by a Park Ranger. This presentation included still pictures of the wildflowers in the park, some of which we had seen that morning, and included facts about the plants and how they came to make their home in Yellowstone. I am always amazed at how knowledgeable the Rangers are and how interesting their 'chats' were. We walked home in the cool night air under a starry sky.

"I don't think I'm going to need to light the heater in the trailer tonight." Eddie reached for my hand.

"That's good; that means we won't have to buy kerosene for awhile."

"But we will need ice," he said and put his arm around me. "And we'll probably need gas in a couple of days."

"Tomorrow we won't need the car." I looked up at him as we turned into our campsite. "I have to do laundry again."

"It seems laundry day comes up often," Eddie said and opened the door.

"I have the extra sheets from our guests and our regular clothes too," I remarked. "I don't want it to pile up."

"Right," he agreed. "We don't have a whole lot of room in here to store up dirty laundry."

Our bed was ready, Eddie slipped under the covers, "Come on, Sweetheart," he lifted the sheet and blanket. "As long as there is room enough for us."

Through our one open window we could hear the sound of crickets as we went to sleep. Morning came quickly and we were awakened by the first rays of sun coming in between the drapes. Eddie was up first and was already dressed in gray slacks and a sweater.

"It looks like it's going to be a beautiful day," I said when I returned from the shower house. "Give me a minute and I'll get some scrambled eggs and grilled toast going."

He had coffee perking on the Coleman burner. "Do you want some coffee?"

"Sure," I replaced the pot with the frying pan and we were ready for breakfast in hardly any time at all. "Looks like we've got this 'one burner' system worked out pretty good."

"Maybe so, but it'll be good to be back to two electric burners and a real toaster again," he remarked.

We ate leisurely, cleaned up the dishes and I was ready for my next chore. The laundry facility was not busy. I brought my dimes, detergent and clothes and was prepared to sit over there for at least an hour and a half. While I waited, I read a copy of Good Housekeeping magazine. The suggestions I read regarding home decoration did not apply to our current living facility. 'Oh well', I thought to myself, 'someday we'll have a larger home; I'll try to remember these ideas.' It was 10 cents for the use of a flat iron so I was able to bring back the basket full of clean laundry ready to put away in the closet and in drawers.

Eddie had been studying our brochures about Yellowstone. "There's supposed to be a scenic stream somewhere near here," he pointed to a picture inside the folder. "Shall we go look for it?"

"Sure," I answered. "I can make sandwiches and we can sit by the water and relax."

We hiked up hills and down hills, walked up this path and that...no stream. At last, as we were giving up hope of finding the stream, Eddie saw a narrow path going through tall grasses and pointed. "Let's try over there." We followed the path for about a quarter of a mile and came to a clearing. "Voila!" he said. "I knew we'd find it."

I had not been as confident. I cautiously looked around for stray wild animals then sat on a large rock near the shore. "It's really beautiful, isn't it?"

"The water is so clear we can see the bottom," he put his hand in the stream. "Brrr this water's cold."

"Good thing we're not planning on swimming." I opened our picnic lunch.

Eddie sat on the pebbled ground next to me. We spent a quiet afternoon watching an occasional fish jump in the shallow water and enjoying the sound of the rippling stream. We chatted about our family and wondered if they had received our letters. "I guess we'll hear from Tante Marie when we get to Montana," I said.

"I hope we hear from your mother before that," Eddie remarked. "Our funds are getting mighty low."

"We'll manage." I answered encouragingly.

We stayed until late afternoon, gathered up our belongings and climbed up the moderately steep hill. I skinned my knee on the way up when I slipped on loose stones. Eddie led, occasionally reaching back to take my hand and we finally reached the top. We looked around, then at each other and laughed. We were directly across the road from our campsite. I turned to look at Eddie, "I don't think you should apply for a job as tour guide here."

"Wise guy," he quipped. "How's your knee?"

"It's okay," I crossed the street feigning a limp. "Nothing our First-Aid Kit can't handle."

Campfire talks were always after dark and each night it was in a different location. Our talk tonight was at the next campground over from ours. It was all about the animals of Yellowstone and the Ranger was Jack Heaton from the University of Missouri. He spoke of bear and bison, deer, elk, prairie dogs and other wild animals, including reptiles. He advised us not to get friendly with any of them but to respect them. "This is their home," he said.

We walked back to our campsite with neighbors, the Linden's from Wisconsin, who had moved into the trailer site next to us that same afternoon. We visited their trailer, which was a little larger than ours, and equipped with propane tanks for heating and cooking. They visited ours and said it was cute and cozy. We spent a lovely evening getting to know each other by the light of our Coleman lamp.

We started the day by cleaning, "It's amazing how much dirt accumulates on the road," Eddie said.

"That's true," I replied, "but fortunately the trailer is small and we can clean up in no time."

We tackled the floors, the sooty wall (from the kerosene heater), and the windows. We hosed down the outside of the trailer as well as the car. "There you are," Eddie announced, "good for another week."

We had a late breakfast after which we drove to Tower Falls. The falls looked like they were sandwiched between two tall rock formations one on either side, and tumbled upon a huge boulder on their way down. They were different and beautiful, but we agreed Lower Falls were more spectacular. We continued on to Mammoth Hot Springs. These were active bubbling pools of hot water fed by an underground river coming from Norris Junction where we had seen the geysers a couple of days before. The springs were red and orange and yellowish in some places and we smelled the same rotten egg odor we had encountered among the geysers. From the parking lot we stepped on to a wooden boardwalk with railings where we got an excellent view of the mostly inactive springs, which had been active in the past and had formed beautiful, colorful, oddly shaped cones of silica some of which were about 15 feet high. We hiked for more than a mile and saw terraces of white limestone formations that looked like cascades of water frozen in time. We saw green and blue pools, their color indicating the temperature of the water was colder than some of the more fiery colored ones we had seen before. By the time we had completed the circle of the boardwalk, back to the parking lot, the sky had become overcast. We returned to the car.

"Mass is at 6:30 a.m. tomorrow in the lounge of Canyon House," Eddie said. "We should get back before the rain comes."

It started to rain before we returned to the campsite. "I guess we'll have a cold supper tonight," I suggested. "No need to light the Coleman burner outside in the rain."

"That's okay with me," he fixed the sofa while I made sandwiches. "We'll have to set the alarm for 5:00 a.m."

We played a game of Rummy by the light of a large flashlight, and then turned in.

There was a heavy frost on the ground when we got up in the morning. The car complained a little before the engine kicked in and we headed out to Canyon House. We were surprised to see how many people had gathered for Mass at this early hour. The altar was set up on two square tables with a white altar cloth. There were two candles set on either side of a gold crucifix which was set in the center back of the altar. Folding chairs were arranged in neat rows with a center aisle facing the altar. Father Reagan, a Dominican priest from Kansas was the celebrant and Eddie volunteered to be the acolyte. I took a seat in the front row. Eddie walked in front of the priest as they came down the center aisle and stood side by side facing the altar to recite the Latin prayers at the beginning of Mass. Eddie had a small bell which he rang during the Consecration of the Eucharist. The congregation came forward to receive Communion via the center aisle and returned to their seats by the side aisles. There was a feeling of awe and reverence throughout the celebration, as people from different places in the country and even the world came to profess their faith in God in this special place. After Mass we met Father Agatha, a Benedictine priest from Saint Anthony's parish in Cody and we drove him to Lake Jet where he was scheduled to offer Mass at 10:00 o'clock. We encountered beautiful scenery in both directions but were happy to return home to have breakfast of eggs and toast, and coffee. It was cold and windy. We attempted to play catch at the campsite, but the wind proved to be detrimental to this activity, so I decided to make vanilla fudge instead. We wore double sweaters to go to the campfire chat after supper. Ranger Heaton was back and he talked about the Geology of Yellowstone. "We have a difficult time," he said, "waiting for something like presents for our birthday or Christmas which we anticipate impatiently every year." He went on, "The formation of Yellowstone took millions of years. I'd say it was worth waiting for." Everyone applauded. He went on to say glaciers, volcanoes and underwater rivers all had a part of the creation of what we see today. He also warned us that it was a matter of time before another volcanic eruption on this site could create more changes in the park, which at this time, we can't even imagine.

There were no stars in the dark sky. We walked at a quickened pace to get home faster. "I'm going to light the heater," Eddie announced. "This place should be warm in no time."

"We'll have hot chocolate and cookies." I reached for the kettle. "That should warm us up too."

"It seems funny we don't have any neighbors," he observed as he lit the Coleman burner. "I guess everyone went home for the weekend."

We played Rummy, ate cookies and fudge and drank hot chocolate before he turned off the heater and we went to bed.

There was no early sunlight to wake us this morning, the sky was still cloudy but the wind had died down. The air was cold when I fixed pancakes for breakfast but we were amazed how the trailer still felt warm. "I guess this little house is well insulated," Eddie said.

"Thank God for that, I'm not really fond of the smell of kerosene."

"After you finish cleaning up in here," he asked, "shall we take a walk up to Upper Falls again?"

"Okay and we can stop and check for the mail," I suggested.

This was a good day for both of us to wear dungarees and warm shirts and sweaters. There was no mail when we checked at Canyon House, so we continued on our walk. It seemed like the farther up the hill we went, the colder the air became. The view was still misty and I was unable to take pictures so we headed back to the trailer. When we got back, there was a tent set up next to us but no car and no sign of occupants. I heated up some soup for supper and cleaned up the dishes. It was getting a little colder now but we decided to wait until we came back from the Campfire talk before turning on the heater. The talk was cut short and it started to rain almost as soon as we got home. Eddie turned on the heater. There was still no sign of our new neighbors.

"Do you think you can beat me at cards tonight," Eddie said smugly.

"You were just lucky last night," I replied. "Go ahead and deal."

In the morning we looked out the window and saw two inches of snow, two very cold little girls and two distressed parents. We invited them in to warm up. Charlie insisted on making breakfast on his propane cook stove but we all ate in the trailer. Charlie and his wife and kids left to go sight-seeing. Eddie went to check the mail: nothing! Our total wealth is now less than a quarter.

Our neighbors made supper and we ate in the warmth of our trailer. They put the kids to bed on our sofa and we played Hi-Lo-Jack, guys against the gals. The men won.

"Let the kids sleep in here tonight," I offered. "We have room."

"Are you sure?" they asked in unison. "We can manage in the tent but I'm concerned it'll be too cold for the kids," Charlie said.

"Sure," I reached for the sheets and blankets in the cupboard. "Come on Ruth, help me make up the nook and Charlie can carry the kids over there."

The kids barely made a sound during the transfer and our neighbors said good night. It was cold all night and there were still snow flurries when we got up in the morning. Charlie was at the door before the girls woke up and announced he was preparing breakfast. The sound of his voice woke his daughters, who were surprised to find themselves in a strange bed. Soon after breakfast, Charlie and Ruth decided to break camp and go home. Their home was in California and they had not expected such a chilly experience.

The campsite next to us was empty again, as were the two others in the area. Eddie went to check the mail again. Nothing! Again! Our entire bankroll consists of nineteen cents, enough for one gallon of gas or maybe one loaf of bread.

"What do you think?" I asked. "Shall we call home?"

"Nineteen cents won't do it." He said.

"I know," I continued, "we'll have to reverse the charges." I was confident. "My mother will accept the call."

"I guess that's the best thing to do," he agreed. "Put your sweater on and let's go."

I reached my mother on the first try.

"Is that really you?" she asked excitedly. "Are you all right?"

"We're fine, Mama, but we did have some tire and car trouble that ate our money faster than we had planned." I answered.

"You should be getting my letter with the money order any time now; I sent it a few days ago."

"We really appreciate you doing this for us; how are you and Pop and Lu?" I inquired.

"We're all fine. Have you seen Uncle Louis yet?" she wanted to know.

"That's where we're headed when we leave the park." I said. "Thanks, Mama. This call is going to cost a lot of money so we'd better make it short. Take some of the money in our fund to pay for the bill."

"Don't worry about it."

"I mean it. I'll write you as soon as I receive your letter. I love you, Mama. Good bye."

"I love you too." We hung up.

We walked back hand in hand. "I miss my mother."

"I know," he stopped, took my chin in his hand and kissed me. "I think the sun wants to come out."

"I sure hope so," I smiled at him. "I'm kind of sick of wearing sweaters in July."

"And I'm tired of lighting that heater."

It was still warm in the trailer when we got back. "It looks like you'll get a break from the heater tonight." I observed.

"Do you have any more of that fudge left?" he asked. "That'll make good munching while we play cards before we go to the Campfire chat."

"You're in luck," I pulled out the candy dish. "The kids left you a few."

We played Rummy, this time I won, and then we headed for the Campfire chat which was about the places to visit in the park. It was especially interesting since we had already visited most of the places he talked about.

There was no snow when we got up this morning but the air was still chilly, not chilly enough for the heater but chilly enough for a sweater. Our ice box is looking pretty empty but we managed to find eggs to scramble and bread to grill and butter to do both.

Coffee is always a morning staple and for two people with nineteen cents between them this was a real feast. We decided to try our luck at the Fishing Bridge. "No one ever comes away from the Yellowstone Fishing Bridge without catching at least one fish," we heard the tour guide say.

"What the heck!" Eddie said. "There's enough butter in the ice-box to fry a fish. I'm going to try."

He walked to the counter where there was a display of fishing rods on the wall and asked the man in charge to borrow a pole.

"That'll be a dollar," the man said.

"I don't have a dollar," Eddie apologized. "But, I'd really like to try my luck at fishing."

"We ask for a deposit of a dollar to borrow the poles," the man said again. "The money is collateral to make sure we get the pole back."

"Well, how about I leave my watch with you?" Eddie offered. "Is that enough collateral?"

The man looked at the watch, then at me, then back at Eddie. "I guess that would be all right." He reached for a pole.

The exchange took place and we headed for the bridge where there was a box with bait and about twenty fishermen. Some anglers displayed their wonderful catch of trout. Eddie threw his baited line in and waited. Nothing! He cast his line again and again, still nothing. After about an hour of casting out and reeling in empty he said, "I have to be the only guy in the world who ever fished from this bridge and never caught anything." He looked discouraged. "I'm going back to get my watch."

There was nothing for me to say. We went back to the car and drove home. There was enough bread and cheese to make grilled cheese sandwiches for lunch and we finished off the lemonade.

"Let's try the mail again," I said. "Maybe we'll be luckier at Canyon Lodge than we were at Fishing Bridge."

Hallelujah! There were letters from both our mothers and a beautiful money order which we were able to cash at the desk. Everyone was fine back home. We answered both letters. I thanked my mother, and promised I'd write again when reached Uncle Louis in Montana. We began to make preparations to leave Yellowstone on the next day. We picked up ice and a few other supplies at the general store, and filled the gas tank. It was a busy afternoon. We skipped the Campfire chat in the evening.

## CHAPTER 9

The temperature was below freezing when we left our campsite at 5:30 a.m. The sun hadn't yet made its appearance and there were still a few stars in the sky. As the morning grew brighter, the now familiar scenery of Yellowstone became more visible.

"I'm going to remember this place for a long time," I said. "Was it what you expected?"

"In my wildest imagination I could not have expected to see all the stuff we've seen here." He held fast to the steering wheel and used the electric trailer brake every now and then. "Since I was a kid I wanted to see this place."

"I know." Just for a moment I put my hand over his on the wheel. "It was quite an adventure."

"It still is," he smiled. "Look around."

He was right; there was scenic beauty everywhere. By the time we reached the West Gate of Yellowstone it was around 7:15. The mountains and valleys were bathed in sunshine and there was a gentle breeze. It was a glorious day.

"Look for a sign to Hot Springs," Eddie said.          "Wait! Come to think of it, you might see signs for Butte first."

I spread the map on my lap. "Oh yes, I see it here." I traced the line of the route with my finger. "Butte is toward the northwest. It looks like Hot Springs is a pretty good distance from there."

The roads were good and well marked with signs. We both saw the sign to Butte at the same time and he made the turn onto the highway easily. The panorama was unspoiled by buildings or bridges, and looked very much like a continuation of the majestic views we had seen in Yellowstone: snow-covered mountains, green valleys, waterfalls and lovely wildflowers by the roadside.

"I think I'm beginning to thaw out," I said. "Shall I open the window a little?"

"Why not? It'll feel good to get some air in here." He nodded toward the dashboard. "See if you can find some music on the radio."

We were still in the mountains and the reception was not very good. We began singing our own repertoire of songs: "A rose must remain in the sun and the rain...To Each His Own!" we sang in full voice. "Let Me Call You Sweetheart..." The morning went by quickly and we arrived in Butte around noon. We found a place to park, unhitched the trailer, had lunch and went to see the city.

We were surprised to see most of the buildings in town were made of brick. The mountains on the outskirts of the city were light in color, carved in layers and flat on top. We decided to explore. We saw a parking area outside a fenced-in work place with heavy equipment trucks and workers. There were no tourists. We walked to the entrance of the work area and met a man wearing khaki pants, a red plaid work shirt and a floppy felt hat.

"What are you folks  doin' here?" he asked.

"We're from Massachusetts," Eddie said. "And we were wondering what all the activity up here is about."

"Well, young fella," he pushed his hat up on his forehead. "What you're looking at is the Richest Hill on Earth."

"We've heard of the copper mines here in Butte," I said. "But why is it called the richest hill on earth?"

"Well I'll tell ya, little gal," he continued. "When the first prospectors came around here around the 1850's, they was lookin' for gold and silver. They dug mines in them mountains and found some. A few people made money."

"But copper is what they're digging for now," Eddie asked. "Isn't it?"

"Oh, yeah," he explained." A man named, Marcus Daly, showed up around these parts and he saw they was lots of copper. They was still gold and silver but a lot less than the copper. They get more copper outa this here mine than any place else in the world."

"Does this Mr. Daly own the mine?" I was curious.

"Naw, he's dead a long time," he answered. "Anaconda Mining Company works it now."

"What are all those men doing on the layers of the mountain?" Eddie wanted to know.

"They's mining the copper," he replied.

"Don't they dig it out from underground?" I visualized a mine like we had seen in Chicago.

"They used to, but now they do what they call strip mining where they dig from the outside of the mountain, get rid of the dirt and take out the copper."

"Do you work here?" Eddie asked.

"Not anymore, but I use to." He adjusted his hat. "I retired from The Company a couple of years ago." He grinned. "Just can't seem to stay away."

"We're glad you were here today," I thanked him.

"Yer welcome," he nodded. "Hey, they's a rodeo just outside of town tonight, ya should come to see it."

"Thanks," Eddie extended his hand. "We just might do that."

I didn't have a cowboy hat but I did have dungarees, a long-sleeved white blouse and loafers. Eddie wore khaki pants and a blue plaid shirt. We may have looked out of place but we didn't care. We knew we were 'tenderfoots' as we had heard easterners called in the movies, but no one seemed to notice or care. We took our seats in the second row of the low wooden bleachers facing the metal tubing area which contained the animals in individual chutes and attending cowboys. They looked very busy as they prepared for the contests which would take place in the large center arena. There were gates at both ends of the rodeo ground; one was the entrance and the other was an emergency exit in case of an accident. Electricity was in the air as the seats filled up and friends greeted one another with loud voices and handshakes. The cattle mooed in the surrounding pens and we heard the occasional whinnying of horses. We didn't know anyone there, but people nodded and smiled at us and reached over to shake our hand as they came in and we felt very much like we were part of the crowd. Suddenly over the loudspeaker came the sound of a band playing 'Stars and Stripes Forever'. Twelve cowboys on horseback rode in, two by two, through the entrance gate. One of the two lead riders carried the American flag and the other carried the Montana state flag. They were followed by the other ten cowboys carrying various types of banners. They circled twice around the field and then lined up facing the bleachers. "Ladies and Gentlemen, please stand for our National Anthem." Everyone stood up, and a hush came over the crowd. Men removed their cowboy hats and placed their hands over their hearts while a bass voice sang out: "Oh say can you see...and the home of the brave." Loud cheers and whistles emanated from the spectators as the riders rode off the field and the gate was closed again.

The first contestants were calf ropers, most of whom were young men. In this event a cowboy on horseback came out of the chute at the same time a calf was released. The rider had to rope the calf, jump off the horse, tie three of the calf's legs with a rope then get back up on the horse. If the cowboy couldn't rope the calf or if the animal got loose, the roper was disqualified. One after another the young men came out, each one trying to rope and tie his calf faster than the one before.

"I can't even ride a horse," Eddie leaned over to me. "Look at those kids; they jump on and off like it's nothing."

"I guess it's second nature to them," I remarked. "They've probably been riding a horse as long as they can walk."

"Hey," Eddie pointed to a figure in the center of the arena. "Where did he come from?"

A clown had appeared on the field from out of nowhere. He was dressed in blue and white polka dot cropped baggy pants, a bold printed red long-sleeved shirt, an oversized green bowtie, a cowboy hat, white gloves and boots. He wore white makeup and a red bulbous nose. He was rolling a barrel painted with large bright flowers, which he alternately jumped into, rolled over, and then dove into shaking his legs at the people and

**85**

rolling over again. It was a great distraction for other cowboys on the field setting up full sized metal barrels around the arena in preparation for the ladies' barrel racing contest.

One by one the girls came through the starting gate wearing a cowboy hat and dressed in western attire. They rode at a full trot as they raced around the barrels in a fixed pattern executing sharp turns expertly and trying to avoid knocking the barrels over. The women demonstrated an incredible skill as one each one tried to better the time of the previous contestant.

A hush came over the spectators when one of the horses slipped and the rider went down into the dust. The clown, ever vigilant, came to the aid of the girl who could have been seriously injured. He picked her up and carried her gently out of the arena as she held on to his neck and waved to the audience. We supposed she was going to be okay. Upon his re-entrance the clown bowed and waved ceremoniously as the crowd cheered.

"That clown is amazing," I said. "Did you see how fast he went from standing on the fence to picking up that girl?"

"And the cowboy who grabbed the reins of the horse to lead it out," Eddie shook his head. "He's no slouch either."

"I guess the barrel racing is over," I pointed to gate on the far side. "It looks like there's a parade of carts to pick up the barrels."

The ever-present clown performed his antics in, around, and over the barrels until the arena was cleared for the next event.

"Look at the fence where the chutes are," Eddie said. "It looks like a cowboy is standing on the bars of the chute just above the horse."

"Yeah," the man sitting next to Eddie said. "He's getting ready to ride the bronc. He'll actually get on the horse only when the gate opens."

"Why is that?" Eddie asked.

"That horse will start bucking as soon as he feels weight on its back. He's going to keep on bucking until he throws that rider off," he explained.

These were untamed horses, we learned, which cowboys attempted to ride for a given period of time. Any rider who stayed on the horse less than, I think it was, 5 seconds was automatically disqualified. The rider who stayed on the longest was determined to be the winner. We sat on the edge of our seats throughout the entire event as each cowboy came out of the chute, holding on to the horse with one gloved hand, trying to outstay all of the other contestants. The clown was on site for this event to create a diversion, if need be, to keep any wild horse from injuring a rider who might be thrown off, and to help guide the horse to the designated exit gate.

"That clown is not only funny," Eddie remarked to his neighbor," he seems to have his eyes everywhere at the same time."

"If you think this was something, wait till you see him with the bulls," he replied.

We didn't have to wait long. The next and final event was the bull riding competition. These animals were huge and mean looking. The preparation was similar to the bronc riding by the fact that the cowboy didn't get on the animal until the gate was opened and the rider held on with one gloved hand. The horns made the bulls look a lot less friendly than the horses and their large bodies made it more difficult for the cowboys to wrap their legs around their mid-section. As soon as the gate was opened and the cowboy sat on the bull, the powerful animal bucked violently and tried to throw the cowboy to the ground. After only one attempt the bull was successful and whirled around to attack its rider. That's when the clown went to work. The clown rolled his barrel between the bull and the rider. In a growing rage the bull now headed for the clown who ran to the side of the arena and climbed a tall ladder set by the fence. The bull attacked the barrel with his horns and the rescue cowboys successfully roped the bull with double ropes and forced him out of the animal exit gate. The clown carefully looked around and tiptoed back to his barrel, got inside, crouched so that only his head was visible, removed his hat and wiped his brow in an exaggerated motion to the sound of loud applause and whistles. The next bull and rider came out of the chute and then the next. The excitement continued with each competitor. A few riders rode a little longer than others, but a few more were thrown and each time it happened the clown distracted the bull away from the rider in a creative way and the animal was successfully led back to its exit.

"I don't know about you," I said as we were leaving, "but I think the clown was the star of the show."

"I'll tell you one thing," Eddie said. "This is the best show I've ever seen in my life, anywhere."

"I agree, I'd like to see that guy we saw this afternoon and thank him." It was a beautiful clear night. "Do you think we'll make it to Hot Springs tomorrow?"

He put his arm around me as we walked back to the car. "If we get an early start we should reach your Uncle Louis' house by tomorrow afternoon."

"I'm looking forward to that," I answered. "I wonder if the hot springs in Montana are like the ones we saw in Yellowstone."

"We'll soon find out," we got in the car. "Won't we?"

The moon was high in the sky when we got back home. "Let's sit outside at the picnic table." Eddie said. "We can have a snack out here."

"Give me a couple of minutes," I looked up at the sky. "It's a beautiful night; we may as well take advantage of it."

I went into the trailer and brought back lemonade on a tray with cheese and crackers. "I still can't get over that clown at the rodeo." I handed him a glass of lemonade.

"Not just the clown," Eddie put cheese on his cracker. "Those pick-up cowboys, or whatever you call them, they were right there moving the horses or bulls right out the exits after each event."

"I know, they worked well as a team," I said, "like they've been doing that for a while."

"I'm sure they have." He stood up, put the glasses back on the tray and brought them back inside. "C'mon, Sweetheart, we should turn in; tomorrow's going to be another busy day."

I looked up at the sky once more and then followed him in.

We woke up around 8 o'clock. We took time for bacon and eggs and toast for breakfast and lingered over our coffee. I finished cleaning up the kitchen while Eddie attached the hitch and brake. Neither of us had to remind the other what to do; our departure routines were very familiar by now.

"I'm all set out here," Eddie announced. "Shall I disconnect the water and electric?"

"Yep, I'm done," I gave a quick look around. "I'm coming out right now."

It's easier to gas up the car without the trailer, so we had filled up the tank before going to the rodeo the night before, just in case the stations might be closed on our way back. It turned out to be a good decision; everything in town was closed after six o'clock. Compared to the likes of busy eastern cities, this part of the country offered wide open spaces, mountains and valleys in spectacular proportions. Except for a rough stretch of road between Perma and Hot Springs we made good time and reached Uncle Louis' and Aunt Elise's Motel just before noon. My mother and Tante Marie (Uncle Louis' sister) had written to them regarding our impending visit.

"We have a room ready for you in the Motel," Uncle Louis said after hugging us firmly. "Oh, no," Eddie insisted. "We can stay in our trailer at a trailer court."

"No," Uncle said firmly. " No trailer court; we want you to say close by,"

"But we don't want to take a room away from a paying guest." I added. "If you have public showers, and can connect us to electricity and water, we'll be just fine."

It was Aunt Elise's turn to hug us, "I'm sure your Uncle Louis can do that."

"See that spot over by the cyclone fence?" Uncle pointed. "That's where we park our car when we wash it; there's a faucet there and a little run-off space for the water to go downhill to the stream."

Aunt Elise put her arm around me, "Come on, dear, let's go inside and I'll show you around." We stepped on to the porch. "That narrow hallway next to our front door leads to the washrooms on the left and the pool area is straight ahead."

The front door of their apartment opened into a large comfortable living room. She showed me two bedrooms; a little girl was playing with her dolls on the floor in one of them.

"This is Carol-Jeanne, our granddaughter," she looked up and we smiled at each other. We continued on to the pink and green bathroom, then into a large bright kitchen painted in yellow and white with small flowers and butterflies on the wallpaper.

"Let me take a minute to make some coffee before I show you the outside." Auntie reached for the coffee pot and set it to perk on her gas stove. "That should do it for now; come on." She led me to the kitchen door that opened into a large foyer which served as an office and reception area. There was a door leading outside on the wall which faced one long side of a moderately sized rectangular cement swimming pool. The door between the kitchen and the foyer was in the center of a knotty pine paneled wall next to a large registration desk behind which were small, square pigeon holes for keys and mail. Outside, the guest rooms faced the other three sides of the pool with flower beds creating a comfortable distance between the rooms and the swimming area.

"You are welcome to use the restrooms and showers and laundry any time you want," Auntie said, leading me back through the hallway. "And, the pool too, of course."

"We're all set," Eddie and Uncle were already in the apartment. "Uncle helped me get connected; this is a nice little place."

"There's mail for you from your mother and my sister, Marie." Uncle handed me two letters.

"Thank you," I put them in my purse. "I'll read them later."

"Come into the kitchen," Auntie said. "The coffee should be ready."

There was a lot to talk about; I wanted to know about his sons who ran the homestead alfalfa farm in Chester, and his daughter, Marie, who lived in Great Falls, as well as Marie's daughter, Carol Jeanne, who I had met earlier while she was playing with her dolls in one of the bedrooms. She had presently emerged into the kitchen. Uncle and Aunt Elise, of course, wanted to hear news about Tante Marie and Sister Saint Illuminat, uncle's sisters in Canada and my mother, Aura. Uncle Louis had thinning gray hair. He stood about 6 feet tall and was of large proportions. He wore dark trousers, a white long-sleeved shirt and blue suspenders. Aunt Elise had short white-hair and wore a blue plaid cotton shirt-waist dress and Cuban heeled black shoes. I fell in love with little Carol Jeanne who was about 5 years old. She had dark curly hair, brown eyes and she wore a blue flower print sun dress. I wondered about the braces on her legs but I didn't ask. I was happy that she found herself comfortable to sit right next to me whenever she could. "Are you coming to the pool with us?" she asked.

"I don't know what Memme has planned." I shrugged.

"We usually take her to the Bathhouse pool a couple of times a week," Auntie said. "And I did promise to take her today."

"You don't mean this pool?" I was curious.

"No," she shook her head. "There's a new bathhouse that opened just two years ago and the pool there is much bigger and filled with mineral water from the hot springs."

"We saw some springs in Yellowstone but they looked too hot to bathe in," Eddie said.

"This water is about 94 degrees," Uncle said. "That's a lot hotter than the pool we have; but the mineral content of the pool seems to be helping our little girl."

"She had polio when she was about three and needs to wear braces," Auntie commented. "We're hoping the exercise in the mineral water will strengthen her legs so she won't need to wear them anymore."

"Do you think that's possible?" I asked.

"The confederated tribes of Salish and Kootanai who built the bathhouse think so," Uncle said. "The Indians have acclaimed the healing powers of the hot springs for centuries; as a matter of fact, that famous athlete, Jim Thorpe, came out here when the bathhouse was first opened."

"Was he from one of those tribes?" I asked.

"I'm not really sure," Uncle said, "but he did come to check the place out."

"We'll take you there and you'll see how close they tried to adhere to the natural settings as much as they possibly could." Auntie stood up. "Let's get our bathing suits."

Auntie picked up some towels and a small inner tube and we all headed for the bathhouse. This was a new experience for me. We entered the bathhouse on the ground level and walked into the large swimming pool area. We were greeted with the odor of sulphur as we entered. I was expecting the smell of chlorine as was the norm in other pools I had been to including, the one back at the motel. There were changing stalls and a showering area for the guests.

"Shall we change now?" I asked.

"We'll come back here after you get the tour of the whole bathhouse," Auntie said. "That way we can stay as long as we like." She waved to Uncle and Eddie. "You show Eddie the men's side and we'll go on the ladies' side."

We walked out of the pool area but the odor of rotten eggs seemed to permeate the entire facility. We entered another room where there was a three foot floor area made of flagstone along the side of the wall where we had come in. The rest of the area was an eight to ten foot pool of smelly mud which came up out of the ground to the level of the floor. There were wide Flagstone steps and a handrail leading into the muck to allow bathers to step safely into the chest high pool of warm mud.

"Yoo-hoo, Elise," one of the corpulent bathers stood up. She was naked and covered with mud. "Are you coming in today?"

90

"No, I'm just visiting." Auntie turned to me, "this is Jeanne, my niece from Massachusetts. "Jeanne, I'd like you to meet my friend, Edith."

"Hi Jeanne," she waved enthusiastically, her heavy breasts swaying with every motion. "You're a long way from home."

"Uh, nice to meet you, Edith," I didn't know where to look. Edith slid back down into the mud. I had never experienced skinny dipping before and felt a tinge of pink on my face. I was hoping not to be invited to join the party.

"Irene, look who's here!" Edith jumped up again. "This is Elise's niece from Massachusetts."

Irene waddled close to Edith. "We're a little too messy to shake your hand, but you're welcome to join us if you like." she announced as she stood up to greet us in her equally generous, equally naked and muddy torso. Both had lovely smiles.

"No thanks." Auntie answered, turning her grand-daughter to face the door, and reaching for my hand. "We're going to the mineral pool with Carol-Jeanne."

"Maybe next time," we heard Irene say as we left the mud room.

We continued our tour of the showers and restrooms on the upper level before we returned to the swimming pool where Uncle Louis and Eddie were already in their swim suits. Everyone took turns splashing around with Carol-Jeanne as she dog-paddled with her inner tube. Auntie and Uncle were the first to leave the pool and Eddie and I stayed with our new little cousin for a while longer. We all hit the showers in the pool area before we left the bathhouse.

"Is there a Catholic Church close by?" I inquired as we were going home.

"Oh yes," Aunt Elise answered. "Sacred Heart Church; we usually attend 8 o'clock Mass. Would you like to come with us?"

"Just tell us what time to be ready," Eddie said. "Shall we follow you in our car?"

"No, no," Uncle answered quickly. "You ride with us; we usually leave at 7:30."

"We'll be ready." We returned to our trailer. I heated leftovers for supper, and then we went to see a movie at the local theater: 'Man in the Saddle' with Randolph Scott and Joan Leslie. We hadn't been to the movies since we had left Rapid City.

Uncle Louis knocked on our door at exactly 7:25 a.m. "Hoo hee come to see, chunky chinky chee chinee…" his crazy little Chinese song made us laugh as we came out to join him and Auntie and Carol Jeanne for the trip to Mass.

"That's a funny song," I said. "I've never heard it before."

"Neither has anyone else," Aunty laughed too. "He makes it up as he goes along."

"Hey, it works to get everybody up and moving." Uncle opened the car door for Auntie. Carol-Jeanne, Eddie and I got in the back seat.

After Mass, Aunt Elise invited us to have sausages and pancakes with them. Carol Jeanne sat next to me while we ate.

"The music was beautiful at Mass this morning," I said. "Your parish has a wonderful choir."

"Yes, for such a small church they do very well," Uncle answered. "One thing about those Latin hymns, they're familiar in Catholic churches everywhere."

"I was surprised to hear a High Mass at 8 o'clock," I remarked. "In our parish back home the choir usually sings at the later Masses."

"This is a small parish," Auntie explained. "There's only one Mass."

"More pancakes, Eddie?" Uncle asked as he offered the platter.

Eddie shook his head, "no thanks, they are great but I've had enough."

"After the ladies clean up, I'd like for us to go up to Flathead Lake," Uncle announced.

I handed the silverware to Carol Jeanne; I picked up the dishes and brought them over to the sink, "After we finish the dishes, I'll go back to the trailer and change. I'll make some sandwiches to bring. It's a great day for a picnic."

"Yes it is," Aunt Elise said. "But Carol-Jeanne and I won't be coming with you."

"Would it be too much for her?" I asked.

"Oh no," she replied. "That's not it. Your uncle's friend Tom will be going with you and frankly, neither one of us likes fishing very much; she'll enjoy the pool over here a whole lot more."

It was about 11 o'clock by the time we were ready to leave. Uncle Louis had changed into blue denim bib overalls and a long sleeve white shirt. Eddie wore tan trousers and a long sleeve blue shirt. Uncle was very familiar with the mountain roads and pointed out various points of interest on the way.

"See those tree-tops over there?" he pointed in the distance. "Those are Tamarack trees; some are more than a hundred feet tall."

"They look like pine trees," Eddie observed; "the way they're pointy on top."

"They are a sort of pine tree," Uncle said. "But these trees turn yellow in the autumn and lose their needles."

"I've never heard of pines changing colors in the fall," Eddie said.

"They don't; but these are not evergreens, they're tamaracks and tamarack needles make this whole mountain look like gold when October rolls around; even the ground is gold from the fallen needles, because their golden color doesn't fade until winter sets in."

"Is it my imagination?" I asked. "These trees look a lot bigger than the pines we've seen in New Hampshire."

"Oh no, it's not your imagination," he answered. "These trees are not only tall but can grow to be over 200 feet around. Some of them are as many as a couple of hundred years old." He laughed, "This is not New Hampshire."

"Look up toward the mountain?" he pointed again. "That snow up there never melts. As a matter of fact, some of what looks like piles of snow are actually glaciers and they don't melt even though it gets to be in the 80's down here. This is Montana; this is God's country!" His face was aglow. "A couple of more turns and we'll be at the lake."

My first glimpse of Flathead Lake was breathtaking. Miles of clear water surrounded by snow crowned mountains, flat land and trees; and in the distance we could see open water where the Flathead River flowed into the lake. Uncle Louis had a corrugated metal house about eight feet tall and five feet square with a peaked, sloped roof. The top corners of the seven foot door just below the peak reached the center of the sloped roof on both sides in the front. The fishing house stood on a jut of land next to a narrow dock where there was a sixteen foot boat tied to one of the pilings. Uncle unlocked the door of the fishing house to reveal neatly stored fishing equipment including an outboard motor. Tom and Eddie carried the engine out and installed it to the stern of the boat. Tom was a quiet man, not as tall as Uncle Louis and much slimmer. They both wore wide brimmed straw hats. Tom wore tan trousers and a long-sleeved shirt. I wore dungarees, a blue plaid shirt and loafers. Uncle carried the poles and a container for bait and we all got into the boat. Tom pulled the rope to start the engine and we were on our way.

"We usually get some pretty good trout out here," Uncle said. "It's a lot different than fishing in salt water, you know."

"I didn't have any luck fishing at the fishing bridge in Yellowstone," Eddie remembered. "I hope I have better luck here."

"We always come back with something," Tom said as we sped away from the dock.

We couldn't have asked for a better day. The sun was high in the sky and although there was a slight ripple on the water, the ride to Uncle's favorite fishing spot was fast and pleasant. We baited our lines and cast them out into the lake, each in turn, one by one, then we settled down to some serious fishing. It was my first time fishing in fresh water. There wasn't much conversation, Uncle had warned; "we should be quiet, too much noise will scare the fish."

"I can't understand it," Uncle said after about an hour of almost complete silence and no activity from the fish; "we usually get at least a nibble by this time."

93

"I'm beginning to think I'm a jinx to trout fishing," Eddie lifted up his fishing pole and reeled in."

"I can't figure it out," Uncle pulled in his line. "We always catch something out here." "Yes," Tom agreed, "even in winter when we drag that old fishing house out here on the frozen lake for ice fishing, we usually catch something."

"I don't understand it either," Eddie shook his head. "I don't have a problem catching flatfish when I go fishing in the bay back home."

"We'd better get back," Uncle shook his head incredulously. "Okay, Tom, get her going."

The men secured the boat, cleaned up the fishing gear and stored everything in the fishing house. "I still find it hard to believe we didn't catch anything," Uncle said.

"Well, think of it this way," I said cheerfully. "We don't have messy fish to clean."

Tom laughed as he took his seat in the car next to Uncle, who wasn't laughing. Eddie and I climbed in the back seat. Uncle continued to point out beautiful waterfalls and rippling streams we had not seen on our way up to the lake. He was clearly in love with Montana and I could see why.

Aunt Elise had prepared a pot roast for dinner. "We've been invited to visit the Marcoux's this evening."

"Are they friends of yours?" I asked.

"Claire is my niece and she and her husband, Emile, are taking care of two teenage girls, Betty and Della," she replied. "The girls both play the piano and love to sing."

"That should be fun," I helped clear the table. By now we had a routine: Auntie washed, I dried and Carol Jeanne told me where to put things away. "Okay, we're done." I held out my hand to Carol-Jeanne. "How about we go to the trailer and I polish your nails?"

She took my hand eagerly and we headed out the door. "Don't be long," Auntie called out. "They're expecting us around seven."

Claire and the girls had made chocolate fudge in the afternoon which they served in a lovely crystal candy dish. There was an upright piano in the small living room and a stack of sheet music on top. Both Betty and Della had good singing voices and they took turns playing their favorite songs on the piano. My favorite was 'Mocking Bird Hill' and we all sang in full voice. The gentlemen were happy conversing with each other and chiming in on the oldies like 'Sweet Adeline' and 'Down by the Ole Mill Stream' every now and then. Every once in awhile Carol-Jeanne lifted her little hands and wiggled her fingers to show off her pretty red nails. Popcorn and punch topped the evening off. As we were leaving, we overheard Uncle Louis say to Emile, "...and we didn't even catch one fish!"

"When are you going to get over that?" Auntie asked. We all chuckled, gave hugs all around and thanked Claire and Emile for a beautiful evening.

"Don't forget," Uncle said on our return to the Motel, "we have an early start tomorrow, there's a lot to see in Glacier National Park."

"Claire said Carol-Jeanne will be spending the day at their house with Betty and Della," Auntie said.

"That's good," I remarked. "I was concerned that it might be a long day for her."

"She'd do her best to keep up," Auntie smiled. "But she loves those girls and she'll have a good time over there."

"We'll set the alarm," Eddie said. "Are Tom and his wife coming with us?"

"Oh, yes," Uncle answered. "They'll be here at the crack of dawn."

"Great!" I said, "I'm looking forward to it."

"Good night," Eddie and I said almost in unison as we left to go home.

We were up and dressed by the time we heard Uncle's knock on our door and his Chinky-chinky-Chinee song. Eddie opened the door for him to step in. "Are you about ready?" he asked sticking his head in the door.

"Yes," I picked up my purse from the table. "Do you think we'll need a sweater?"

"That might be a good idea," he stepped back. "Sometimes it can get a little chilly up in the mountains."

I pulled out two sweaters from the closet and followed Uncle to his 1950 four door Buick special deluxe. "We'll use my car," Uncle said. "It will accommodate six passengers more comfortably than yours; men in the front and ladies in the back."

Tom and Grace and Auntie were standing next to the car when we got there. Uncle opened the trunk and Eddie put the picnic basket I had prepared inside. "It looks like we're all set to go," Auntie said. "Come on Grace, let Jeanne sit in the middle and we'll sit next to the doors."

We were on our way. "We're going to be heading north," Uncle said. "Glacier Park is part of the Rocky Mountains and stretches past the border to Canada." From the center of the back seat it was somewhat difficult to get a full view of the beautiful scenery Uncle was pointing out. "We passed these forests on our way to Flathead Lake yesterday," Uncle reminded us. "Kalispell is about an hour's drive up from the lake; we're going to stop there so we can stretch our legs."

**95**

Kalispell was a rustic town with old fashioned looking buildings. We didn't go shopping but walked around and peeked in store windows. After about a half hour Uncle announced.          "Okay! Everybody back in the car; up ahead I want to show you an impressive Victorian mansion. It's only a few blocks from town; it was built by one of the early settlers of Kalispell, named Charles Conrad. He raised his family there and one of his daughters still lives there with her husband."

"Do they have any kids?" I asked.

"That, I don't know," he answered. He slowed down as we passed the house, "But if they do, between the size of the property and three floors in the house, I'm sure they'd have enough room to run around."

As we drove farther away from the city we could see mountain peaks every-where. Some were snow capped, some not, but snow was visible everywhere on the slopes and in the crevices. I could only imagine what it might be like in winter when everything is blanketed in white. It wasn't long before we reached the park. Our first stop was Logan's Pass. There was a water fountain near the entrance not far from the Ranger Station. The snow, or hardened glacier, was up to our hips in the unplowed areas. A path had been cleared to the stone bubbler. Uncle stood on top of the pile of frozen snow to show us how hard it was packed. It was a beautiful July day and surprisingly warm in spite of the large piles of snow we observed everywhere. Beyond the parking area we could see Reynolds's Mountain with its intermittent snow patches on the slopes. Beneath the mountain there were fields of wild, pale yellow flowers. At the Ranger Sta-tion we learned they were called glacier lilies. They were hardy plants which came up out of the ground soon after the snow disappeared and lasted all summer long. Uncle picked up a map of the park. "One thing you probably didn't know," he looked at Eddie and me, "these mountains go clear across the border. And I have to tell you, they are just as pretty on the other side of the lines."

"I can vouch for that," Auntie agreed, "Some of my family still lives there."

Eddie took charge of the map while Uncle kept a close watch on the road. Ever-green trees grew between the mountains; there were spruce trees, pines, fir trees and larch trees (also called tamarack), throughout the region. There were many campsites, as there had been at Yellowstone Park and each area had at least one picnic table. Uncle Louis suddenly stopped,

"Don't get out of the car," he said firmly. "Look!"

I sat up straight. Everyone's eyes followed his pointing finger. There was a tent set up on the ground near a picnic table. A Mama bear and her two cubs had climbed on the table and were busy scavenging through an unattended picnic basket. They didn't seem to notice us watching them as they feasted on the contents of the spilled basket. There was no sign of the campers anywhere near the campsite.

"Now, that wasn't wise of these people to leave their food out on the table and take off." Tom observed. "That's an invitation for bears to come visit."

96

"I think we'll look a little farther for a spot to have our picnic," Uncle said as he drove ahead slowly. "We'll look for a table without wild and furry diners."

We continued on and found an unoccupied campsite. Uncle took the basket and soda tub out of the trunk and we ate in the shade of the evergreens surrounding us. I was grateful for the grocery store Auntie had introduced me to. There was an ample supply of sandwich meat, and Wonder Bread as well as Hostess cupcakes and Twinkies. These provided a wonderful variety of sandwiches and dessert for our picnic. Eddie had chipped some ice off the block in our icebox to keep our soda bottles cold in a small tub Uncle had given us.

"You're tempting me," Uncle said. "Twinkies are my favorite but I'm not supposed to eat them because I have sugar."

"I'm watching you," Auntie gave him a warning look. "You'd better move the cakes closer to Tom and Grace."

"She's a kill-joy!" Uncle took another spiced ham and cheese sandwich.

"This park is different than Yellowstone," I commented. "The mountains are different and the waterfalls seem narrower."

"That's because both parks were formed in a different way; Yellowstone developed from volcanic action while Glacier Park developed from what you'd expect, because of its name, ancient Glaciers." He looked out over the forest. "Even the trees are different; I don't remember seeing Tamarack trees in Yellowstone. At least I don't think so."

"Where are we going next?" Eddie asked.

"I'd like to drive toward Lewis Range, that's the source of the Continental Divide," he answered.

"I wondered about that," Eddie said. "I've read about that place where the water from the mountains separates and flows either toward the Pacific or the Atlantic."

"That's right," Uncle nodded his head. "Well, right there at Lewis Range, that's where it happens."

Grace and I picked up the wax paper sandwich wrappings and empty bottles, returned them to the basket and Tom carried them back to the trunk of the car. We returned to our places in the Buick and Uncle continued his drive east toward Lewis Range which runs north to south along the eastern side of the Continental Divide. The highest mountain we saw was Jackson peak which is 10,052 feet high. From our lookout area we could see mount Jackson's black peak peeking above a huge glacier at a lower level nearly surrounding it giving it the appearance of being completely surrounded by snow. Mount Jackson is the fourth highest mountain in this range but probably the most spectacular. The melting snow from the mountains created waterfalls flowing down to the foot of the range; from there the water flowed east toward Hudson Bay, the Missouri River, the Mississippi and eventually to the Gulf of Mexico before reaching the Atlantic Ocean.

"We're going to go west again toward Kalispell," Uncle said. "The Flathead River is near the border of Idaho."

"Is that near Flathead Lake where we went fishing?" I asked.

"Yes, it is." Uncle further explained. "The waters flow along the border of Idaho into the Flathead River, through Flathead Lake heading toward Clark Fork River and the Columbia River and eventually to the Pacific Ocean."

"That's amazing," Eddie observed.

"That's nothing," Uncle said. "I'm going to show you Montana's newest project."

"Are you going to Hungry Horse Dam?" Tom asked.

"Yes," Uncle answered. "I want to show them how the Flathead River is being diverted during construction over there until the project is completed."

The dam was covered with wooden forms for the pouring of the concrete. There was no water in the basin above the dam except for a few trickles here and there and the wider flow of the Flathead River forced over to the right of the dam. "The concrete was poured a couple of weeks ago," Uncle said. "I'm not exactly sure, but, I think the forms have to stay on for at least a month to make sure the concrete is completely dry."

"Do you need the water for irrigation?" I asked.

"Oh no," Tom answered. "The dam is mainly being built for hydro electric power and it's also expected to help prevent flooding in this area during the spring thaw."

"That's quite a project," Eddie remarked.

"You're right," Uncle said. "When it's done, the Flathead River is supposed to flow over the dam to more than 400 feet below. The highest in the world;"

"I've never seen a dam under construction before," Eddie said.

"You're an ironworker, aren't you Ed?" he didn't wait for an answer. "Maybe you should consider settling down in Montana. I'm sure there's enough work around here to earn a good living."

"It's a beautiful state all right," Eddie agreed. "The thought is very tempting, but, both our families are back east, and I would like to see more of the U.S. before I decide."

"We hope to have kids someday," I added. "And I agree this would be a great place to raise a family."

"Think about it." Uncle said as we headed toward Kalispell and Hot Springs.

It was still light when we got back to the Motel. We emptied the trunk, thanked Auntie and Uncle for the wonderful day. We hugged them and Grace and Tom too then headed back to our trailer.

"We'll have to get some ice in the morning and start thinking about leaving in a day or so," I said.

"Yeah," Eddie answered. "I do like this place but it's time for us to move on."

We cleaned up and stored our picnic equipment, listened to the radio while we ate graham crackers with milk, and then opened the sofa. "It was a great day, wasn't it?" I commented.

"It sure was; goodnight Sweetheart," he put his arm around me. "Maybe some-day we'll come back."

It was around eight o'clock in the morning when Uncle knocked on our door and sang his Chinky, chinky, Chee, Chinee song. Eddie opened the door and he stepped in. His head almost touched the ceiling. "Sit down, Uncle," I pointed to the breakfast nook. "I'll get you a cup of coffee."

"I wondered if you'd like to see another part of the mountains, today," he said." I want to show you a couple of lookout points up there."

"That sounds interesting," Eddie replied. "But this afternoon we have to get ice and groceries before we leave tomorrow."

"Not so soon?" Uncle sounded disappointed. "We like having you here."

"And we like being here too," I sat next to Eddie across from him. "Who knows? Someday we may be back."

For a minute or so it appeared that we might become teary eyed, then Eddie said,"What time do you want to leave this morning?"

"How about nine-thirty?" Uncle finished his coffee and got up.

"Sounds good," I answered. "We'll be ready."

I had time to mop the floor and clean up the kitchen before it was time to leave. I made a list of the supplies we would need to shop for in the afternoon in preparation for leaving on the next day. Then we walked over to Uncle's car. I sat between Uncle and Eddie on the front seat. Uncle took a different road into the mountains this time. We didn't adhere to the main road but took side roads that led up to the lookout points then returned to the main road. Most lookout areas had a wooden cabin, some more rustic than others. All had a good view of the forests below and were set up to communicate with fire apparatus in the event of a fire. I was surprised to learn that people actually lived in some of the cabins, especially in the summertime. I could only imagine what disastrous results could occur if there were ever a fire in these beautiful forests. Yet it was comforting to know that there were people who watched out for any impending emergency.

When we returned to the Motel, Carol-Jeanne was waiting. "I've been waiting for you," she said. "Betty and Della want you to come to their house again tonight."

"That's great," I replied. "That sounds like fun. Auntie, is it okay for Carol-Jeanne to come to the market with us this afternoon?"

"Please, please, can I Memme?" she pleaded.

"Of course," she agreed. "She didn't have lunch yet, though."

"That's okay, we'll be having lunch when we get back and she can join us," I said.

It was settled. Eddie was ready when I came back with our little cousin. It didn't take us long to shop. I brought in the bags of groceries, Eddie put the large piece of ice in the icebox and Carol-Jeanne helped me put everything away before the three of us sat down to eat our hot dogs and beans for lunch. The afternoon went by quickly as Carol-Jeanne and I played cards: first War, then Old Maid. Auntie made soup for supper and then we were off to another lovely evening with Claire and Emile and the girls. We said our good-byes and thanked them again for their wonderful hospitality.

"It's going to be hard to say good-bye to Auntie and Uncle and Carol-Jeanne tomorrow," I said while we prepared our bed.

"I know," Eddie put his arm around me. "This has really been a great visit."

HOUSE ON WHEELS

CHAPTER 10

"You know you're welcome to stay longer," Uncle said as he disconnected the faucet.

"I know, Uncle Louis," I felt my heart grow heavy. "You and Aunt Elise have been wonderful. We can't thank you enough."

"We enjoyed your visit too," Auntie said as she put her arm around me. "Carol-Jeanne is going to miss you too."

I bent down to kiss my little cousin, "I'll remember you always, Sweetie." We hugged each other.

"I didn't know my grandmother," I said to Uncle, dabbing my eyes. "But having spent time with her sister, Tante Marie and you, her brother, somehow I feel close to her. And I have you to thank you for that."

"Okay, Sweetheart, the trailer is hitched up, "Eddie shook hands with Uncle and hugged Auntie and Carol-Jeanne. "We should get going. Thanks for everything."

"Think about what I said," Uncle walked us to the car. "This is a great place to live.

"We'll remember," Eddie said.

It was a cloudy day. We drove northwest toward the panhandle of Idaho, that narrow part of the state between Montana and Washington. Uncle had taken us by this road before when we went to see the Hungry Horse Dam project. We drove straight on the main road hoping to cross into Washington State by mid afternoon. We had no sooner crossed into Idaho when we felt that old familiar shaking of the trailer.

"Uh-oh, I don't like the feel of that," Eddie said. "I think one of the trailer tires has gone flat."

"Maybe it's trying to tell us something: like we should have stayed in Montana," I commented. "Should we pull over and take a look?"

"I haven't seen any repair stations on this road, but I'll stop when I find a shoulder wide enough."

Eddie slowed down to keep the shaking at a minimum but had to continue a few more miles before he could stop to assess the damage. "The tire's not completely flat yet, but we're going to need a new tire," he said. "We don't have a spare for the trailer. We'll just have to keep going the way we are until we come to a town."

"I hope that'll be pretty soon," I said as I sat down in the car.

We continued on for another few miles before we came through a small town and we saw a gas station on a side street off the highway. I think the town was Wallace but I'm not really sure, and at that time I didn't really care. Eddie talked to the attendant who wore dark blue coveralls, and was very courteous but couldn't accommodate us by providing us with a new tire.

"The best I can give you," he said with his thumbs in his belt loops, "is that old recap." He rolled out a sorry looking tire. "I don't really know why I kept this thing," he scratched his balding gray head. "But you're welcome to it for two bucks; it'll probably get you as far as Sandpoint."

"It's better than nothing," Eddie said. "Let's mount it on the rim."

I thought two dollars was highway robbery for the old tire but Eddie said it was better than the one we had. "Let's make the best of it," he said. "If Sandpoint's a bigger town they'll most likely have what we need over there."

It was about two hours later by the time we reached Sandpoint and found a service station. The attendant approached the car wearing a blue and gray striped uniform and a hat with a peak. "Do you realize how lucky you are?" he asked as he looked around the trailer. "This right tire is ready for a blowout and the other one is losing air."

Eddie and I looked at the second tire more closely. "Goll dang it!" Eddie turned to me. "There's a bloomin' nail stuck in this one too."

"Like I said," the attendant repeated. "You're lucky you made it here; I'd say it was a miracle."

It was more than a miracle. The attendant had two tires for sale, our tire rims were still in decent condition and within an hour we were on the road again hoping to reach Washington State before we stopped for the night. Eddie had the Spokane address of a Mr. Young, from back home, who was a fellow ironworker. We located the address but his friend had moved away two weeks before. Another disappointment! In our search for a trailer park, we ended up in an area of untended vacant land and ran over a big boulder. It didn't take us long to realize the brakes weren't working. Using the electric brake on the trailer wasn't ideal but it worked as we drove around unfamiliar streets looking for a repair shop. We found one, but it was past closing time and no one was in sight. We continued to look for both a repair shop and a place to stay for the night. We found a station where the attendant, looked like he was getting ready to close.

"We've got no brakes on the car," Eddie said. "And we'd like to find a place to park the trailer for awhile."

"Let me put up this 'CLOSED' sign and I'll see what I can do," he answered.

Eddie followed the attendant inside. "I sure appreciate your taking the time to do this," he said.

"It's going to take a while, you've damaged the brake line and there's no more brake fluid." He wiped his hands on a rag that had been sticking out of his pocket. "I'll tell you what," he continued, "I can fix it temporarily and you can come back in the morning."

"That would be great," Eddie said. "Once we're settled for the night we won't be going anywhere anyway."

"Okay," the man disappeared under the car on a flat board and re-emerged about 15 minutes later. "It's okay for now," he said. "I'll see you around 8:30 in the morning."

He gave us directions to a trailer court just outside of the city but when we got there, they were filled up for the night. The manager was kind enough to direct us to another park on the other side of town. It was beginning to get dark by the time we found the High Bridge Trailer Court.

"How long will you be staying?" the manager asked.

"I don't know," Eddie looked at me. I shrugged. "Probably a couple of weeks."

"Okay," he placed the registration book facing us. "That'll be five dollars, in advance for the first week and the same due at the beginning of each additional week."

Eddie signed the register; we drove to our assigned spot. Eddie backed the trailer in, next to a wooden picnic table. He unhitched the car and parked it on the road in front of our little yard that had a low white picket fence on both sides our area. The manager hooked up the electricity and water. "Okay," he said. "You're all set. If you need anything, give a holler." He waved to us and headed back to the office.

We were home.

"This was a tough day," I said as I began to prepare dinner.

"You can say that again," Eddie unfolded the newspaper he had picked up at the office. "Don't make anything heavy for supper; a cheese omelet will be good enough."

"We have a lot to be thankful for," I kissed him on the lips. "With everything that went wrong today, we can thank God we're safe."

"I'll go along with that." He put the newspaper aside. "There's not much going on in Korea except a lot of talking."

"Let's hope they get that conflict settled before many more guys get killed over there," I said as I buttered the toast.

We listened to Hank Williams while we ate and then cleaned up the dishes. It felt good to slip under the covers and listen to the gentle rain coming down on the roof.

"I'm glad the rain held off until tonight," he said.

"Me too, it would have made our day a lot worse if we had to deal with the rain too."

"Right." He kissed me. "Good night, Sweetheart."

"Good night, Hon,"

We were up and ready long before our eight thirty appointment to have the car fixed. Eddie has a good sense of direction so we found the garage without a problem. While the car was in the shop we walked around Spokane in the vicinity of the garage. It looked like a nice well laid out city and we noticed many buildings were constructed in marble or brick. We went back to the shop after about an hour and the car was ready.

"Hey, thanks a lot, Buddy," Eddie paid the repairman and shook his hand. "You've been a lifesaver."

"Glad I could help."

"By the way," Eddie asked, "Could you tell me how to get to the Ironworkers Hall?"

The garage owner gave him clear directions and we arrived at the business office of Local 14 in about 10 minutes. Eddie parked near the curb in front of the building and we went in. I sat on a wooden chair against the wall while he walked up to the desk. He knew that at most union offices, workers are sent out early in the day, so he simply introduced himself and presented his International Journeyman card to the Business Agent.

"You're from Rhode Island," the B. A. said. "You're a long way from home." He looked at me.

"Actually, we live in Massachusetts, this is the wife," he nodded toward me. "But the Providence Local is closer than Boston; I know this is Friday and the men are already out on jobs today, but I was hoping there would be a job I could go to on Monday."

"Did you bring your tools?" the B.A. asked.

"Oh yeah, I never go to work without them."

"You're in luck," the B.A. answered. "There's a new building going up and it's just starting on Monday."

"Thanks, I'll see you on Monday around seven," Eddie extended his hand to the B.A., and then we walked out to the car together.

"It looks like I'll be going to work on Monday," he said. "Let's go have lunch then take in a movie."

We saw two movie theaters in the center of town. Each ran its own particular feature continuously and each theater featured a different movie. One was showing

'Tarzan's Peril' with Lex Barker and Dorothy Dandridge and the other featured Randolph Scott, David Brian and Phyllis Thaxter in 'Forth Worth'. We didn't have to wait for a start time. It didn't matter what time we entered the theater, the movie was usually in progress. We watched the movie from whatever point the story was at when we came in, up to the end. Then we waited until the movie, usually preceded by Selected Short Subjects, started again and continued to the place it was when we had arrived. If we really liked the ending, we could stay and watch the ending a second time. If it was a really good movie we could even stay and watch the whole thing over again. (We didn't) The 'Three Stooges' was the short subject before the 'Tarzan' movie and 'Fort Worth' showed 'Movietone News'. Eddie's favorite was always 'Tarzan', but he also found it hard to pass up a good western. The decision was easy: we went to both and didn't get home until nine-thirty. It had been a hot day, in the 90's, but by the time we got back to the trailer the temperature was in the low 70's.

"I'll open the windows while you get the graham crackers and milk."

"The breeze feels good in here," I said as I set the glasses and snack tray on the table. "The cool night air will be good for sleeping."

Eddie turned on the music before he sat down at the table. "It's going to seem funny going back to work after all these weeks."

"I'm sure it will," I said. "It's been two months if you count the time you were in the hospital before we left."

"I might be a little rusty."

"You'll do fine," I put my hand over his. "I'm sure the work here will be the same as it was back home."

"I guess." He got up from the table and brought his glass to the sink. "Let's walk over to the washroom together."

Saturday was a day to explore the city of Spokane. It was a quiet town, well laid out and it had many parks and each one had a swimming pool and all the pools were equipped with high and low diving boards in the deep end and there was a shallow end for the smaller swimmers. All the pools were free and provided lifeguards which made them a popular site for families on hot summer afternoons. We decided to go to the Comstock Pool. Eddie swam a few laps while I splashed around the shallow end; swimming was not my forte although I did enjoy the cool water. When we climbed out of the pool we sat on our towels on the opposite side of the lifeguard's chair.

"What's all the commotion? I asked. "Why are those people gathering near the entrance?"

"I don't know," Eddie answered.

"Wait!" I pointed to the entrance. "There's a big guy coming in over there."

He was wearing a one piece swim suit with dark blue trunks and a Kelly-green sleeveless top. The children seemed to know him and flocked all around him. The life guard stepped down from his perch in the lifeguard chair holding a microphone in his hand.

"Here he is, boys and girls, come gather around the edge of the pool." It took only seconds for the children to respond excitedly and make room for each other around the pool. "Here comes Corky, 333 pounds of swimming energy!" he announced as Corky dove into the deep end of the pool with a big splash. Corky didn't need a microphone. He sang, tossed large beach balls to the children, dove underwater and emerged spewing water out like a whale. The children were mesmerized as Corky seemed to be able to entertain each child as though he or she was the only one there. Eddie and I were equally fascinated as Corky swam gracefully around the pool tossing an inflated ring now and then to invite a child to swim along beside him. It was beautiful to see their broad smiles and hear the "me too" shouts from the edge of the pool. Corky was clearly the hit of the afternoon. The show lasted about an hour and we left shortly afterward.

We looked for a church on the way home. We checked the schedule for the morning Masses and arrived in the trailer court around six o'clock. We had our usual Saturday night supper of beans and hot dogs. The temperature was in the 90's while we were at the pool but it had cooled down to around 73.

"You know," Eddie observed. "It was around 55 degrees when we got up this morning. That's like a 40 degree temperature change in one day.

"I don't think we've ever experienced that much of a temperature change in the same day," I answered. "Not even in Yellowstone Park."

Eddie tuned in on 'The Grand Ole Opry' our favorite Saturday night show on the radio and we played rummy while listening to the music until it was time for bed.

The alarm woke us up at 7:00 a.m. It didn't take long for us to shower and get ready for 8:30 Mass at Our Lady of Lourdes Cathedral. It was a beautiful Romanesque style church built in red brick and marble. A set of stairs as wide as the church rose from the street level to the entrances. There were two square steeples at the two front corners of the church and a circular stained glass window beneath a pointed pinnacle with a cross in the center in between. The three entrances were sculptured bronze doors, about 14 feet high. There was one door in each steeple and one in the center below the pinnacle. All three doors had sculptures of saints carved in their design, and a statue of a saint above it. Inside there were stained glass windows on all sides of the worship space. The altar and altar rail were made of marble and trimmed in what looked like black onyx. Although the bishop was the celebrant, it was a low mass and the altar boy responded in Latin to all the prayers. The choir was not there. From the top level of the stairs there was a lovely view of the neighborhood. We stopped to pick up a newspaper in the trailer park office when we came back. It didn't take us long to get changed out of our 'church' clothes and I put on a pink short-sleeved dress with a wide collar. Eddie wore gray trousers and a short-sleeved green shirt. Eddie glanced at the paper while I made pancakes for breakfast. "There's still not a lot of news about the Korean War," Eddie remarked. "They're still talking."

106

"From what I can see they don't even want to call it a 'War'," I said. "They refer to it as the Korean 'Conflict'.

"You're right, but it doesn't seem to make a difference what they call it, they're still sending young people over there and young people are still getting killed or maimed every day."

"Could you put the paper aside?" I had a stack of pancakes on a platter with bacon and waited a minute or two before placing it on the table.

I handed him the plates and utensils while I retrieved the syrup from the icebox.

"These are really good," he said. "My compliments to Aunt Jemima again."

I poured the coffee, "what do you want to do today?"

"I don't know," he took a sip of his coffee. "Maybe we could go to one of the other swimming pools around here."

"There are lots of them," I replied. "We can drive around and go to one that is not so crowded."

I picked up the dishes from the table and Eddie returned to reading the newspaper. The comic section was open in front of him when we heard a knock on the door. I went to answer it.

"Hi," the man in a navy blue business suit and red striped tie, carrying a briefcase said. "I'm Jim, your new neighbor," he extended his hand. "My wife and I just moved in yesterday and we'd like to get acquainted." I took his hand cautiously.

Eddie stretched his neck to see who our caller was and said, "Sure, come on in. The name's Eddie."

I didn't close the door and watched as the two men shook hands. "Nice place you got here," Jim said. "Our trailer is a bit bigger, but hey," he chuckled, "how much room do we really need?" He placed his briefcase on the table and sat down.

"I see you have a cross up there above the cabinets," he observed. "That tells me you are people of God."

I continued to wash the dishes and Eddie and I glanced at each other.

"You know lots of people believe Sunday is the Lord's Day," he pulled out a bible and some literature from his briefcase and continued. "In fact I have proof right here, in this holy book, that Sunday worship is an error."

"What do you mean an error?" Eddie asked. "Everyone I know except Jewish people go to church on Sunday."

107

"Yes, the Jews get it right from the Bible; they go to the Synagogue every Saturday, the Sabbath. Right here in the book of Genesis it says: God created everything in six days and on the seventh day he rested." Jim said.

"And Jesus died on the Cross on a Friday and Resurrected on a Sunday," Eddie replied.

"Yes he did, but that didn't give anyone the right to change the Sabbath Day from what's written in the Bible," Jim went on.

"Well, I guess you have a right to believe what you want." Eddie said.

"And, there's more. I believe I detect the odor of bacon." Jim sniffed.

"Yes," I agreed. "That's what we had for breakfast. So what?"

"Bacon comes from pork," Jim declared. "And it's clearly stated in the Biblical dietary laws, that pork is a forbidden meat." He fanned through the Bible. "Here let me show you."

Eddie stood up, stuffed Jim's papers back in his briefcase. "Well, neighbor, I've already heard a good sermon by the bishop at the Cathedral this morning." Eddie handed Jim his briefcase, he was still holding his bible, and gently pushed his elbow and escorted him toward the door. "I've never heard of neighbors coming to visit carrying a briefcase. If you expect to convert us to whatever your faith is, I think you should go now before you leave here a Catholic." Without further discussion, Jim was out the door and Eddie returned to his seat at the table where he resumed reading the newspaper.

"Is there any more coffee?" he asked.

I had to admire how Eddie handled this whole situation. He was calm as he listened to Jim's presentation but he wouldn't be shaken from his own beliefs. It was a side of him I had not seen before and I deeply respected my husband for his sincere faith.

I put his cup of coffee on the table. "Did you decide which pool you wanted to go to today?"

"I thought we'd go to the Liberty pool for a short while, and then take in a movie," he answered.

"That Donald O'Connor movie 'Francis' about a talking mule is playing downtown," I said. "What do you think?"

"Sure," he agreed. "We'll bring our bathing suits and we'll have popcorn at the movies and eat supper when we get home."

I joined him for a second cup of coffee and read the 'funnies', "Okay, while you finish reading the paper, I'll get the suits and towels and we'll be ready to go."

It was a lovely summer afternoon with the temperature in the upper 80's. It felt good to cool off in the pool. By two o'clock the pool was beginning to get crowded so we decided to follow through with our plan to go to the movies. Donald O'Connor was as funny as ever and the short subject was Desi Arnaz in one of his Cuban 'Ba-ba-lou' presentations. When we returned home it was around six thirty. I made American Chop Suey while Eddie got his work clothes and tools ready for work in the morning. It was a warm evening so I set the tablecloth and plates outside on the picnic table.

"Did you find everything you need for work tomorrow?" I asked as I brought out the pot of hot tea.

"Oh yes," Eddie said. "I put my clothes on the seat of the breakfast nook and my tools are in the trunk of the car."

"It will seem strange for me not to have you around all day," I commented. "I know I'll find stuff to do, but I'll miss you."

"I know what you mean," he reached for a slice of Italian bread. "It's going to be different for me too. I'll be working with guys I never worked with before."

"I'm sure you'll do fine." I tried to reassure him. "I'll be fine too."

We sat outside for awhile after dinner. The air began to get cooler as the sun started to go down. We brought the dishes in before it got dark, and then went out again to sit out under the starry sky as the moon shone down upon us. We were on the brink of a new experience. Most of our neighbors were working people who had chosen to live in mobile homes, whether for economic reasons because it was more affordable than buying a house, or whether their work required them to move from one place to another, or like us, settling here in this city temporarily, only long enough to save sufficient funds to allow us to travel on to a new adventure. We sat in silence for a long time, and then Eddie said, "Come on Sweetheart, five o'clock will come soon enough." He put his arm around me. "We should go in."

By the time Eddie showered and shaved, had breakfast and was ready to leave it was close to six o'clock. He picked up the lunch I had packed for him and was on his way to the union hall for directions to his new job. I settled in to cleaning, washing and ironing and getting accustomed to my new surroundings. I met Mrs. Kennedy in the laundry room. She spoke with a French accent and she told me she was a salad chef at one of the local restaurants. "Your name sounds French," she said. "Parlez-vous français?"

"Mais oui," I answered.

We began a conversation in French. She and her GI husband met during WWII and married soon after the war ended. She had attended culinary school in France and looked forward to a higher position in a restaurant someday.

"A wooden bowl is best for making a salad," she directed. "And most important," she emphasized. "You must always rub the inside of the bowl with garlic before you put any greens into it."

"Thank you," I said. "Next time I make a salad I'll remember that."

"Well, Chérie," she picked up her laundry basket. "Au revoir. I have to get ready to go to work. I hope to see you again."

When Eddie returned from work that evening I had our bathing suits and towels ready.

"What do you think?" I asked. "How about we go to the Liberty Pool where you can shower and swim before supper?"

"Good idea," he answered. "It was pretty hot out there on the steel today and the water will feel good."

"And you're probably feeling bones you didn't remember you had," we headed back to the car. "Are you too tired to go to the movies after supper?"

"Me?' He laughed. "Too tired for the movies?"

"That's what I thought." I sat next to him. "'Fabiola' is playing, that's a story about the persecutions of Christians in Rome."

"Sounds interesting!"

Everything was going as planned until we sat down for supper. It was terrible. I tried to take a short cut with tuna and noodles. I hadn't got the hang of the stove-top oven yet so I opted to use a saucepan. I don't know how I managed to make such a sticky, unsavory sauce but…Yuk…there it was!

"What the heck is this?" Eddie examined a forkful of the moosh after his first bite.

"It's tuna sauce with noodles; our neighbor gave me the recipe and said to put it in the oven," I explained. "But I wanted to save time."

"Well, I'll do us both a favor and throw this stuff out," he scraped our plates into the garbage. "And while we're at it, you can get rid of the recipe too. Let's have a baloney sandwich and get going to the movies."

'Fabiola was wonderful: enough love interest for me and enough action for him and by the time we came home from the movies, we both appreciated our snack of Ritz Crackers and cheese with milk before heading for bed.

We fell into the routine of trailer living. Most of the men were off to work during the day and the women stayed at home. There were a few young children and the summer vacation routine seemed to be to get chores done in the morning and to go to one of the parks in the afternoon. Our trailer was one of the smaller ones in the court. Everyone went to the community house at some point during the day or evening. The laundry room was on one side of the facility and the toilets and showers on the other. In the center there was an activity room with card tables and a pool table. Against the wall there were cue sticks and shelves with decks of cards and board games including checkers, chess and parchesi.

Dolores' and George's trailer was two spaces down from us. George had a construction job on a different site than Eddie. He was a carpenter. Dolores and I made bread pudding in the afternoon and we had spaghetti and meatballs ready for the guys when they came home from work. We played Canasta at their trailer in the evening (the girls won). We were making new friends and soon learned that each one of us had something to contribute to mobile family living because for most of us, our own families were far away.

I drove Eddie to work on the next day so I could run some errands with the car. Dolores came with me to show me where the market was and where we could pick up some ice for our icebox. When we came back I invited her to have lunch with me. While we ate our tomato soup and grilled cheese sandwiches, she told me George's job was almost done and they were planning to leave in a couple of days. I picked up Eddie after work. I brought our suits and towels and we splashed around a bit before going home. It was my birthday so we stopped to eat 'Chinese' on the way back.

George was standing behind his trailer when we pulled into our parking space. "Hey, Ed," he called out. "I'm having a problem with my rear trailer lights. Can you have a look-see?"

"Sure," Eddie walked over. "What seems to be wrong?"

"I don't really know," he scratched his head. "I think maybe there's a loose wire or something."

Eddie said, "You get a flashlight, I'll get the old blanket out of my trunk and we'll check it out."

Dolores and I figured this was a 'guy thing' and we sensed there was nothing we could do to help so we came over to our trailer while they fixed the lights on hers and we made Rice Krispies squares. We figured by the time they fixed whatever was wrong they'd probably be ready for a snack and voila! By the time they were done, Eddie needed another shower from having been under the vehicle and the evening had long past its prime time. No card playing tonight. Dolores brought some of the squares home to share with George. Eddie and I prepared the sofa and went to bed.

One day was pretty much as the day before except some trailers moved out and new ones came in. We never did meet Jim's wife because they left the day after Jim had come to visit. Bernie and Richie had been at the park for about a month. He was working on an electrical project in town. Bernie invited me to go with her to the V.A. hospital where she visited a couple of times a week. Some G.I.'s were casualties from the Korean Conflict and others were patients requiring care on a regular basis since WWII. I was a bit timid at first because I had never visited injured servicemen before.

"Be cheerful," Bernie said before we got to the wards. "And smile a lot. These guys have been through enough, they don't need to see 'I feel sorry for you' faces."

I learned from her that these brave men looked forward to having someone talk with them and listen for a while to take their minds off their suffering. She introduced me to patients she had seen before and introduced herself and me to newly admitted men.

Some appeared to be barely out of their 'teens' and had to adjust to a future with missing limbs. I was deeply touched by some of the stories I heard that day. I'll never know if my visit was ever meaningful to the men I visited that day, but I know their courage and hope will inspire me for the rest of my life.

"What time does Eddie get home?" Bernie asked on the way home.

"Around five usually," I answered.

"Richie gets home around that time too and we usually like to go to the pool before dinner," she said.

"We like to do that too," I remarked. "Want to go together?"

"Sure," she turned into the park. "Shall we say around six?"

"Sounds good to me," I got out of the car. "I'll get our stuff ready."

"Good; six it is; and Richie will drive." She waved as she walked toward her trailer. "Thanks for coming with me this afternoon."

"It was my pleasure; we'll see you at six." I waved back. I saw Dolores standing in her doorway as I passed her trailer. "Hi," I stopped for a minute. "What are you up to?"

"We're definitely leaving on Sunday," she said. "So I've been busy getting things ready."

"Want to come to the pool with us around six?" I asked.

"No, we'd better not." She answered. "There's still so much to do."

"I understand," I continued to walk toward our trailer. "We'll probably see you when we get back."

I made a quick stop at the office to pick up a newspaper and checked the mail. There was a belated birthday card from my mother with a newsy letter inside. I hurried home to read it. Then I peeled potatoes and chopped onions to save time for when we'd return from the pool. Corned beef hash was one of Eddie's favorites and, with all the preparation done; it wouldn't take long to get supper on the table while Ed read his Spokane Daily Chronicle.

We met Bernie and Richie at their trailer, and we left just before six. I was always amazed at the number of people who were at the pools, no matter which one we went to, or whatever time it was, there were usually at least twenty or more people there, even at suppertime which is when we generally went. On weekends there were always a lot more bathers when parents came with their families. Richie stopped for Bernie to buy watermelon on the way home and invited us to join them for dessert. "I'm going to ask Dolores and George to come over too," Bernie said. "I'm going to miss them when they leave."

"Me too," I said.

It was still light at eight-thirty when we gathered around Bernie and Richie's picnic table. It's really funny how fast people can get close to one another under certain circumstances. Each one of us came from somewhere else, Dolores and George from California, Bernie and Richie from Colorado and we were from Massachusetts. All of us found friendship here in Spokane. We had no idea whether we would meet again after we left Spokane and yet, for a time, this time, we were family to one another. We ate water-melon, talked about our hometowns, Richie talked about serving in Europe during WWII and George talked about the Navy. Eddie was too young to serve during WWII and the threat of Korea still hung over our heads. We listened to each other's stories until the stars and the moon made their appearance. It was a beautiful night. The girls hugged, the guys shook hands as we told each other, "See you tomorrow," and went our separate ways.

Bernie and I planned to have a pot-luck supper for Dolores and George on Sat-urday night. We were pleased that Mr. and Mrs. Kennedy (I never did learn their first names) had the night off and would be able to come. Mrs. Kennedy prepared her famous salad, and her husband baked rolls for the occasion. (He was a baker at the restaurant where they both worked). It was a real feast with fried chicken, potato salad, baked ham and beans. Mr. Kennedy also provided choux à la crème (cream puffs) for dessert. George surprised us all when he pulled out his guitar. Not to be out done, Eddie brought out his harmonica and we had a 'sing along' well into the night.

The park was quiet when we left for eight-thirty Mass at the Cathedral. One of the curates was the celebrant, he wore a green chasuble. I think he probably could have taken the record for shortest Mass ever. He gave a short sermon after the gospel and zipped through from the collection to the final Amen. He plopped his biretta on his head at the end of Mass; genuflected with the two acolytes who wore black robes and a white surplices, followed them to the sacristy and was gone. We were out of church before nine o'clock. By the time we returned home, George was already hitched up and was testing the lights. Bernie and Richie weren't up yet. Dolores and I hugged each other, and the men shook hands, we wished each other well and they were on their way. I made scram-bled eggs and ham for breakfast with toast and coffee.

"Want to go to the Comstock Pool today?" Eddie asked while I washed the dish-es.

"Okay," I replied. "The Liberty Theater is showing 'The Great Caruso' with Mario Lanza do you want to see it?"

"We'll go right from the pool," he said. "We can eat when we get home."

The day went by quickly and we commented on how empty the spaces next to us looked now that Dolores and George were gone. "I wonder if we'll ever see them again," I said.

"They were nice people," Eddie replied. "I wouldn't mind if we did." He opened the icebox. "In the meanwhile let's dig into some of the leftovers from last night's supper, I'm pretty hungry."

113

A cold supper with lemonade was just the right meal after our hot leisurely afternoon. We were still sitting at our picnic table when Bernie and Richie came home and we chatted for awhile before saying goodnight. The men had to go to work in the morning.

While Eddie was at work a new family moved into the empty spot next to us. We didn't get acquainted with them until Eddie and I came home from the pool after Eddie's work day was over.

"Hi," Eddie extended his hand. "The name's Eddie and this is the wife."

"Welcome to High Bridge," I shook our new neighbor's hand. "My name is Jeanne."

"Mandy and Stanley here and these are our kids." There were two beautiful blond blue-eyed children. "This is Sherry who is 10 and Billy he's 7," Mandy said.

"That's a pretty big trailer you've got there," Eddie observed.

"Yeah, well, with these two guys we sure need the room," Stanley said.

"You're lucky, those kids look pretty special." I started to walk toward our trailer. "We'll let you get settled. If you need anything knock on our door." By this time we felt like old time residents. Eddie took my hand and we went home for supper. We listened to music on the radio until it was time to walk over to the community room before going to bed. It was a cool night as usual and there was still no sign of rain.

Stanley's car was already gone when I came back from driving Eddie to work. I didn't see Mandy or the children until after ten o'clock. By then I had already done laundry and a quick clean-up in the trailer.

"Hi," I called over to her. "Are you getting settled in okay?"

"Oh yes," she replied as she put down her laundry basket. "We all slept well but the kids were still asleep when Stanley left for work so I decided to sleep in too."

"After the long trip yesterday," I said, "I'm sure they are still pretty tired."

"It wasn't so long; we only drove up from Oregon." She told me. "Stan is a stone-mason and his contractor sent him up here on a job for a few weeks and we decided to come up with him."

"You're going to like it here. I'm sure the kids will enjoy all the swimming pools they have around here."

"That's what Stan said," she closed her trailer door. "And it beats staying home alone with the kids while he's working up here."

"Good thinking." I observed. "I'm going to Liberty Pool this afternoon if you and the kids would like to come along?"

**114**

"What do you say kids?" she asked. "Wanna go swimming this afternoon?"

"Yeah, Yeah!" Sherry and Billy danced around, "Can we, Mom, can we?"

"I guess you've got your answer," I smiled at the kids. "How about one o'clock?"

I had beef stew cooking for supper since around eight o'clock. It smelled good and I went in to check on its progress. I figured there would be time enough to cool it in a bowl and refrigerate it in the icebox before leaving for the pool. I still had clothes to iron and put away before we could leave.

Mandy and the kids knocked on the door a few minutes before one o'clock. I had my towel and changing clothes ready in my large beach bag. Mandy sat up front with me and Sherri and Billy sat in the back. It was a short ride to Liberty Pool. We found a parking spot close to the entrance and climbed the few short steps to the swimming area. We were there only a few minutes when 'Corky' showed up to entertain the swimmers as he had at Comstock the first day we came to Spokane. It was Liberty's turn to host the "333 pounds of swimming energy". Again he called the children to the edge of the pool and played catch with them, juggled balls and tossed out floating rings to invite the kids to join him in the water. Billy caught one of the rings and splashed around delightedly from one side of the pool to the other with Corky. Our 'mini-whale' sized friend put on a show for about an hour and left. Then Billy and Sherry talked about the experience all the way home. By the time I dropped Mandy and her kids off it was time for me to pick up Eddie at work. I stopped at the bakery and bought some French bread on the way to the job site.

"Do you want to stop at the pool before we go home," I asked when Eddie got in the car.

"No, not tonight," he said. "I'll shower at the court while you get supper ready."

"Okay," I replied. "In a way that's good because I went this afternoon with Mandy and the kids next door; and guess what?" I didn't wait for an answer. "Corky showed up."

"I bet the kids liked that," he was quiet again.

"Is something wrong?" I was concerned because he seemed to have something on his mind.

"No, not really," he was quiet again.

I didn't say any more. I turned into our parking space. He got out of the car and headed for the showers while I heated up the stew for supper.

"Okay," I said during the meal. "What happened at work?"

"How do you know something happened at work?"

"Because you're not usually mopey, and tonight you are."

**115**

"Well aside from it being hot as heck," he finally confided. "When the crane tried to pick up a beam off the ground it rolled over a guy's legs. The guy, his name is Gerry, was in a lot of pain. It took a while to replace the snapped cable so they could lift the beam off of him and for the ambulance to come. They took him to the hospital but nobody seems to know how he is."

"Well look at it this way," I tried to encourage him. "He was on the ground. He's alive and; whatever injuries he has, the hospital will be able to help him. You know how that goes; out of work a few weeks, time to heal and Gerry will be back to work in no time."

"I know you're right," he said. "But it's always tough when someone gets hurt on the job."

"Is the job almost over?" I asked.

"Yes, we should have all the iron in place by Friday."

"Are you going to try to stay on for another job?" I wanted to know.

"No, I'll be ready to move on," he admitted. "I'm looking forward to see the Pacific Ocean. I want to see for myself if it's really as blue as they say." He took a bite of buttered French bread. "Hey, this stew is good."

"Welcome back, Honey," I smiled. "Now you sound like your old self. I'm sure you'll find out that Gerry is okay when you get on the job tomorrow."

After he read the newspaper we played rummy and listened to the radio. It had been an emotional day for both of us. We were grateful for the time alone.

Eddie found out at work that although both Gerry's legs were badly bruised, only the left leg had broken bones and would need a cast. The good news was that he might be able to return to work in about six weeks.

The next few days were quiet. I went to the V.A. Hospital with Bernie once more. Some of the patients were still there, a few had gone home and there were a few new patients in the wards. It was still an emotional experience.

Friday was Eddie's last day of work and we planned supper with Bernie and Richie on Saturday night. We hadn't seen much of Stan and Mandy and the kids, nor the Kennedys. I replenished our staples in the cupboards, and made sure all our clothes were washed and ironed and ready for traveling. Our plan was to leave on Sunday after Mass.

CHAPTER 11

At 9:30 a.m. the temperature was already in the low eighties. There was still no sign of rain. "Why don't we spend one more day here in Spokane?" Eddie suggested.

"I don't mind staying here another day," I said, "any particular reason?"

"Some guys at work told me we should see Manito Gardens before leaving Spokane," he shrugged. "They said the park is really worth seeing."

"To be honest, between you working and our going to the pools almost every day we didn't do much sight-seeing here," I realized. "That's a great idea."

"I think so too," he agreed. "It's getting kind of late to hitch up and leave at this time," he reasoned. "If we leave tomorrow we can get an earlier start."

"Shall I pack a lunch for a picnic?" I asked.

"Good idea." Just then Bernie and Richie came walking toward us.

"Do you need any help to hitch up?" Richie called out.

Eddie looked over at me and smiled. "We decided to stay one more day and go to Manito Park. Do you care to join us?"

"What changed your mind?" Bernie asked.

"Well, for one thing," Eddie replied. "I really like to get an early start on the day we travel and here it is close to 10 o'clock. Then, for another thing, someone at work told me about the gardens and said we shouldn't miss going there."

"We haven't been there either," Richie said. "Sure, let's do it."

"Give me enough time to put a couple of sandwiches together," Bernie said. "What do you think, a half hour?"

"That sounds about right," I headed back to the trailer and Bernie did the same.

The gardens were in the South Hill section of the city. We followed 17th avenue until we reached Grand Boulevard. As we entered the 90 acre park we were greeted by a profusion of brightly colored flowers arranged in large concrete edged flower-beds. We reached the Visitor Center in time for a guided tour of the gardens. From our guide we learned that the name 'Manito' in the Algonquin language means 'spirit of nature'. In one area of the gardens, called Rose Hill, there was a large variety of roses.

"This year, 1951, Rose Hill was selected for the planting of experimental types of roses in Spokane. As you walk through the garden, you'll see hybrids of varied shades

**117**

of pink, yellow and red all over the place," he took a deep breath. "And I don't have to tell you, let your nose treat you to the wonderful fragrance that permeates the air."

In the 3 acre area called Duncan Gardens there was a beautiful granite fountain and a wide walkway that ran through the center of that portion of the park. On either side of the concrete walk the flower beds and trees were symmetrical with respect to the species and colors of the flowers. Whatever flowers were on one side were reflected on the other; even to the shapes of the trees.

"The flowers you see here will be removed and replaced by new flowerbeds throughout the growing season," the guide told us. "As these flowers fade, a new species is planted so that there are always flowers in bloom."

We walked past the symmetrical flowerbeds and the guide pointed to a rusting iron bar that was stuck in a rock. "There used to be a zoo located in this park, and this is the remnant of a bear cage from that time."

The only animals we saw were ducks in and around a pond within the park. At the end of the tour we stopped in a rest area to have our picnic lunch before driving over to the undeveloped area of the park where we saw rock formations and cliffs in their natural state.

"These rocks and cliffs sort of remind me of the landscape we saw in South Dakota," Eddie remarked.

"There are rocks and cliffs similar to this in Colorado too," Richie said. "Except over there, a lot of the dirt is reddish-orange."

"Really!" I was surprised. "I've never seen orange dirt."

"You'll see it for sure if you ever get to Colorado," Bernie assured us. "And some of the cliffs are formed like arches."

"Yeah," Eddie said. "We saw some arches in the badlands, but they were the same grayish color as these rocks."

"I'm glad we didn't miss this place," I said. "And I'm glad you guys came with us."

"It was a great day, all right," Bernie said. "Let's have supper together when we get back to the court."

Everyone nodded. "We'll eat at our trailer," Richie said. "I'm sure you guys are pretty much packed up over there."

"Well, kind of," I said. "But that's okay."

"Our place," Bernie said firmly.

Bernie fried hot dogs and warmed up Campbell's beans. We had potato salad and pickles on the side and hot tea. It was like a feast. We ate and chatted into the evening until it was time for us to go home.

"We probably won't see you when we leave tomorrow," I said.

"Probably not if you're leaving around 5:00 a.m.," Bernie agreed.

"That's the plan," Eddie said. "I'd like to make it to Grand Coulee Dam before noon."

"You should be able to get there by mid morning," Richie said.

There was an awkward silence. It was a little sad to say good-bye to Bernie and Richie, they had been wonderful neighbors.

"Thanks for all your help," I hugged Bernie. "I really enjoyed our visits to the hospital. I'll miss you a lot."

"Me too," she was teary-eyed. "Drive safely and all that good stuff."

"It looks like Stan and Mandy are still out," I nodded toward the quiet trailer. "Please tell them and the kids good-bye for us."

Eddie and Richie shook hands; "This place won't be the same without you guys," Richie patted Eddie on the shoulder.

"We'll miss you too, Buddy." Eddie looked at me. "We'd better get home, kid."


As had been pre-arranged, the manager met us at the trailer at 5 o'clock to disconnect the water and electricity. Eddie had already hitched up the trailer and connected the hand-brake. We were officially checked out. We got in our car and headed out of the court, turned on to the highway and headed North West toward Grand Coulee Dam. We drove through mountainous areas where there were deep canyons and winding rivers. The road was smooth and there was very little traffic. We arrived at the dam much earlier than we had expected. We parked in the nearly empty parking lot and walked up to the visitor area. Eddie had a million questions many of which were answered in a brochure we picked up in the lobby. The dam controls water from the Columbia River just below the Grand Coulee River.

The foundation of Grand Coulee Dam is a natural solid granite base and built up with iron and concrete to a height of 550 feet. It is the largest dam in the Columbia River Basin and one of the largest in the world. It began to produce hydropower in 1941 and is also used for irrigation and flood control. Above the dam is Lake Franklin Delano Roosevelt which extends almost to the border of Canada. It was still morning when we drove to the lake; the temperature was already in the upper 80's so we decided to go in for a swim in one of the many areas set aside for public bathing. The water was clear and warm and refreshing. The good part about hauling a trailer is that we are always 'home'. We can stop, have a snack or change our clothes anywhere, anytime and be ready to move on to our next destination in a short period of time.

We continued on to Sun Lake and Dry Falls near Coulee city. This was an amazing place. In an area just above where Grand Coulee dam is located today, during the ice age, more than 12,000 years ago when the Columbia River, the Missouri, the Colorado, the Clarke and Grand Coolie Rivers were dammed up by ice, the force of the water carved out deep canyons and an enormous flood occurred creating a waterfall ten times larger and more spectacular than Niagara. These spectacular falls disappeared when the ice melted and the rivers resumed their natural flow leaving the ragged cliffs, taller than three hundred and fifty feet and wider than three and a half miles. We drove by the beautiful clear water of Sun Lake located in the basin below the cliffs. It was hard to imagine this area thundering with waterfalls when we were seeing a beautiful calm lake and what appeared to be narrow streams flowing through the basin. The raging waters were gone and peace filled the valley. We continued on the highway and headed southwest toward Mount Rainier.

"It's unbelievable to see how straight the roads are out here," Eddie said. "Back in Fall River, we're lucky to find a stretch of five miles that's totally straight; and that's usually on a highway."

"I know what you mean," I looked around. "Out here even in the cities the roads are straight and well laid out."

"The sign we just passed said to bear left. Mount Rainier is about two hundred miles from here," he observed.

"How long do you think it will take us to get there?" I asked.

"Probably we'll get there around six or seven o'clock," he guessed.

"It's amazing how every state we travel in is different than the other," I said.

"They're alike in some ways too, but not at all like the New England States," he approached the fork where he followed the left arrow indicating the direction to Mount Rainier.

"Look up ahead," I pointed to a snow covered mountain peak directly in front of us.

"That must be some big mountain when we can see it from this far away," he remarked.

"We still have about a hundred eighty more miles to go."

The road was so straight that the mountain was in our sight for most of the distance we traveled to get there. We stopped once at a gas station to fill up the gas tank and freshen up. We could feel the slow, steady climb toward the mountain and the air felt cooler too. We listened to the radio and sang along with Lefty Frizzell as he sang "I Want

To Be With You Always" (one of our favorites), and chimed in with Eddie Arnold and Hank Williams as they sang out a few other western songs. The miles slipped by as we enjoyed the music, the scenery and each other. I sat close to Eddie on the bench seat of the car as we cruised along heeding the call of the beautiful mountain ever before us. We arrived at the campground of Ohanapecosh near Hot Springs at about six-thirty in the evening. There were rest rooms and showers but there was no facility to hook up to water nor electricity so we didn't unhitch the trailer. It was considerably colder up in the mountains than it had been earlier in the day and much colder than we had experienced since we had been in Washington. We didn't bother lighting our heater. We wore warm sweaters as we ate a cold supper, and played rummy by the light of our flashlight lamp until it was time for bed.

We didn't set the alarm but we were up early and decided to walk around our campsite area. There was a trail by the Ohanapecosh River that led through huge old trees; Douglas Firs, Red Cedars and Western Hemlocks. The river was calm and the area was lush and beautiful. We walked for about a half mile before we saw signs pointing to a Hot Springs Resort area. We opted not to check it out and instead walked back through the trees to the campsite.

Eddie checked around the car and trailer before we left. As we were turning to head southwest, the mountain looked different.

"Check the brochure," Eddie said. "Either Mt. Rainier is very wide or there's another mountain there."

I spread the brochure out on my lap. "You're right, what we're actually looking at are two volcanoes."

From the angle where we came in, it looked like Mount Rainier was one high, wide mountain. Now as we were driving south we could see two distinct snow covered caps one higher than the other.

"It says here," I continued. "Mount Rainier is over 8,000 feet high and Mount Saint Helens is more than 5000 feet high. They're separated by only 35 miles." I looked up from the brochure. "They look so beautiful and majestic it's hard to imagine what kind of activity might be going on way below ground. Although it says here neither volcano has erupted since 1857."

"I don't think I want to be around if ever one of those guys decides to blow its top." Eddie said.

"I agree," I folded the brochure. "I think they could cause a lot of damage. But they sure are pretty, aren't they?"

We continued driving through picturesque areas in the state of Washington. We passed little towns and stopped only to gas up, to stretch our legs or grab a snack. We crossed the Columbia River and drove down a two lane highway which followed the river along the southern part of Washington toward the border of Oregon. There were cliffs and waterfalls and green fields and wildflowers. With each curve of the road the land-scape changed and each turn was as beautiful as the one before. We got our first glimpse of the blue Pacific Ocean when we reached the coastline and Route 101. We stopped at a scenic overlook on the edge of the highway. We stepped out of the car and walked to the edge of a high cliff. It was a bight sunny afternoon and the water gently washed against the rocks below where we stood. Eddie put his arm around me. We stood alone before the breathtaking view of the blue sea stretching to the far horizon. From our viewpoint looking south, we saw a lighthouse down the coast in the distance.

"Look at that ship," Eddie pointed toward the sea. "I wonder if that's a cargo ship headed for Alaska." There was a large ship several miles out to sea heading in a northerly direction.

"I guess it could be," I replied. "It's surely big enough."

"The water is not too rough," he observed. "Look how smooth it's moving."

"I never pictured the water to be this beautiful color of blue," I said.

"We've been looking at the Atlantic all our lives," he commented. "And it sure isn't like this."

"Well, for one thing," I observed. "This ocean looks a lot cleaner."

"That's true; I wonder what the fishing is like over here?"

"I guess you'll find out when we get to California." I kissed his cheek. "We'd better get going."

We drove south down Route 101 until we reached Newport, Oregon where we stopped for the night. It had been a long day so we opted to go to the movies to see 'I'd Climb the Highest Mountain' with Susan Hayward, William Lundigan and Rory Calhoun. It always felt good to walk around a new town after a day's driving. Walking home from a movie and holding hands, felt like we were out on a date. Lingering over a late supper, chatting about the events of the day, listening to the radio; everything was perfect. We were in a world of our own.


We didn't leave Newport until around 8 o'clock. We were surprised at how chilly the night had been for the month of August, but were confident the sun would warm the day as we traveled south along the Oregon coast. As we neared Florence we began to see signs announcing the Sea Lion Caves.

"Are Sea Lions another name for Seals?" I was curious.

"I really don't know," Eddie answered. "There will probably be some informa-tion at the viewing point. I imagine there will be a place where we can stop to see the animals."

We drove a little more slowly. We didn't want to miss the observation area. We need not have worried; it was well marked. Eddie drove to the side of the parking lot; we got out of the car and walked to the rail at the edge of the cliff.

"Wow!" I exclaimed. "Look at 'em all. There must be more than a hundred sea lions down there."

The animals were lying in the sun, on a wide flat rock ledge. The adult sea lions were whiskered and a blonde-reddish-brown color. The pups were darker, almost black. When they walked they turned their back flippers forward and seemed to strut from one place to another.

"How much do you think these guys weigh?" I wondered.

"I think those big ones are males and they could go as high as about half a ton, maybe more," Eddie estimated. "The females look smaller; I'd say maybe 650 or 700 pounds."

"This brochure I picked up says sea lions belong to the Pinniped family." I remarked. "I never heard of Pinnipeds."

"Whatever family they belong to, they sound like a bunch of barking dogs."

"I'd say a little more high pitched than dogs though; wouldn't you?"

"I guess so," he conceded. "What else does that brochure say?"

"It says here they have flaps over their ears," I pointed out. "I've heard of 'eared seals' but I didn't know that was a distinction of sea lions."

"I don't see any ears from here," Eddie said.

"Neither do I, but I'm guessing that's because they're too far away and the ear flaps are probably small and flat against their heads." I checked the brochure again. "It says here the sea lions come here from May to October every year." I looked at Eddie, "Funny how they know when it's the right time to come here. I wonder where they go in the off season; it doesn't say anything about that here."

"I don't see any caves either," Eddie looked around. "They must be hidden in the rocks of the cliffs below us."

"It's still kind of cold up here," I shivered. "I'm glad we wore our heavy sweaters. Let's get back in the car."

We continued on Route 101 toward California. For the first time ever, we saw piggy-back trailers of logging trucks. There were two; long flat-bed trucks piled high with huge logs, held secure with strong chains, hauled by a single truck cab from the forests (we supposed) to the mills to be processed. Route 101 was not a straight highway. Rather it followed the rugged Pacific coastline from Washington State down to Mexico going gradually toward sea level.

"That has to be some good driver," Eddie commented. "Going uphill, riding close to the inland road would be tough on the engine of the truck but probably safer. Going downhill, however, there's always the danger of misjudging a turn or the brakes failing and kaboom! You're flying over the edge of the road into the Pacific."

"That does not sound like fun," I touched his arm. "Promise me you're not going to apply for that job."

"Don't worry about that," he assured me. "Hey, look at that sign. We're only 25 miles from the California border."

"We must be getting close to the Redwood Forest." I looked around. "It's so pretty on this highway. The beautiful ocean on one side and trees as far as we can see on the other."

"We're steadily going down," Eddie said. "But even so, it's not very warm."

"You're right; so far we haven't seen any evidence of this sunny, warm California everyone talks about," I agreed. "It's been sunny all right but not nearly as warm as I expected, especially for the month of August."

"Maybe it's going to start getting warmer," Eddie observed. "It looks like we're almost down to sea level. There's a lighthouse over there and a big curved beach."

"The sign back there said Crescent City is the next town," I said. "I don't know that it's any warmer but I see sandy beaches and people in bathing suits."

"That's a good sign," he pointed ahead. "Speaking of signs, how about that one: Crescent Beach Trailer Park?"

"Sounds good to me; it'll be a good time to stretch our legs and maybe even go for a swim if it's warm enough." The blue Pacific looked inviting.

The trailer court was not far from Crescent Bay. In the lobby of the main office we saw a poster advertising a seal exhibit in a building on the outskirts of the city.

"What do you think?" Eddie asked.

"It sounds interesting," I checked the map on the wall. "It looks like the building isn't very far from here."

"Okay," he agreed. "We'll get settled, maybe go for a swim and then we'll go see the seals."

It didn't take long to unhitch the trailer and get hooked up to the water and electric. We were walking on the golden sand by two thirty. The waves rolled gently onto the shore creating a lacy greenish-blue crown within the bay. There were sunbathers lying on wide towels along the beach. We walked into the Pacific for the first time. Eddie swam out a short distance; I was always impressed by his graceful mobility in the water. I splashed nearer to the shore until he returned; then we spread our towels and stretched out on the sand to dry off a little before going to see the seals. From the shore we had a clear view of the Battery Point Lighthouse we had seen driving down. It looked like a big white house on an island close to shore. The beacon was set in what looked like a 'widow's-walk' type structure with a red roof at the very top of the house.

"Look down the coast," Eddie observed. There's another lighthouse." He turned to a gray haired man sitting on a beach chair next to us. "What's the name of that lighthouse?"

"That's Saint George Reef Lighthouse," he answered. "That thing is very old and it's about 16 stories high."

"It looks like there might be a lot of history there," Eddie said.

"Oh yeah!" the man replied. "It was built in the late 1800's on the site where there had once been a shipwreck. That beacon has been warning ships away from 'Dragon Rocks Reef' for all these years. You can't always see it because it's often foggy out there; but that beacon never fails."

It looked like it was made of stone, wide at the bottom and narrowing toward the top where the beacon was set to light up the sky.

"How far is that island from the coast?" Eddie wanted to know.

"About six miles, I'd say. But the island has a pretty rocky terrain and the water's very rough around there," he shook his head. "It's a good place to stay away from."

"I can see why," Eddie agreed.

"But this other one, Battery Point," the man continued. "This one you can walk out to on the causeway; you can't see the roadway now because it's high tide. It's only visible and accessible when the tide is out."

"You seem to know a lot about this town," Eddie said.

"Lived here most of my life," he picked up his beach chair. "I work in the Redwoods just up the road. Nice talking to ya."

"Thanks," Eddie stood up. "C'mon Sweetheart, we'd better get going if we want to see those seals."

We walked up to the trailer together, went to the showers and then headed for the seals exhibit. The building was on the other side of the bay on a beach a short distance down the coast. As we entered the lobby we saw lifelike framed posters of many different kinds of seals: the Elephant Seal was the largest. It looked like it had a stunted elephant trunk for a nose, the Leopard Seal was the next largest, then there were posters of Harp Seals with whitish and black or brown fur, and many more. The Hawaiian Monk Seal was sleek looking and very different from any of the others. When we walked out to the beach side of the building we saw many Harbor seals. They were reddish-brown in color; they had fewer whiskers compared to sea lions and smaller flippers. When they moved around they flopped on their bellies. They didn't have ear flaps, only little holes on both sides of their heads. They mostly lay around in the late afternoon sun on the

**125**

sandy beach or on the concrete slab which stretched out across the entire width of the building toward the water.

"These seals are much smaller than the sea lions," I remarked.

"Yeah," Eddie agreed. "I'd guess they go about 300 pounds."

"They may be smaller but, they don't smell very good."

"Maybe the sea lions didn't smell so good either," Eddie reasoned. "But we weren't this close to them and we were in the open air."

"That makes sense," I concurred. "Okay, the seals are cute, they have no flaps over their ears, they stink, let's go home."

Eddie laughed, "We'll pick up some ice on the way back. I think we've seen enough Pinnipeds for a while."

We spent a quiet evening playing Rummy and listening to the radio before calling it a day.


We woke up to a dense fog. It was not exceptionally cold but it was definitely light sweater weather. I made hot oatmeal for breakfast with toast and coffee to warm our bones. We were on our way by eight o'clock and continued to follow the coastline south down Route 101 toward the Redwood Forest. The fog continued for most of the morning. The forest covered an area of about 40 miles. We drove along a two lane highway through the enormous trees and stopped in a large rest area where we could walk around and get a better look. The ground was covered with ferns in varied shades of green but we were able to follow a clearly defined path among the trees.

"Here touch my fingertip and see how far we can reach around this tree," Eddie extended his arms around the tree.

"Are you kidding?' I touched his fingers and extended my arms around as far as I could. "We could have your whole family reach around this tree with us and we probably still couldn't reach all around."

"You're probably right, between the two of us we can probably reach around ten and a half feet; we'd probably need another 40 people touching fingertips to reach all around."

"Not only that," I looked up pressing against the rough bark. "Try looking straight up; we can't even see the top."

He stepped back a few feet and sat on the mossy ground. "Come on, sit over here next to me, lean back on your hands and look up." We could see light coming through the upper branches. The sun was still hidden in the clouds, but it was bright enough for us to appreciate how high these trees were. "This place is incredible," Eddie said. "Can you believe some of these trees are more than 3000 years old?"

"If we think about it, these trees were probably seedlings at the time of the Roman Empire and during the time Christ was on earth," I reasoned.

"Yeah, that's a long time ago." Eddie got up and held my hand to help me up, "Let's get back to the car. I'd like to see some other areas of the park."

We passed a sign announcing the town of Klamath and a Paul Bunyan attraction. When we reached there, amid more giant trees, we stopped in a rest area to walk around. We followed the path to a clearing among the trees. Suddenly, there before us was the giant 30 foot tall figure of Paul Bunyan and his equally large blue ox, Babe. There were more trees beyond the clearing. The tallest tree we saw was about 364 feet high. One tree was hollowed out at the base and large enough for a car to drive through. We didn't go through it because our trailer was too tall. There were a couple of other trees that were also carved out and used as gift shops. We stood in awe among the giants.

"When I read about these trees I couldn't imagine them to be this big and this many," Eddie said.

"It's not just the trees," I pointed in the distance. "Look at those lush fields out there and the wildflowers. I don't know about you, but, I think I know what an ant might feel like standing next to us eating crumbs off the kitchen floor."

"I know what you mean." Eddie headed back to the car. "Let's see if we can find that place called 'Mystery Spot'. It's in the forest somewhere near Santa Cruz."

The sun had finally made its way through the clouds. The road continued to wind among the trees until we came to 'Mystery Spot'. This was an area within the forest, approximately 150 feet in diameter where, for no known reason, gravity didn't seem to exist. There was a little cabin there and a docent who demonstrated how a rubber ball placed on a narrow flat board rolled uphill. The same board had a two inch trough in the center which ran the length of it and when he poured water into it, the liquid flowed upwards to the edge of the plank and dripped to the ground. Another demonstration involved two people. They stood back to back to show they were of approximately the same height. When the docent led them to stand a few feet from each other on a spot of apparently level ground and one appeared taller than the other. When they switched places, their height seemed to change too; these phenomena could not be explained except that there may have been some unknown magnetic fluke. "No one knows for sure," the docent said. We left there amazed, not knowing any more than we did before but realizing there were some questions in life that cannot be answered.

We continued to drive south. We passed through a town called Cummings and stopped at a trailer park about 30 miles south of there. They advertised a quiet spot among the trees and a fresh water creek. We were ready for both. We went through the usual routine of unhitching and hooking up, then got changed into our bathing suits, grabbed our towels and headed for the creek. The water was clear and cool. The late afternoon sun penetrated the treetops and created a wonderland of light and peek-a-boo shade. After our initial tooth chattering dip, the creek didn't entice us to stay in any longer. We sat side by side on our towels, and I put my head on his shoulder as we listened to the sounds of the forest. The birds sang sweetly, the water rippled softly and the trees waved gracefully in the gentle breeze.

"This is great, isn't it?" Eddie whispered contentedly.

"It's beautiful for sure," I remarked. "It almost feels like we're part of the forest and we're the only people on earth."

"Well," he thought a minute. "I don't know about that, but it sure is quiet." He stood up, picked up his towel, held his hand out to help me up. "The fact is, however, I'm getting hungry."

"You sure know how to pop a girl's bubble," I teased; "always thinking of your stomach."

"That's not it at all," he laughed. "I think I hear the ham and cheese calling: 'You need a sandwich'. How can I ignore that?"

We walked back to the trailer, hand in hand. I always enjoyed our quiet time at the table during our meals. It was a time to talk about the events of the day and to look forward to another adventure on the next day. After supper we played ping-pong in the community house before settling down for the night. The truth is, I am not a good player and Eddie won every game. It was clear night; the stars had already begun to decorate the sky.

"Let's set the alarm tonight, Sweetheart," Eddie suggested. "I want to get an early start in the morning."

"Where are we headed for tomorrow?" I asked.

"I'd like to make it up to Yosemite National Park and I'm not sure how long it will take us to get there." He took the map out from the drawer.

I took out a pen and pad to write down highlights of what landmarks we needed to look for and placed the notes with the map on the counter. We prepared the sofa-bed together and snuggled in until it was time for 'Big Ben' to ring in a new day.


We were back on the highway before six o'clock. There was a slight fog but not as dense as it had been the day before.

"I hope this pea-soup is gone before we get to San Francisco," Eddie said. "I'm looking forward to getting a good look at the Golden Gate Bridge."

"How long do you think it'll take us to get there?" I had the map and the note-book in my lap.

"I think maybe a couple of hours," he sounded confident. "We're back on 101 and it should take us directly to San Francisco."

The sun was trying to make an appearance through the fog and by mid morning we had a clear view of the rugged coast and the ever present Pacific Ocean as far as we could see.

"Do you remember when I told you I wanted to see the 'Wonders of the United States?"

He didn't wait for a reply. "Golden Gate Bridge is considered one of them."

"How do you know that?" I wondered.

"Back in the thirties, there were a lot of people who said building a bridge here couldn't be done; and then this guy, I think his name was Strauss, he got a team together and they figured out how they could do it. And here it is; the longest suspension bridge in the world," he said.

"You always amaze me at all the stuff you know," I looked at him and shook my head.

"This was a big project for Ironworkers," he reminded me. "I know most of the steel was manufactured at Bethlehem Steel in Pennsylvania and brought all the way over here either on trains across the country, or by ships through the Panama Canal," he continued. "My old man and my older brothers would probably have worked on it if they could have figured out a way to get here."

"That was during the depression," I reminded him; "and people didn't travel much back then."

"Do you realize we will be the first from our family to actually cross over it?" he beamed.

"Well get ready," I pointed ahead. "I can see the orange towers up ahead."

"That's another thing," he announced. "That's called International Orange, a unique color for this particular bridge."

"Well, whoever declared this bridge a wonder is right," I sat up higher on the seat of the car for a better view. "It's the most beautiful bridge I've ever seen."

It was an incredible feeling to drive over the 4,200 foot expansion. We were hundreds of feet above the gateway of San Francisco Bay where it meets the Pacific Ocean. We could see the city of San Francisco at the far end of the bridge. As we drove off the bridge we followed the signs through San Francisco, crossed the Bay Bridge into Oakland; and then headed toward the Sierra Nevada Mountain Range to begin our ascent to Yosemite National Park. The road seemed to be steeper than when we were climbing the Big Horns. The engine heated up several times but Eddie stopped now and then to allow the car to cool down before we could incur any damage. We proceeded on our upward climb until we reached an area about 20 feet from top of the last hill before the entrance of the park.

"Uh-oh! Eddie exclaimed. "We've got big trouble."

"What's wrong?" I could tell he was getting more than a little concerned.

129

"The engine is vapor-locked," he pulled on the electric trailer brake but the steep incline caused the car and trailer to roll back and jack-knife across the two lane road. Eddie pulled the emergency brake to prevent us from rolling down any further. He quickly got out of the car and pulled out two wooden blocks from the trunk of the car and placed them behind the trailer wheels.

"I saw an emergency phone by the side of the road a mile or so back," I said. "Do you think I can reach the ranger station from there?"

"It's worth a try," he answered. "For sure, we're not going to make it up the rest of the way without some kind of help. Be careful."

I started down the hill. A few cars were climbing up toward the entrance. I knew they would be blocked as they drove closer to our vehicle but I soldiered on. The phone was farther down the road than I thought. When I finally reached it, I called the ranger station and was disappointed to learn they had no emergency vehicles available to help us. There was nothing else to do but to walk back up the mountain and hope for the best. A black Packard with two men and two women stopped next to me. They had strong British accents.

"What are you doing by yourself on this road?" the driver asked.

"Our car and trailer jack-knifed across the road up near the top," I explained. "And I came to call the Ranger Station." I was on the verge of tears. "They can't help us."

"Get in our vehicle," one of the ladies said. "You can't walk all the way up there by yourself."

It took me half a minute to decide between accepting a ride from strangers, foreign strangers at that, and whose English I could hardly understand, or walking up that hill alone for more than a mile. "Thank you very much," I said as I squeezed in the back seat between Philip and Kate.

By the time we reached the area where Eddie had been, the car and the trailer were gone. I had visions of the car and the trailer having fallen off the cliff, down to the depths below. "He's not here!" I exclaimed.

"Are you sure this is where he was?" Nigel, the driver, asked.

"Yes," I pointed ahead. "See, there's the top of the hill; the car and the trailer were blocking the road," I was more than a little worried.

The Packard continued up the mountain to the entrance of the park. "There's a red caravan parked on the side of the road over there," Nigel said. "Could that be it?"

I sat up higher in the back seat to see between Nigel and Jane. "There he is," I said. "There's my husband; he's standing next to the car." I couldn't wait to get out of the car.

Nigel pulled up behind the trailer and Kate opened the back door of the car. I scrambled past her to get out.

"How did you get up here?" I ran into his arms and he hugged me.

"A guy in a big Buick came down from the top," he explained. "He saw the traffic was backed up on both sides of the road and horns were honking; he got out of his car and asked if he could help. I got some rope out of the trunk, we hooked up the two cars and he hauled me right up here."

"When I didn't see you when we were driving up, I really got scared because the rangers told me they couldn't help us."

"I found out they just don't have the equipment or the manpower to help stranded motorists; thank God the guy in the Buick stopped to help." "Come to think of it, I don't even know his name," he took my hand and guided me toward the Packard. "Who are your friends?"

All four, the men dressed in suits and wearing checkered caps, and the women wearing A-line skirts and blazers were standing next to their car.

"Nigel is the driver and this is his wife, Jane," I said. "And this is Kate and Philip; they're on holiday from England."

"Thanks for helping the wife," Eddie extended his hand. "I was getting pretty worried about her." The men shook hands.

"Nothing to it," Nigel said. All four waved as they got back in the car. "Have a jolly good trip."

We watched and waved to them as they headed toward the park entrance. I looked around the trailer and the car. "Is the car okay to drive now?" I asked.

"I don't think we'll have any more problems," Eddie motioned me to get in. "The engine is cooled down and I think we're going to be all right. I'll have the attendant check it out when we stop for gas."

We stopped at the Ranger Station at the entrance of the park where we picked up a map and information about sights to see and to locate a campground to park our trailer. There was one continuous paved road that ran through the center of the park and around the main places of interest, and then returned to the point of origin. From that road there was access to all the numbered campgrounds as well as hiking trails or bridle paths if anyone wanted to climb higher up the mountains (we didn't). There were beautiful groves of trees as we drove down toward the campgrounds. There was room at the first site we came to so we decided to stop for the night. The arrangement was similar to the campgrounds in Yellowstone; there was a large facility for showers, a country store and a game room. We hooked up to water but there was no electricity available. The first thing we did after we unhitched the trailer was to drive down to the service station to check the water in the radiator and whatever else we might have needed. Eddie was right, so we added a bit of water to the radiator but other than that everything else checked out okay.

We filled the gas tank and headed back to the campsite. Eddie pulled out our trusty little Coleman stove and I prepared grilled cheese sandwiches which we washed down with milk.

Eddie examined the brochure we had picked up earlier, "Hey! There are Campfire talks here too, just like there were in Yellowstone; want to go?"

"Sure," I answered. "They were interesting. Let me get this stuff cleaned up and I'll be ready to go."

"It looks like the designated campground isn't very far from here," he said, "just a couple of numbers over."

When got to the campsite, it was just dusk and there were already a few people. The ranger had a beautiful campfire going. El Capitan was in full view and it was a beautiful quiet evening. The stars began to dot the sky in the deepening twilight and the circle of visitors around the campfire was complete.

"Welcome to Yosemite, I'm Ranger Paul Scott and I'm going to tell you a little bit about the history of this beautiful place. We owe a great debt of gratitude to John Muir, a man who was born in Scotland and migrated to the United States with his family as a child of 11. His interest in nature began after he attended the University of Wisconsin. He walked from Indiana to Florida and drew maps of the places he traveled. Eventually he made his way to San Francisco, California by ship through the Panama Canal. He did some more walking and found this place. That was in 1868. When he saw the beauty of Yosemite he knew he wanted it to be preserved for future generations so he sent ecology essays regarding the protection of this area to the New York Tribune who published them. Behind me you can see El Capitan which is the largest rock in the world. Muir studied and mapped out this area and was instrumental in preventing it from being sold to private enterprise. In 1903 he invited Theodore Roosevelt to come on a three day camping trip to Yosemite. Roosevelt was equally impressed with Yosemite and realized the need to protect this area from any kind of exploitation. Once back in Washington he started the process of cutting through a lot of red tape of common ownership. Yosemite became a National Park in 1906." The ranger stopped and turned and pointed toward El Capitan. "If you look to the top of the rock you'll see a campfire lit by the rangers up there."

The huge campfire (it looked more like a bonfire) glowed in bright reds, golden yellows and oranges in the dark night.

"Keep watching," Ranger Scott directed.

At a given moment the blazing fire was pushed over the cliff and the embers became a spectacular, glowing fire fall which illuminated the cliff more than half way down, then began to darken gradually as it fell close to the bottom. We were in awe.

"Beautiful, isn't it?" Ranger Scott stood up. "I never tire of that glorious show," he continued. On Sunday we'll be at Camp Curry. We'll talk about the layout of the park. I hope we'll see you there. Thank you coming."

"Wow, that was sure interesting," Eddie said.

"That guy, John Muir, must have worn out a lot of shoes with all the walking he did."

"Yeah, I bet." He reached for my hand and we headed for the car to go home. It was a cool clear night. The stars seemed so close it almost felt like we could reach up and grab a few. "This was quite a day,"

"It was an adventure for sure," I sat in my seat in the car. "But, here we are safe and sound in God's country."

"I'm sure we'll sleep well tonight."


There was hardly anyone in the Community Room when we walked up to the showers in the morning. We had an early breakfast and headed out to do some sightseeing. We headed for Tuolumne Grove where we saw giant Sequoias that were at least as wide and tall as the Redwood trees we had seen in the northern part of the state. We saw another tree that was carved out large enough for a car to pass through, similar to the one we had seen before, except that the top of this one had been lopped off unevenly. The one we had seen in the Redwoods was still a full tree. It was still impressive. We had to lean backwards to be able to see the tops of the trees. The mountain air was clear and fresh as we walked along the footpath among the trees on the soft terrain. The sunlight filtered through the tall trees creating golden dainty patterns on the ground around us and then, suddenly we were fully bathed in sunshine as we came to a clearing, surrounded by a field of green grass and flowers. Then the path led us back through the trees and eventually to the parking area.

We drove up to Glacier Point which is 3,000 feet up in the Sierra-Nevada Mountains. There, we had a beautiful view of Yosemite Valley. We could see the granite Half Dome which dominated that part of the park and Bridal Veils Falls which were wide and lacy and fell around 650 feet. It seemed like we saw breathtaking scenery at every turn of the road. From our high perch we could also see Camp Curry, Mirror Lake and the Nevada Falls.

It was getting late in the afternoon. "This is all so beautiful," I said. "But I think we should be getting back to the campsite."

"Okay," he agreed. "We still have tomorrow to drive around after Mass."

"Right, and tonight I'd like to catch up on laundry before we leave here."

"Good Idea." He started down the two lane mountain road toward home.

We were turning into the campsite when I asked, "Want an omelet for supper, Hon?"

"Nah, a can of beans and hot dogs are good enough."

"Great," I said. "I'll throw in a load of laundry to wash while we eat, and by the time we're finished cleaning up, the sheets will be ready to make up the bed."

Everything went as planned. "Come on, Sweetheart," he said. "I'll help you with the bed. Don't bother with the alarm. It's been a busy day."

"Sunday seems to come awfully fast," I said as we closed up the sofa.

"I know," Eddie said as we collected our clothes to bring to the Community room shower. "Mass is at 9 o'clock in the Old Village Pavilion, we have plenty of time to get there."

It was another beautiful day and we took advantage of it. The celebrant was already in the Pavilion when we arrived. He was from a parish in San Francisco. We were surprised to see the large number of people in attendance. The hall was similar to the one in Yellowstone. Because we had to fast in order to receive Holy Communion, we went back home for a late breakfast. It was late morning by the time we returned to explore Old Yosemite Village which dated back to 1918. The Sentinel Hotel was in the center of the village and there was a clumsy arrangement of rustic wooden houses in the neighborhood. There was an administration building, a small post office, a museum and a gift shop as well as a large building used as housing for Park Rangers. We walked leisurely through the village poking our noses into the museum to examine the artifacts on display, and perused the gift shop where we bought salt and pepper shakers resembling miniature sequoias.

When we left the village we drove along the Merced River which flows throughout the park. We came to a narrow part of the river which had a sandy beach on both sides. The water was crystal clear and people were sunning themselves on both sides of the river. No one was in the water, yet there were no 'NO SWIMMING' signs.

"I wonder why nobody's in the water." Eddie questioned. "The water is so clean and inviting." He had his bathing trunks on under his clothes and decided to take the plunge. He was very good at shallow diving and dove into the calm clear water from the shore. In less time than it's taking me to tell you about this, he was already out on the other shore, headed for the narrow foot bridge to come back to where I was sitting. "Gimme a towel, quick," he said shivering. "Now I know why nobody's in the water. It's like diving into a river of ice."

It was a warm day and it didn't take long for his suit to dry. We ate our peanut butter and jelly sandwiches and drank lemonade, all the while admiring the landscape and enjoying the afternoon sun before driving up to Camp Curry.

That evening, Ranger Scott greeted us again in full uniform including his wide brimmed hat. He had already started the campfire when we got there. Visitors trickled in, a few at a time, and soon the campfire circle was complete.

"Good evening, I'm Ranger Paul Scott. Welcome to Camp Curry. I see some familiar faces here tonight; it's good to see you again and a special welcome to our new

134

visitors. As you have no doubt noticed, El Capitan dominates the scenery almost everywhere in the Park. Unfortunately, at this time of year, the most spectacular falls, Yosemite Falls have dried out. But had you been here in May when the melting snow finds its way down the cliff, you would have seen an incredible waterfall of 2,400 feet which is the highest waterfall in all of North America. Half Dome is not quite as spectacular but in the spring it also has many waterfalls caused by the melting winter snow. Half Dome is solid granite and looks like half of it is missing. Yosemite Park is actually 1200 miles; unfortunately it is not totally accessible by car. But for those of you who like to hike or ride on horseback, there are many trails where you can get to see more of the hidden areas higher up in the mountains. I hope you got to see the Giant Sequoia trees, if not put this forest on your agenda for tomorrow. Look around, you'll also see some beautiful flowers and at times wild animals that make their home here."

Again Ranger Scott pointed to the top of El Capitan. Again we saw the huge campfire and witnessed the unbelievable sight of the fire fall as the glowing embers tumbled down the cliff. We were entranced once more.

Ranger Scott stood up, "I never get tired of that beautiful fire fall coming down the cliff. Thanks for coming and enjoy the rest of your visit in Yosemite."

"Well, I have to say, Ranger Scott seems to know his stuff," Eddie said.

"And that fire fall," I remarked. "It was every bit as beautiful as it was the other night."

'We were lucky there wasn't any wind," Eddie noted. "I would think it could be dangerous and a possible cause for a forest fire if the wind should carry those fiery embers into the woods."

"I'd hate to think of this beautiful place going up in smoke." It made me sad just to think of it.

"I'm going to stop for gas on the way back," Eddie announced. "We should get an early start in the morning; we're still a good distance from Los Angeles.

CHAPTER 12

The sun was barely rising in the eastern sky when we began our descent through the Sierras. There were beautiful evergreen trees on both sides of the two lane road as we drove south toward Los Angeles. The trees became scarcer as we continued down the mountain and in the increasingly barren landscape we began to see a few Juniper trees which looked like small conifers, maybe about nine feet high, with 'leaves' that resembled long pine needles.

"There's no traffic on this road," I said. "Can we stop to look at those trees?"

Eddie pulled over on the shoulder; we got out of the car and walked closer to the trees. "They look like misshapen pines."

"Look at these little bluish fruits," I observed. "They kind of look like oversized blueberries."

"I wonder if they're edible."

"Leave it to you," I teased; "always thinking of something to eat."

"They ARE kind of pretty," he looked more closely. "It seems like somebody, somewhere at one time or another might have found some use for them."

"There are not that many of those trees around," I said. "It doesn't look like it would be practical to depend on those berries to keep alive."

"Probably not," Eddie put his arm around my waist and led me back to the car. We got going again and soon we began to see signs telling us we were approaching the Mojave Desert. We saw a few more Junipers and then started to see another type of funny looking tree. It had a round grayish fuzzy looking trunk with a few thick branches that extended out like arms. There were deep perpendicular ridges up the trunk and also along the length of the branches. There were nest-like clusters with sharp pointed green leaves on the very ends of the branches and on top of the trunk.

Eddie slowed down in front of one of them and pointed. "What does that sign say?"

"It says this is a Joshua tree," I shrugged. "I've never heard of it; but according to the sign it only grows here in the Mojave."

"That's interesting," Eddie remarked. "They must like this hot dry weather. I don't think this place has seen rain in a long time."

The day was ungodly hot but the road was good and there were very few cars on the road. We saw the remnants of what might have been a town a long time ago: the slanted frame of a windowless building, a free standing hitching post in front of a collapsed cabin and now and then we saw a few cactus plants with golden fruit as well as Yucca plants. Occasionally we saw small patches of yellow or blue flowers where once there may have been a garden. I felt a little sad about the lackluster nature of this place. I wondered out loud, "where did the people come from who lived in this town and where did they go? Who were they?" Eddie didn't respond. There were more questions than answers.

"Look at the map," Eddie said. "It seems to me we should be getting close to Route 101 and Redondo Beach."

I pulled the map out from the glove compartment and spread it on my lap. "Are you planning on stopping to see Charlie and Ruth and the kids?"

"They did make us promise to stop by when came through this area," he reminded me.

"I know, but I don't like arriving unannounced." I said.

"They may not even be home and we can just leave a note."

"You seem to have a sixth sense," I pointed to a sign, "Route 101, 25 miles."

Greener vegetation began to appear as we got closer to the coastline. We turned south on 101 and stopped at the first gas station we came to. We called Charlie and Ruth from a pay phone and learned we were only a few miles away from their home. We gassed up and were on our way.

"It's so great to see you," Ruth said. "Are you going to stay the night?"

"No, no," Eddie and I said in unison.

"We'd like to make it to L.A. by tonight," Eddie continued.

"That won't be a problem," Charlie said. "I hope you haven't had lunch; we have to have a barbecue before you go."

We nodded to each other. "If it's not too much trouble," Eddie said.

"Tell us about your trip home after you left Yellowstone," I suggested.

"I don't think we warmed up until we got back to California," Ruth said.

"We never expected it to be as cold as it was for the Fourth of July," Charlie added.

"Neither did we, "Eddie replied. "It got even colder after you left."

Their two blonde pony-tailed girls helped carry out the hot dogs, hamburgers and buns. We ate around a large picnic table under a cool umbrella. We chatted like old friends and time flew by. We didn't realize it then, but that was our first experience of true California hospitality. We hugged each other and promised to keep in touch.

Palm trees became more prominent as we drove closer to Los Angeles. We didn't stop in L.A. but stayed on the highway. In the late afternoon, we were on the road to San Pedro when we saw a sign advertising 'Shady Grove Trailer Park' in Torrance.

"Shall we give it a try?" Eddie asked.

"Why not?" I said, "If we don't like it we can look for another place tomorrow."

There was a line of Palm Trees along the edge of the highway as we approached the wide entrance. We turned in and stopped at the large ranch style house which was the office and attached Community Center. We were delighted to learn there was a space for us. The manager directed us to space number 5. He removed a section of the low white picket fence adjacent to a rose trellis which was the entrance to our space. Eddie backed the trailer, unhitched, hooked up to the water and electricity and replaced the little fence.

"What do you think?" Eddie asked.

"I think we're home," I looked at the card the manager had handed me. "22733 Main Street #5, Torrance California is going to be our address for a while."

We had a small lawn to mow and pretty geraniums growing on both sides of our short flagstone walkway.

"Hey, Sweetheart, come here," he called me to the back of our trailer spot. "We have a goldfish pond; look at 'em all!"

Sure enough, there was an eight feet by four feet oval cement pool right there in our back yard. The fish weren't large enough to be Koi fish, but some were close to five inches long.

"This is amazing! I wonder if we have to buy fish food for these guys." I wanted to know.

"It beats me," he replied. "We should call Aunt Bina and Uncle Victor in San Pedro to let them know we're here. I'm sure there's a pay phone at the Community Center; while we're there we can ask the manager."

"The phone is in the game room," the manager said. "Do you need change?"

"I think we're all right," Eddie said. "By the way, do we need to buy fish food for our new pets in the back yard?"

Bill, the manager, laughed. "Nah, that's all included in your thirty dollars a month rent fee. Go ahead and make your phone call."

We reached Aunt Bina on our first try. Aunt Bina was Eddie's aunt who had relocated to San Pedro from New Bedford Massachusetts with her husband, Victor Martin and their family before WWII.

"It's still early," she said. "I can't wait to see you, come on down right now. Here, talk to Uncle Victor, he'll give you directions."

"Uncle Victor said he was familiar with our location. We're only about a half hour away from where they live," Eddie said as he hung up.

By the time we arrived, Auntie had prepared little square slices of assorted cheeses and Ritz crackers for a snack.

"Eddie, it's so good to see you." Auntie hugged him. "And this is Jeanne," she took me in her arms. "I've heard so much about you; I'm glad to finally meet you."

Uncle Victor hugged us warmly, "I can't believe you're here." He led us through the dining room to the small kitchen. "Come, sit, eat and tell us all about the family back east."

"I'm so sorry my son Albert couldn't come over tonight," she said. "But he and his wife, Bonnie, want us all to go over there for supper tomorrow night."

"That would be great," Eddie replied. "I haven't seen him since I was a kid."

"Of course," she reflected, "we've been out here in San Pedro for quite a while. It'll be good for all of us to be together again."

"That place where you're staying is a nice little trailer park," said Uncle Victor. "We've passed it a couple of times on our way to L.A."

"We were lucky to find it," Eddie replied. "You'll both have to come up to see our little place."

"How about we pick you up tomorrow night when we go to Albert's," Auntie suggested.

"Good idea," said Uncle. "It's all settled, we'll see you tomorrow around five."

It was time to get home. They walked us to our car. What a day it had been: from the Sierra-Nevada Mountains to the shore of San Pedro; from having been alone in the wilderness to the warmth of home and family. Does it get any better than this?

Main Street was a busy highway but the date palms that lined the edge of the trailer park cushioned much of the sounds of traffic. It was a clear night and we slept well as we breathed in the fresh California air coming in through our open windows.


"What's on the agenda for today?" I asked as I fried sunny-side eggs.

"I want to drive around L.A. to see what kind of construction is going on around here."

"You don't mean sight-seeing?" I wanted to know.

"No," he answered quickly. "There's plenty of time for that; right now I have to locate the Union Hall of Ironworkers' Local 433 and make arrangements to go to work."

**139**

"You're not wasting any time," I placed his plate of toast, bacon and eggs on the table in front of him.

"I've missed going to work," he took a sip of coffee. "You know how much I like construction work."

"Yes, I do," I sat across from him. "But I have to admit I've liked having you all to myself every day these last several weeks."

"I know," he agreed. "It's been fun; but we'll still have evenings and weekends to visit and sight-see around here. There are a lot more places we want to see on our way back east and while I'm working here, we can save up for that."

"You're right." We finished our breakfast.

Eddie went to the car to check on the city map of L.A. By the time we headed for the city it was after 9 o'clock. It was an interesting city, well laid out and very modern. We drove up and down through the city, located the Union Hall, but the Business Agent wasn't there. We saw a few places under construction and Eddie stopped to look around at some of the sites but didn't make any inquiries.

"I'll go back to the hall tomorrow," he said, "now that I know how to get there."

"Good," I replied. "We can go to early Mass in the morning."

"It's not Sunday tomorrow," he answered quickly.

"I know," I reminded him. "It's a Holy Day of obligation, the Assumption."

"I forgot about that," he said. "Let's drive back through Torrance to see if we can find the church."

We drove back to Torrance and located the Church of the Nativity on Engracia Avenue. It was a lovely white stucco church with a square entrance beneath a tall bell tower reminiscent of and old Spanish Mission Church.

We were beginning to get acquainted with our new surroundings. We reached home in plenty of time to shower and get ready to be picked up to go to Albert's. When the Martins arrived we gave them a quick, half hour tour of our trailer and the Community House before we started off on our dinner date. It was clear Uncle Victor knew his way around this area. We drove past Signal Hill on our way to Huntington Beach. I was surprised to see the large number of oil towers up there. As we got closer to Huntington Beach we saw what looked like giant iron grasshoppers constantly moving up and down like devouring monsters in a science fiction movie. It seemed like they were everywhere.

"What are those?" I wanted to know.

"They're oil drills," uncle said. "Albert works for an oil drilling company in this town. Those things go on day and night."

"I didn't realize there was oil in California," Eddie said.

"Oh yes, this area has some of the largest oil producing wells in the country," he told us.

"Albert and Bonnie live only a couple of miles from here," Auntie said. "We're almost there."

Their large sprawling home was in the suburbs of Huntington Beach. There was a lovely latticed entrance with beautiful flowers on both sides of the flagstone walkway. They greeted us warmly and we were ushered into their pale green living room with a large picture window draped in white curtains.

"We're so glad you could come," Bonnie said after Auntie had introduced us. "Al, why don't you give Ed and Jeanne a quick tour of our home?"

"I'm not great at this tour-guide stuff," Albert said as he led us from one beautifully decorated room to another, each one done in its own pastel color.

By the time we returned to the living room Bonnie called out from the lemon colored dining room, "dinner's ready, come on, let's sit in here where it's comfortable."

We sat around a large oval oak table. She served a Caesar salad on crystal plates to start, followed by baked French onion soup and the special main course was prime rib roast with baked potatoes, green beans and carrots. For dessert there was homemade Apple pie or Pecan pie with a choice of ice cream or whipped cream. Bonnie was a gourmet cook and a gracious hostess. Eddie and Albert had a lot of catching up to do. As we ended the evening, we promised each other this would not be the last of our family get-togethers. Albert kissed his mom, "make sure you bring these guys back."

"It was a great evening," I said. "Thank you for everything."

"We'll see you soon," Uncle Victor said to our hosts as we took our seats in the car.

Bonnie and Albert waved to us and we were on our way.

"Tomorrow night Eva and her two kids will be back at our house," Auntie said. "She's looking forward to seeing you, Eddie."

"It's been a long time since I've seen her too," Eddie nodded his head. "Her kids must be pretty big."

"Teenagers, both of them; they live with us," Uncle said. "They've been away for a few days."

"We'll be having supper around six," she announced. "Don't expect a feast like you had tonight; think more like hot dogs or hamburgers."

"Maybe beans and potato salad," Uncle laughed.

"Sounds good to me," Eddie said. "We'll be there."

The trip home seemed shorter than our way over to Albert's. "Thanks for a beautiful evening," I said.

"It was our pleasure," Auntie hugged me "we'll see you tomorrow."

"I've only just met your aunt and uncle and they already seem like close family," I said as we arrived home.

"Oh yeah, they're good people all right," Eddie put his arm around me. "Let's go in, I'm going to set the alarm for Mass tomorrow; did you say it was at 6 o'clock?"

"Yes," I reached under the sofa to retrieve the blankets and pillows. "You'll be able to get an early start to go to the union hall."

It didn't take long for us to get settled for the night. We laid out our clothes for the next day; we made our last trip to the Community House before we snuggled in our comfy bed.


"I'm glad the Mass is early," Eddie said as he was shaving. "We'll be able to come back here and have breakfast before we head for L.A."

"We? You want me to come with you?" I asked. "Don't you think they might want to send you out on a job today?"

"I doubt it." He wiped his face and splashed on Old Spice. "The B.A. will send out the local guys first, and then check around to see about other jobs." He hung up his towel on the rack next to the sink. "I thought we'd look around the town and maybe take in a movie this afternoon."

I put my hat on and picked up my purse, "Okay, I'm ready to go."

Torrance is a small town and it seems like everything is close. The church was about three quarters full and the mass lasted less than a half hour. We didn't bother to change our clothes when we got home; we had a quick breakfast of Rice Krispies and milk and were on our way to the big city. Our first stop was the union hall. I waited in the car while Eddie went in to see the Business Agent. He had been right, the local ironworkers had already been sent out on jobs for the day. The B. A. located a job that was set to begin the next day with Bethlehem Steel and Eddie received his instructions about the location of the job site and instructions on how to get there.

"Okay, Sweetheart," he said. "I start work tomorrow, so let's go have a look at this town."

We knew Sunset Boulevard was one of the main thoroughfares of the city and was part of the Hollywood Scene where many famous stars lived. We had no idea of one end of Sunset from the other but headed in the direction of Figueroa Street where Sunset Boulevard began or ended; for us it was the beginning. Palm trees were featured prominently on both sides of the boulevard. We came to Vine Street and saw the Capitol Record Tower, the Pantages Theater and NBC West Coast Radio City.

"I think we're going to have to come back another day to really look at these places," Eddie said. "Otherwise we'll never get to the end of this street."

"Maybe when we come back we can park the car somewhere and just walk around to see these buildings up close?"

"If we keep going we might be able to see some of the fancy Hollywood homes," I said.    On the corner of Ivar and Sunset we stopped at a huge car dealership called 'Muller Bros. Oldsmobile'. It was not only a place where you could buy a car; it was also a car wash and a place where you could purchase gasoline and household appliances. It seemed like a good place to fill our gas tank. We were fascinated by the layout of this place. There was a control tower in the center of the dealership and the various sections offering different services radiated from that point. They were advertising a beauty contest to promote the 3,000,000th customer to use the car wash.

"Hey, Honey," I called to Eddie. "Come look at these pictures."

"Interesting names," he commented. "Look at that: Miss Control Tower, Miss Auto Accessory, Miss Lube Rack, Miss Gasoline Station and Miss New Car Department."

"When is the contest going to be?" I wanted to know.

"I don't know," Eddie shrugged. "I guess when the 3,000,000th car wash person shows up. We're not going to wait that long. Let's get back in the car."

We continued up Sunset Boulevard. We saw some impressive looking homes but had no idea whether any movie stars lived there. We turned on the highway and drove toward Torrance, stopped at home for a sandwich then went to the Stadium Theatre on the corner of Craven and Gramercy Avenues in the center of Torrance. It was a modern building with a tall perpendicular Marquee which spelled out 'Stadium' in large letters. Beneath it, over the entrance, was the three-sided marquee announcing the movie 'Frogmen' with Richard Widmark and Dana Andrews. We picked up some popcorn at the lobby snack store before we went in. 'Popeye' was the Selected Short Subject and there was a showing about the Korean War on the Movietone News. The movie was a captivating story about Navy Frogmen during World War II. These were men whose lives depended on each other during their dangerous missions regardless of any personality differences they may have had when they were off duty.

"I see those guys diving underwater wearing only bathing trunks, flippers and a mask and I wonder how they can hold their breath for such a long time underwater," I observed.

"Yeah, although on one of their missions they wore triple tanks on their backs; it didn't look like they had an easy time of it, "Eddie continued. "I wonder if my brother Del and the other Seabees wore similar gear or if they were dropped off by boat when they landed on Guam."

"However they got there," I touched Eddie's arm. "I'm sure it was a tough experience no matter how much training they had to go through. You still miss him a lot, don't you?"

"Yeah; I always looked up to him. It seemed like he was good at everything he ever tried to do," he hesitated. "I wanted to be like him." We walked back to the car; he held my hand. "We should head over to San Pedro, it's almost 5 o'clock."

Uncle Victor had the grille going in the small back yard when we arrived. "Go right on in," he said. "Your aunt and your cousins are inside."

"Here you are," Aunt Bina handed Eddie a tray with hot dogs and hamburgers. "You're just in time; you can help your uncle with the cooking. You can talk with your cousin later."

The kitchen was buzzing, "Come on in, Jeanne," Auntie took my elbow. "This is Eddie's cousin Eva and her two kids, Loretta and Billy."

"Hi. It's nice to finally meet you and your family," we hugged each other.

Eva handed me an apron. "Don't think you're getting away that easy," she smiled. "We still have carrots and celery to fix."

Everyone had a job to do and within a half hour we were all sitting at the dining room table eating hot dogs, hamburgers, potato salad, veggie sticks, chips and pickles. "Notice the paper plates and cups," Auntie said. "This is hospitality, California style. Billy and Loretta will be in charge of cleaning up while we go to the living room and watch Lawrence Welk on TV."

"Who's Lawrence Welk?" I asked. "Is he a cowboy star?"

Everyone laughed. "He's got an orchestra and plays the accordion," Auntie explained. "He comes on every week."

"You're going to like him," Loretta said. "He makes bubbles and plays good dance music."

"Yeah," Eva added. "He even dances the Polish Polka; I know you'll like that, Eddie."

"My mother says you like to dance the polka, Eddie," Loretta said.

"The good old Polish Home on Montaup Street in Fall River," Eddie laughed. "That's where we all learned."

"He's right, you know," Eva agreed. "Sssh, the show's starting."

Auntie's TV screen was about 12 inches, rounded on the sides and straight on the top and bottom. Every once in a while the screen was snowy but for the most part it was clear. In between the musical numbers Eddie and Eva had a chance to catch up on

144

the years that they had not seen each other. Eva's husband, Loretta and Billy's Dad, had been killed in WWII. Aunt Bina and Uncle Victor were helping Eva raise the kids.

It was a pleasant evening for Eddie as he renewed his relationship with his Aunt and his cousins and for me too as I was being absorbed into the family.

"Sunday," Uncle Victor said as we were leaving. "We'll go to Mass together here in San Pedro and we'll go to Knott's Berry Farm."

Eddie and I looked at each other "Whatever and wherever that is; we'd love to," I said. What time should we get here?"

"Eight-thirty will be fine," Auntie said. "It was a nice evening, thanks for coming."

"No," I hugged her, "it was a pleasure for us to be here; thank YOU."

"We'll see you Sunday," Eddie shook hands with Uncle. Loretta and Eva walked us out to the car. We waved to each other as we turned out of their driveway.

Eddie checked the trunk for his work belt and tools before coming in, laid out his work clothes in the breakfast nook for the next day and set the alarm for six a.m. We walked up to the Community room for our last bathroom visit before going to bed. We held hands on our way back to the trailer. "What are you going to do tomorrow?" Eddie asked.

"I'll find enough to keep busy," I said. "The laundry has piled up since we left Yosemite and there's always cleaning up to do. Maybe I'll get to meet some of the neighbors."

"That's one good feature about the Community room; you get to meet people from the other trailers."


Brrring! Big Ben roused us from a deep sleep. Eddie got dressed in his work clothes and went up to the washroom. I fixed oatmeal, coffee and toast for breakfast. He kissed me and I watched him leave on his way to work. This was the first of many similar days to follow during our stay in California. I gathered the bed linens and other soiled laundry and made my way to the Community House to begin my chores. This day was apparently not the day I would meet new neighbors. I had the laundry facility all to myself. I put dimes in the washers, grabbed a Good Housekeeping magazine and read until the washing and drying of my clothes was done. During all this time, not a soul came in sight. I went back to the trailer, put the clean sheets on the sofa-bed, did the ironing from that day and finished up a little pile I had hiding from another day. The morning was shot!

I ventured out to a market that the manager, Bill, had told us about. "It's only about a quarter mile down the street," he had said. "They've got fresh fruit and veggies, a deli counter and a few canned goods. The prices are pretty good too."

**145**

I decided to check it out. It wasn't a long walk. There were small strawberries for 10 cents a basket; I bought two. I paid 25 cents for 5 pounds of potatoes, 10 cents for a bunch of carrots and 39 cents for a pound of stew beef (I already had onions). What a find! I made beef stew for supper and while it was cooking in the pot on one of the two burners of the hot plate, I used my small oven on the other burner and baked a cake. Strawberry shortcake for dessert!

Eddie was tired after his first day of work but he was exhilarated. "We're working on a new school," he said. "Bethlehem Steel is a big company."

"How is the gang you're working with?" I wanted to know.

"They're a bunch of good guys," he said. "I like being back to work and, you know, Ironworkers are pretty much the same everywhere. They're good in Rhode Island, they were good in Spokane and they're good here."

"I knew you'd say that," I said. "Get cleaned up, I just have to add the dumplings to the stew and supper's ready."

It was a quiet evening at home. We played a few games of rummy and then repeated the ritual of the night before: work clothes, alarm, walk to the washroom and settling in to bed.

It didn't take long to clean up the dishes and straighten out the trailer after Eddie had left for work. I was dressed in my dungarees and was prepared to do yard work. I walked over to the Community House and asked the manager about yard keeping tools. He led me to a storage area where he kept a few lawn mowers, clippers, rakes and hoes for our use to keep up our little plot of land. I came back with a large cardboard box, a hoe and clippers. I knelt on the flagstone walk and began to pull up weeds between the pink and red geraniums. It's truly amazing how weeds can hide the beauty of the flowers in a garden. I managed to accumulate quite a pile of unwanted greenery and felt quite proud of myself until I stood up and noticed the dead branches and leaves overcrowding the puny-looking roses on the trellis. I went inside the trailer and got the step ladder so I could reach the top of the trellis. I was ruthless! I clipped away until the rose bushes began to look bald. It was time to carry my weeds and clippings to the trash bin at the Community Center. I brought the cardboard box and a mower back to our yard and started to cut the grass. I was thankful we had a small area; the mower was hard to push, especially as I carefully rolled it behind the fish pond and then around the rest of our little plot. I must admit, I was tempted, more than once, to quit and leave all this care taking for Eddie. But, I reasoned: if I leave this for him to do we may not be able to go to the movies or do something else more fun. Reasoning won out. I brought the lawn mower back to the storage area and brought back a rake to gather up the grass clippings and put them in the box. Done-dee-done-done! I had to admit the yard looked pretty good but I secretly prayed the 'pruning' on the rose bush would help revive the sorry looking plant. Only time would tell.

"What happened?" Eddie said when he came home. "It looks like the roses got scalped!"

146

"I thought I'd do a little yard work and I got carried away." I was hoping he'd be more pleased.

"The yard looks good," he commented, "but I don't know about the roses."

"Let's just give them some time," I crossed my fingers. "If they don't get better, we'll ask the manager if we can buy new ones."

I fixed ham sandwiches while Eddie got cleaned up and we decided to go see 'Alice in Wonderland' at the Lakewood Drive-In. We were surprised at the long line of cars waiting for admittance to the outdoor theater. We supposed it was because it was a Friday night and the feature was a new Disney film, perhaps families thought it was a good time to go to the movies with their kids. There was a short Gene Autry movie too and of course Movietone News (we noticed parents used this time to bring their kids for a restroom break). The traffic moved slowly as we left the theater and made our way back to the highway.

"Uh-oh!" Eddie said after we had driven a few miles.

"What's wrong?" I saw the worried expression on his face.

"The car is beginning to overheat," he pulled over to the side of the road.

"I'll let it cool down before we get going again," he looked under the hood and did the stuff guys do to check the water and whatever. I looked over his shoulder.

"We're losing water," he said, "it's a good thing I still have that metal can of water in the trunk from when we had that problem in the Sierra's."

He checked the trunk, retrieved the can, and then poured some of the water into the radiator. "You know what this means," he said.

"I guess we find a shop to get the radiator fixed," I offered.

"Yeah," he said, "good thing it's the weekend; I won't be losing any days of work."

We made it home safely, without overheating, and in the morning Eddie called Uncle Victor to see if he could recommend a good shop to bring the car to.

"I'll be right over," Uncle said. "I'll call my friend first and I'm sure he'll take you today."

True to his word, Uncle was at our trailer within the hour with instructions from Aunt Bina to bring us to their house while the car was being repaired.

"Guess what, Sweetheart!" Eddie said as they came in the door. He didn't wait for an answer. "The radiator is okay, we only need a new hose."

"That's good news," I answered. "For one thing it should cost us a lot less."

147

"My friend, Bob said the car should be ready in a couple of hours," Uncle said. "He didn't have a hose in stock."

"Well, good," Auntie put her hands on her hips. "While you're waiting for the car, you can both go to Safeway's and pick up a few things." She handed them a list. "Jeanne will help me prepare the vegetables for the soup I'm making for supper."

She was amazing; she had the ability to adapt to any situation. We had not planned to spend the entire day at her house, but as soon as she learned of our predicament she organized and planned the whole day. Eva and the kids did the cleaning chores while Auntie and I took over the kitchen to prepare supper for the whole family, which included Eddie and me.

"Of course you're staying for supper," she insisted. "You have to stay and see the Wrestling Matches," she said. "I'm sure you've never seen anything like it."

She was right. We were completely fascinated by this new media: TV! Baron Leone put on a good show, beginning with his grand entrance wearing a cape and long coiffed hair, to his grand gestures in the ring. 'Wild' Red Berry was a master blabbermouth and spent much of his time in the ring trying to avoid the Baron and complaining the entire time. Needless to say the Baron pinned Berry nobly and lorded over him while the 'Berry' was still crying foul.

"It's a great show," Eddie said. "But I wonder how real these matches are."

"Everybody talks about that," Uncle said. "But, whether the matches are set up or not, they still put on a good show."

No one could argue with that. We thanked Auntie and Uncle again and they reminded us about our date for the next day to go to Knott's Berry Farm.


We were up early to get dressed church. I wore a pale blue waffle pique dress with a mandarin collar and cap sleeves, with red high heeled sandals and a red hat. Eddie wore light blue trousers and a white shirt and tie. We arrived on schedule and everyone greeted us in their finery. Eva was wearing a pink flowered print dress, high heels and a close fitting hat; Loretta wore a pale green skirt and white blouse penny loafers and a skull cap. Billy and Uncle wore tan trousers and an open collared sport shirt. Auntie wore a navy-blue shirtwaist dress and a straw hat, white shoes and gloves. Sunday Mass was a family ritual.

"I think we're going to need both cars for church," Uncle said.

"I want to ride with Eddie and Jeanne," Loretta called out.

"If that's okay with your mom," Eddie replied, "it's okay with us."

"It sure is," I piped in, "everyone looks so nice."

"The church isn't far," Uncle said, "just follow me."

**148**

Loretta climbed into the back seat of our car and we headed for Mary Star of the Sea Church on West 8ᵗʰ Street following the rest of the family in Uncle's car. The old Spanish Mission Style Church built in pink stucco was filled to capacity. Some worshippers were standing in the back near the confessionals and some even spilled to the outside of the open doors. The High Mass was celebrated in Latin and enhanced by a beautiful choir singing Latin hymns.

"I'm glad we got to the church early," Auntie said after Mass, "otherwise we might not have gotten a seat."

"She's right, you know," Uncle said, "that's why we always leave for Church early."

"What's for breakfast?" Billy asked as we reached their house.

"I was wondering how long it was going to take you to ask," Auntie said.

"Well," Uncle repeated, "what IS for breakfast?"

"Give me a minute to put my hat away," she said, "and I'll fix sausage and pancakes."

A chorus of: "Sounds good to me" followed almost as though on cue. Auntie put on her apron, set up the pancake grille on the gas stove while the rest of us 'girls' prepared the table. The conversation was rich in what everyone planned to do who was not coming to Knott's Berry Farm with us. Billy was going to a baseball game and Eva was going to take Loretta to the movies in L.A. With everyone pitching in to help, brunch was cooked and eaten and the kitchen was cleaned up in record time. Uncle led the way to his driveway, "I'll drive," he said. "You can sit up front with me, Eddie, and the girls can sit in the back."

It seemed to me that wherever our starting point was, we were usually close to a highway. This time was no different. "We're going to head toward Buena Park," Uncle said to Eddie. "What do you think of these roads compared to New Bedford?"

"Well for one thing," Eddie remarked, "the roads are much wider and straighter too."

"That's what I find remarkable," I chimed in. "No matter where we go the roads are straight for miles."

"That's true," Uncle agreed. "That's what helps us get to our destination a lot faster."

"Tell me about this place we're going to," I suggested to Uncle.

"The farm goes back to the 1920's." Uncle said. "A man named Walter Knott and his wife Cordelia first leased this large farm where they met a Mr. Boysen who had been working on developing a new berry. Mr. Knott called it a boysenberry."

"A boysenberry?" I asked, "I never heard of it."

"Boysenberries are a cross between raspberries and blackberries." Auntie said. "The fruit is dark purple and larger and juicier than either one of them."

"It turns out they were able to produce a lot of those berries during the short growing season between May and July. Cordelia made preserves of the fruit and sold them, as well as homemade sauces and candy at a stand by Highway 39, which runs along the property," Uncle said. "They did so well, that they ended buying the farm."

"Cordelia was pretty resourceful. During the off season she prepared chicken dinners which she served in her dining room for sixty-five cents a plate," Auntie said. "They were pretty good too, eh Vic? We came here a couple of years ago, soon after Walter had started to build his 'Ghost Town'."

"We haven't been here in awhile," Uncle said. "I bet the orange trees are producing fruit by now."

"I wouldn't be surprised." Auntie pointed to a sign. "There's the entrance just ahead."

We followed the road leading to the parking lot and walked through the large wooden gate under a hand crafted sign: KNOTT'S BERRY FARM. There were rustic signs on a perpendicular pole with arrows pointing in different directions: Pan for gold, Ghost Town, Butterfield Stage, Orange grove. We saw a large crowd of people gathered by a narrow river which flowed from a higher elevation. It was guided through wooden sand-filled boxes creating a trough which leveled at about the height of our hips for about twenty five feet in length before spilling into a stream below. Gold 'prospectors' wearing red plaid shirts, pointy black felt cowboy hats and suspendered Levis, were on one side of the long wooden troughs instructing the visitors on how to pan for gold. Eddie and I were handed metal pie pans which we sank in the sand, shook very gently, and allowed the flowing water to gradually wash the sand away to reveal small specks of gold. It worked! I proudly walked off with my lipstick size vial containing river water and a few tiny sand-sized pieces of gold. What a treasure! We moved on to 'Ghost Town' which was very different from the remnants of life we had seen in the desert. This one was modeled after the ones Walter Knott had seen in Nevada. Here the buildings were rustic but still standing. There were cowboys roaming around, some carrying lassos, and there were a few saloons. We went into the Calico Saloon where Auntie and I had boysenberry juice and the men had drinks of sarsaparilla as we 'bellied up' to the bar and the piano tinkled "My Darling Clementine".

We stepped out in time to see the Butterfield Stage Coach making its way through the town. On a platform outside one of the buildings in 'Ghost Town' there were life sized carvings of two cowboys in chatting positions, set up for visitors to 'chat' with them for a keepsake photo. We happily obliged and also posed later on with Indian Joe who was standing by a tom-tom, wearing a full feather headdress in front of a latticed building not far from the entrance.

We wandered through the groves and saw for the first time, oranges actually growing on a tree. We resisted the urge to pull one off and eat it right on the spot but waited until we were able to buy a small basket of them at a makeshift stand, as well as a jar of boysenberry preserves.

150

"What do you think? Auntie asked.

"This place is amazing," I said, "I'm sure glad we came."

We walked back to the parking lot. "It goes to show you how somebody can start out with nothing like the Knott's and end up with a place like this," Eddie said.

"I think his wife was incredible," I remarked, "Did you tell me they had four kids?"

"Yes they did," Auntie said, "and you're right, she managed to take care of her family, and still was able to make and sell all that stuff in her little farm stand."

"They don't make 'em like that anymore," Eddie chuckled.

"Oh you!" I said, "When's the last time you invented a berry?"

We chatted about our afternoon all the way home. "See this warm sunny day," Uncle said. "This is real California weather. Now you know why we like it here."

"I can see that," Eddie said.

The day ended too soon. When we were back in their driveway Auntie said," Make sure you come to see us during the week."

"Of course we will," I said. "Thanks for a great day."

"I think I could get used to this California life," Eddie said.

"I know what you mean," I agreed. "This would be a good place to raise a family."

He put his arm around me, "That's a good thought."

We walked up to the Community House. The following day would be another workday for Eddie and another day for me to become more familiar with our new surroundings.

CHAPTER 13

We are settling in to a regular routine. Eddie goes off to work early each day and I begin my chores soon after he leaves. Today I learned a hard lesson: don't leave any improperly closed food packages or leftover snacks around unless you are prepared for an invasion of ants. I am not fond of creepy crawly things of any kind. I reached under the sink and found my bottle of Lysol and used it, undiluted, which seemed to do the trick, for the moment, but when I came back from the Community House after doing laundry, the critters were back. There was a small army of ants moving from the counter opposite the sink into the cupboard above it. I found an unsealed package of graham crackers on which the ants were feasting. I threw the whole box in the rubbish and carried the bag to the outside trash bin. I walked back up to the manager's office to complain of my dilemma.

"You're in California," Bill said. "These things happen."

"But," I moaned, "I've never had a problem with ants before."

"Do you have any 20 Mule Team Borax?" he asked.

I shrugged. "I don't know what that is."

"You can get some at that market up the street. It's pretty cheap and you just have to sprinkle some on your shelves and counter." He nodded. "That'll keep them away."

I thanked Bill, picked up my purse from the trailer and headed to the store with a short grocery list that included borax. When I got home I washed the counter again with a solution of borax, and then cleaned out the shelves checking all the items to make sure there were no more uninvited guests. Next I sprinkled some dry powder in all the seams (as I had been directed by Bill). The ant population had dwindled to zero. It was my intention to keep it that way. Supper was cooking on the hot plate. The counter and the cabinets were neat but I was not. I had barely time to get cleaned up and changed before Eddie came home.

"What did you do all day?" Eddie asked when he returned from work. "Everything looks the same as when I left!"

"I had a battle with ants," I started to complain.

"It couldn't have been too bad," he remarked. "I don't see any ants now. What's for supper?"

I suppressed an inner growl; I wanted to let him know about my bad day.

He lifted the cover of the pot, "American chop suey. Good," he kissed me on the cheek. "Let me get cleaned up. Want to go to the movies tonight?"

He was definitely a mood changer. Going to the movies was exactly what I needed to expunge the memory of my challenging day. But before we left for the theater, I took my precautions: the leftover food was in the ice box and the dishes were washed and put away.

On our way to the theater Eddie looked in the rear view mirror. "There's a police car following us."

"I wonder what's wrong," I felt a little nervous. "I know you weren't speeding"

"We'll soon find out;" he pulled over to the side of the road. "The car is stopped and the officer is coming toward us."

"Hi," the officer said, "don't worry this isn't an official stop. I noticed your Massachusetts license plate and wondered what part of the state you come from."

"Fall River," Eddie answered.

"Oh yes, that's about 50 miles south of Boston: Hills, Mills and Pork Pies."

"That's what they say about Fall River all right," Eddie nodded.

"I come from Massachusetts too," he smiled. "I've been here a few years. I come from Brockton."

"I know that area," Eddie said, "It's on the way to Boston."

"Oh yeah! It's a good place to be from. Are you planning to stay in California?"

"We don't know yet," Eddie looked over at me. "We've only been here a couple of weeks."

"I've been here a couple of years," he said. "I'm never going back to the snow and ice over there."

"I know what you mean," Eddie answered. "My aunt and uncle in San Pedro say the same thing."

"Listen to them," he lifted his hat to the back of his head. "Where are you off to?"

"The Stadium," Eddie answered, "there's a double feature tonight."

"What's playing? "he asked.

"Cyrano de Bergerac and Peking Express"

"I didn't see those two; Hey! Nice to meet you;" he extended his hand to Eddie and waved to me. "Enjoy the show and enjoy your stay," he called over his shoulder as he walked back to the police car.

The theater was less than half a mile away. I quickly forgot about the events of my day as I sat close to Eddie while we ate popcorn and watched Jose Ferer and Mala Powers in Cyrano, then Joseph Cotten with Corinne Calvet in Peking Express.

"Do you think TV will ever feature movies?" I asked Eddie on the way home.

"I doubt it," Eddie answered, "the screens are way too small. It's fine for shows like sports and comedies, but movies? I don't think so."

"Look," I observed, "there's a trailer in the space next to us."

"They must have come in while we were at the movies," Eddie reasoned as he parked the car.

"I guess we'll find out who they are tomorrow," I said as I stepped into the trailer.

"It'll be good for you to have a new neighbor to talk with while I'm at work," Eddie remarked.

"I hope they're as nice as the ones we met in Spokane." It was a lovely evening as we proceeded hand in hand, to and from the Community House. I took one final look around the counters and cupboards before I went to bed. The battle of ants was really over. "Move over, Honey," I picked up a corner of the blanket. "Here I come."

"What's taken you so long?" he made room for me.

Lying comfortably in his arms was the perfect ending for this day.


Our new neighbor was in her yard when I came back from the Community House this morning. She is a pretty girl, around five feet five, who looks to be in her early twenties with blue eyes and long auburn hair. She was wearing blue Bermuda shorts and a sleeveless print blouse.

"Hi," I called to her, "welcome to the neighborhood, my name is Jeanne."

"Hi, my name is Julie," she extended her hand. "Darryl and I just moved in last night."

"Where are you from?" I asked.

"Right here in California," she said, "We just got married in Reno and this is our first home."

154

We were still standing in our respective yards with the low white picket fence between us when another neighbor from a trailer across the way came toward us. She was slightly shorter than Julie, with freckles, grey eyes and short dark hair. She was wearing dungarees and a pink flowered blouse.

"Hi, my name is Joan," she extended her hand, "it's great to see neighbors. My husband Jesse and I live in the second lane. There aren't a lot of people around during the day."

"I know what you mean," I shook her hand. "Eddie and I have been here a couple of weeks and you're the first neighbors I've met. My name is Jeanne; this is Julie. It looks like the guys are all off to work for the day," I offered, "would you both like to come in for a cup of coffee?"

Our trailer was actually smaller than either Joan's or Julie's but the breakfast nook was quite adequate to accommodate all of us to sit and enjoy coffee and toll house cookies. They both wanted to know about Massachusetts and found my 'accent' quite funny. 'You pahk yaw caah in the front of the traylah!' they teased. This was not new for me or Eddie; as soon as we got past Chicago we had begun to hear similar teasing. The funniest thing was: it seemed to us that everyone else had the 'accent'. Joan's husband Jesse had been transferred from the Texas oil fields to L.A. and they were seriously considering relocating in California. Our twenty minute coffee break turned into an hour.

Julie noticed the time; "it's already 11 o'clock," she looked at her watch. "We're just got back from a vacation in Reno and I've got a lot of catching up to do before Darryl gets home."

"Thanks for coming over," I said. "We'll have to do this again."

"We'll have to figure a way for the guys to get to know each other," Joan said. "We've been here over a month and don't really know anyone yet".

"Today was a good start," I said. Maybe we can plan something soon when we know all the guys will be home."

"Sounds good to me," Julie said.

"Me too," Joan waved as she walked back across our lane to her trailer, "see you soon!"

Eddie was home before 5:00 p.m. His usual routine was to go up to the Community House to clean up before supper. I laid out a clean set of clothes for him on the sofa.

"What do you think about going back to L.A. to see a little more of the city?" I suggested. "I thought maybe we could head toward Wilshire Boulevard."

"Didn't Auntie mention something about some old mansions over there?" he asked.

155

"She did," I pulled the leftover chop-suey out of the icebox." "I figure if we go into the city in the evening a couple of times during the week, we'll be able to see L.A. a little at a time; then maybe we can take longer trips down the coast on weekends."

"Good idea," he was off and back by the time supper was on the table.

"I met some of our neighbors today," I told him. "The girls are about our age and we were talking about having a get together for you guys to meet. Their husbands work all day, like you do."

"We did that in Spokane and it worked out well," he said finishing off the chop suey.

"That's what I thought too." We finished dinner and cleaned everything up before leaving. "Let's not forget to pick up some ice on the way home," I reminded him.

Torrance is a suburb of Los Angeles. It was a short ride to Grand Avenue, where Wilshire Boulevard begins, in the center of L.A. This part of the Boulevard appears to be the old section of the city. Some of the buildings look like they may have been built in the late 1800's although there were a few tall modern buildings in between. As we continued up the Boulevard we came to a couple of interesting looking structures which looked like very old residences. One was a large Mission style white stucco house with a Spanish tiled roof and an ornate façade over a white columned entrance. There were chimneys on all four sides of the house indicating the possibility of cozy fireplaces as features for this home. There was a large 3 feet by 5 feet sign in front of the house. We stopped and got out of the car to get a closer look. A young man dressed in gray slacks and a white short-sleeved shirt with a plaid bow tie came down the steps of the front entrance. I asked him about the house.

"This place used to be the home of General Harrison Gray Otis. He built it in the late 1800's," the young man said. "He called it the Bivouac."

"Does anyone live there now?" I wanted to know.

"Oh no," he pointed to the sign; "it's and art institute. There are art exhibits in there and classes here too."

"Are you a student here?" Eddie asked.

"No," he shook his head, "I'm interested in the art exhibits. I'm an artist, myself."

"There are a lot of old houses on this street," I observed. "It makes you think that back in the day, this might have been a lively neighborhood full of kids."

"I suppose so," our new friend pointed to an old brown, partly shingled and partly dark brick house closer to the next corner. "That old house was built by Edwin Earle; he's the man who invented refrigerated railroad cars to transport fruit from California to the east coast."

"It doesn't look like anyone lives there now," Eddie remarked.

**156**

"You're right," he said. "Nobody's lived there in years. As a matter of fact they use that house as part of this Art Institute."

"That's interesting," Eddie noted, 'they're so different in design."

The Earle house was more rustic. It had a pointed arch above the entrance just off center of the front of the building and there was greenery, resembling ivy, growing over the roof of the arch. There were chimneys on all sides of this home too. A few palm trees graced the property and the lawn was well manicured.

"As you drive down the boulevard you'll see a few more large buildings that used to be homes," he informed us, "and you'll see many styles of architecture. That's why I like to come down here; there's a lot of history in this neighborhood."

"Thanks for taking the time to talk with us," Eddie extended his hand. "You'd make one heck of a tour guide."

"No problem," he smiled and shook Eddie's hand, "I'm always happy to talk about my town."

There was still more to see on this amazing boulevard. We passed a place called Ralph's Market which had high white arches on the sidewalk like an arcade but we didn't stop in. We crossed the causeway which divided McArthur Lake and continued west.

"There's an interesting looking place," Eddie pulled over to the side of the road. We were nearing the corner of Alexandria Avenue. "That has to be the Brown Derby Restaurant. I've heard of it, but I didn't expect the building would be shaped like a brown derby hat."

It's hard to tell how large it was. It was round and perhaps a hundred-fifty feet in diameter, and about two stories high. It was cocoa brown and had an upturned brim all around except at the canopied entrance which extended to the street. There were greeters in uniform to meet the diners as they arrived.

"That is one huge hat," I noted, "and look there's a small tower on top with a brown derby shaped sign above it."

We watched people come and go. "I don't recognize anyone famous," Eddie looked around, "do you?"

"I don't expect we will," I said, "I think it might still be too early for elegant dining."

There was a white stucco and brown wood, flat-topped coffee shop adjacent to the main restaurant which extended to and around the corner. Tall Queen Palm trees stood at intervals for the whole length of the restaurants.

"Did you want to get out of the car?" Eddie asked.

"I don't think so," I looked around, "we can see okay from here, and we're not going inside anyway."

157

"Okay," he started the engine and re-entered the line of traffic. "You know what I find funny around here?"

"Well for one thing," I observed, "the buildings are not the same as we've seen in other large cities."

"That's true there are old buildings and newer ones too, all in the same block," he agreed, "but that's not what I mean," he pointed to a hotel on the next block. "See, even the older hotels or apartment buildings, whatever they are, look like the high rises in New York and Chicago, but they're not as high."

"You're right," I sat up higher in my seat. "Slow down see if I can count the floors...one, two..." I continued to count one window above the other as he drove slowly toward the corner of the street, "I count twelve...how many floors are there in the Empire State Building?'

"I'm not sure, but I think there's about a hundred."

"That would definitely make New York buildings a lot taller, and even the ones we saw in Chicago," I remarked. "I wonder if there's a law that restricts the height of the buildings."

"I have no idea...What do you say?" he asked. "Shall we head back to Torrance.

"Sure, why not? Tomorrow you have to get up early again and I want to get some yard work done before the weekend."

We put the ice we'd picked up in the ice box, and then settled easily under the counterpane until 'Big Ben' jolted us up into a new day.


California is certainly conducive to new growth. There are new green sprouts on the climbing rose bush, and a few new weeds to pull up in the flower bed. I was busy with yard work for most of the day and checked up on the fishes. I didn't see either of my new neighbors. When Eddie came home and suggested a movie, I showed him the advertisement in the Torrance Herald: "'David and Bathsheba' with Gregory Peck and Susan Hayward is playing on a new widescreen at Grauman's Chinese theater on Holly-wood Boulevard. What do you think?"

"I don't see why not," he answered, "what's for supper?"

'Ham and cheese sandwiches okay?" I asked.

"Sure," he picked up his clean clothes on the sofa, "we can eat when I get back from the shower."

Our timing was perfect; I put the plates on the table just as he came in. He put his work clothes in the laundry bag; we sat down to eat our sandwiches and had milk and cookies for dessert. Paper plates and cups and napkins made for a fast clean-up and were easily disposed of in the rubbish bin on our way out to the car.

By now he knew the short cuts in L.A. and the layout of the numbers according to the city blocks. If # 3200 was on the corner of one street, then that same number would be on all the parallel streets after it, this layout made it easy to locate almost any place we wanted to find. We were looking for Hollywood Boulevard and found it easily enough. We saw the tall perpendicular 'GRAUMAN' marquee in bright lights hanging on the outer right side wall of the white building as we approached the theatre. The center was like a tall Chinese pagoda and another identical white wall with another brightly lit marquee stood on the left side of the picturesque yellow and orange center. The center roof was pointed and gracefully sloped on four sides ending with four turned up corners. Slim black poles, bearing four flag-like pennants, stood erect on each of the corners of the tangerine upper structure. Beneath this roof, a huge oriental design in yellow, orange and green, resembling dragons, decorated the face of the pagoda above the wide, maroon, arched doorway, which was the entrance to the theater.

"Sweetheart, look at this! It's Al Jolson!" He pointed to the sidewalk. There were neatly arranged 30 inch by 30 inch cement panels with the signatures as well as hand and foot prints of celebrities. "We're standing on the 'Hollywood Star Walk'.

"I've heard of it," I said, "but I never thought I'd ever see it."

"Here's, Douglas Fairbanks. I think it must be the father," he called.

"You may be right," I said. "Look at the date, 1927 and here's Mary Pickford, I think she was his wife."

We continued to walk around and found the small imprints of Shirley Temple and Freddie Bartholomew. We "ooh'd and aah'd" as we continued to discover the panels of Eddie Kantor, Jeannette McDonald, Joan Crawford and many others; some from the silent movies we had never heard of.

"These are amazing," I said, "but a line is starting to form over there."

"I see that," he said, "Some people are already going in." He held my hand and we took our place in line to purchase our tickets at the free-standing ticket office (also in the oriental theme) before entering the theater. Inside, the walls were decorated in deep red and gold panels and the viewing area was furbished in comfortably cushioned, deep red velvet seats. There were gold oriental designs on the red proscenium arch from which the red curtain decorated with several varied types of gold embroidered trees hung gracefully. We were escorted to our seats by ushers wearing ornate red uniforms with gold braid and epaulets. When the movie was about to begin the curtain parted to reveal the widest movie screen we had ever seen. We were amazed when the first previews appeared. The pictures were larger than we had ever seen before.

"When we go back to the Stadium," I whispered, "the screen is going to seem kind of puny."

"I know what you mean, this is quite the place!"

The theater was full and chatty but became hushed as the first strains of music accompanied the title and credits at the opening of the film. Susan Hayward was exquisite as the beautiful Bathsheba and Gregory Peck was the perfect David. We were completely mesmerized as we watched the biblical story unfold before us. It was a perfect example of how God is always there to pick up the pieces and forgive us even when we make a mess of our lives.

"It's hard to imagine watching this movie on a smaller screen," Eddie said.

"I don't think it'll be very long before most of the other theaters will follow suit."

"You're probably right; they'll most likely be making a lot more movies for the widescreen," we walked hand in hand back to the car.

I was in a romantic mood. The love story of the parents of Solomon had been larger than life. The ride home seemed short and Eddie reminded me we had promised Aunt Bina that we would come over to watch the wrestling matches on the next night.

"Time is flying by," I said. "We're coming up to the weekend; it's time to think about taking longer trips if we're going to see more of California."

"Maybe we can start doing that next weekend," he suggested. "I saw an advertisement for the Sheriff's Rodeo at the Coliseum in L.A. that's going on this Sunday."

"That sounds like fun," I was interested, "I wonder if it'll be like the one we saw in Butte, Montana."

"I don't know," he shrugged, "but I imagine all rodeos have the same kinds of competitions; we'll check out the ad when we get home."


Sunday came fast enough. We went to Mass at the Church of the Nativity in Torrance. When we came home, I changed into a navy blue A-line skirt and a short-sleeved blue striped buttoned blouse and Eddie changed into a green short-sleeved shirt to go with his tan trousers. We wanted to reach the outdoor stadium before the parade of the main participants. The Coliseum was a large oval arena enclosed in a white wall with narrow arched windows all around and a seating capacity for thousands. Our seats were half way up on the right side of the main entrance. Two flag bearers on horseback, wearing cowboy outfits and black hats carried the California flag and the American flag respectively and led a local high school band in the parade around the perimeter of the arena. They were followed by the Grand Marshall, Randolph Scott (screen actor) riding in on a silver saddled white horse. He was wearing a glitzy cowboy outfit and a white hat. Behind him were Rodeo Queen, Lucille Norman (singer/actress) dressed in white with a white cowboy hat and also riding a silver-saddled white horse. She was escorted by Gene Autry (of singing cowboy fame) who was wearing black and white, a white hat and riding his silver-saddled horse, Champion. They lined up facing the American Flag and behind them, on horseback, stood the cowboys and cowgirls who would be competitors in this day's rodeo. We all rose up from our seats as Lucille Norman sang the Star Spangled Banner; this was followed by loud cheers as the celebrities took their places in the Grand

Stand while their horses were led out of the arena. The flags were secured near the entrance, and the band led the participants out of the arena to prepare for the competition.

Once the arena was cleared from the opening ceremonies the work crew came out with their equipment to set up the barrels for the first competition. The crowd cheered as each cowgirl maneuvered her way around the barrels and raced back to the starting point; each one trying to better the time of the others without knocking over the barrels.

The Coliseum was larger than the arena in Butte Montana. There were white fences made up of horizontal boards on both ends of the arena and the small pipe enclosures with the wide metal gates which confined the animals until they were ready to enter the arena. The calf riders were next.

"Hey, that's new," Eddie said. "I don't remember young boys riding calves in Montana."

"Maybe this is how they learn how to ride bulls when they get older," I guessed.

One by one each teenage boy came out of the bucking chute astride a bucking calf, holding on for dear life with one gloved hand gripped on the calf's rope while waving the other in the air for balance, hoping to stay on for the required number of seconds needed to qualify for a prize.

A tall clown in baggy jeans, a bright orange flowered shirt and a cowboy hat rolled out a large beer keg. His face was made up in white around his eyes and mouth. He stood the keg up. The clown inside popped out and we could see from his waist up that he was made up and dressed in a more traditional clown attire with a bulbous nose, a yellow and white polka dot top, a ruffled red collar and a pointed green and yellow hat. He grabbed on the top of the barrel and flipped himself out just as the first boy was thrown off the calf. Like lightening he rolled the empty barrel toward the animal to distract it from the boy who hightailed himself onto the fence. The cowboy clown waved his hat and a red bandana like a matador while the barrel clown chased the calf toward the exit, back to the enclosures. It was amazing teamwork.

"Those guys sure know what they're doing; don't they?" Eddie observed.

"They sure do," I agreed. "You know it's a dangerous job they're doing but they make it look so easy and funny besides."

Following the calf riders there were the contests for the calf ropers. Each in his turn, a cowboy rode in, chasing a calf. Once he roped it, the horse stood still holding the disabled calf on the rope while the cowboy firmly tied three of its legs, then remounted his horse and released the calf. One after the other each competitor tried to accomplish the feat faster than the others. The center clowns were especially alert when it came time for the bull riding and bronc bustin'. We had seen the bull riders in Butte but it our first time watching the bronc bustin' which was bareback riding of bucking horses.

"That horse looks like it's trying to fold itself in half," Eddie said.

161

"It looks pretty mean all right," I said, "but look at the big spurs on the cowboy boots; I don't imagine they'd feel too great on the horse."

"Watch the teamwork of the clowns," Eddie said, "they don't take their eyes off those animals; ever."

"Oh my God!" I yelled. "The horse bucked the cowboy up into the air!" His hat landed on the ground before he did.

Within the protection of the barrel the clown rolled toward the angry horse while the rider lay on the ground until two other cowboys ran to his side to help him up, one handed him his hat and they both supported him under his arms as he limped between them on his way out of the contest area. The clown stuck his head out of the barrel and crawled out, the cowboy clown roped the horse and, as a team, they were able to escort the animal back to the enclosures.

"I said it before and I'll say it again," Eddie's eyes were on the now subdued horse with the clowns. "Those guys sure know their stuff."

There was enthusiastic applause as the winner of each contest was announced. When it was over, the flag bearers retrieved the flags, followed by the cowboys escorting the celebrities' horses to the grand stand. This time there was no band, only shouts and cheering from the fans as the celebrities mounted their silver saddled horses and rode off through the exit. The crowd began to disperse.

"This was quite an afternoon," I said. "Do you want to stop in Redondo Beach before going home?"

"Yeah, that's a good idea," he took my hand, "we haven't seen Charlie and Ruth in a while."

"We won't stay long," he said. "Who knows when we'll be up here again."

They were sitting on lounge chairs in the back yard when we arrived. "What a great surprise," Charlie said.

"We went to the Sheriff's Rodeo this afternoon," Eddie explained. "We were so close we decided to take a chance you might be home."

"Come right in," Ruth hugged me. "Charlie, get a couple of chairs."

We sat on the patio chatting about what had been going on since our last visit. We gave them our new address, sipped on lemonade while the kids played on the swings in the back yard. Eddie talked about his construction job and Charlie talked about his work.

Ruth chatted about how the kids were looking forward to going back to school in a few weeks. "They miss their friends," she said.

"You're so lucky to have these beautiful girls." I said. "Eddie and I would love to have a family, but so far, it's just not happening."

162

"It will," she smiled encouragingly, "just be patient."

"Okay, ladies," Charlie called over to us. "It's time to get the salad ready for the barbeque; I'll get the grille."

"We hadn't planned on staying for dinner," I said.

"Nonsense," Ruth said, "I need help in the kitchen; and you're it."

She had potato salad already made and I helped cut up the vegetables for the tossed salad. The girls brought out the plates and napkins and before long we were feasting on perfectly grilled cheeseburgers and salads and lemonade.

"Now you know our address," I said, "next time we'll get together at our place."

"You've got a deal," Ruth said.

After dinner I helped Ruth clean up, we said our good-byes and headed back to Torrance. "That was a great visit," Eddie said. "I hope they do come down to the trailer park with the girls one of these days."

"We don't have a barbeque grille but I can make something up pretty fast," It'll bring back memories of our first meals together in Yellowstone Park."

"Yeah," Eddie reminded me, "only you couldn't use your electric hot plate over there; only the Coleman stove."

"Ah yes," I nodded. "I remember it well."

"We're home," Eddie announced. "I'm glad we made it back before dark."

"There's a note on the door," I walked through the trellis.

I picked up the envelope and opened it. "It's from Uncle Martin, he was here this afternoon."

"I told them we were going to the Rodeo," Eddie said.

"The note says he wants us to come over to their house tomorrow, they have something they want to tell us." I handed the letter to Eddie.

"It must be important," Eddie looked concerned as he re-read the note. "We were there just a couple of days ago."

"I don't think we should call them at this hour," I reasoned, "we'll go over there when you get home from work tomorrow."

CHAPTER 14

"Hello, is this Loretta?" I asked. "Is your Papa home?"

"Hi," Loretta responded, "is this Jeanne?"

"Yes, Uncle Victor left us a note at the trailer last night," I said. "Is everything all right over there?"

"Grandma's in the hospital," Loretta informed me. "Papa said to tell you he'll fill you in about her condition when you come over this afternoon."

"You don't know what's wrong? Is she going to be okay? When did she get sick?" I had so many questions.

"I wish I could answer you, I'm sorry, I really don't know what's wrong," she apologized. "But Papa said he wants to talk to you in person."

"I understand; I'm sorry if I'm putting you on the spot, Loretta. We'll see you when Eddie comes home from work. Thanks."

It was a long day. Julie and Joan and I met in the laundry room and had coffee at Joan's trailer while our clothes were in the dryer. I was grateful for the company.

"How about we get together with the guys on Friday night?" Joan suggested.

"Good idea," Julie said, "Darryl was asking me this morning about when he was going to meet everyone."

"Friday's fine with me too," I answered. "What time is good?"

"How about here, around six," Joan offered. "Our dining area is the largest and six o'clock will give the guys enough time to change out of their work clothes."

"Shall I make macaroni and cheese?" I asked.

"That sounds good; but I think my oven is bigger, maybe I should make that," Joan said. "How about you make the salad and Julie can make the dessert."

"Okay," I agreed, "and I'll fix peas and carrots too. Consider me the vegetable girl."

I think that's the fastest menu planning I've ever seen," Julie said. "Never mind a dinner for six."

We each picked up our cups and saucers, rinsed them and put them in the dish draining rack. It was time to walk up to retrieve our clothes from the dryers.

"I'm really looking forward to Friday," I said, "and I'm sure Eddie will be too."

"I think we all are." Julie said.


By the time Eddie came home from work the laundry was ironed and put away. I had made corned beef hash for supper and heated a can of green beans. We had tapioca pudding for dessert and we were on our way to San Pedro as soon as everything was cleaned up.

Uncle Victor hugged me as soon as we came in the door. "I'm glad you're here," he said. "I just got back from the hospital. Aunt Bina's in surgery."

"What happened?" I was concerned. "She seemed fine when we were here on Saturday."

"You know she doesn't tell us everything," he reminded us. "I guess she's been having some discomfort in her stomach for awhile without complaining." He sat in his rocking chair and motioned for us to sit down. "Sunday morning she started to feel severe cramps and was vomiting," he continued, "she didn't want to go to the doctor's but I called him anyway and his answering service told me to take her in to the hospital."

"I'm sure she didn't like that idea," Eddie said.

"You're right," Uncle replied. "But I insisted and it's a good thing I did. The doctor met us there. He took some tests and they showed she has a gastric ulcer which needs surgery. They were able to calm her down and scheduled her operation for this afternoon." He had tears in his eyes. "That's where she is now."

"Are you going back?" Eddie asked.

"Oh yes, Eva and Loretta are still over there," he said. "I came back for you; I knew you'd want to be there when she comes out of the operating room."

"Shall we leave now?" I wanted to know.

"Yes," he stood up and started toward the door. "She's been in there for more than an hour and a half."

It took about twenty minutes to get to the hospital. By the time Uncle parked the car and we made our way to the waiting room we still had to wait another forty-five minutes before a nurse from the O.R. came to tell us all went well; but it would be another hour before Uncle was allowed to see her.

"Papa," Eva said, "we're not going to be able to visit with Mama tonight, so Loretta and I will go on home." She turned toward Eddie and me, "do you want to come with us?"

"No," Eddie replied, "we'll wait here with Uncle Victor."

By the time the nurse returned to escort Uncle to the recovery room, he was looking pretty tired. "You'll only be able to see her for a few minutes," the nurse said, "she's still pretty sleepy." They left together.

"I'm glad Uncle Victor is finally able to see her," I said. "He looks very worried."

"Why wouldn't he be?" Eddie walked to the doorway of the waiting room. "The operation took a long time; I'm not surprised he's so concerned."

The nurse was right, Uncle returned about 15 minutes later, "How is she?" I asked.

"The doctor said she's going to be all right," Uncle told us, "but she can't have visitors until tomorrow when she goes into a regular hospital room."

"We'll come directly to the hospital tomorrow," Eddie told Uncle. "In the meanwhile we should all go home and you need to get some rest."

"I'll meet you here when you get off work," Uncle headed toward the exit. "The doctor said she'll be asleep for the next couple of hours and she won't even know whether anyone's here."

We hardly spoke on our way back to the parking lot or to Uncle's house to retrieve our car. "Do you want to come in for coffee before going home?" Uncle offered.

"No thanks," I answered. "You need to rest and Eddie has to get up early in the morning."

"We'll see you at the hospital tomorrow after I come home from work."

Uncle walked us to our car, kissed me on the cheek, "Take good care of this girl," he said to Eddie as we backed out of the driveway.

"Don't worry about that," he answered, "I will."

"I hope your aunt's going to be okay."

"I do too," he replied. "You know, you always think someone is indestructible until something like this happens; and it sure makes you think."

"I know what you mean, she never ever complained about having pains or anything," I agreed. "Loretta and Billy are sure lucky to have her."

The drive home was short. It was a beautiful starry night and we took our time walking to and from the Community House. Most of the trailers were in darkness and we didn't meet any of our neighbors on the path. "Do you want a snack of milk and grahams?" I asked.

"No, not tonight; it's late," he laid out his work clothes on the seat of the breakfast nook. "I just want to get to bed. Morning will come fast enough."

166

I lay awake for a long time before falling asleep. I silently prayed for Aunt Bina's recovery as I listened to Eddie's rhythmic breathing.

Dear Lord, watch over Auntie and heal her, please. And give Uncle Victor the strength he needs to help her through this illness. Amen.


"You don't have to get up," Eddie was already dressed. "I can get my own breakfast. I only want Corn Flakes and milk."

"I didn't hear the alarm."

"No, I woke up before it rang," he kissed me. "Go back to sleep, I'll be leaving in a few minutes; see you this afternoon."

I sat up on the edge of the bed. "I'm already awake, don't you want any coffee?"

"No, I'm serious. Try to get some rest," he put his bowl in the sink. "I hope we'll be able to see Auntie tonight."

"Me too," I walked him to the door and decided to make the bed rather than get into it. It was a good day for outdoor work. The roses on the trellis were not in bloom yet but there were a few new shoots and that was encouraging. I weeded the flower bed and cut the grass. Joan came over, I took a coffee break.

"Jesse and I were thinking about going over to Catalina Island one of these weekends," she said. "We wondered if you and Ed would like to go too."

"That sounds like fun," I replied, "but we can't go this weekend because Eddie's aunt is in the hospital."

"That's okay, we can go anytime, and we thought it would be more fun if the four of us went."

"What about Julie?" I asked.

"They're usually busy with family and they've probably already been there; you know, they grew up in this area."

"I'll ask Eddie and if he agrees, I'll take him to work tomorrow, and then we'll have the car so we can go buy the tickets for next week, Saturday."

"That sounds good," She took a sip of coffee. "What's wrong with Ed's aunt?"

"She had surgery for an ulcer; we're going to the hospital when he gets home from work."

"I hope she's going to be okay," she put her cup in the sink. "If I see Julia today I'll mention our plans to see if she and Darryl want to join us."

**167**

"That's a good idea," I walked her to the door and then I went outside to resume my yard work. It was good to keep busy because it made the day go by faster.

When we got to the hospital we were directed to Auntie's room. Uncle Victor was already there. Auntie was still connected to tubes in her nose and she was resting quietly. "She's been through a lot," he told us.

"I didn't expect to see all those tubes still there," I commented.

"The doctor said it was to help her breathe," Uncle explained. "They'll probably come out tonight."

"Any news on when she might be going home?" Eddie asked.

"Friday or Saturday if she can keep soft food down; right now she's only getting liquids."

Auntie opened her eyes, "Hello you two," she said in a whisper.

"Hi," Eddie kissed her cheek. "You gave us quite a scare."

"I'll be fine, just fine," she attempted a smile, "as soon as they get this thing out of my nose."

"She must be getting better," Uncle remarked, "she's starting to complain."

We all suppressed our concerns. We knew very well she was still quite sick, she would be facing a strict dietary regime, at least for a while. And yet it was good to see her fighting spirit, the very attitude that would help her heal and get home so she can be in charge again. We didn't stay long; it was clear she needed to rest.

"We'll be back to see you tomorrow evening," I promised. "By that time, hopefully that tube will be gone."

"I hope so," her voice was scratchy.

I hugged Uncle Victor, kissed Auntie on the forehead and waited for Eddie to say his goodbyes before reaching for his hand to walk toward the door.

"It's hard to see her so sick," Eddie said when we reached the hallway.

"It is," I agreed, "but, you know she's got a lot of spunk and if anybody can get through this, she can."

"You're right." We drove in silence for most of the way home then Eddie remembered; "if you're going to keep the car tomorrow we should gas up now and pick up some ice at the same time."

"Does that mean you want to go to Catalina with Joan and Jesse?"

"Of course, it sounds like a nice trip."

168

"Auntie should be home by Saturday," I reasoned, "so by next week she should be much better."

The lights were on in Joan and Jesse's trailer. It was still early so we knocked on their door. We bribed them with a blueberry pie I had made that afternoon and we were invited in for coffee. "I'll have the car tomorrow, Joan; what time do you want to go to Wilmington?"

"Does 11 o'clock sound okay?"

"Sounds good to me," I took another bite of pie. "We should be back in plenty of time for me to pick up Eddie at work."

"That's a great idea you guys came up with," Eddie said.

Jesse nodded his head, "Joan and I have wanted to go to Catalina since we moved to California; I'm glad we're finally going to get there."

"Me too, the wife will tell you how much I like boats and from what I hear the S.S Catalina is a good sized vessel."

"We have a small two person kayak at home; if I listened to him we'd be out paddling on all the rivers around Fall River and Swansea, Massachusetts every weekend."

"She might be exaggerating just a little, there," he laughed. "Anyway, it's time for us to get home."

"Thanks for the coffee, Joan," I picked up the empty pie plate. "I'll see you tomorrow."

"We haven't seen much rain since we've been in California," I said on our way home.

"It's a good thing," Eddie remarked, "that means I haven't lost any days of work because of rain."

"You really like working here don't you?"

"Yes I do, Bethlehem Steel is a good company to work for and the work crew is good too."

"Would you consider staying here?"

"I might," we walked under the trellis into our yard, "it would be a great place to raise kids."

"If we ever have any," I walked into the trailer and put the plate in the sink.

"Of course we will," he took my chin in his hand, turned my face toward him and kissed me. "I promise to do my best."

169

We both laughed. "Get your clothes ready for tomorrow while I clean this pie plate."

Joan and I went to Wilmington, as planned, to pick up our tickets for the Catalina Island Steamship. San Pedro and Wilmington abut each other and sometimes it's hard to tell whether you're in one community or the other. Both are part of Los Angeles. Joan was more familiar with the area than I, so I followed her directions and we arrived there easily. I parked the car in front of the office and we went in, bought our tickets and decided to look for a place to have lunch.

"Hey, do you like tacos?" Joan asked.

"I don't know," I shrugged, "I don't know what they are."

"Nobody doesn't like tacos," she nudged me toward a little Mexican looking shack.

"Tell me what they are," I said looking at an assortment of bowls containing hamburger meat, onions, lettuce, tomatoes and cheese. "Are those pancakes on the grille?"

"No, those are corn tortillas," she informed me, "the guy's going to fold one up and put all that other stuff inside with some hot sauce; they're really good."

"Okay, if you say so," I guessed it was probably a local food; what harm could there be in trying it?

We sat on one of the nearby benches with a cup of root beer and our taco wrapped in a paper napkin. "This is pretty good," I said after my first bite.

"Oh yeah," Joan agreed, "tacos are sort of a Spanish thing from Mexico, they're a favorite with Jesse; we had them in Texas too."

"They look easy enough to make," I observed. "Do they sell tortillas at the market?"

"Sure, most markets carry them; I like the soft tortillas best; I buy them all the time."

"This gives me a great idea for supper tonight," I said. "We'll stop at the market on the way home."

We ate at leisure and then went to pick up the groceries we needed at the store. I dropped Joan off at home and I chopped the cold fillings for the tacos. I was hooked on a new food, I was sure Eddie would be too. I picked him up at work, and by the time he was back from the Community House, the tortillas and hamburger meat were ready.

"What's this stuff?" he examined the folded tortillas.

170

"You're about to make a taco: fill up the tortilla starting with the ground beef and onions, then all the other stuff," I directed. "Add the cheese last and then the sauce; don't forget the sauce."

He followed the directives and took a bite, "hey! This is good!"

Holé! Another favorite has been created! "I'm glad you like it."

When we saw Auntie Bina at the hospital after supper, the tubes had been removed and she was sitting up. Her color was better and she was showing signs of healthy progress.

"They gave me a puree kind of soup for lunch," she said, "I don't know what it was but it tasted okay and it didn't make me sick."

"Well that's good," I chuckled, "I made tacos for Eddie for the first time today; they turned out pretty good."

"It'll be a while before I can have those" she nodded toward her husband, "your Uncle likes tacos too."

"I like hearing you talk about food," Uncle Victor smiled at her, "It's a sign you're getting better."

"I think I'll be able to go home on Friday," she announced. "I'll have to watch what I eat but it'll be good to sleep in my own bed."

We had visited about a half hour when Eva came in with Loretta and Billy. The hospital restricted the number of visitors per patient so; Eddie and I gave hugs all around and promised to return the next day.

"It's still early," Eddie looked at his watch as we reached the car. "Do you want to go to the Stadium?"

"Do you know what's playing?"

"I don't know," he closed the car door. "Does it matter?"

"I guess not," I settled in my seat, "we'll see when we get there."

It was a short ride to Torrance and as we approached the theater we saw the marquee: 'Frankenstein Meets the Wolf Man'. "I think I saw that when I was a kid," Eddie said.

"Was it any good?"

"I think it was scary," he was trying to recall, "but I don't remember much about it."

"Well," I shrugged, "the popcorn's always good."

171

Before I met Eddie, I was not an avid movie-goer; and horror movies have always been my least favorite. In my opinion, this movie left much to be desired as entertainment but I did enjoy the Movietone News with Lowell Thomas and the cartoon featuring Bugs Bunny was really cute.

"I have to admit," Eddie reached for my hand as we left the theater, "that movie wasn't so hot. It's no wonder I didn't remember much about it."

"I did like the cartoon," I chuckled, "that carrot eating rabbit cracks me up. He reminds me of you when we were dating. You always had a carrot in your pocket for your walk home."

"What can I say?" He made a face like he had buck teeth. "I like carrots." We both laughed at the memory.

We arrived home at a reasonable hour; I fixed longhorn cheese and saltine crackers for a snack. We sat in the nook and drank hot chocolate before we went to bed.

"It's good news that Auntie's going home on Friday." I handed him a paper napkin.

"She looked a lot better tonight," he reached for a cracker. "Maybe on Saturday morning we can make a short visit and you can bring her some tapioca pudding."

"Sure why not?" I agreed. "We won't stay long, and then we'll have the rest of the day to ourselves."

"Tomorrow night is when we're supposed to have dinner with our neighbors," I reminded him.

"I had almost forgotten about that," he pulled out the sofa-bed. "I guess you're going to have a busy day cooking while I'm at work."

"I'm only bringing salad and veggies for the dinner, but I'll be able to make something to bring to Auntie's on Saturday," I washed the dishes and put the crackers in the cupboard before going to bed.


The neighborhood market opened at 8 o'clock. I walked over to pick up the stuff I needed for tonight's salad, and for the spaghetti and meatballs I planned to bring to Auntie's on Saturday. I bought enough ground beef to make extra meatballs for our dinner with the neighbors. The day flew by and Julie and Joan and I checked in with each other at intervals to make sure no one had forgotten anything.

When Eddie came home from work I walked up to the Community House with him. While he was in the shower I called Auntie's house. "Hello," Uncle answered.

"Hi, it's me, Jeanne; I called to ask if Auntie was released from the hospital today."

172

"Yes, she came home around three o'clock."

"How is she doing?"

"Right now she's lying down, she's pretty tired."

"I can understand that, she's been through a lot," I said. "Eddie's in the shower right now," I explained, "he said to tell you we'll be coming over around eleven tomorrow"

"Your Aunt will be glad to see you."

"Don't fix lunch," I told him, "I'm bringing over spaghetti and meatballs for the family and tapioca pudding for her."

"We'll all look forward to that."

"See you tomorrow," I hung up.

I waited to walk back to the trailer with Eddie. There was still a little time before we were supposed to meet with our friends. I pulled out some meat balls and sauce from the pot to put in the ice box to bring to San Pedro the next day and saved some to reheat for tonight's dinner. I made the salad in a large wooden bowl and put the vinaigrette dressing in a jar to be added just before serving and left the peas in the can. At six o'clock Eddie carried the pot with the meatballs and a smaller pot with the cooked carrots; I brought the peas, the salad and dressing. Julie and Darryl arrived a few minutes after six with a lovely chocolate cake. Joan had decided to put in a loaf of Italian bread to warm in the oven with the macaroni. We introduced the men to each other; I added the salad dressing to the salad while the meatballs and veggies heated up. Joan took the macaroni and the bread out of the oven. We sat around a drop-leaf wooden table and placed the food in the center, family style.

"Darryl, the wife told me you and Julie come from California," Eddie said.

"We've lived here all our lives," he answered, "Julie and I went to the same high school."

"My parents moved from Nevada when they were first married," Julie passed the salad bowl, "and Darryl's parents have always lived here; the farthest place we've ever been is Nevada.

"Joan grew up on a cattle ranch, she's a real country girl," Jesse took the bowl, " but I was raised in Dallas; I met her when she worked in the five and dime store in my home town after she finished high school."

"My aunt lives in Dallas and I stayed with her," Joan said. "Jesse's uncle got him a job on an oil rig just before we got married," Joan said.

"Do you like that kind of work?" Eddie asked.

173

"Oh yeah," Jesse answered, "but the work is very different in Texas than it is here; how about you, Ed?"

"I'm a journeyman ironworker out of Local 37 in Providence, Rhode Island but we live in Massachusetts; I like the work and I like California, it wouldn't take much to convince me to stay here."

"What's it like in Massachusetts?" Darryl wanted to know.

"It gets pretty cold in the winter and we usually get a lot of snow," Eddie said, "but the summers are hot and sometimes the temperature gets into the nineties; I notice it doesn't get that hot over here."

"No," Darryl volunteered, "it's always around 75 to 85, even in winter."

"I can handle that," I said.

Everyone went back for seconds, "What do you think," Joan suggested, "should we save the dessert for a little later?"

"It's okay with me," Jesse answered, "the wrestling matches are on TV; us guys will watch while you gals clean up in here." The men gathered on the couch.

"That figures", Joan said, "the ladies work while you guys relax."

"You want me to be a good host, don't you?" Jesse teased.

Joan gave him a 'yeah right' look and proceeded to get containers for the food. Julie and I cleared up the dinner dishes and Joan put away the leftovers. We finished in time for the ending of the wrestling program and gathered at the table again for the cake.

"This evening went by too fast," Joan said, "we'll have to do this again."

"Oh yeah"…"Great idea"…"Name the day"…"Anytime you say"…everyone said almost in unison.

We all carried our respective containers home and agreed this had been a good evening.

"Do you have everything ready for Auntie tomorrow," Eddie asked as he opened the sofa.

"Oh yes," I said, "we won't have to rush in the morning; It's been a busy day and I'm ready for a good night's sleep."

We made our visit to Auntie's around 11 o'clock as we had planned. Eva met us at the door and took the meatballs, "I'll put these in the kitchen," she said.

"Here," I handed her two boxes of pasta, "I didn't cook the spaghetti, I figured it would be better to cook it up fresh."

"Good thinking," she put the boxes on the counter.

"I'll put the pudding in the refrigerator," I looked for a spot on the top shelf, "I hope your mother will like it."

"She's been doing pretty well," Eva remarked, "she'll probably be able to eat a little spaghetti too."

"That's great; she had us pretty worried for awhile."

"That very true," Eva reached for the coffee pot. "How about a cup of coffee before you go?"

"Sure, let me get the cups." It was good to see things were beginning to get back to normal in that house. We had our coffee with Auntie and Uncle in the living room and left San Pedro about an hour later to head for Los Angeles.

Eddie was familiar with the area so it didn't take us long to find Valley Boulevard and the entrance to Lincoln Park. There were cars parked along the side of the road and Eddie found a space to squeeze in. We walked up the sidewalk to the wide concrete entrance. We passed a stone retaining wall and a few banana trees. We passed an occasional palm tree along the flowered pathway and stopped to admire a simple statue of Florence Nightingale.

"This is interesting,' I said, "I don't remember ever seeing a statue of Florence Nightingale."

"I don't think I ever did either, I wonder if she had a special connection to this place."

"I don't see a sign anywhere; if she's the aunt of somebody in L.A. I guess we'll never know."

As we continued through the park we came to a large lake where there was a boat house. There were a few small boats out on the water and one or two tied to a wooden dock. In the distance near the shore of the lake there was a white, open sided, domed bandstand. We walked along the beautiful flower gardens and came upon a statue of Abraham Lincoln.

"Now that's an unusual sculpture," I stopped in front of the president. "I've never seen a statue of him from the hips up with his arms crossed."

"And no top hat," Eddie observed. "Come to think of it, except for the Florence Nightingale Statue we saw before, there doesn't seem to be a lot of statues in this park."

"You're right," I looked around. "What does that sign say?" I pointed in the distance.

He walked ahead of me to check it out, "there's an ostrich farm and an alligator farm on Mission Boulevard, across from here."

I caught up to him, "That sounds interesting, do you want to go?"

"Sure; I don't think we'll have to move the car, it's only a short walk."

It was a lovely afternoon; the temperature was a cool 75 degrees and the Ostrich Farm was across the street and right around the corner. Ostriches are awkward looking birds. I had never seen one before and it was amazing to be looking at so many of them in one place. Some of the Ostriches roamed together in groups in a large fenced-in area of the park. Some were sandy gray in color, others were black and some were black and white. All were at least six feet tall with a long skinny neck, a small head, with golf-ball sized eyes and a wide beak, tinged with red. They had large roundish feathery bodies with bushy tails and long spindly legs.

"I didn't realize those birds are so strong," I observed an ostrich harnessed to a small cart, containing four children as passengers.

"That guy holding the leash on the harness had better hope the ostrich doesn't decide to run or everyone's in trouble."

"I know, I read on a description back there that they can run up to 60 miles an hour."

"That's pretty fast; it's a good thing the cart those kids are riding in is sturdy," Eddie said.

"I wonder how long it took for the trainers to teach them to pull carts like that."

"I'm sure it took a lot of time and patience and maybe a few pecks on the head." Eddie laughed.

Tucked in a corner of the farm there was a nursery with baby ostrich chicks all fluffy and freckled barely as tall as an adult ostrich's knees. In the large incubator we saw oval ostrich eggs which are about six inches around and I would guess six times larger than a large chicken egg. "That would make some big omelet!" I remarked.

The alligator farm was right next to the ostrich farm; separated by a high wooden fence and trees.

WARNING

DO NOT PET

THE ALLIGATORS

"Do you really think that sign is necessary?" I asked as we entered the farm.

"The people who own this place must think so," Eddie shrugged. "It's possible some former visitors may have tried to get friendly with the animals and maybe had a limb chomped off."

"What an awful thought!"

We were surprised to learn that these animals can live to be 400 years old. One on this particular farm was 425. The animal caretakers were everywhere. They watched the alligators and the visitors closely to ensure they didn't try to get too close to each other. We were surprised to learn that alligators can also be trained. A pair of gators was harnessed to a four wheeled cart and was pulling passengers around the farm. We chose to walk. There were concrete ponds in different locations and at various times we saw a few gators lumber in for a swim. We were fascinated with a long wooden ramp where gators, prodded by trainers, climbed up to the top and then slid down a giant wet concrete slide into a large pool.

In a separate, fenced-in, shallow, concrete pool about twenty feet round we saw a sign which read 'Billy Ponchetrain'. We were curious. Inside the pool there was a single alligator and a trainer who had just entered the enclosure.

"Gather around folks," he addressed the visitors who were coming close to the fence. "I'll give you a demonstration of this wonderful fighting enemy of Tarzan."

"Tarzan!" Eddie was all ears. He was Tarzan's biggest fan.

The trainer stepped into the pool, wrapped himself around the animal, pulled what looked like a knife from his belt and began to strike at the gator. Both whirled around in the water until the animal 'gave up' and crept out of the pool. "...and that's how it's done," the trainer announced, "this is the very alligator Johnny Weissmuller, as Tarzan, wrestles in all his movies." Everyone applauded wildly as the trainer pointed to the alligator, "let's hear it for the star: Billy Ponchetrain." There was louder clapping as the trainer bowed and waved to the audience. "Thank you all for coming."

The crowd began to disperse. "I know it's all fake," Eddie said, "but when he pulled out the knife that looks so real and rolled around like he did, it sure gave me an idea of how they film those dangerous looking scenes."

"You'll probably think of this day every time you see another Tarzan movie," I predicted.

"You may be right," we were ready to leave the reptiles. "Speaking of movies, while we're in town do you want to go to the Palace?"

"Do you have any idea what's showing?"

"We'll know when we see the marquee," he said, "if we don't like it we don't have to go."

"I'm not ready for another horror show."

We drove up Broadway and saw the cursive word 'PALACE' on the three sided marquee in front of the theater, and beneath it in large letters: 'Moonlight Bay' with Doris Day and Gordon Mac Rae. "That sounds good to me," that settled that as far as I could tell. Eddie parked the car; we bought the tickets, watched a great movie, and ate popcorn; nothing could have been any better. We chatted about ostriches and alligators on our way home and topped off the evening with a light supper of grilled cheese sandwiches and hot chocolate.

"Shall I set the alarm for early Mass tomorrow?" Eddie asked.

"I don't think so," I didn't have to think long, "we usually wake up early anyway, and if we don't, we'll just go to a later Mass."

"After we have breakfast we can check up on Auntie Bina."

"I thought you might say that," I put the dishes I'd just washed into the cupboard. "I'd like to see her too, but I don't want to tire her out."

"We won't stay long," he assured me, "I just want to make sure she's doing okay."

We transformed the sofa into our bed and slid under the covers. "It's been a great day," I kissed him 'good night', "let's see what tomorrow brings."


We usually tried to attend an early Mass on Sunday. Because we had to fast from midnight if we intended to receive Holy Eucharist, we waited until after Mass before we ate breakfast. This Sunday was no different, we woke up around 6 o'clock and had plenty of time to shower and get dressed before the 8 o'clock Mass at Nativity Church. I wore a yellow shirtwaist dress with a white pill box hat, and sandals, and carried a small white purse; Eddie wore tan trousers, a pale blue shirt with a red and blue striped tie and a dark blue sports jacket. I always found it interesting to see the assortment of head wear the ladies wore on Sunday morning. The variety of head fashions went from a simple beanie, to a tam, to a picture hat (with or without flowers and ribbons), a cloche, a kerchief, a lace doily, or even a mantilla. Since the priest celebrated the Mass in Latin with his back toward the assembly, and the only English we heard was in the sermon, I have to confess, even though I fingered my rosary to keep me in a prayerful mood, I often found myself distracted by the hats until I heard one of the two acolytes ring the bell alerting us to the Consecration; the sound brought me back to my reason for being in Church: to worship God. Mea Culpa. Eddie always seemed to be more focused than I, perhaps it was because he remembered all the Latin responses from his altar boy days. I remembered the Latin hymns from having sung in the choir, but music was ordinarily sung only at the High Masses celebrated later on in the morning.

"That was a fast Mass," Eddie said as we left the church. "It couldn't have been more than a half hour."

"That's because there was no singing," I walked beside him, "and there were a lot of people too; it took a while for everyone to line up and kneel at the altar rail to receive Communion."

"That's true; it's amazing how many people attend the early Masses." We got in our car and he started the engine.

"Maybe they don't like to eat a late breakfast either." I rolled down the window.

"Speaking of breakfast, do we need to stop at the market on the way home?" He followed the line of cars out of the parking lot.

"We should pick up some ice; and maybe bacon, bread and cheese," I noted.

"I may as well get gas too, in case we want to go somewhere after we see Auntie."

We didn't encounter very much traffic and our errands took less time than we had expected. We were home by 9:45. We put the food away and got changed into more casual clothes. Eddie read the Torrance Herald while I fixed breakfast and we were ready to leave for San Pedro around 11:30. As we turned the corner onto Auntie's street Eddie recognized Albert's car.

"Albert's here, I wonder if Bonnie came with him." Eddie parked behind Albert's car.

"I hope so, we haven't seen them for a while," we went up the stairs and then knocked on the door.

"Come on in," Bonnie greeted us, "you're just in time; Albert and I brought lunch for everyone."

"What a nice surprise to see you," I hugged her, "it's been a while."

Albert extended his hand to Eddie, "we were hoping you'd drop by today."

"Oh yeah, I have to check up on my favorite aunt," he smiled at Auntie who was giving him that 'aw get out of here' look.

"Bonnie made some of her great fried chicken," Auntie pointed to the table, "come join us."

"We'd love to," Eddie shook his head, "but we just finished a pancake and bacon breakfast."

"Nonsense, there's always room for Bonnie's chicken," Uncle took us each by our elbows and led us to two places at the table.

Eva and the kids had gone off for the day and the six of us had much to chat about while platters of chicken and assorted veggies were being passed around. Auntie had her special pureed lunch while the rest of us enjoyed the incredible feast. Uncle was right: 'there was always room for Bonnie's chicken'. Everyone unanimously decided we should wait until later before we had dessert. Bonnie and I cleaned up the table and the kitchen while Auntie supervised the men as they set up for six-handed Hi-Low-Jack: girls against the guys. The afternoon went by quickly, the guys won two games to our one.

"We should leave," I said after we finished playing cards, "Auntie is getting tired.

"Not before you have apple pie and ice cream," Albert said.

"How can we refuse that?" Eddie asked.

"You can't," Bonnie already had the dessert plates, napkins and forks on the table.

"I'll sit right here," Auntie announced, "I'll have some Lipton tea and then I'm going to lie down; that pie sure looks good, though."

"Don't get any ideas," Uncle warned, "tea is all you're getting for now."

Auntie was true to her word, when she finished her tea she stood up. We took our cue and said our good-byes. We hugged and shook hands and were on our way.

"I didn't expect we'd stay at Auntie's as long as we did," I opened the door to the car.

"Neither did I, but it was great to see Albert and Bonnie," Eddie adjusted the rear view mirror. "Boy; that woman can sure cook."

"You said it; I know I'm not going to do any snacking tonight."

"Did you want to go anywhere before we go home?" he pulled away from the curb.

"I don't think so, I've got some letters to write; and you still didn't finish reading this morning's Herald," I reminded him.

"Okay, tomorrow's Labor Day, the job will be closed and we'll have the whole day to do whatever we want."

"I think I saw an announcement in the paper about a beauty contest in Santa Monica tomorrow," I wasn't sure.

"We'll check it out when we get home."

It was still light when we got home. We changed into our comfy night clothes and got settled at the table; I with my Esterbrook fountain pen and stationery and he with the newspaper. I had letters to answer from our parents and relatives. I loved receiving letters from home and having a permanent address helped to keep the correspondence active, as long as I kept up my end of the writing.

"Here's the ad about the beauty contest in Santa Monica," Eddie turned the paper toward me. "It's going to be in Ocean Park and that wrestler Baron Leone is going to be a special guest."

"That should be interesting," I looked at the picture of the contestants. "I wonder if the Baron will be wearing regular clothes or his wrestling attire."

"We'll find out tomorrow," he turned the paper to the comics section.

"Honey, I think you've got an internal alarm clock," I said sleepily. I heard him filling the coffee pot with water. He was fully dressed and was whistling happily. What he didn't say is: "Okay, Sweetheart, it's time to get up." But that was the message that came through; loud and clear. I put on my bathrobe, picked out the clothes I planned to wear for the day and went up to the Community House. He had already picked up the newspaper and was settled at the table with a cup of coffee when I returned.

"Nothing much is happening to end the Korean War," he put the paper down and looked up. "The peace talks at Kaesong that started in July are at a standstill since August 19th when the Communists accused the UN Forces of some kind of violations," he shook his head. "You know; if this war goes on much longer, I could still be drafted into the military and become part of it."

"Don't talk like that, it scares me," I sat at the table across from him with my hands around my cup of coffee. "This is not a good way to start the day."

"I know," he reached over and covered my hands with his, "but we both know that this could happen."

I choked back the tears and changed the subject. "What would you like for breakfast?"

"Adam and Eve on a raft!" he chuckled.

"What?"

"For those who don't know anything about eating in a diner; that would be two poached eggs on toast."

"Does that include oars?"

"Oars...what do you mean?"

"Two crisp slices of bacon for paddling of course," I teased. "Gotcha!"

We had had a couple of days of rain the week before but not enough to prevent Eddie from working. Today promised to be a bright clear sunshiny day, a perfect day for the beach and an outdoor beauty contest. I cleaned up the trailer after breakfast while

181

Eddie checked on the goldfish and the yard. We left for Santa Monica around 10:30 o'clock. From Torrance we drove northwest toward the ocean for about 20 miles until we saw the beautiful beach at Santa Monica.

"There it is," I pointed toward the water, "see if you can find a parking place so we can walk on the beach."

"The sign over there says 'Muscle Beach'," Eddie said. "I wonder if we're in the right place."

"Maybe we should ask somebody if this is where the contest is," I suggested.

The golden sand extended as far as we could see. There was a large white stucco building near the shore which advertised Royal Crown Cola for 5 cents and hot dogs for a dime.

"Let's ask over at that store," I started to walk in that direction, "somebody over there should know."

We decided to buy 2 cones of vanilla ice cream. "Is this where the beauty contest is going to be this afternoon?" Eddie asked the server.

"Oh no," he handed Eddie one of the cones; which he handed to me, "that would be at Ocean Park about two miles further up the beach."

"This is Santa Monica, isn't it?" Eddie took the other cone and gave the man twenty cents.

"Yes it is," he smiled and pointed up the beach, "and that's Santa Monica too, this beach is about three miles long; there's a lot of stuff going on everywhere."

"This sure is a popular place for families," I looked for an unoccupied picnic table for us to eat our ice cream. Children ran along the shore chasing the ebb and flow of the blue foamy water while their parents kept watch from blankets close to the shore. Some parents were farther from the water in a play area where there were swings, seesaws, and monkey bars, and still others played volley ball. We hadn't come prepared for swimming but we did take our shoes off to walk in the sand and explore the area. We walked past sunbathers on blankets and saw palm trees here and there. We came to an area where there was a large concrete platform with all kinds of body-building equipment on it, including stands with exercise rings and free standing exercise bars and a trampoline. We saw some men flipping their bodies using the exercise bar or the rings. In the weight-lifting area there were mostly men, but there were some women too, lifting various types of weights. Their well toned bodies were evidence of their frequent use of this place.

"I guess we should put our shoes on before we go back to the car and go up to Ocean Park," Eddie said.

"I suppose you're right," I sat on a bench near a palm tree. I brushed the sand off my feet and put my sandals on.

182

The ride to Ocean Park was short. "It looks like there are a lot of people here," Eddie said as he followed behind a line of cars between the two 12 foot stone pillars with tiki torches on top at the entrance. "What time is it?"

I looked at my watch, "I have 1:25; the contest starts at 2:00." We drove past some low, uneven, rough-barked trees to a clearing where we could see the beach and a pier.

"There's the parking lot," Eddie nodded ahead of us," it looks like it's pretty full."

"I'm sure we'll find a place, even though it may not be close to the beach," I looked for a space with him.

"Okay," Eddie turned into a spot about four rows toward the back part of the lot. "This is close enough. It'll be a little walk, but I'm sure we're up to it."

"This place looks like it might have been an amusement park at one time," I observed as we got closer. "See over there on the pier?" I pointed; doesn't that look like it might be a Ferris wheel?"

"It does," Eddie agreed, "but it doesn't look like it's working now."

As we got closer to the pier we noticed there were smaller amusement rides for children and they were very popular. "Look," he pointed to a tall sign atop two long poles, "'Lick Pier.' That's a funny name for a pier."

"I wonder if that's somebody's name," we continued to walk along the pier.

There was an elegant looking building with a sign in large letters above the theater style doors. 'ARAGON BALLROOM' The sign near the entrance advertised Lawrence Welk every Saturday night. "This is where the TV shows we watched at Auntie's are broadcast," I said. "We'll have to tell them that we saw this place."

"I'm sure they'll be interested," Eddie said, 'but then again maybe they already know."

"I wonder where the beauty contest is," I looked around.

"There are a lot of people standing by that large white building near the beach," he said.

"Let's go over there and find out."

There was a large domed stage area in the center at the front of the building with arch openings on both sides for the full length of the structure. The activities were held outdoors. The contestants lined up on one side of the stage behind the arches before strutting before the judges one at a time; they posed and turned, smiled at the judges and the audience then waited on the other side to return to the stage as a group before exiting behind the curtain to change for the next event. There was an evening gown contest, a talent show and finally the bathing suit competition. The contestants were the only ones we saw go inside the building in between events. Prominently located in front, facing the stage, were the judges as well as special guest, Baron Leone, the wrestler we had seen on TV. His long dark wavy hair hung down his back, his mustache was neatly trimmed and he wore his wrestling attire complete with his championship belt with a diamond design on the front. The judges and the Baron went up the stairs leading to the stage to announce the runners-up and winner of the contest. Fans and children crowded up on stage to congratulate the winner and to shake hands with the special guest.

"Do you want to go up on stage?" Eddie asked.

"No, it's ok," I pulled out my Brownie camera, "I can take a picture from here."

We walked around the pier a little longer before going back to the parking lot. "There will probably be a lot of traffic as we get out of here," Eddie said, "there's no sense rushing to get back to the car."

"Good idea." I stopped to watch the children riding in little cars attached to the thick stationary spokes of a large wheel. "I like seeing the faces of the kids; they hang on to the steering wheel like they're competing in a drag race."

"That's how kids are, they think they're driving on their own," he reached for my hand. "Look over there," he pointed to a circular structure filled with water and small, four passenger boats also attached to a wheel. "I bet the kid holding the steering wheel on that red boat feels like the captain of an ocean liner."

"You're probably right, look how he's grinning from ear to ear."

We started to walk toward the parking lot. "I suppose we should be heading home." Eddie reached into his pocket for the car keys. By the time we reached our car most of the lot was empty. The ride home was short. I fixed leftovers for supper and we played a few games of Rummy before calling it a day.


By the time we visited Auntie later on in the week we found there was quite an improvement. She had begun to eat more substantial food and was healing very well.

"We're glad you came over tonight," Uncle said. "We're planning to go to Pasadena on Sunday and would like you to come with us."

"Really," Eddie was surprised. "You're feeling that well, Auntie?"

"It's Fall River day at the park in Pasadena," she told us. "We go every year."

"Do you mean Fall River, Massachusetts," I wondered.

"Oh yes," Uncle answered, "we were surprised at how many people from Fall River have settled down in California."

"Is there anyone you know?" Eddie asked.

"Actually, we've met people who know people that we know back there," Auntie added.

"Yes," Uncle said, "we know them now and we look forward to seeing them again every time we go to the reunion."

"That's why we try not to miss it," she was enthusiastic, "I know by Sunday I'll be feeling a lot better; I'm feeling much better right now."

"We're going to Catalina on Saturday with some friends," Eddie said, "but we're returning the same day; it sounds like we have a date for Sunday."

CHAPTER 15


"What time are we meeting Jesse and Joan?" Eddie asked as he poured milk into a bowl of Rice Krispies.

"Eight forty-five, the ship leaves at 10:30," I tucked the pillows under the sofa and pushed it closed. "Joan said Jesse wants to drive."

"That's okay. I'm not wearing a jacket," he announced, "I think this long-sleeved green shirt will be warm enough."

I wore a navy-blue pleated skirt and a white blouse, "I'm going to wear my tweed coat; it might get chilly on the ocean." I joined him at the table with my bowl of cereal.

"This will be our first cruise out on the Pacific," Eddie said. "Just imagine, if we could stay on the ship heading west for six days we'd be pretty close to Hawai'i."

"Hawai'i! That's not even part of the United States," I exclaimed. "And, if I'm not mistaken, I think we'd need a passport to go there."

"Hey, it's only a dream," he smiled, "I dreamed about this trip, didn't I? And here we are."

"That's true," I finished cleaning up the dishes, " here we are. Let's go meet our friends."

Joan also wore a skirt and a blouse and both she and Jesse wore short jackets. The men sat in the front seat of Jesse's car while Joan and I sat in the back.

"I can't get over the price of these tickets," Jesse said, "I never would have believed we could get round trip tickets to Catalina Island for under six dollars each."

"It's a bargain all right," Eddie agreed. "It's a little foggy this morning, I hope it clears up."

"You know how it is over here," Jesse said, "the fog usually clears up around noon."

When we arrived at the pier in Wilmington, the tall, white, majestic S.S. Catalina was tied next to the dock with its gangplank extended to receive the passengers who were already beginning to line up.

"How big do you figure this ship is, Jesse?" Eddie asked.

"I'd say about 300 feet, easy, and maybe around 50 some feet wide, don't you think?"

"That sounds pretty close," Eddie looked around. "What do you think? I'm guessing there's around five decks."

"We'll know when we get aboard," Jesse nodded toward the gangway. "We'd better head over there, the line's moving pretty fast."

"Look at the big tan smokestack on top of the middle of the ship, it's got a blue flag painted on it with a big white 'C' in the center," Joan waved a pointed finger.

"That has to be the bridge right in front of it," Jesse declared. "That's where the Captain handles the ship."

Eddie reached for my hand, "Come on, Sweetheart, we've got to keep moving."

We followed the other passengers up the gangplank, I'm sure there were more than fifteen hundred people boarding the ship. As we stepped on board, we were greeted individually by members of the crew, wearing navy and white uniforms, who handed us brochures about the ship and the city of Avalon. It was still a little hazy when we shoved off but clear enough to see several pleasure boats out on the water.

Jesse was right; we boarded on 'A' deck (also called the Promenade deck) which was equipped with oak benches for open seating from the bow of the ship to the stern and there was a railing all around. The bridge was forward of the smokestack, one level above the 'A' deck. It housed the wooden pilot house and the captain's quarters. 'B' deck forward could be accessed by a wide staircase where there were a few staterooms and private restrooms. Another staircase aft from 'A' deck led down to the 'Saloon deck' side of 'B'. There were glass windows all around and a bandstand on one end with a dance floor and a bar for those passengers who preferred to stay inside. 'C' deck was where the purser's office was located and where the life boats and life rafts were lined up on both sides of the ship. The engines were below 'C' deck and inaccessible to passengers. Although we explored the decks open to passengers, we preferred to stay topside and enjoy the open sea for our two hour voyage.

"I didn't think there would be so many boats out here," I said.

"Why not," Eddie stood next to me at the railing, "I bet the fishing's pretty good out there."

"Some of those boats look too fancy for fishing," Jesse observed.

"It's clearing up pretty good," Joan said. "I can see a couple of sailboats out there."

"As the sun gets stronger the fog will be completely gone," Jesse predicted.

"It'll be beautiful by the time we get to the island," Joan said confidently.

"For those of you standing near the railing of the ship," the captain's voice came over the loudspeaker. "Look for the flying fish…you can see them from both sides of the ship. They like tropical waters and are found in very few places in the world. Enjoy!"

"I heard about 'flying fish' in that song 'On the Road to Mandalay', "I recalled. "I wonder what they look like." I moved closer to the railing. The water was some distance below our viewing point but we could see the fish moving under the surface of the clear ocean at a fast rate of speed.

"Look at that little son of a gun," Eddie exclaimed. "It looks like a little foot-long torpedo leaping out of the water with its long fins extended like wings."

"I know," I agreed. "Look there's more of them over there."

"Wow," Jesse said, "some of them fly about twenty feet or more into the air before plunging back into the water."

"It's amazing they can fly such a long distance," Joan observed.

"They've got two sets of wings," I exclaimed, "Look the smaller ones are near the tail."

"And the fins don't flap;" she noticed. "They look sort of rigid, like a glider's wings."

"The water's so clear out here we can actually see the sleek fish speeding with the fins tucked in just below the surface before flying out," I was fascinated.

"I don't imagine anyone would try to fish for these guys," Eddie said. "For one thing they're probably hard to catch."

"They're most likely not good for eating either," Jesse shook his head.

"I'm glad that's settled, aren't you, Joan?" I rolled my eyes.

The flying fish kept us mesmerized until there were fewer and fewer and we were past the school. The fog was completely gone and we could see the large round white casino on the island situated close to the harbor. There were mountains in the distance, not as spectacular as the ones we had seen in the national parks we had visited, but they were beautiful, and picturesque.

"Hey!" I yelled. "What are those kids doing?"

"They're diving off the dock," Eddie answered.

"That doesn't seem like a good idea," I was concerned. "The ship is headed right toward them."

"What are you doing?" Jesse saw one of the passengers throwing money into the water.

"It's an old custom," the man answered. "See that kid over there; he's waving a coin in his hand."

"That doesn't look like it's very safe for the kids," I said.

**188**

"The water's clear and shallow over here," the man continued. "These kids dive for coins all the time; I'm sure the captain's watching for them and going a lot slower."

Eddie put his arm around me and said, "These kids look like they know what they're doing; I'm sure they'll get back on the pier as the ship gets ready to tie up."

He was right, when we finally docked at Steamer Pier in the small city of Avalon; the teenagers were walking around the dock, soaking wet, and probably waiting to get back into the water to search for coins they might have missed.

"Okay," Jesse asked, "glass bottom boat first?"

"According to this brochure, we should be able to find the 'Torqua' right on the other side of this pier," Eddie showed Jesse the picture.

"It must be close to the ocean end of the pier," Joan walked in the opposite direction of the crowds walking toward the city. We followed.

At the very end of the pier we saw the 'Torqua', a long white boat with a blue cabin. There were a few other people lined up ahead of us for the tour. We were greeted by a couple of divers, a man and a woman, wearing full underwater deep sea diving gear, except for the helmets. We purchased our tickets at the little wooden kiosk at the edge of the pier and were directed on board to the blue cushioned seats along the inner perimeter of the boat, outside the cabin. There was a railing around the rectangular glass bottom area of the boat. Here the passengers could stand safely away from the glass to get a better underwater view during the tour. We waited a few minutes until the seats were full and the divers came on board. "Welcome aboard," the man in the diving suit said. "We'll be shoving off in a few minutes. We ask that you do not roam about the boat. You are free to stand next to the railing in front of your seat at any time. My partner and I are wearing diving gear similar to what divers wore during World War II. We'll be going out a half mile or so where we'll go down to the bottom and show you a world you've never seen before. Here we go, sit tight and enjoy the wonderland of the sea." The boat was underway and they disappeared into the cabin.

The boat headed out to sea, past some pleasure boats that were tied to buoys, the breeze was refreshing as we neared our viewing destination in the open sea. The divers re-appeared wearing round brass colored helmets with a wire and an oxygen tube attached. The glass protectors over the ears had little grids inside that looked like a 'tic tac toe', and the face mask was clear. They threw a rope ladder over the side of the boat and descended into the sea. The first thing we noticed was a green forest of kelp swaying with the movement of the water. The divers bounced toward the undersea plants and when they parted the kelp they pointed to a few orange fish. "These are Orange Garabaldi," the lady diver said in her microphone. She followed one with her hands on either side as it swam gracefully and she walked on the bottom with her weighted feet to keep up with it. As the divers walked along the sea bottom they pointed to debris which could have come from ancient disasters at sea,

"We don't know how long this stuff has been here," the man said. "Look at this, these are encrusted metal straps."

189

"These things look like they might have been parts of a chair or a table," she held up a rounded piece of wood, "or maybe even a part of a wheel; no one can tell for sure."

"Look at these low coral formations," the man said. "I'm not going to touch them because they are living organisms and very delicate."

Both divers avoided walking on the colorful and delicate coral. Some were like little pink fingers coming out of the sand, others were a deep fuchsia and flower shaped; some looked like a small pink brain and still others were a brownish tan color and looked like huge sponges. Beautiful yellow and black striped angel fish and other colorful fish swam profusely around the undersea garden nibbling at the coral as though it were a salad bar. "It's one whole community," the lady said, "the fish are like caretakers of the coral."

"But these guys," the man carefully picked up a spiny sea-urchin with his gloved hand. "Don't be fooled by their delicate appearance. You can do some serious damage to your foot if you should accidently step on one of these things," he said.

"He's right," she replied, "sea urchins are creatures you want to avoid." She took some food out from the bag she was carrying on a strap over her shoulder and waved her hand as she released it. Soon they were surrounded by hundreds of colorful fish ready to glop up their free meal. There was one group of grey fish which I found to be different than the others. They were about a foot long and not overly fat for their size, but they had little white rectangles in three neat rows along the full length of their bodies. They swam among the black fish and the yellow ones but their markings were certainly distinctive. I don't know what they were and no one who was watching seemed to know.

"This water is way clearer than the Atlantic," Eddie observed, "and I don't see any quahogs down there."

"What the heck are quahogs?" Jesse asked.

"They're hard shell clams we have back home; we can eat them either cooked or raw," Eddie said. "I don't see any clams at all, as a matter of fact."

"Are they like oysters?" Joan wanted to know.

"No," Eddie explained, "oyster shells are wavy, like on a 'Shell Oil' sign. Quahog shells are smoother."

"I've looked in the markets around here and I've never seen any of the kind of shellfish like we have back home," I said.

"You would think an ocean is an ocean and the same kinds of creatures could be found in both," Joan said, "but I guess not."

"Speaking of same kinds of creatures," I observed, "I know that lady is holding up a starfish but I've never seen one the color of aquamarine."

190

"Yeah," Eddie agreed, "the ones we have back east are red; I don't see any red starfish down there either."

There was some unidentifiable debris that perhaps could have come from ship-wrecks but much of it was half hidden by the plants growing out from the sandy ocean floor, the divers didn't elaborate on any of it. They climbed the rope ladder and came aboard and then pulled in the ladder. The lady diver emptied her feed bag over the side before they both went into the cabin to remove their diving helmets and heavy boots. We continued to watch through the glass as schools of colorful fish came to feed below us. The boat circled and we headed toward the island. The fish became fewer and fewer as we got closer to the dock. There was already a line of people waiting to take the next excursion out to sea.

We exited the boat and headed toward the city of Avalon. The small city was filled with tourists. The roads were dirt and the primary mode of transportation was mostly bicycles. We saw very few cars (under five) and not a single traffic light. We boarded a small bus which took us on the short ride to Bird Park in the Canyon surround-ed by mountains. The bus stopped in front of a long white stucco building built in Span-ish architecture with arches on the outside and a concrete walk along the front of the arched entrance. The roof was covered with red Spanish style tiles. The Park was built by William Wrigley, Jr., of chewing gum fame. He had ordered birds to be imported to Catalina from all over the world. There was no admission charge and we could roam about as much as we liked. In the center of the park there was a large octagonal screened aviary where all kinds of birds flew about. There was a small, mounded island in the center, with tropical plants including Ti and Bird of Paradise. It was completely sur-rounded by a circular pond and two bamboo bridges, one on either side of the island. We saw a white peacock, dragging its long tail across one of the bridges as it traveled from the outer perimeter of land to the center island where there was a large tree extending almost to the ceiling. We saw a few white cockatoos with flashy red headdresses.

"It's impossible to tell which birds are native to this region," Jesse remarked, "from here it looks like they all feel at home in and around that tree."

"I see Robins and Cardinals and Baltimore Orioles; and I don't know what those black birds are," Joan looked quizzically at her husband.

"I dunno," Jesse shrugged. "I'm just kind of listening to all of them, it's a won-derful sound."

"My mother had a canary once," Eddie said, "she used to love listening to it; she'd probably go nuts listening to all these birds at once."

"Look at those graceful white Swans swimming around the island and under the bridges," I said   .

"There are big black Swans over on the other side," Joan pointed, "aren't they gorgeous?"

"What is that funny looking white bird with a yellowish shaggy head splashing around over there?" Jesse wanted to know, "It looks like it needs a new hairdresser."

**191**

"The picture in this flier says it's a Cormorant," we all looked over Eddie's shoulder, "it doesn't say what part of the world it comes from."

"Well I know what these are," I was confident, "These are ducks and geese and they look like they're all peacefully enjoying their surroundings."

We left the large aviary to walk around the park. There were a few smaller aviaries which we observed from the outside. We saw Toucans and Cranes and Tropical Penguins.

"Oh!" I exclaimed. "Stop! Look at the teal Peacock with its tail spread."

"It's just roaming around free," Joan observed, "now I understand what they mean when they say 'proud as a Peacock'; just look at the way that bird is strutting."

We all laughed but kept our distance.

"If we're going to see more of the town before the boat leaves," Eddie said, "we should think about taking the bus back to Avalon."

"Good idea," Jesse agreed, "but let's go back to the exit by another path; I'd like to see the Bald Eagles."

The view was breathtaking on all sides of the park. As we walked back to the stucco building, we passed the aviary where the Bald Eagles were kept. There was ample room for the birds to fly around and we saw a few eaglets.

"I read in the flier that our national bird was near extinction and this park was working to help increase the Bald Eagle population," Eddie said.

"I heard that before," Jesse nodded, "one thing I didn't know is that Bald Eagles mate for life; so I'm guessing the adult birds in here are probably permanent residents and the young ones are released into the wild."

"That makes sense," Eddie agreed. We continued on to the bus stop.

We didn't wait long for the bus which took us the short distance from the park to Crescent Avenue. We visited the Catalina Souvenir Shop. We didn't actually buy anything but it was fun to look through the wonderful assortment of pottery and gifts from the island and imported gifts from exotic places. On our walk back to the ship we stopped to buy hot dogs, soda and chips and sat around a picnic table while waiting for our ship to board for our trip back to the mainland. It was late afternoon when we sailed for home. There were fewer boats on the moorings and more boats out on the water. The flying fish made their appearance as expected but there were fewer than earlier in the day. From the Promenade Deck we could hear the band playing on the Saloon Deck.

"Shall we dance?" Jesse said to Joan.

"Why not?" she answered, "Come on, you guys."

"Sweetheart...?"

"Sure," we all walked down to 'B' deck together, piled our coats and jackets on the chairs surrounding one of the small tables along the bulkhead. I took Eddie's hand and we danced until the ship docked in Wilmington.

"It seems like the ride back was shorter than the way over to the island," Eddie held me close as the band played 'Good Night, Sweetheart 'til we meet tomorrow'.

"It does seem that way," I looked around the dance floor and saw a few people, who had been sitting at the tables, starting to ascend the stairs up to the Promenade Deck. We weren't in any hurry to join the line of passengers headed for the gangway.

"I picked up your coat, Jeanne," Joan said as she and Jesse met us edging our way toward the stairway.

"I guess it's that time," Eddie helped me with my coat. "It's been a great day." We were among the last passengers to leave the ship.

"Funny how everyone rushes to be first to get on the ship," Joan observed, "then everybody rushes to be first to get off."

"You're right, but I'll tell you the truth," Jesse announced, "I'm not in any rush to get into the parking lot traffic."

"Maybe it won't be so bad by the time we get there," Eddie said, "we'll just take our time to walk over."

None of us wanted the day to end as it was evidenced in the chatter on the drive home. Each one of us had a favorite moment to share with each other: "I can't get over the wingspan on those bald eagles"…"what about those colorful fishes"…"how about those flying fish?"..."and hardly any cars, only bicycles!"…"not even a traffic light"…"somebody said the Chicago Cubs are not going to have spring training on Catalina any more"…"I would have liked to see the baseball field"…"I guess we'll just have to go back on another day."

"Good night you two," I hugged Joan and Jesse. Eddie did the same.

"It was a great day," Jesse said as we headed for our respective trailers.



Eddie had set the alarm for us to attend an early Mass in Torrance. We went to eight o'clock Mass at the Church of the Nativity. As usual it was a Low Mass and well attended but done within thirty-five minutes.

"Shall we stop at the store?" It was still fascinating to me that all markets were open for business on Sundays. This is a luxury we could not expect to have once we got back to Massachusetts. Over there, the Blue Laws prohibited any kind of business on Sundays, except for gasoline stations, and this did not include any type of repairs unless there was an absolute emergency like a flat tire.

193

"I noticed we need ice," Eddie answered. "Didn't Uncle Victor say he wanted to go to Pasadena today?"

"Yes, he said this is the annual Fall River, Massachusetts day."

"If we plan to bring a lunch, then," Eddie said, "we should stop."

"I don't want Auntie to make anything," I told him, "I just want her to enjoy the day."

"You're right," Eddie agreed. "We'll call them when we get back to the Community House to see what time we should pick them up."

We picked up extra ice to put in our tin picnic basket to keep the cold cuts and cheese and potato salad cool. The potatoes were cooking for the salad while we ate Kellogg's corn flakes for breakfast. "Uncle said Pasadena isn't far and if we leave about one o'clock we'll get there plenty early enough."

"I'll chill the potatoes with ice and drain them before I make the salad," I said. "I've decided to keep the cold cuts and cheeses, lettuce and tomatoes separate and everyone can make their own sandwiches on the bun."

"Okay, I'll put some mayo and mustard in the basket," he pulled the condiments out of the icebox. "I've got plenty of ice; everything should stay nice and cold. Don't forget the lemonade."

"I think we're pretty much ready to go," I picked up a sheet to use as a tablecloth and put it in a separate bag with the sandwich rolls, napkins, paper plates, cutlery and cups. "Wow! It's already noon. I don't think Auntie and Uncle will mind if we're a little early; do you?"

"No they're usually ready on time," Eddie took the bag from me. "And if they're not ready I don't mind waiting."

"Neither do I," he started loading up the trunk. "I wonder if we'll meet anyone we know from Fall River."

Eddie was wearing tan slacks with a green checkered short-sleeved shirt. He was already sitting behind the wheel of the car when I emerged from the trailer wearing a red and white polka-dot sundress with white sandals. I locked the door, took my place beside him in the car and we were on our way. It was just as Eddie had said; Auntie and Uncle were ready when we arrived. I stepped out of the car for Uncle Victor to sit up front with Eddie. I opened the back door for Auntie Bina to get in and walked around to the driver side to sit next to her. "Everybody in?" Eddie asked.

"We've got a great day for a picnic," Auntie said. "I know you said you'd bring everything, but Eva made these nice chocolate chip cookies so I brought some along."

"That's good; I didn't think to bring dessert."

"Do you know the way to Pasadena?" Uncle asked.

194

"Not really," Eddie answered, "I was hoping you could be the co-pilot and guide us there."

"It's not difficult to find," Uncle assured him, "Pasadena is just outside of L.A. it's a nice ride. Like I said before, we go up to this event every year. Oh turn up ahead on Grand Avenue, there's a place I want you to see."

Eddie drove only a block or two when Uncle shouted, "There it is," Uncle waved his hand and pointed. "That big whitish stone building over there is Vista del Arroyo."

The building was six stories high with a narrow square tower in the center with two angled wings on either side.

"Is it a hotel?" I asked.

"It was built as a hotel around 1930," Uncle said, "but the army took control of it during the war and turned it into a convalescent hospital for wounded soldiers."

"After the war, the government took it over and now it's a courthouse, and there are federal offices in there," added Auntie.

"That's an interesting transition of uses for a single building," I noted.

"I guess it shows how well it was built for it to be able to sustain all those changes," Eddie remarked. "It's a beautiful building all right,"

"Just a few more blocks to Brookside Park, it's on Arroyo Avenue," Uncle said.

There were large cardboard posters to guide us to the entrance of the reunion area:

MEET YOUR FALL RIVER, MASSACHUSETTS FRIENDS...A GOOD PLACE TO BE FROM

"I guess we'll be meeting a lot of people who've taken up permanent residence in California," I said, "like you."

"Well," Auntie hesitated a little, "I have to admit, I do get homesick for the old Bay State, once in a while, although I think Eva and her family will make this their permanent home."

We drove into the park and found an empty picnic table among lots of occupied tables. The reunion was very well attended and people were mingling with each other. Uncle and Auntie met some people they had met in previous years. Eddie and I didn't recognize anyone we knew but as we roamed around and chatted, I came upon the cousin of one of my classmates from Dominican Academy, Gerry Belisle. We talked for awhile and then we were off to meet a few of Auntie and Uncle's friends before we decided to sit and eat our picnic lunch. Eddie unloaded the trunk and set up the picnic basket on the tablecloth.

195

"Don't you touch a thing," Uncle said to Auntie. "Just tell me what you want in your sandwich and I'll fix your plate."

"Stop spoiling me," she smiled coyly. "When did you start being a chef?"

"This is your day off," he said. "And just making a sandwich doesn't exactly qualify me for a chef; you'll get your old job back soon enough."

We all laughed, Eddie poured the lemonade. Someone had set up a three legged race in a field beyond the picnic area, and another group had a sack race for the children after that. Now and then people would stop by our table to tell us what part of Fall River they were from, and it was interesting to hear the stories they had to tell about our home town.

Auntie was getting a little tired so Uncle suggested we head for home. It had been a pleasant afternoon; we shook hands with a few people and said we hoped to see them again next year.

"Here, put the rest of these cookies in your bag," Auntie said, "Eva made enough for an army and I'm sure she'd want you to have them."

"Thanks," Eddie said as he packed them away with the rest of the buns in the bag with assorted stuff.

We drove home by a different route so Uncle could point out the route for the Rose Bowl Parade and we drove past the field where the football games were usually held every year. We didn't make any stops on our way to San Pedro and arrived there close to 5 p.m. Uncle was right by Auntie's side as she got out of the car, visibly tired but still smiling.

"We had a great time," she said, "come, give me a hug; I think I'm ready for a little nap."

"It was fun," I said, "now go on in and take it easy."

""We'll see you sometime during the week," Eddie shook Uncle's hand.

"Sure thing, thanks for everything."

When we reached the trailer park Darryl and Julie came to meet us as we were unloading the trunk.

"Hey, strangers," Darryl said, "we haven't seen you guys for awhile."

"We were on a picnic with Eddie's Aunt and Uncle," I replied.

"Feel like playing some cards tonight?" Julie asked.

"Sure," Eddie emptied the water from the picnic basket. "Just give us a half hour or so and we'll be ready."

"If you didn't have dinner we still have the fixin's for sandwiches and salad if you care to join us," I offered.

"Great!" Darryl said. "We'll see you in a little while."

Left over picnic! Could we ask for any better? No dirty dishes to wash...everyone could choose their favorite sandwich filling and we were done...ready for a couple of hot games of Hi-Lo-Jack. We could not have planned the evening any better. Eddie and Darryl had to get up early for work the next morning so we made it an early night and our guests left around 10 p.m.

The week went by fast, there were the usual things to do during the day, like laundry and ironing and cleaning and I managed to spend some time with Julie and Joan. Eddie worked overtime for two of the evenings. On one evening we watched TV with Joan and Jesse. On another night we went to the movies in Torrance with Darryl and Julie to see a double feature: Betty Grable in 'Meet Me After the Show' and Ricardo Montalban with Cyd Charisse in 'Mark of the Renegade'. We munched our 10 cent boxes of popcorn in rhythm with the music and were greatly impressed with the beautiful costumes in both movies: Hollywood style glitz in the first and Classic Spanish attire in the other. Movietone News showed scenes from the Korean War, and the golden voice of Lowell Thomas gave us news about the passing of the 22$^{nd}$ amendment to the Constitution, "The term in office for the President of the United States will be limited to two four year terms; and cannot be re-elected for a second time once this eight year term has been served." There was also a clip about Julius and Ethel Rosenberg, being sentenced to death for treason. They were the two American spies who were convicted of selling secrets of the Atomic Bomb to Josef Stalin's Union of Soviet Socialist's Republic. On a happier note Bugs Bunny was still getting into trouble and chomping on his carrots.

"We should get over to San Pedro tomorrow evening," Eddie said as we walked in the trailer. "We won't be able to get over there on Saturday if we plan to go down toward Mexico."

"That's a good idea," I fixed crackers and cheese for a snack. "I'll give Auntie a call tomorrow."

"In the meanwhile, Sweetheart, it's time to call it a night," he opened the sofa. "The old alarm clock isn't going to give us a break in the morning."

"You're right about that," I finished tidying up, "move over, here I come."

I made Eddie's lunch and packed a thermos of coffee for him. "I'll pick up some fish for supper and we can go to San Pedro after we eat."

"That's a good idea," Eddie kissed me on his way out. "Call them up today and see if Auntie's up to watching the wrestling matches tonight."

It's amazing how there is always something to do, even though our living accommodations are small there's always cleaning, laundry, ironing or cooking to keep me busy. After sweeping out the trailer and dusting, I walked to the market to pick up the fixings for supper. I found a new thing in the produce section. There were pint-sized baskets of small strawberries. They were smaller than the end of my little finger and were selling for ten cents a basket. I bought some heavy cream to whip and decided strawberry shortcake would make an excellent dessert. I bought four baskets; I set some aside to eat fresh and cooked two baskets to make a sauce to eat with toast. What a find! As usual, I made the bags heavier than I had intended, and it was a struggle to carry them home. I sure could have used the old Red Coaster Wagon I used to have when I was a kid and shopped for my mother. Oh well, someday I'll learn.

Eddie came home at the regular time, supper was on the table by the time he came back from the Community House. We ate and then went to see Auntie and Uncle. I brought them some of the strawberry shortcake. We watched the wrestling matches with them as planned and told them about our plans for going to Mexico the next day.

"Be careful," Uncle warned, "hold on to your pocketbook. People have been known to steal things down there."

"Thanks for the warning," Eddie said. "Have you been down there?"

"Oh yes," Auntie said. "It's going to be fun; most people are nice; they try to sell you all kinds of stuff. But Uncle Victor is right; there are some who try to take advantage of people from the states."

We said our 'good-nights', hugged and were on our way. We were satisfied Auntie was feeling much better and we were always appreciative of their sound advice.

CHAPTER 16


"Here we go again," Eddie was outside standing next to the goldfish pond. "Just like on the day we went to Catalina; pea soup fog."

"It'll clear up," I said from the doorway; "you know how it is around here; foggy in the morning and by eleven o'clock the sun's out."

"I know, but I was kind of hoping it would be sunny first thing today for our drive down the coast."

"Come on in," I said, "I've got ham and eggs ready and the toast is about done. I thought we should have a good breakfast before leaving."

"Are you packing a lunch?"

"I think I should," I buttered the toast, "don't you?"

"Yeah, we don't need a lot of stuff," he dipped his toast in the soft egg yolks; "but if we get hungry we can eat in the car."

"How far are we from the Mexican border?" I took another sip of coffee.

"It's not that far, you know, only about one hundred thirty some miles," he took his last mouthful of toast and thought a minute or so. "We could probably get there in about three hours."

"Okay, then," I suggested. "Why don't you go gas up the car and check the tires or whatever while I clean up and fix the lunch. We can leave when you get back."

He gave me a quick peck on the cheek as he was leaving and was back within forty-five minutes. It was just enough time for me to pack the lunch, and for the fog to have lifted a little. I was wearing a straight grey and pink checkered skirt with a pink cap-sleeved blouse, white sandals and a kerchief to hold my hair back. He wore grey trousers and a white shirt with the long sleeves rolled up to below his elbows. He picked up the tin lunch basket and put it in the trunk, "This is it," he said, "let's get going."

This was our first time to drive down Route 101 south from Los Angeles. We had driven from Washington, through Oregon and Northern California but this was new territory. Eddie had picked up a map from the gas station and checked out the directions to San Juan Capistrano which was about 55 miles south from Torrance. We didn't know much about this mission except from a song we had heard when we were kids: 'When the Swallows Come Back to Capistrano' written by Leon René. We were curious about this place.

"I don't remember where I read it," I said, "but this article I was reading told about how every year, on Saint Joseph's Feast Day (March 19), the Swallows return to Capistrano from their winter home in Goya, Argentina."

"That's in South America," Eddie remarked. "That has to be all of 6,000 miles from here."

"It's amazing that such small creatures can find their way between both places, and have the stamina to make such a long journey."

"I agree," he laughed, "we're having trouble finding the place and we've only gone about 40 miles."

"According to the map we have to look for a turn off this road and head toward San Juan Road," I refolded the map on my lap. "I hope there are signs to tell us which way to go."

We need not have been concerned; our turn was marked well ahead of time and we arrived in San Juan Capistrano around 11 o'clock. We drove through the small town. It wasn't hard to find the Mission; it was the tallest building around. The designated parking was on the street. Eddie turned our car diagonally to face the white stucco wall surrounding the area. The entrance was a six foot wide opening in the wall with a tall pointed arch and a cross on top. The wide gravel path inside was bordered on both sides with football sized rocks. It was large enough to accommodate a car but there were no vehicles on the Mission grounds. We saw graceful Palm trees and tropical plants everywhere. There was an old, long, Spanish style building reminiscent of a monastery, with a series of arches along both sides of the walkway. The ruins along the inner side looked like there may have been workshops or stores flourishing in the Mission at some time in the past. The walkway led to the tall Mission Church where Father Juan Junipero Serra had once said Mass. This was the seventh Mission established by Father Serra in California. There were pews on both sides of the chapel, separated by a center aisle, leading to the altar. Behind the altar, the wall was ornately decorated in Baroque style art with hand carved cherry wood with gold overlay. There were small window-like niches displaying statues of saints. To the left of the altar, against the wall, near the first rows of pews was an ornate canopied wooden pulpit which was accessed by a narrow eight foot semi-circular staircase.

"Funny, you know," I sat in the front pew for a few minutes. "I can almost picture the priest up there giving his sermon; his voice bouncing off the canopy and reaching all the way to the back of the church."

"Leave it to you," he took my hand, "I agree this place is more than I ever expected; but I can wait until Sunday before I listen to another sermon. Come on, let's go see what else there is around here."

The cemetery was next to the chapel and, a short distance away, there was a large cement enclosure filled with water with colourful fish swimming around and graceful lily pads floating here and there. Plants and flowers grew profusely around the low outer rim. Deeper into the property we saw the ruins of the Old Stone Church which had been destroyed by an earthquake in 1812. We were surprised to see small mud nests among the stones in the ruins as well as hanging on the outer walls of the chapel. There were tiny elusive birds of blue and white, and a few with a peach colored breast hovering about the nests. When I asked one of the groundskeepers about them, he told us these were the Swallows who return each year to find and reclaim their nests from the previous year.

"They've been doing this for a couple of hundred years," he said.

"They're smaller than I expected," I observed. "What are those large white birds we saw near the chapel?"

The groundskeeper adjusted his brimmed straw hat. "Those are Pigeons; they don't go anywhere. The little ones over here are Swallows."

"I noticed the Pigeons like to hang around the visitors," Eddie said.

"They go wherever the food is," he smiled. "Here, let me get you guys some seed."

He disappeared into a wooden garden house for a few minutes and returned with a small paper sack half full of seeds. "Here, go on over to the gravel path and hold these in your hand, you'll see how fast those Pigeons come to you. Have fun!" He was gone.

The caretaker was right. We walked back toward the entrance and we crouched near the large stones on the gravel path. With an open hand full of seeds the Pigeons were literally eating out of our hands. We moved to another spot as we continued toward the exit and the Pigeons came right along with us. We were friends forever (as long as the seeds held out).

"I read the sign over near the chapel; it says this is the oldest building in California," I said.

"They've done a lot of restoration," Eddie looked around, "but there's still a lot more to be done."

"You're right," I nodded toward the chapel, "but there's not much they can do to improve the inside of the church; especially that 400 year old Baroque wall behind the altar. Now that is really something!"

"I suppose we should get going," Eddie suggested. "We still have another 75 miles or so before we get to the Mexican border."

"We may as well," I agreed, "the seeds are gone and the Pigeons are bored with us anyway."

Eddie took my hand and we walked toward the car. We stopped under the arch at the entrance and looked back. "This is a holy place," I said, "I'm glad we came here."

"I am too." There were more cars parked on the street than when we had arrived. Eddie took his place behind the wheel and started the engine. "Look at that blue sky; you'd never guess how foggy it was this morning."

"I know; it's amazing how few clouds there are up there. How long do you figure it'll take us to get to Mexico?" I asked.

"No more than two hours, I figure."

"According to this map, we should be going through San Diego; are you planning to stop there?"

"I don't think so," he said. "We stayed in Capistrano a little longer than I figured; when I see a nice spot we'll stop for lunch and then drive directly to Tijuana."

I think he has a sixth sense regarding travel directions. The highway followed the coastline for much of the way and of course provided scenic viewing areas at various intervals. "Point Loma," Eddie read the sign "Check the map to see what's over there?"

"Sure," I noticed the sign indicated a turn toward the coast. "The writing is small, but there's a picture of a lighthouse."

"Let's check it out," he turned onto a narrower road that led toward the ocean. We saw another sign: 'Ballast Point Lighthouse', "I guess we just have to follow this road."

He was right, of course, the road ended when we reached a wide, white, horizontal wooden fence on two sides with an opening in the center, large enough for vehicles to go through. There was a car parked facing the fence so we decided to do the same. A large sign at the entrance read 'Ballast Point Light Station'. We didn't see any 'NO TRESPASSING' signs and saw a few people walking around in the yard so we figured it would be okay to have a look. The point of land extended into the ocean and we could see a large city across the bay. There was a large square two story building with one window on three sides of the first level and double windows on three sides of the second level. Above the second level there was an octagonal, peaked, red roofed tower with a low wooden fence on all the outer edges which housed the light. This structure was attached to a two story residence with attractive landscaping including flower beds, a lawn and palm trees. There was another residence on the property and a small boathouse. While we were standing in front of the tower a gentleman walked over to us.

"Hi," he adjusted his green, narrow brimmed, cotton fishing hat. "Are you new around here?"

Eddie extended his hand, "Yeah, I'm Eddie; we're from Massachusetts. This is quite a place; are you the Lighthouse Keeper?"

"Yes, my name is Jack. I live in this house near the tower," he motioned toward the red roofed tower building. "My friend, Frank and his family live in that house over there," he pointed to the house closest to the entrance. "We share the responsibilities around here. He has the day off today."

"Hi, I'm Jeanne," I shook his hand too. "This looks like a peaceful location to live."

202

"For the most part it is," he admitted. "But when we get a big storm it takes both of us to make sure the generator keeps working to keep the light on, and the bell on the second level of the tower has to be rung when the visibility is bad."

"That sounds busy all right. What's that city on the other side of the bay?" Eddie asked.

"San Diego," he said," during storms those waters can get more than a little treacherous and we are kept pretty busy. Come on, it's pretty quiet today, let me show you around."

The blue Pacific water washed lazily upon the golden sand along all three sides of the peninsula. "Are you headed for San Diego?" Jack wanted to know.

"Actually we would like to make it all the way to Mexico," Eddie told him.

"You shouldn't have any problem with that," Jack said, "it's only about 45 minutes from here."

"We don't really plan to stay very long," I said. "We want to get back to Torrance tonight."

"There's a lot to see down there," he nodded his head. "You won't see it all in just a couple of hours."

"I guess we'll just have to come back this way again," Eddie decided, "next time we'll stop in San Diego and then go directly to Mexico earlier in the day."

Jack walked us back to our car, "it was good to meet you guys." The men shook hands. "Drive safe."

"This was an unexpected bonus," Eddie said as he sat behind the wheel. "I've never been this close to a lighthouse before."

"I guess they don't get many visitors," I remarked, "I don't imagine the lighthouse keeper would be able to give a grand tour to large crowds of people."

"We were lucky to be there at the right time; Jack really knows his stuff."

It didn't take long to get back on the highway to Mexico. "I'm getting hungry," I said. "How about stopping at the next viewing area?"

"We're almost in San Diego; shall I look for a park over there?"

"I really don't care where we stop," I was getting a little irritated. "I don't know how you can go so long without eating and going to a rest room."

"Okay, okay, I get it," he replied. "I'll see what I can do."

We came through San Diego, as he had predicted, and found a park with picnic benches and rest rooms. He pulled in the small parking area and brought the picnic basket from the trunk and placed it on one of the tables. I didn't see a sign with a name for the park but it was near the water and had a few palm trees scattered here and there. I have to admit food was a great remedy for my malaise, and the lemonade improved my attitude.

"This is a nice spot," Eddie munched on his baloney sandwich and picked at the tomato and cucumber wedges. "It's always nice when we can sit by the water."

"It seems wherever we go, here in California, the scenery is beautiful."

"I agree," he sipped his lemonade. "We should be in Tijuana in about ten minutes. I think I'll gas up before we leave here and we should be all right for the ride back home."

"Good idea." I picked up the wrappers and cups and put them back in the basket before Eddie returned it to the trunk.

There was a bit of traffic but we moved along steadily and arrived in Tijuana in about 15 minutes. We didn't have a problem crossing the border; we each showed our driver's license and the customs agent waved us through. It was close to 4 o'clock when we drove into town.

"We won't be able to stay very long," Eddie said as he looked for a place to park on the street. "It will take us a good three hours to get home."

"I guess we can see quite a bit in a couple of hours," I looked at my watch. "If we leave by six we should be okay."

He found a spot in front of a leather shop. "We'll just have to remember where we left the car."

"Don't forget to lock it," I warned, "I don't really relish the thought of having to walk home."

"Neither do I," Eddie put the car keys in his pocket. "Let's go in this leather shop first."

The shop keeper was working on a hand tooled purse. There were many different styles on sale. It was interesting to see the way he made beautiful designs on the leather. Some were floral designs and some were animals all carved by hand with tools that looked like a chisel and a small hammer. The purses were held together with strips of rawhide woven through holes that had been punched with an awl. It was incredible workmanship.

"Hey, Sweetheart, look," Eddie pointed to a sign on the sidewalk. "There's going to be a bullfight to night."

"Let's walk down toward the arena," I suggested.

"We can do that," Eddie said, "but we won't be able to go in; the sign says the show starts at 7 o'clock; we wouldn't get home until around one in the morning."

"Well," I was disappointed, "at least we'll see where the fights are and maybe next time we come they'll have contests in the afternoon."

There were many different types of shops: A Spanish dressmaking store which specialized in colorful tiered skirts and matching off the shoulder blouses, another featured hand crocheted lace scarves and doilies, and, of course many Mexican food stands where there was a variety of tacos, enchiladas and fajitas. As we were walking hand in hand through the city, a little boy, about 7 or 8 years old approached Eddie and tugged on his sleeve. He stayed close to Eddie keeping pace with him for a few steps then tugged again and said something to Eddie. Eddie did not let go of my hand.

"Uh, no thanks," Eddie said and pulled me quickly away from the boy in another direction.

"What was that all about?" I asked.

"He wanted me to meet his sister," he answered.

"What?" I turned to see if the boy was still there. He wasn't. "What did he say?"

"He told me, 'my seesta, she give you one good time,'" he said.

I was at a loss for words. "It must be close to 6 o'clock."

"You know!" he remarked, "even if it's not, I think I'm ready to leave this place for now."

"Me too," I looked at my watch again. "It's already 5:30, by the time we get to the car it'll be time for us to head home."

We had no problem re-entering the United States. We showed the border guard our birth certificates and Massachusetts driver's licenses. We hadn't bought anything so we didn't have to deal with customs. The guard waved us on back to California. We followed the signs pointing toward L.A. and began our trek northward. It didn't take long for us to get through San Diego. We passed through small towns and open areas.

"There's a police car behind us," Eddie said. "He's been following us for awhile."

"I wonder why? You weren't speeding."

"We'll soon find out," the police car flashed its lights and Eddie pulled over to the side of the road and rolled the window down on the driver's side. There were no other cars on this stretch of the road.

"You're a long way from home," the officer looked in, as if to see what we might be hiding in the back seat. "May I see your driver's license?"

Eddie obliged.

205

"Please step out of the car and open your trunk," the officer stepped back toward the rear of the vehicle.

Eddie stepped out and unlocked the trunk, "What's wrong?" he wanted to know. "I know I wasn't speeding."

I was too nervous to stay in the car.

"Where are you coming from?"

"Tijuana," Eddie answered.

"What were you doing there?" he asked.

"Just visiting," Eddie said. "It's our first time in Mexico; we were only there a couple of hours."

"Did you meet anyone there?" He moved the picnic basket and poked his head around the trunk.

"Not really," Eddie closed the trunk.

"Tell him about the little boy," I said.

"What little boy?" the officer looked in the back seat again.

"I don't think that's important," Eddie commented, "he was just trying to drum up business for his sister and we didn't pay any attention to him."

"That's not uncommon down there," the officer said, "actually, I'm checking to see if you have any Wetbacks."

"Wetbacks? What's a 'wetback'?" I looked at Eddie. "What does he mean?"

The officer adjusted his cap, looked at me and shook his head. "It means you haven't got any."

"Wetbacks are Mexicans who are trying to get across the border illegally," Eddie explained.

"Yes," the officer opened the door for me. "They often hide in out of state cars."

Eddie got back in the car. "Are we okay to go?"

"Where are you headed?" He asked.

"We live in Torrance," Eddie said.

"You still have a couple of hours to go. Have a safe trip home," he tipped his cap and walked back to the police car.

206

Dusk soon turned to dark. The road was good and the traffic was light. Everything looks different at night. We listened and occasionally sang along with the music on the radio.

"It's good to see the lights of the trailer park," Eddie said as we drove down our street.

"It won't take us long to get to sleep tonight," I said. "You must be tired after all that driving."

"It wasn't so bad," he pulled the picnic stuff out of the trunk. "We saw a lot of great things today."

"Are you hungry?" I put the small block of ice from the picnic basket into the icebox. "There are still a couple of sandwiches."

"Nah, let's just have graham crackers and milk," he wiped out the basket and put it away. "Shall I set the alarm for church tomorrow?"

"Auntie said Albert and Bonnie invited us all to dinner at their house tomorrow," I reminded him. "So maybe we should go to a later Mass in San Pedro? What do you think?"

"Great! No alarm," he sat at the table and buttered his crackers. "Let's finish our snack and get to bed."


It was good to see Auntie Bina feeling well again. We met her and Uncle Victor at church and followed them home after Mass. "Bonnie is expecting us around 2 o'clock," Auntie said, "she's preparing a ham dinner and says she wants to play Hi-Lo-Jack after we eat."

"Are you up to it?" Eddie asked.

"What! Girls against the guys?" she laughed. "You haven't got a chance; get your nickels ready."

Eva's son Bill and his wife Elaine dropped in for a short visit to see his Mom and his sister Loretta; they all decided to go to the beach. "Hey, it was good to see you guys," Bill said as they were leaving. "It's been a while."

"I know," Eddie shook Bill's hand. "With both of us working and your Grandma being sick, it's been kind of tough for us to get together."

"Well, she's feeling better now," Bill looked over at her, "let us know when it's a good time for all of us to come over."

"Okay," Auntie gave him and Elaine a hug, "we'll make it soon."

**207**

Loretta was laden down with straw mats and beach towels to put in Bill's trunk. Elaine and Bill sat in the front and Eva and her daughter sat in the back.

"Come on, Uncle," Eddie walked over to our car. "I'll drive."

As usual, Bonnie was the perfect hostess and the dinner was scrumptious. I felt like family because she allowed me to help her clean up the kitchen before we settled down to play cards. The guys won the first game and the girls won the last two out of three. Auntie Bina beamed.

"Come on," she held out her hand, "put those nickels right here." It was good to see her looking so much better.

"We should get going," Uncle Victor said.

"Oh sure," Auntie teased. "You just can't stand losing."

Everyone laughed. "Nobody's going anywhere until I serve my apple pie and ice cream," Bonnie announced. "Albert, you collect the cards and Jeanne will bring out the dessert plates and forks."

"Only a small piece for me," Auntie said, "I'm still watching what I eat."

"Whatever you're doing seems to be working," Albert said. "You'd never know by looking at you today, how sick you've been."

"And I want to keep it that way," she passed on the ice cream too.

The rest of us ate with gusto and left shortly afterward.

"It's been a great day," Eddie said when we dropped Auntie and Uncle off in San Pedro. "We'll give you a call during the week."

We were home by 8 o'clock. Eddie had to get his work clothes ready for the next day.            "No snacks tonight," I picked up the dishes from the drying rack and put them away. "I think we ate enough for two days."

"I said it before and I'll say it again, that Bonnie sure can cook."

"You'll get no argument from me." I sorted out the laundry in preparation for the next day's chores.

Eddie hadn't read the Sunday paper before we went to Mass. He picked up the front section.

"The Korean War is still in the headlines," he said. "I wonder if they'll ever get that conflict resolved."

"I don't know what the difference is between a conflict and a war," I put the laundry basket on the floor. "It seems to me, though, that things aren't going so well over there since Truman took General MacArthur out of there."

"I think Truman was afraid MacArthur was being too pushy and his tactics might get us into another World War with the Soviet Union and China."

"Who's in charge over there now?" I asked. "And what's this 38th parallel they're always talking about?"

"That's the division between Soviet backed North Korea, led by Communist Kim Il Sung, and pro-western South Korea which is led by Syngman Rhee," Eddie explained. "General Ridgeway is now in command over there and, with the help of NATO has succeeded to push the North Koreans back behind the 38th parallel." He put the paper down and looked at me, "I don't care what they call it, a war or a conflict, men and women are still getting killed over there."

"I know, I was thinking about your brother, Bob, it's possible he could be called into that mess."

"Don't think that hasn't come to my mind." He folded the paper. "It's time for bed."

"Are Baloney sandwiches okay for lunch today?" I poured hot coffee into the thermos.

"Sure, Baloney sandwiches are always okay," he pulled his plaid work shirt out of the drawer and put it on. "You can throw in a few cookies with that too."

"Weekends seem to go by so fast, don't they," I closed his lunch bag.

"Yeah, they do," he plopped his striped, railroad engineer styled cap on his head; "but we manage to do a lot of different things in just a couple of days."

"You're right about that," I walked him out to the car.

"I'll see you tonight." He kissed me on the lips.

I went back into the trailer, cleaned up the breakfast dishes and gathered up the laundry. I picked up a box of stationery and a little pile of unanswered mail and then headed for the Community House. It was a wonderful time to catch up on writing letters while I waited for the wash to get done. There was a lot to write about. Neither of our families had ever been much farther west than New York and some not even that far. I wrote about our visits to Capistrano mission and the lighthouse. I mentioned our short trip to Mexico but did not mention a word about Eddie's young enterprising friend. Some things are better left unsaid. It was sufficient to talk about the aroma of Mexican food which permeated the air and the amazing craftsmanship of the shopkeepers in Tijuana. My mother said she found our letters very interesting. She wrote wonderful letters and was always very conscientious in reporting news of the family. 'When are you coming home?' was her most frequent question. She was also faithful about forwarding important mail as promptly as she could. So far, nothing earth shattering had occurred over there which would require our immediate attention. Eddie's mother had written that Eddie's Godchild Bruce, who had just turned five, and who was a huge fan of 'Howdy Doody', was preparing to enter kindergarten. Letters about our nieces and nephews always make me nostalgic. The timing was good. By the time the dryer buzzed the end of the cycle, I was done with my correspondence: signed, sealed, addressed, stamped and mailed at the desk. I carried the basket of clean laundry back to the trailer. It was a good morning's work done. I had barely enough time to put the towels, socks and underwear in their proper drawers when, as I was getting ready to set up the ironing board, Julie knocked on the door. I opened it. "Hi, come on in."

"Did Joan tell you she and Jessie are buying a house?" She seemed to be upset.

"She told me they were looking at homes in Torrance," I moved the pile of ironing to the sofa and then put a pot of coffee on the hot plate. "I guess they've decided not to go back to Texas."

"She said the oil company made Jessie a great offer so they're looking to buy a place out here," Julie crossed her arms and rested them on the table.

"I'm going to miss them," I set out the sugar and cream, mugs and napkins.

"So am I," Julie put sugar and cream in her empty mug; "maybe, if they find a place in town, they might still come to visit."

"That would be good," I leaned against the counter. "That's the problem with living in a trailer park; you just get to know people and you get to like them and then they move away."

"That's true," she stirred the cream and sugar pensively. "You and Eddie will probably do the same thing." She looked up, "your family is all back in Massachusetts isn't it?"

"Yes it is, but we really like it out here." I set out a plate of Lorna Doone cookies. "It wouldn't take much to convince us to stay."

"Aren't you having a Stanley Party this week?"

"Yes, on Thursday," I was glad she changed the subject. "Joan has the day off; she said she'll come." I poured the coffee.

"That's good," Julie took a sip from her cup. "She hasn't been around much since she started her new job."

"Things change," I looked up at her, "I've been thinking about getting a job."

"Darryl and I talked about that too," she put her elbow on the table and held her chin in her hand. "We could both go tomorrow; I can drive Darryl to work and keep the car."

"Okay," I picked up a cookie. "I'll look through the ads in today's paper and see what's available."

"I'm getting excited already."Julie said. "What time is it?" she looked at her watch. "I've got to go."

I finished my cup of coffee and ate my cookie before putting the cups in the sink. I decided to wash them later. I pulled out the ironing board to finish pressing the freshly laundered clothes before putting them away. I made corned beef hash for supper and Eddie and I spent a quiet evening playing Rummy and listening to the radio.


Eddie wanted Cheerios for breakfast. That was quick and easy. I packed his lunch and filled his thermos. It was a beautiful morning; I was still in my bathrobe when I walked with him to the car. I decided not to mention my intention to go job-seeking today and went up to the Community House as soon as he left. Julie was at the door around 9:30 a.m. and we were off to Los Angeles armed with the 'Help Wanted' section of the paper. My previous experience at work had been calculating piece-work payroll in a dress manufacturing shop in Fall River. Julie's experience was nil. We went together to a few places that were looking for office clerks, and then we applied to a couple of companies looking for experienced workers. We didn't qualify for anything, anywhere.

After our eighth attempt I decided it was time to go home, "I guess we'll just have to leave our job search for another day." I led the way back to the car.

"Maybe my mother is right," Julie sat behind the wheel and started the engine, "she keeps telling me I should go back to school to learn typing or something."

"Not a bad idea," I commented, "you're not that long out of high school. I bet a business college would be a good place to learn office skills."

"What about you?"

"Eddie and I want a family," I told Julie, "and if we do go back east, I know I can get my old job back."

"There you go," she shook her head, "talking about going back east again."

"Never mind that," it was my turn to change the subject. "I've got a Stanley party to plan for; can we stop at the market on our way home?"

"Sure," she seemed to perk up. "Is the market near home okay?"

"Oh yes, they have pretty much everything." I took a pad and pencil from my purse. "Now, let me see, what will I need for this party anyway? Give me some hints; after all you were the one who talked me into this."

"Moi?" she tried to look innocent. "It wasn't me, it was that new resident, or should I say that salesman at the Community House; he offered to shake YOUR hand first."

"Yes, Mr. Larsen, but when he told us about the Stanley products and the party, YOU were the one who said it would be easy to get people to come and it would be fun."

"As a matter fact, I still think it will be fun and I'm looking forward to seeing this Stanley stuff that isn't sold in stores. I've never been to a house party that sells its products directly to the customers in their homes," she drove into the parking lot of the market, "and Mr. Larsen did say everybody present will get a gift, who knows; we might even like the stuff."

"Okay, okay, I get it!" I admitted. "New product, new sales promotion, games, free gifts and so forth…now help me prepare a list for this shindig."


Thursday turned out to be a hot afternoon, in the low nineties. I had all the windows open. Julie had been right about getting guests to come. We were a group of eight

212

people, including Joan, in our small trailer. We squeezed five people in the breakfast nook and three on the sofa.

Mr. Larsen lined the Stanley products on the counter. He explained the purpose of each one. There were silver polishes, floor cleaners, and every kind of cleaner one could possibly think of for the upkeep of anything from dishes to furniture and cabinets. He showed us how easy it was to clean the kettle, the table, the naugahide and the cabinets. We played several games, he booked another party with one of the guests, and then he presented me with a lovely hostess gift of a silver plate salad set. All those present received various samples of give-away Stanley products or some type of brush. A few of the ladies had questions for Mr. Larsen while he tallied up the orders and then began packing his wares into his large black rectangular case: "Are these products fully guaranteed?" "Can we have our money back if the stuff doesn't work like you say?" "If I like the product how can I reorder?" "Will you accept a check?"

"When can we expect our orders?" I asked.

"In about three weeks," he turned to the ladies, "I prefer a cash payment and you can pay your hostess for what you purchased. I will collect the money from her when I bring the merchandise."

"That sounds easy enough," I remarked. "Now, Mr. Larsen, please join us in a little snack before you leave."

"As soon as I tally these orders, it will be my pleasure," he said.

I had prepared lemonade and small sandwiches of tuna salad and ham and cheese, and a tray of sliced cucumbers, celery and carrot sticks. Of course the old standby of sugar cookies was available for dessert. I waited until the presentation was over before I pulled the goodies out of the icebox. In spite of the hot day, there was a slight breeze and we were comfortable. Mr. Larsen didn't stay very long after his drink of lemonade. He gathered his orders and his case and was gone. A couple of the ladies were Julie's friends; one of them had booked a party. They chatted with her while munching on the snacks and then they left together. The other neighbors went home soon after. Joan lingered for a little while longer.

"Can I help you clean up?" she offered.

"There's not much to do," I put the used paper plates in the waste basket. "Sit and talk to me while I prepare some potato salad for supper. Tell me about your new job."

"Sure," she sat at the table. "I like it a lot. I'm the receptionist in an insurance office and I get to meet new people every day."

"That sounds interesting," I rinsed the peeled potatoes and put them on the hot plate to boil, "do you have to sell insurance too?"

"No, the salesmen do that," she explained, "but I do accept premiums when customers come in."

213

"Julie and I went job hunting this week but we didn't have any luck." I said.

"Don't get discouraged; it took a few times of trying for me, before I got this job."

"I know I'll try again." I put ice on the cooked potatoes, drained them and added the onions and stuff to the salad and then cooled it in the ice box. "There, with the few leftover sandwiches and veggies, this will be a nice cool supper for Eddie after having worked in the hot sun all day."

"What time will he get home?" she wanted to know.

"He usually gets home about four thirty."

"Why don't you guys come on over to watch TV after you eat?" she suggested.

"That's a great idea, Eddie loves TV, and he always likes to visit with Jessie. I've got plenty of lemonade, I'll bring some over."

"Great!" she started toward the door, "we'll see you later."

As it turned out Eddie worked overtime and didn't get home until after 6. He took the time to shower and welcomed the light meal and the cool breeze of the early evening. It was a little after seven when we got to Jessie and Joan's trailer. The Jack Benny show was already in progress.

"Hey, there you are," Joan said, "we're glad you could come."

"I had to work a little overtime," Eddie said, "you know how that is."

"It's okay," Joan said, "it's been a while since we've been able to get together."

"Thanks," I handed her the lemonade and some napkins I had brought over, "I'm afraid we'll see each other a lot less when you move away."

She filled our glasses, "There's a bowl of pretzels on the counter, Jeanne; will you put it on the coffee table."

"We're going to miss you guys," Jessie said.

"It won't be the same around here without you," I took a sip of lemonade.

"We won't be that far away," Joan offered, "you can still come over and watch TV."

"With both of you working," I observed, "it may be a little difficult to find a convenient time for visiting."

"I'm glad for you, though," Eddie said, "we've thought about settling down out here too but, there's still the threat of the draft for me in Massachusetts; and if that happens we won't have a choice. We'll have to go back east."

"Yeah," Jessie reached for a pretzel, "I'm a little older than you so I'm not concerned about that."

"Hey! Never mind that gloomy talk." Joan commanded. "Let's enjoy being with each other while we can and make the decision to stay in touch."

"Amen!" we toasted with our lemonade glasses and continued to watch TV.

The Jack Benny show was just ending. In his deadpan fashion, he said: "Say good night Gracie."

She answered "Good night Gracie," there were roars of laughter and the show was over.

"I always liked Jack Benny on radio but on TV he's even funnier," I remarked. "He doesn't even have to say a word; just his blank look is hysterical."

"There's a new show we've been watching," Jessie said. "It's 'Dragnet' starring Jack Webb and Harry Morgan."

"It's pretty good," Joan added, "the stories are supposed to be about real people and real events."

"That sounds interesting," Eddie munched on another pretzel. "We may as well stay to watch it before saying good night." Which is what we did.

It was a clear night. Eddie held my hand and we were quiet as we walked up to the Community Room before going home. He opened the door to the trailer and we went in. "You don't have much to say," he let me go in first.

"No, I was thinking about Jessie and Joan's decision to settle in California and I guess I'm torn between wanting to stay here too but concerned that we may not be able to." I reflected a little, "and, of course, I think about how much I miss my mother and my family."

"We've been talking about having kids," he took my chin in his hand and turned my face toward him. "This would be a great place to raise a family."

"I can't argue that," I looked in his eyes, "but I can't help wondering if that's ever going to happen."

"I think both our mothers are storming the heavens for us," he chuckled. "How can it NOT happen?" There was a twinkle in his eyes, "in the meantime, let's see what I can do to help move their prayers along." He opened the sofa, grinned at me and lifted the sheet, "Après vous, Madame."


Friday's usual routine was to visit Aunt Bina and Uncle Victor to watch the wrestling matches. This week was no exception. We ate a quick supper of grilled cheese sandwiches and Campbell's tomato soup before heading over to San Pedro. Eva and

Loretta were there and Loretta volunteered to make a bowl of popcorn for munching during the exciting bouts and some of the not so exciting ones. We looked forward to these Friday evenings. Auntie always got so excited over the matches, often yelling during the entanglements: 'Fake! Fake! It's all a fake!' Her favorite wrestler was Baron Leone who, in her eyes, could do no wrong. He strutted around the ring with his long wavy hair brushing his caped shoulders, and then he settled in his corner before removing the embroidered cape to begin the match. Each near pinning of his opponent was an occasion for the Baron to strut around arrogantly some more before getting back to the business of wrestling and finally pinning his opponent to win. Auntie didn't particularly like Gino Garibaldi or Gorgeous George, she called them show-offs. These evenings always flew by and drew cheers and jeers from our small devoted group of wrestling fans, this Friday was no exception.

"The wife and I are going to the Pomona State Fair on Sunday," Eddie announced as we were leaving. "Does anyone want to come with us?"

"I'm sorry," Uncle answered, "I'd really like to but I've kind of neglected some stuff around here while your Auntie was sick, and I plan to do some 'catch up' while I can."

"I understand," Eddie said, "we want to go early and make a day of it."

"You'll have a good time," Uncle walked us to our car, "It's the largest fair in the country, and maybe the largest in the world. We've been there before and there's a lot to see."

"We'll catch up with you during the week and tell you all about it," I hugged Uncle Victor.

"Sounds good to me," he closed the car door. "Have fun."

Eddie had to work on Saturday, which was unusual. It turned out to be a good day for me to work in the yard. The roses on the trellis needed trimming and the flower gardens needed weeding. Yard work took up a large part of the day. We had a light supper when he came home from work and then we went out to see movie in Torrance. Jane Powell and Wendell Corey and Vic Damone were starring in the musical 'Rich Young and Pretty'. One of the songs featured in the movie was 'Deep in the Heart of Texas'. Neither Eddie nor I realized Wendell Corey could sing, yet there he was, in his mustachioed best, singing a duet: 'The stars at night are big and bright...clap-clap-clap- clapping' away right along with cute little Jane in her soprano voice. It was a fun movie and as always we enjoyed the Movietone News and a cartoon, this time it was Betty Boop.

"I'll set the alarm for seven," Eddie said as we were having our cocoa and grahams.

"Okay, I can get a quick shower before we go to church." I kissed him before he went to bed and I finished cleaning up the cups and plates before turning off the lights.

Eddie woke up before the alarm and was up and dressed before I rolled out of bed at seven o'clock. He had picked up a copy of the Torrance Herald and settled down to read it while I went to shower at the Community House. Mr. Early Bird was always ready, often before the crack of dawn. He was also au courant of the most recent events of the day. I liked the funnies. I was ready to leave on time for the eight o'clock mass. He was wearing gray trousers and a yellow short-sleeved shirt. I had on a red polka dot sundress with a white bolero and a white beanie and sandals. Mass was short and we had time for a leisurely breakfast at home before leaving for the 50 mile ride to Pomona around ten. We headed northeast which was new territory for us but the scenery did not disappoint. There were flowers and palm trees in great profusion and lovely homes along the way. The Pomona State Fair was an annual event held in September or October every year on what used to be a beet farm. The Fairground consists of 543 acres of land and impossible to take in on only one visit. The first thing we saw was a large arch with 'Fun Zone' spelled out in neon lights at the entrance to the carnival area where there was a huge Ferris wheel which could be seen from almost anywhere at the fair. There were flower gardens and small ethnic villages scattered throughout. In the Mexican village we saw a tall four sided clock tower. It looked like it was built out of tan colored stucco; the walls seemed to curve inward; I really don't know how tall it was but it looked to be about 40 feet high.

In the livestock area there were pens for sheep, cows, pigs and poultry that would be competing in blue ribbon contests. The best cooks in the county displayed their best preserves and pickles on tables in numbered Mason jars ready to be judged. Not to be outdone the bakers also had their best pies and cakes on display numbered and ready for judging. It was a hot afternoon and it looked like the judges were about to start the judging for the baked goods but we didn't wait for the final results.

There was a horse racing track but we opted not to go. There was so much more to see. We came to an area where a huge ski jump was being prepared. When we first saw it, it was a high, bare, wooden structure built on top of interwoven slats like you'd see supporting an old fashioned piazza or a high roller coaster. There were people at the very top and we assumed there must have been stairs or some sort of elevator behind the platform but we couldn't see it from where we stood. There were huge 500 pound cakes of ice which were fed into a machine to be ground up into snow and then blown onto the molded wooden slope. People with tamps and rakes moved and smoothed the soft snow to even it out all over the wood. It took several hours for the ski jump to be covered with this man-made snow. The in run area was a wide, smooth, slightly sloped section where the skiers could generate speed to reach the jump area where they jumped off and became airborne over the sharp, snowy decline in an attempt to land as close as possible to the landing slope near the bottom at ground level where they would come to a stop. The skiers who were going to use this slope were aspiring to qualify for the 1952 Olympics in Oslo. It was the highest and the largest man-made ski slope in the world. It took several hours for it to be completed. It was an interesting project to watch; we stayed there for a while and then walked around to see the judging of the various animal contests and came back to the slope to check the progress. As the project moved along to completion, some skiers wearing tee-shirts appeared on the slope and stomped down sideways, using their skis to help tamp down the snow. It was an awesome sight to see this mini-mountain of snow in this 85 degree afternoon with palm trees and flowers in the not so distant back-ground. The area began to fill up with spectators in the mid afternoon as it got closer to

217

the time of the competition. We watched a few skiers do a trial run but we decided to leave before we got swallowed up in the crowd.

"Let's go see if we can find a hot dog stand," Eddie said, "I'm getting sort of hungry."

"I think I saw one near the Spanish village," I was getting hungry too. "I'd like to walk through that little village before we go home."

"Let's check out what kind of food they have over there, maybe they've got tacos," he took my hand and led me toward the little food stand. "Hey, here's something different: 'Tortilla Espanola'"

"It looks like a taco with eggs inside." I asked the server, "What's in the filling?"

"Potatoes, onions and spinach whipped with eggs," the man said.

We looked at each other, "why not?"

We watched the man make the omelets and fill the soft, warm tortillas, he handed them to us in paper napkins and I went to find us a seat at one of the small tables while Eddie paid him and picked up two root beer sodas.

"This is different," I said.

"It needs a little hot sauce," Eddie reached for the bottle of Tabasco sauce on the table, "you want some?"

I nodded, "this is good stuff," I took the bottle and sprinkled a few drops on my tortilla.

"This has been an interesting afternoon," he took a sip from his cup of root beer. "I think after we finish eating we can look around the rest of this area and then make our way to the parking lot; is that okay with you?"

"Oh yeah, it's been a great day," I took another bite of my tortilla, "but I'm ready to go home."

"Did you want to go to the movies before going home?" he asked.

"No," I finished up my root beer, "maybe we can play cards for awhile and by the time you get your clothes ready for work tomorrow it'll be time for bed."

"I guess you're right," we started out toward the parking area. "It'll take us about an hour to get home; by the time we go to the Community house and back to the trailer we may not even feel like playing cards."

We listened to music on the way home. The road always looks different when it's dark. The traffic was light and, as it often happens, the way home seemed shorter than our trip going to the fair. It had been a great day but we were ready to call it a night soon after we got back.

218

"Do you have any plans for the day?" Eddie asked as he poured the coffee.

"Not really," I buttered the toast, "Julie wants to go to Torrance to get her car checked up and registered. She asked me to go with her."

"Pick up some breakfast sausage on the way back," he suggested. "We haven't had sausage and potatoes and brown gravy for awhile."

"I'm sure Julie won't mind," I put two plates with fried eggs and toast on the table.

"How is that job coming along?" I wanted to know, "is it almost finished?"

"I'd say there's maybe two more weeks before we top it off," he said. "The boss at Bethlehem Steel asked me to stay on with them after this job is done."

"And, are you planning to?" I took a sip of coffee.

"I haven't decided," he was silent for a few minutes, "Let's wait and see."

He picked up his work hat and lunch bag, he kissed me and was out the door before I could ask any more questions.

I met Julie at her car around 8:30. We first went to the shop where Julie's car checked out okay and she received the papers she needed to get it registered.

"My cousin, Mildred, is expecting us for lunch around noon," she announced, "I hope it doesn't take us long at the Registry."

"If this place is like the one we have back home," I warned, "we'll probably be there for awhile."

The Registry of Motor Vehicles annoyed but did not disappoint. We stood in line for more than an hour and a half before Julie was able to get her car registered.

"Hallelujah!" she exclaimed. "It's only 11:45; we won't be keeping Millie waiting too long."

"Do you want me to help you put the new plates on?" I offered.

"No," she put them in the trunk. "Darryl can install them when he gets home."

We drove straight to Millie's house where she had chicken and rice soup and tuna salad sandwiches on a roll waiting for us as well as a pleasant afternoon. Millie is a quilter and she showed us some of her home sewn pillows and quilts. Her motifs were varied; she displayed a pillow and quilt set in a patriotic theme and another set in different styles of lighthouses. There were sunflowers and wild flowers, and even one quilt

**219**

which depicted embroidered names of members of her family. She did incredibly beautiful work.

"Who are you making all these quilts for?" I was curious.

"I give some away as gifts," she said, "but I also make them to sell when I get special orders and sometimes I donate one or two for our annual church bazaar."

"Didn't I tell you Millie was great?" Julie beamed.

"You didn't exaggerate," I took another look around at the beautiful craftsmanship. "Thanks for lunch; it's been a great afternoon."

Julie hugged her cousin and she accompanied us to the car.

"We'll go straight to the market and then I'll drop you off before I pick up Darryl," Julie said as we started for home.

"Great idea," I said, "if there's any corn on the cob I'll get some of that too."

"I love corn on the cob."

"Would you like to join us for supper?" I asked.

"Thanks but Darryl said he has something going on in L.A. tonight. Sausage and gravy sound great too but I'll have to take a rain check," she drove into a parking space close to the entrance of the market.

"You've got it." I went in and picked up what I needed while she waited in the car. Then she dropped me off at home and was on her way to meet her husband. I unloaded the groceries and got busy. First I put the sausages on to boil while I peeled the potatoes. I drained the meat and set it aside while I cooked the potatoes. I shucked the corn and then browned the sausage. With only two burners to work with on the hot plate I had to cook everything in stages. When the potatoes were cooked, I set them aside in the hot water to keep warm until I was ready to mash them; and then I put the pot of water on to cook the corn. After the sausages were browned I made the gravy.

"Something sure smells good," Eddie said as he came in from work. "Do I have time to clean up before we eat?"

"Sure," I put the plates on the table, "I'll mash the potatoes when you get back; everything else is ready."

He picked up his clean clothes from the sofa and was off in a second. It could have been my imagination, but it seemed to me he was back from the Community House in record time.

"This is really good," he took a bite of sausage. "I was getting my taste buds ready for this all day."

"I have to admit," I put a little more gravy on my mashed potatoes, "this stuff isn't bad at all."

"Is there any more tapioca pudding?" he pushed his empty plate back after his second generous helping.

"Yes," I got up to get the pudding container from the icebox. "Let me get a little bowl from the shelf."

There is no doubt; tapioca pudding was one of his favorites. A cup of coffee topped off the meal. "Do you feel like going to the movies tonight?"

"Sure, give me a few minutes to clean up the dishes." I set the kettle of water to heat while I put the leftovers away. "Someday we're going to have running hot water and dishwashing will go much faster."

"The movies don't start until 6:30 so we still have a little time," he pulled a dish towel from the drawer. "I'm all set to dry when you're ready."

There was a double feature at the Stadium again tonight: 'Cattle Drive' with Joel McCrae who was the trail boss and young Dean Stockwell who started out as the lost bratty kid of a railroad owner. When Dean is found wandering, he learns the hard way, under the guidance of Joel and the other cowboys, how to become a responsible individual. The second feature starred the Bowery Boys with Huntz Hall and Leo Gorcey in 'Let's Go Navy'. It was hilarious throughout. From their antics while swabbing the decks on the ship; to their exotic leave on a tropical island they were constantly befuddling the Captain and their superior officers.

"Do you have any big plans for the rest of the week?" Eddie asked on our way home.

"Not really," I pondered for a few minutes, "I'd really like to clean the fish pond; there are a lot of dead leaves in there."

"That's going to be an all day project."

"I know, I've attempted it a couple of times before but I had to quit because I got started on the project too late in the day."

"Maybe the manager can give you hints on how to go about it," he turned into our trailer park.

"I can ask," it seemed like a good idea. "I'll go up to the Community House early in the morning and see him."

"In the meanwhile," he set the alarm, "let's have some Ritz crackers and cheese and milk before we go to bed."

As usual, Eddie was up before the alarm and was returning from the Community House as I was starting to make breakfast. I made a few potato patties, heated up some sausages and fried a couple of eggs. He made the toast.

"Are you still planning to clean out the fish pond?" Eddie took a bite of toast.

"Yeah," I poured refills in our coffee mugs. "As soon as I get dressed I'll check with the manager for any hints he might have."

"Good luck with that," he finished his breakfast, gave me a quick peck on the cheek and was off to work.

It was my turn to go up to the Community House. I was dressed for work. I wore a short sleeved blue cotton blouse and dungarees and sneakers. It was still too early to see the manager so I got a large galvanized pail and filled it with clean water. I located a pocket net in the storage room and returned to the trailer. I started to pull the fish out from the pond and put them in the bucket. The fish were squirmy and the water was murky but I managed to get them all out along with some goopy stuff that clung to the net. They were a little cramped in there but I hoped to be able to get their pond cleaned up in short order and put them back before they experienced too much discomfort. Then, as Eddie had suggested, I went to see the manager and started to tell him about my wonderful accomplishment.

"You what!" the manager yelled. "You put the fish in a pail? Are you trying to kill them? Of all the asinine…" He stomped into his office as he screamed at me. "Don't do anything else! I'm coming right over there."

True to his word, the manager put his secretary in charge and he was on my heels just as I arrived at the trailer. He headed straight for the pail.

"Those fish will die if you leave them in this bucket." He said sternly.

"But is that dirty water any better?" I yelled back. "I just came to ask for your advice! I didn't expect to be yelled at! Look at all that junk in the water!"

"Okay, okay, calm down," he stood about six feet tall, and was dressed in a long sleeved gray sweatshirt and dungarees. He walked around to examine the pond, "let me get some leaf nets from the storage room so we can clear out this debris. I think the fish will be okay once we get the leaves cleaned up."

He returned within a few minutes, handed me a net and kept one for himself. He proceeded to give me instructions on how to skim the leaves off the surface of the pond.
"Here, hold it like this," he demonstrated, "see how the leaves stay on the net? Then pull it up flat so the leaves don't fall back in the pond." He had brought a large box to deposit the soggy leaves and woody stems.

He skimmed the leaves skillfully off the surface while keeping a close eye on my netting progress, to make sure I was following his directions, and after a while the pond began to look a lot better.

"As long as the fish are still out of the pond, let me check the pump and filter, they could be part of the problem." He lay flat on the ground, pushed his sleeves up, past his elbows, and reached underwater with his two hands. The water reached up his arms almost to his shoulders.

"#@*&#!" He did not look or sound happy. "There's a pile of 'crap' (not the exact word he used) stuck on the filter!" He continued to work with his arms inside the pool, tugging and pulling at whatever was in there and finally maneuvering out some long stringy dark gunk. "Aha!" he said. "Here's the #&*#@#%! This is what's been keeping the water that 'crappy' color." He stood up holding the culprit in his wet hands.

"Yuk!" was all I could say.

He turned to look at me like he had forgotten I was there, "Oh, sorry," he plopped the gunk in the box and then nodded toward the bucket with the fish. "Okay, you can put the whole bucket in the pond and let the fish swim out on their own."

I walked over to the bucket and started to reach for it.

"Wait!" He had a second thought, "Wait, that might be too heavy; let me help you." He lifted it up and gently lowered it into the pond at an angle until it was completely submerged. "See you have to tip it just right so the fish don't get shocked by the temperature of the water." He held it down until all the fish swam out of the pail and began swimming around happily in their somewhat cleaner home.

"It'll take a day or two before the water clears out completely," he pulled his shirt sleeves down but they were still dripping. "I've got to go change my shirt." He carted the nets, the leaves and the gunk back with him up to the Community House.

It had taken us a good part of the morning to clean the pond. Even though the manager had done most of it; I still felt it was a good job done and I know I could never have done it by myself. I decided right then and there that outdoor fish ponds were not going to be a priority in the landscaping of my future home, if we ever were fortunate enough to own a house. This was hard work! It was getting close to lunch time. I felt a little unkempt so I picked out a clean dress from the closet and fresh underpinnings. Armed with a towel and soap I went up to the Community House to shower before going to the market to pick up something to cook for supper.

"Where are you going?" Julie asked as I walked past her trailer on my way back to mine.

"I'm going to the market as soon as I put this stuff away." I still had an armful of dirty clothes wrapped in the towel.

"Did you have lunch yet?" she wanted to know.

"Nah, I figured I'd make a grilled cheese sandwich later." I continued to walk toward our trailer.

"I've got egg salad already made," she offered, "want to join me?"

223

"That sounds really good," I nodded my head, "let me put my stuff away."

"Great," she said, "I have to go to the market too; we can go together."

"I have iced tea, shall I bring some over?"

"Sure, that'll be great." She went into her trailer and I went home to put my laundry in the basket and pick up the drinks. It was a great impromptu lunch.

It was a cool day with the temperature in the mid seventies, a good day for walking. Julie was good company. When we reached the market we separated and each of us shopped for what we needed. I decided on pork chops, mashed potatoes, carrots and applesauce, she decided on hot dogs and beans. We both picked up some Twinkies for dessert. We were not overburdened with packages to carry home and were back in ample time to prepare supper before our guys got home.

"What happened to you?" I looked at the lump on Eddie's forehead when he walked in the door.

"One of the guys was climbing a column and dropped his spud wrench. I happened to be in the wrong place; I was lucky, though, I ducked fast enough and it just nicked me."

I picked off a chunk of ice out of the icebox and wrapped it in a dish cloth, "Here let me put this ice on it, it'll help get the swelling down."

"Quit fussing around," he held the ice in place, "it's gonna be all right."

"Right and the next thing you're going to tell me is that it doesn't hurt." I tied a red bandana around his head to hold the ice in place.

"Well maybe it hurts a little."

"That's typical; if you ignore something, and tell yourself it doesn't hurt it'll go away."

"No, really, it's not so bad," he insisted. "What's for supper? Do I have time to take a shower?"

Grrr, I was thinking, this is such a guy thing. "Supper's ready; it's probably a good idea to keep the ice on for a while and you can take a shower after we eat."

He cleaned up at the kitchen sink and we sat down at the table. It turned out to be a quiet evening. When Eddie came back from the showers I told him about the pond cleaning experience.

"I wonder how long it's been since he had cleaned that filter," he said. "It hasn't been done in the last couple of months since we've been here."

"I know," I fixed another ice pack and tied it on with a clean bandana, "and from the language he was using; I can tell you it's not his favorite project."

"I didn't get a chance to look at the pond tonight," he took a deck of cards from the drawer. "I'll take a look at it in the morning."

We played rummy for a while. His wounded head did not affect his card game. He won two games straight. He removed the bandana and the ice pack and put them in the sink before we went to bed.

"I hope your head feels better in the morning," I pulled the pillows out from under the sofa.

"It's not so bad now," he pulled back the sheets. "By the way, how's the ice holding out?"

"We'll need a block by tomorrow," I slid under the covers, "would you mind picking some up on your way home from work?"

"Sure," he kissed me, "that won't be a problem. Good night."


The week went by fast, there were the usual laundry and cleaning and cooking chores to be done and all of these made the time to fly by. On Friday evening we went to San Pedro again. Eddie's head was healing well; the swelling had gone down completely and, except for a few scratches, the evidence of his encounter with the spud wrench was almost gone. Neither Auntie nor Uncle seemed to notice. After all, we did come over to watch the wrestling and so who pays attention to little scratches.

"The Baron's not wrestling tonight," Auntie announced. "The main feature is between Wild Red Berry and Fred Blassie."

"Red Berry," I questioned, "isn't that the guy you don't like?"

"He's got a big mouth," she replied, "right in the middle of the match he steps out of the ring and yells at the spectators."

"Is that allowed?" I wanted to know.

"He doesn't always do what's allowed," Uncle answered, "and the referee seems to be blind when 'Big Mouth' is pulling the other wrestler's hair." He turned to Auntie, "Isn't that true?"

"Oh yeah," she agreed. "It's crazy, I know, but I like to watch anyhow."

We watched a couple of matches before the main event. The TV cameras showed the audience and I was surprised to see so many women at the event and, for the most part, the ladies were wearing stylish dresses and hats as they watched the wrestlers from front row seats or wherever they happened to be sitting throughout the arena.

Auntie was enthusiastic during every match but really got fired up when Wild Red and Fred came into the ring. "What's the matter with that referee?" "Can't he see Red stepping on Fred's hair?" She shook her fist at the TV: "Shut your mouth and get back in the ring!" She motioned to us and pointed to the screen: "Look at him; he keeps wrapping his legs in the ropes; get back in there and wrestle!"

Finally the match was over and Red Berry was declared the winner because he succeeded in pinning Fred's shoulders to the mat for a count of three. I had never seen wrestling before we came to California. I was amazed at Aunt Bina's love for this sport. As far as I was concerned, I'd rather see Ted Williams hit a home run out of the park at Fenway for the Red Sox than to watch these wrestlers slam each other brutally; 'each to his own taste'.

"Do you have any plans for tomorrow?" Uncle asked as we were leaving.

"As a matter of fact, yes" Eddie answered. "A guy I work with, Jerry, wants us to meet him and his wife at the Hollywood Riviera Beach Club tomorrow; have you ever heard of that place?"

"Oh yes," he nodded knowingly, "it was quite an elite club in its heyday in the 1930's when it was first built."

"Were you living here then?" I asked.

"Oh no," Auntie said; "We didn't come to California until much later."

"You have friends in Redondo Beach," Uncle tilted his head, "don't you?"

"Yes, we do," Eddie reminded him, "we met them in Yellowstone Park."

"Well, the Hollywood Riviera Beach Club is on the shore of Redondo Beach on the North to Torrance on the South; it kind of sits on the edge of both cities."

"Jerry said it was closed during the war."

"That's what I heard too," Uncle said, "the army put some anti aircraft guns in the hills on the Torrance side. They used the guns for training purposes and the building incurred quite a bit of damage from the shaking during the gunfire." Uncle was a wealth of information.

"Have you ever been there?" Eddie asked.

"No, your aunt and the girls aren't much for swimming," Uncle explained, "it used to be a private club, but somebody bought it after the war and reopened it to the public just last year."

"We'll be seeing the place tomorrow and we'll let you know what it's like," Eddie started out toward the car.

"Good night, Auntie," I hugged her.

"I'll walk out with you," Uncle put his arm around my shoulders, "we're glad you came."

Eddie took his seat behind the wheel and Uncle held the door for me. It always felt like a home visit when we came to San Pedro. In only a couple of months we had become family. I kissed Uncle on the cheek and then sat next to Eddie. Uncle closed the door and waved as we backed out of the driveway.

"I really like your aunt and uncle," I said on the way home, "and I'm always impressed at how much your uncle knows about this part of California."

"They've been here for a while," Eddie reminded me, "and he's always made it a point to learn what was interesting about this place."

"What time are we supposed to meet Jerry in the morning?" I walked into the trailer ahead of Eddie as we came back from the Community House.

"He said he'd be there around 11:45" he put the keys on the table. "I think he said the pool opens at noon."

"Were you planning on having lunch there, or should I make a big breakfast?"

"I think we should eat home," he pulled out the sofa, "if we get hungry after our swim we can always get a hot dog or something."

"Sounds good to me," I put the pillows on the bed and crawled under the covers, "I'll let you turn off the lights."

By the time I woke up, Eddie had been to the Community House and back. He was already dressed and sitting at the table reading the newspaper.

"Good afternoon," he said, "are you planning to make coffee sometime today?"

I looked at the clock, "it's only seven o'clock; what time did you get up?"

"I guess it was around five, I didn't really notice."

"I'll put the coffee on before I go up to the Community House," I reached for the pot. "It should be ready before I get back."

"Okay, no need to hurry" he spread the paper out on the table, "we've got plenty of time."

I pulled out a blue and white checkered dress from the closet, and clean underwear out of the drawer. I grabbed a towel and was off to get ready for the day. I made breakfast when I returned and by the time the kitchen was cleaned up it was time to get going to meet Eddie's friend and his wife.

Shady Grove Trailer Park was about 15 minutes from the ocean. Charlie and Ruth lived on the north side of Redondo Beach and each time we had visited them we had gone a different route. Truthfully, other than finding the church and the theater we had not explored much more about Torrance; so, today, we were seeing a new side of our not so little city. Jerry and Eddie had agreed to meet in the parking area of the Club. We saw the sign in neon lights as we turned down the street: Hollywood Riviera Club, we pulled into a parking space and then stood outside our car while we waited. It was only a few minutes before Eddie's friend showed up.

"I hope you weren't waiting long," Jerry was about five feet ten inches tall with sandy hair and blue eyes. "I had a little trouble finding the place."

"No we've only been here a few minutes ourselves," the men shook hands. "This is the wife."

I extended my hand, "hi, my name is Jeanne."

"Good to meet you," he put his arm around his wife's waist, "This is Phyllis."

"This is quite a place, isn't it?" she stood about five feet five and had blonde hair and gray eyes. "I've never been here before; have you?"

"No, we've only been in Torrance for a couple of months," I explained. "There's still a lot about this town we don't know."

"We've been in L.A. for a few years," she volunteered, "But we don't get down this way very often."

We walked ahead of the guys on an upward ramp toward the large white stucco, Spanish styled structure with a red tiled roof, which straddled the city line of Torrance and Redondo Beach above the sandy shore, just as Uncle had told us. There were several levels in the structure. The swimming pool was on the first level. It was a long rectangular pool that stretched 75 feet from the front of the building out toward the ocean. There was a lounging area on the three sides away from the walking area next to the structure. There were wooden chaise-lounges arranged neatly all around. For a fee of twenty-five cents we were allowed the use of the changing rooms and the chaises. A tiny concession stand just past the changing area sold hot dogs and soda and ice cream.

"Somebody told me this place was closed for eight years and an old Navy man who was in WWII bought it and fixed it up." Jerry said.

"He did a good job," Eddie remarked, "you can tell there were cracks in the walls, but they're painted over pretty good."

"Where's the night club?" Phyllis looked around. "I heard it used to be quite elegant."

"It's in the very center of the building," Jerry pointed down the hall from the pool area. "Actually part of it is in Torrance and the other is in Redondo Beach."

"That's interesting," Eddie said, "I wonder which city police goes there if the patrons get a little wild."

"That's a good question," Jerry laughed, "I'm afraid I can't answer it though; and as a matter of fact, I've also heard the club isn't quite so elegant anymore."

"Does anyone live here?" I pointed to an upper level balcony.

"You'd think so wouldn't you?" Jerry replied, "but I don't think that part of the building's been done on the inside yet. The place only reopened last year."

We chose lounge chairs on the ocean side. Eddie is a strong swimmer and he swam the length of the pool a few times. Phyllis and I dipped our toes in the shallow end and eventually plunged our bodies in for a short dip, and then decided to sunbathe on the lounges. Jerry and Eddie alternated swimming back and forth or sitting on the edge of the pool or resting on the lounges. The water was warm, the sun was hot, and there was a cool ocean breeze. For a few hours on this Saturday afternoon, we had a taste of what it's like to enjoy life like the elite.

"I hate to see this afternoon end," Phyllis stood up and picked up her beach bag.

"Now that we know what this place is like," I reached into my bag for a comb. "Maybe we can get the guys to come here again."

"Hey," Jerry said, "I'm game. Eddie and I can set a time when see each other on the job."

"Okay with me," he took my hand.

We all walked to the bath houses to change out of our bathing suits. We met outside the changing area and then went down the ramp into the parking lot. We hugged each other and promised we would do this again sometime in the near future.

"I like your friends," I said as we drove out of the parking area. "Jerry's wife is really nice, and she's cute too."

"Yes she is."

"I should have known that you'd notice," I felt a pang of jealousy.

Eddie laughed, "But she's too tall."

We had barely passed the beach area when Eddie slowed the car down. There was a little boy on the side of the road. He was sitting next to a box with a sign over it. We couldn't read the sign until we came next to it because it was facing the road.

229

"Puppies for Sale, $10.00" the sign said.

Eddie stopped a little past the box and looked at me, "What do you think?"

"I don't know, the last dog we had was Mickey that was three years ago." I wasn't sure we should have a dog in the trailer.

"It can't hurt to take a look," Eddie got out of the car.

I got out and joined him. There were three Doberman puppies and one sad little freckle faced boy.

"Hi," Eddie greeted the boy, "it kind of looks like you don't want to get rid of these little guys."

"I don't really," he admitted. "But my mother says I can't keep them because we can't get the papers to sell them for more money."

"See?" he held up one small dog. "His legs ain't quite straight, he can walk ok, but we can't get papers for him. Ma said we'll have to put him down if I can't find a home for him."

"What about the other two?" Eddie asked.

"They's somethin' wrong with them too," he handed me the puppy and petted the two in the box. "That one is my favorite."

Eddie and I looked at each other, I held the puppy. He licked my face. "Can we?"

"Ten bucks, is that it?" Eddie asked.

The boy nodded.

"I think the wife likes him." He pulled the money out of his wallet. "I guess we've got a dog."

He lay comfortably in my lap all the way home. We stopped to pick up some dog food, a leash and a collar at the dime store in town.

"There's no sense buying him a bed right now," Eddie said, "he's going to be a big dog and he'll be outgrowing it in no time."

"Do you have a box we can use for a bed for our puppy?" I asked the clerk.

"Let me see," she went to the back of the store and returned with a cardboard box. "Will this do?" She held it up at arm's length.

"It's perfect," I nodded to Eddie, "the sides are a little high so he won't be able to get out."

"At least not for a week or so," He paid for our purchases. "Okay, let's go home."

We were only about 15 minutes from home. I was anxious to settle in with the newest member of our family.

"What are you going to call him?" Eddie asked.

"We bought him in Torrance so I thought maybe that's what we should name him," I suggested. "What do you think?"

"Torrance," he nodded, "we can call him Torrey for short. Yeah, that's a good name."

I carried Torrey into the trailer when we got home then handed him to Eddie. I pulled out a beach towel and folded it to fit the bottom of the box and used newspapers to cover the towel. "Okay, Honey, you can put Torrey in his new bed."

"Maybe we should walk him around outside a little in case he needs to go," Eddie said.

"Hand me the collar and the leash."

"I'll go up to the Community House first while you walk the dog," I watched him adjust the collar, "then you can go up. I'll fix supper while you're up there and I'll feed Torrey before putting him in his box."

CHAPTER 18

Torrey had a restless night. "I think he misses his brother and sister," Eddie said.

"I heard him whimpering after you put the lights out," I put the pillows under the sofa before I closed it, "then I heard you slide the box."

"Yeah, I pulled the box up close to the bed and put my hand inside. He was quiet as long as I rubbed his neck," he attached the leash to Torrey's collar. "I'll take him out to do his business."

"What Mass do you want to go to?" I asked as he was leaving.

"I guess we can go to 8 o'clock," he called from the yard. "You take your shower first. I'll come up after I put him back in his box."

I picked up a towel and the other stuff I needed and went up to the Community House.

I met him on my way back. "How was he?"

"He was okay," he smiled, "I was surprised his box was dry when I went to change the newspapers in it."

"Let's hope he keeps it up," I continued my way back to the trailer where I found Torrey with his nose in the air, trying to see over the side of the box.

I finished getting ready and we left for church soon after Eddie returned from the Community House.

"Do you think Torrey will be okay?" this was the first time we were going to be leaving him alone.

"I'm sure he will," Eddie reassured me, "he can't get out of the box and we won't be gone for more than an hour and a half; he'll be fine."

Of course Eddie was right. Torrey's head popped up from the box when we came home and his tail was wagging. "I think he's happy to see us," I rubbed behind his ears.

"You worry too much," Eddie laughed, "I can just see you when we have kids."

"Well, for one thing," I took my hat off and put it away, "I won't be leaving them in a box."

"Touché; now what's for breakfast?" he pushed the box next to the sofa.

I proceeded to cook eggs, bacon and home fries, "You're in charge of feeding the dog and making toast."

"What do you say we go show off our pup to Aunt Bina today?"

"I think that's a great idea," I put the plates on the table.

"We won't stay long," he said. "I'd like to go to see that new movie 'Kon Tiki' this afternoon."

"I think that movie is continuous," I figured we could catch it at any time. "We can bring Torrey home and then go to the theater."

"That's what I thought too." Eddie put Torrey's bowl of food on the floor next to the table. He made sure the screen door was closed to prevent him from going out.

It was amazing how quickly this little puppy had already worked his way into our hearts. However, he wasn't eating as heartily as I thought he should.

"I'm going to take him to the vet's tomorrow," I announced. "I want to make sure he gets started on his shots."

"That's a good idea," he poured coffee in both our cups.

We finished our leisurely breakfast and cleaned up the kitchen before leaving for San Pedro. We decided to put Torrey and his box in the back seat for traveling. He slept most of the way but every once in a while I looked back to see him pop his nose up over the side as if to say: "are we there yet?"

We stayed at Auntie's for about an hour. Loretta immediately fell in love with Torrey and insisted on attaching his leash to take him for a walk. Torrey cooperated nicely, and enjoyed playing ball with her when they came back.

"It looks like your dog has a friend for life," Uncle Victor said. "Loretta always wanted a dog, but it just isn't practical here, where we live."

"I don't how practical it will be in the trailer," I said, "but we won't be in a trailer forever."

We said our good-byes and brought Torrey home before going to the movies. "Kon Tiki' was the story of Thor Heyerdahl and his crossing of the Pacific Ocean on a Balsa wood raft in 1947. This was a courageous attempt on his part to prove that it was possible the first settlers in the Polynesian Islands came from South America instead of from the west as currently thought; but I guess we're too young to understand the need to find out who the first people were who came to Tahiti or for that matter, even care. Six people and a parrot on a raft was not your typical action movie. We left the theater while the rafters were still in mid-ocean.

Julie was in the yard when we came home. "Hey, you guys are back early!"

"Yeah," I said, "we weren't crazy about the movie so we walked out."

"We went to see 'Kon Tiki'," Eddie explained. "There was a lot of talking and not much action watching a raft floating around on the high seas."

"Did you guys have supper yet?" I asked Julie.

"No, we just got back from visiting Darryl's family," she answered.

"I'm going to make sandwiches," I said, "would you like to join us?"

"Sure," she accepted, "maybe we can play cards after?"

"Give me about a half hour," I suggested, "I think I can get a salad together too."

Our neighborly pot-luck was on. She brought over the iced tea and cup cakes and we had a feast. After supper we played three games of Hi-low Jack. The girls won two and the guys won one.

"I think you girls were just lucky tonight," Darryl commented. "There was no real skill involved."

"Oh, please!" Julie rolled her eyes, "are those 'sour grapes' remarks I'm hearing?"

"Darryl's right," Eddie picked up the cards to put them away. "Your winning was just pure luck. Just wait until the next time." He waved the deck of cards as he watched them walk through the trellis.

"Okay," I said to Eddie, "you have won the privilege of walking the dog while I go to the Community house. I'll open the sofa when I get back."

We had begun a new routine: I go to the Community House, he walks the dog, and then he goes to the Community House or vice versa.

Eddie was awake before the alarm. He was up and dressed and out for his morning walk with Torrey by the time I got up to make the coffee.

"Good morning," he untied the leash and let the dog play on the floor when they came in. "The coffee smells good."

"What do you want for breakfast?" I poured a cup of coffee for both of us.

"Not much," he put a bowl of water on the floor for Torrey. "I was thinking maybe two sunny sides and toast?"

"Give me a few minutes to finish fixing ham and cheese sandwiches for your lunch and then I'll make the eggs."

"Sure," he settled at the table and sipped on his coffee, "no rush."

"How was the dog when you went out this morning?"

234

"He was acting funny, as a matter of fact," he took a sip of coffee. "I'm glad you're taking him to the vet today," he looked concerned. "He was dragging his rear end on the grass. I think you should tell the doctor about that."

"That is strange," I put the toast in the toaster. "I'll mention it to him."

We sat and ate together. "I'm going to need the car today," I said after we finished breakfast. "I have to go to the Community House; I'll be right back and then I'll drive you to work."

Torrey was in his box and Eddie was behind the wheel of the car when I returned. It was a half hour ride to L.A. and Eddie drove straight to his work site. He opened the door; I slid over on the bench seat to sit behind the wheel, he kissed me before he closed the door. "I'll see you around 4 o'clock." He waved as I left.

When I got back to the Community House, I looked in the telephone book to try and locate a vet. I found one in San Pedro. I called Dr. Angelo's office and was able to get an appointment for one o'clock. I went back to the trailer, I picked up the basket of laundry; I got it going in the washer and was able to get the kitchen cleaned up before the clothes were ready to be put in the dryer. There would be no time for ironing today. I wanted to give myself enough time to locate the vet so I wouldn't be late. The manager provided us with another box for Torrey; this one would stay in the car. I put towels and extra newspapers on the back seat, just in case we should need them.

"Look who we have here," Dr. Angelo said as he picked Torrey up and looked in his eyes. "He's only a little guy."

"He's the runt of the litter," I told him. "His back legs are a little crooked but he seems able to walk okay."

"Let me look at him," he set the dog on the examining table. "For one thing he'll need his first puppy shot."

"He's been kind of sluggish and my husband said he was dragging his rear end in the grass this morning," I explained.

"That's a symptom he may have worms," the doctor looked concerned. "We'll give him his first puppy shot today, and I'll also give him some medicine for the worms; but, you'll have to make another appointment for Thursday so we can really get him completely cleaned out."

"Is he going to be all right?" I was worried.

"Oh yes," Dr. Angelo assured me, "once he's rid of the worms he'll be able to digest his food and grow stronger. You'll see a big difference."

I made the required appointment at the front desk and returned to the car with Torrey in my arms. I settled him in his box and decided to bring him home before picking up Eddie from work. I hadn't gone far when I heard whimpering from the back seat. I pulled over to the side of the road to check out what was going on. Torrey was a mess.

235

There were short worms on his face and all around him. I picked up one of the towels to wipe him down and before I got him settled he vomited another mouthful of slime. I reached for a clean towel, wiped him again and pulled him out of the box. The wormy towels stayed inside. I wrapped him up tightly in a fresh towel and lay him on newspapers on the floor. Then I lifted up several layers of newspaper in the box to wrap up the dirty towels and the bunch of slimy stuff that was gunked up on the top layers. Fortunately the towels covered most of the goop and I was able to avoid touching any of it. Yuk!! I added more sheets of newspaper to fix the box at least well enough for Torrey to make the rest of the trip home. He seemed to be comfy in the towel so I put the whole little bundle in and he slept the rest of the way back to the trailer park. My first stop was the rubbish bin and the second was to fill a wash basin with warm water for my poor little puppy. I gave him a bath before I placed him in his clean box at home. By the time I got all that done it was time to go pick up Eddie in L.A.

"You're right on time," he put his tools in the trunk, "how was your day?"

I moved to the passenger side of the front seat. "It was a little hectic. Now I know why we were able to buy Torrey so cheap."

"What are you talking about?" he sat behind the wheel and started the car.

"The poor dog is full of worms," I told him. "He spit out a pile of them today and I have to bring him back on Thursday to clean out the rest."

"Why couldn't the doctor get them all out today?"

"Dr. Angelo said he suspects two different types of worms," I shrugged, "so he'll need two kinds of medicine I guess."

"Where's Torrey now?" he asked.

"At home in his box," I proceeded to tell Eddie all about the dog's afternoon ordeal. "He seemed to want to sleep so I chose not to disturb him."

"It sounds like it was not a fun afternoon for you either," he reached over and patted my thigh. "But, at least we have an idea of why he's been acting so sluggish."

"The doctor said he should be all right after the next treatment and we'll see a big difference," I assured Eddie.

"Why don't we stop at the market and pick up something easy for you to fix for supper before we go home?" He offered.

"Sure, we need a block of ice anyway," I said, "how about tomato soup and grilled cheese sandwiches?"

"Sounds good to me," he pulled into a space in the parking lot. "I'm kind of dirty from work, do you mind going in alone? I'll get the ice at the gas station."

"No, I'm okay."

236

One more quick stop to pick up the ice and we were home. Torrey heard us come in and was peeking over the side of the box. Eddie went over to him immediately, reached for his leash and they went for a short walk before he went up to the Community House to clean up before supper. We ate leisurely; Torrey ate a little from his bowl then lay on the floor next to Eddie's feet. He didn't move until Eddie put on his leash to go for another walk while I cleaned up the kitchen.

"I don't know what kind of medicine that doctor gave the dog," Eddie commented as he came in the door, "but this little guy is really tired."

"I know what you mean," I put the last of the dishes in the cupboard. "He's been doing a lot of sleeping since we came home."

"Do you feel like playing cards?" He opened the drawer to take out the cards and pulled out a pad and pencil.

"Sure, are you ready to get beat again?" I drew lines on the score pad; he shuffled the cards.

It was a quiet evening for all of us. Torrey slept on the floor, while Eddie and I played Rummy until it was time for bed.

This day started out pretty much like every day since Torrey became part of our lives. Eddie was up and dressed first, he and the dog went for a walk, and he put a fresh bowl of water on the floor for the puppy. I made Eddie's lunch and fixed breakfast while he went up to the Community House and then we ate; he picked up his lunch box, gave me a kiss, and went off to work. Then it was my turn at the showers and the routine of my regular chores. Today I had some catching up to. Right after cleaning the kitchen I still had the ironing to do from yesterday's laundry. I remembered it was Julie's birthday; so before I got involved with anything else I baked a vanilla cake. The pureed tomatoes and spices were already simmering on the hot plate and I began to prepare the meatballs to simmer in the gravy for our supper.

"Something smells good in here," Julie called as she knocked on the door.

"Happy Birthday," I held on to Torrey's collar before I let her in, "I'm making spaghetti and meatballs for supper, I hope you and Darryl are still coming over."

"My parents invited us to their house but that's not until 7 o'clock," she said. "What time will Eddie be home?"

"He's usually home by 4:30," I stirred the gravy, "we should be eating by five."

"That's perfect; Darryl should be home by quarter of."

The timer rang and I put the cake on a cooling rack on the counter and shut off the oven. "You weren't supposed to see that."

"I didn't see a thing," she laughed.

I finished rolling the meatballs and added them to the simmering tomato gravy and replaced the lid, "with a little stirring now and then, these should be done long before suppertime."

I sat at the table, across from Julie. "Do you feel like having some coffee?"

"No, not really," she looked over at Torrey. "You didn't tell me how your visit at the vet's went yesterday."

"I have to go back on Thursday," I told her. "He's got worms and that's what's making him sick."

"He'll be okay won't he?" She sounded concerned.

"The doctor thinks so," I continued, "he said once the worms were gone he should start to eat better and get stronger. I hope he's right, we're sort of getting used to him."

"I can see that," she smiled. "He IS a cute puppy." She looked at her watch and got up suddenly, "Hey, I've got to go, I'll see you around quarter of five."

After I cleaned up the preparation dishes, I put Torrey back in his box while I set up the ironing board; I didn't want him to get tangled up in the electric cord. He didn't seem to mind. I guess he figured it was nap time because when I peeked over at him he was sleeping. I put the cooled oven away after I finished the ironing; I stirred the meatballs, I iced the cake and then ate cottage cheese and fruit for lunch.

Torrey was peeking over the side of his box so I picked him up and tied on his leash so he could come for a walk with me to go pick up the mail. There were letters from both our parents and one from Eddie's sister Evelyn. I opted to wait and read them when I got back to the trailer. My mother's letter was fat and in a large envelope. Usually, this was how she sent forwarded mail. This was no exception. There was one letter enclosed, addressed to Eddie from the Selective Service office. Could this be the dreaded draft communication? I put it aside. My mother's letter was full of news about the grandchildren and how fast they were growing up. I missed my nieces Claire and Thérèse and my nephews. Eddie's mother wrote about our God children, Bruce and Alan and I realized how much I missed them too.

Eddie's sister, Evelyn, was a faithful correspondent. She wrote amusing letters and kept us abreast of what was happening on Ed's side of the family. I missed her too. What's happening here? Am I getting nostalgic? Is California losing its enchantment? I looked at the clock and realized it was time to put the pot of hot water on the burner to cook the spaghetti. I made a salad and sliced the Italian bread we had picked up at the market the day before. I glanced at the sealed letter and wondered if its contents was about to change our lives. I stirred the meatballs.

The table was set for four when Eddie came in. He petted the dog, and then picked up his clean clothes that were laid out on the sofa. I didn't mention the letter until he came back from the Community House.

"This came today," I handed him the letter.

He looked at it and at me before he opened it, "Greetings," he said aloud. He read the rest of the letter to himself and then he looked at me again. "This is it. We have to go back."

"Just like that?" I took the letter to read it for myself. "It says we have a few more weeks before you have to report to the draft board."

"Yeah," he took the letter and put it back in its envelope. "The job I'm working on is almost done; we can make plans to leave as soon as it's over."

"So much for our plans to stay in California," I said.

"Hey," he put his arms around me and lifted my chin, "When we started on this trip we knew I might be called up. We started out to see the country and we've seen a lot of it." He gave me an extra squeeze and then he looked in my eyes. "We still have a lot of the country to see and I think October will be a great month to travel. Now come on, company's coming, get rid of the gloomy face."

He gave me a quick kiss and there was a knock on the door. Eddie opened it and Julie and Darryl came in. "Happy Birthday, Julie, I hope you folks are hungry," Eddie shook her hand first and then Darryl's. "The wife's got a feast prepared, come on in and sit down."

"I know, I've smelled it since this morning," Julie said.

I hugged Julie and shook Darryl's hand and hoped they hadn't noticed my teary eyes. I set out the salad bowl with my new silver salad spoon and fork on the table so we could serve ourselves family style, and then I put the spaghetti in the boiling water. The chatter was light during the meal, I didn't have candles for the cake but we sang 'Happy Birthday' anyway. Julie and Darryl left on time for their date with her parents.

"You didn't say anything about the letter," Eddie remarked.

"We don't have to tell them right away," I replied. "I think I first have to get used to the idea myself."

"There are still a couple of places I'd like to see before we leave California," Eddie said.

"Here," I handed him the other letters we had received that day. "I'd like to see Charlie and Ruth in Redondo Beach before we leave California."

"That's a good idea; and we'll also have to make sure Torrey's okay to travel," he put the letters on the counter. "I'll read these when I come back from my walk."

"Tomorrow I'll make a list of things we need to do and then check them off as we get them done," I anticipated a very busy couple of weeks.

I finished cleaning up the kitchen while they were out. Our lives were about to change but for the time being the leftovers needed to be stored in the ice box and the dishes still needed to be washed and put away. Eddie's timing was good, I was just finishing up when he came in and picked up the letters to read and then sat at the table.

It was Torrey's turn to have supper. I put his bowl on the floor. He still wasn't eating much.

"I'm going up to the Community House while you finish reading the mail, we can open the sofa when I get back."

"When are you taking Torrey to the vet?" Eddie asked when I came in.

"On Thursday," I put my soiled clothes in the laundry basket. "I plan to start getting the trailer ready for traveling tomorrow."

"We'll have to check our supplies too," he reminded me. "It's going to be like when we first started out in June."

"You're right," I agreed, "except now we have a better idea of what we will most likely need."

"Are you going to write home and tell them we're coming back?" he opened the sofa.

"I'll answer the letters," I pulled out the pillows, "but I don't think I'll mention anything about the trip back, I think our parents would worry too much about us being on the road."

"I suppose you're right," he put Torrey in his box. "I'll turn off the light."

I heard him slide the box close to the bed as I slid under the covers.

"Good night, Honey," I whispered as he lay down beside me.

"Good night, Sweetheart," he kissed me. "Don't worry everything will work out."

Torrey woke us up with his whimpering.

"I wish you were going to the vet today," Eddie put the dog's leash on. "It's the first time I've heard him cry like that."

240

"I know," I pulled on my robe. "I'll be sure to mention that to the doctor when I see him tomorrow."

"I'll tie his leash to the fence while I go up to the Community House; maybe he'll feel better if he runs around a little."

I made coffee and took out the ham and eggs to prepare for breakfast. By the time he returned I had the table set and was filling his thermos with coffee.

"Do you have a place to warm up a meatball sandwich?" I wrapped the stuffed Italian bread in waxed paper.

"Yeah, I can put my lunch pail on the crane," he buttoned his green plaid work shirt.

"The motor gets pretty hot, it should get warm enough."

"Don't forget to take the cake and the thermos out," I finished wrapping the cake.

It only took a few minutes to cook sunny side eggs and ham. Eddie made the toast; we ate and then I handed him his lunch.

"Thanks," he kissed me and walked out to the car carrying his pail.

It was another beautiful day. I put down a towel and a bowl of water in the grass and checked Torrey's leash on the fence before I took down the drapes and pulled off the sofa cover. He looked happy lying in the sun so I walked up to the Community House to do laundry. It was a busy day. I washed the windows and venetian blinds and hung the drapes back up, and then I put clean sheets on the sofa-bed before I put the cover on again. Except for changing the bed sheets, I wouldn't have to do this kind of major cleaning again before we started our trip home. The walls and floor would have to wait for another day.

"How about going to a movie tonight?" Eddie suggested after supper.

"I guess we could," I hesitated, "do you think Torrey will be okay?"

"Sure he will," Eddie sounded certain, "he stays all night in his box; he'll be fine for a couple of hours."

There was a double feature at the Stadium. The main feature was 'The Day the Earth Stood Still' with Michael Rennie and Patricia Neal. This was a movie about a saucer shaped vessel from Mars that landed on earth. As you would expect, army tanks and armed soldiers were waiting to destroy them. The sleek, robot-like Martian characters had come in peace, to warn our world that unless we get rid of our weapons we will, in time. destroy our own planet. The aliens zapped the guns right out of the hands the soldiers with a powerful beam without injuring anyone. I thought of the imminent possibility of Eddie having to go to war in the Korean conflict. This message of peace in the world sounded very attractive. I wonder if there will ever come a time when all nations will get along and there will be no need for arms.

241

The second feature was 'Disc Jockey' featuring Nick Lucas. It was not exactly a thought provoking film, but it was different and gave us an insight into the job of the guys we listened to on the radio every day.

"I wonder if they'll ever find out if there are really people on Mars," I said as we left the theater.

"I don't know," Eddie held my hand as we walked to the parking lot. "There would have to be some pretty powerful telescopes to be able to see that."

"Silly! I didn't mean actually see them walking around the planet through a telescope; I mean if they can imagine a space ship from Mars landing here on Earth," I opened the door to get in the car, "don't you think someone could build a rocket or something like Jules Verne writes about and we could go up to another planet; like Buck Rogers maybe?"

"You know what I always say," he put the key in the ignition, "if someone can imagine it someone else can figure out how to do it."

"Right," I laughed, "and some day someone will figure out a way to land a man on the moon."

"Hey, you never know," he backed out of our parking space. "In the meanwhile, what can we have for a snack when we get home?"

"I have Fig Newton's" I suggested. "Would you like that with a glass of milk?"

"Sounds good, I'll take Torrey for a walk first," he parked the car.

I walked in the trailer first. Torrey was peeking over the side of the box. I picked up his leash and tied it on him as Eddie came in. Torrey's tail was wagging and Eddie rubbed him behind the ears before he picked him up and adjusted the leash. I ran clean water in Torrey's bowl and put it on the floor and then proceeded to prepare our evening snack. The pre-bedtime ritual had begun: fix a snack, walk the dog, eat the snack, fix the bed, put the puppy back in his box for the night and then we would settle down under the counterpane to dream our dreams of adventures still to come.

Eddie was up and dressed by the time I rolled out of bed. "I'll take the dog out while you go up to the Community House."

"Okay," I stored the pillows under the sofa and adjusted the cover. "I need to take you to work today so I can take Torrey to the Vet."

"Yes, I know," he held the leash as we walked together. "Don't fuss about breakfast, toast and strawberry jam will be fine with coffee."

"I'll fix your lunch when I get back," I held a navy blue and white striped dress over my arm.

"A peanut butter and jelly sandwich will be okay," he said as I went toward the showers.

When I returned Eddie was seated at the table with the newspaper spread in front of him. Torrey lay at his feet. "Don't forget to tell the Vet about the whimpering," Ed reminded me.

"I'm also worried about his lack of appetite," I refilled Ed's coffee cup and made sandwiches while waiting for the toast to be done. "I'll also have to find out how soon he'll need his next shot."

"Torrey can stay in his box while you take me to work," Eddie picked up the puppy. "What time is his appointment?"

"Not until 11:30;" I put the breakfast dishes in the sink. "I'll have time to clean up the kitchen when I get back, before I have to leave for San Pedro."

"I'll drive over to the job," he put his lunch pail on the floor of the back seat.

I grabbed my purse from the closet and joined him. "What do you want for supper?"

"You'll be gone most of the afternoon," he pulled out of the trailer park. "Let's just have hot dogs and beans."

"Okay," I agreed, "I can pick that up on the way home."

When we reached the job Eddie got out of the car, I slid behind the wheel; he kissed me and closed the door. "Good luck at the Vet's. I'll see you around four."

While I was at the market I picked up a roll of paper towels; I remembered the mess after Torrey's last treatment for worms. I wanted to be prepared. I cleaned up the kitchen when I got home and then put Torrey's box, extra newspapers and the paper towels in the back seat of the car, just in case we had a repeat of regurgitated worms. Torrey walked out with me, attached to his leash, and I put him in his box when we got to the car.

We got to the Vet's a few minutes before 11:30. We didn't wait long before being led to the examining room. Dr. Angelo came in and rubbed Torrey behind his ears, "hey, little fella, you haven't grown much since I last saw you."

"He's not eating that much," I answered, one morning a few days ago he woke us up with his whimpering."

"I'm surprised it happened only once," the doctor felt his abdomen. "I'm sure the worms have something to do with that."

243

I proceeded to tell him about the wormy experience after our last visit. He listened and said, "That's not unusual, but that treatment was for only one type of worms."

"I remember you mentioned he might have two kinds of parasites the last time I was here," I petted my puppy. "Will you be able to get rid of the rest of them this time?"

"Yes, but it's going to be messy again; I hope you're prepared," he motioned for me to hold the dog on the table while he went to get the medicine.

"Yes I am," I stroked Torrey's back, "I've got paper towels and newspapers in the car."

Dr. Angelo returned quickly, he gently held the dog and put the medicine in his mouth and held it shut while he gently rubbed Torrey's throat, "okay, little guy, it won't be long before those nasties are out of you and you'll start feeling better." He turned to me, "this stuff works pretty fast, it might be a good idea for you to stay in the parking lot with him until he upchucks; you'd better have your clean-up stuff ready."

"I do," I assured him, "it's all in the back seat of the car.'

"Torrey will need another puppy shot in about three weeks," the doctor said. "You can make an appointment at the front desk."

"My husband and I are planning to leave California in a couple of weeks," I told him. "It will take us about a week and a half to get back to Massachusetts."

"Two weeks will be too soon for the shot," he thought for a minute, "I'll give you his records if you wait a few minutes." He wrote on the papers in front of him. "You'll need to find a Vet in three or four weeks who can give him his shot. When he looks at this file he'll know what to do."

"Thank you," I extended my hand. "Then you think he'll be okay to travel?"

"Oh yes, he should be fine once this medicine does its job." The doctor shook my hand, "this is a lucky puppy; he might not have made it without you." He re-attached the leash, "It was nice to meet you, have a safe trip."

I took Dr. Angelo's advice. I opened all the windows in the car, put Torrey on the newspapers on the back seat and waited. It wasn't long before he started to retch and expel long squiggly worms by the mouthful. I picked up the mess with paper towels and threw it in a doubled grocery sack I had brought just for this purpose. No sooner had I gotten rid of one mess there was another. I was glad I had postponed eating my own lunch because I'm sure it would have become fodder for the expelled worms, I gagged more than once. Finally Torrey stopped retching and calmed down, I waited to make sure he was done vomiting and then put him in his clean box. I looked for and found a trash barrel to dispose of the disgusting slime. Torrey slept all the way home. I parked in the space in front of our trailer and brought his box in the yard. I thought, perhaps, lying in the fresh air and sunshine for a while might be good for him. I sat on a folding chair next to him and read for awhile until it was almost time to pick up Eddie. I put the box back in the car, took Torrey for a walk and then brought him with me for the ride. I wanted to make sure the wormy episode was really over.

When I reached the job site I got out of the car to peek in the back seat to check the dog. Torrey's eyes were still droopy, he lifted his head and then positioned himself to go back to sleep. I was acting like a doting parent, this little puppy had 'wormed' his way into my heart; no question about it. All I wanted now was to see him hungry and happy.

"Here you are," Eddie opened the driver's side door. "You're right on time. How did it go at the Vet's?"

"It was a mess again," I sat next to him on the passenger side. "This time was worse, but Dr. Angelo said this treatment should be the end of the worms."

"That's good; did you ask about traveling?" He started the engine.

"Yes, he gave me Torrey's records and he said we'll have to get him another puppy shot in three or four weeks, wherever we are." I rolled down my window. "He said any Vet would know what to do when he looks at the file."

"That's good to know," Eddie lifted his head toward the back seat. "I noticed you brought him with you."

"After this afternoon's episode, I didn't want to leave him alone," I replied. "He's been sleeping most of the time."

"Did the doctor say how soon we would see a difference?" He asked.

"He didn't really give a time exactly," I looked toward the back seat. "I guess we'll notice a change when he starts eating better."

"Speaking of eating," he turned down our street. "I'm getting hungry."

"To tell you the truth," I said, "I haven't felt very much like eating today."

"Maybe once we get home," he drove in the driveway of the trailer park. "You'll feel better."

After he parked the car he picked up the dog and brought him for a walk while I went in the trailer. I washed my hands in the kitchen sink and began to prepare supper. I put the beans in a small saucepan to warm and fried the hot dogs in the frying pan, Eddie liked them browned but not burned to death. I opened one end of a can of brown bread and stood it up between the burners on the hot plate to warm it up a little. There would be time for all this to be done by the time Eddie would come back from the Community House after his walk with Torrey. I put Torrey's dish on the floor. To my surprise and pleasure he went over to it and actually ate some of it.

"It smells like supper's ready," Eddie put his work clothes in the laundry basket.

"Yes it is," I put napkins next to our plates on the table. "And look, Torrey's eating pretty good too!"

"He didn't clean his dish," Eddie sat at the table.

"No, but it's more than he's eaten before," I opened the other side of the brown bread can, pushed it through and sliced it. "Maybe he'll start growing a little now."

"Yeah, but not too fast," Eddie buttered a slice of the bread, "or else he won't fit in his box for the trip home."

"You've got a point!" we both laughed and enjoyed our supper.

It was another quiet evening; Eddie finished reading the newspaper while I cleaned up the kitchen and then we played rummy again until it was time for bed.

The next day was busy with chores such as laundry and ironing and the time went by fast. I made chowder from canned clams and we had tuna fish salad sandwiches for supper. Since it was wrestling night, we went to see Aunt Bina and Uncle Victor. We told them about the letter and our upcoming trip back east.

"I'm really sorry to see you go," Auntie sat up in her rocking chair. "We've gotten used to having you around and we like it."

"We like it here too," Eddie said, "as a matter of fact we've talked about settling down here. Bethlehem Steel told me I had a job with them for as long as I want."

"Uncle Sam has another idea," I interjected. "It's that Korean conflict, no one seems to be able to agree on any kind of solution."

"I understand what you're saying," Uncle remarked. "Nobody wants another world war."

"When do you figure you'll be leaving?" Auntie asked.

"Probably around two weeks," Eddie said, "the job should be done this week and it'll take us at least another week or so to pack up for the trip back."

"I'll call Albert," she announced. "I'm sure he's going to want to see you before you leave."

"We'd like that too," I agreed, "we're going to miss him and Bonnie."

"Next Friday, Eva and Loretta will be here," she said, "so don't eat supper before coming over. We'll all eat together."

"That sounds like a great idea, what shall I bring?"

"Yourselves and maybe the puppy," she laughed, "you know how much Loretta likes that dog."

"We didn't watch much of the wrestling tonight," I commented. "It doesn't look like we'll be seeing much next week either."

246

"I don't care about that," Auntie said. "But you're leaving, that I do care about."

It seemed like we hugged each other a little harder at the end of the evening. Uncle had been very quiet most of the night, "I hope you'll find a way to come back someday," he had tears in his eyes.

"You never know," I said, "I told you before; Eddie and I both like it here, and part of the reason for that is you and Aunt Bina."

"Come on, Sweetheart," Eddie took my hand. "We're going to see them next week, there's no need to get emotional now."

I could always depend on my Honey to bring me back to reality, even amid my tears. Uncle walked to the car with us and opened the door for me. "One more hug," he held me for a few seconds, I sat in the front seat, then he closed the door. "See you next Friday."

"Are you okay?" Eddie started the engine.

"I'm really going to miss your aunt and uncle," I put my handkerchief in my pocket. "They are really great people."

"I'm going to miss them too," he said. "It's been good to have family around."

It was a clear night and the drive home seemed short. As usual, Torrey heard us come in and was peeking over the side of his box. "We've got a welcoming committee of one," I laughed when I walked in the door.

"He knows he's going out for a walk," Eddie said. "I'll get the leash."

"It's a nice night, I'll come with you."

We walked up to the Community House together and Eddie and I took turns using the facility while the other stayed with the dog, we walked around the trailer park a little more before going home.

"What a beautiful sky" I remarked.

"We can almost count on one hand the number of rainy days we've had since we've been here," Eddie looked up at the sky. "You know," he reflected, "I'd like to see the telescope on Mount Palomar before we leave California."

"Is that near here?" I wanted to know.

"It's close to San Diego," he said. "I figure when we go to the zoo down there and to Tijuana, it wouldn't be that far out of the way to go to the Planetarium."

"It's amazing how you figure all these things out," we walked under the trellis into our yard.

247

"Hey," he opened up the door to the trailer, "while we're here we may as well see as much as we can."

"Right again," I put the leash away. "Do you want a snack?"

"Got any more of those Fig Newton's?" he asked.

"Sure," I reached in the cupboard for the cookies. "I'll pour us some milk too."

Torrey took a few laps of water from his dish on the floor and settled down next to Eddie's feet.

"What do you think about going to Redondo Beach tomorrow?" Eddie suggested.

"That's a good Idea," I replied. "I'd like to see Ruth and Charlie and the kids before we leave."

"We won't stay long," Eddie said. "We'll bring Torrey; I think the kids will get a kick out of meeting him."

"Okay," I agreed. "We'll bring our bathing suits too in case they feel like going to the beach."

"Pack a lunch anyway," he decided, "we don't want to be pushy; if they have other plans we can go to the beach on our own."

"Okay, Puppy, back in your box," I said. "It's time for us to get to bed, we've all got a big day tomorrow."


We left for Redondo Beach around 11 o'clock. It was another glorious day. Charlie's car was in the driveway when we got to their house. The kids were playing on the swings in the back yard and Ruth was hanging clothes on the line to dry.

"What a great surprise," Charlie came to meet us as we got out of the car. "We haven't seen you guys for a while." The men shook hands.

I walked toward Ruth with Torrey on the leash and the girls ran up to meet him. "Take it easy, girls," Ruth called out, "that puppy is kind of small."

"Can we take him for a walk?" they pleaded, "can we?"

Torrey's whole body was wagging and it was clear that he was happy to be around the children.

"If it's okay with your mom," I answered, "he does like to go for walks."

"You know the rules," she warned, "no going in the street. Stay on the sidewalk."

"They've been begging us to get a dog," Charlie said, "but we just haven't found the right one for us yet."

"We just happened to find this one," Eddie told them, "he was the runt of the litter and, as a matter fact, he was sick. He seems to be doing all right now."

"He's really cute," Ruth said, "the girls like him already."

"Have a seat at the picnic table," Charlie offered. "What are you up to these days?"

"This is kind of a good-bye visit," Eddie sat next to Charlie. "I got my draft notice and have to report to the board in Fall River, Massachusetts."

"I thought you were settled in with Bethlehem Steel," Charlie looked puzzled.

"Oh yes," Eddie answered, "we even began to think about settling down in California; but this notice sort of changes things."

"That would have been so good," Ruth looked at me, "we could have become neighbors."

"Yeah," Charlie said, "they're starting to build a lot of homes in this area and they're not that expensive."

"I hear what you're saying," Ed shook his head, "but who knows how long this Korean War is going to go on and where I'll be sent once I'm in uniform."

"It's a threat for all of us, isn't it," Charlie looked concerned. "I served during WWII and I wouldn't look forward to going back."

"Enough of this gloomy talk," Ruth interrupted, "have you had lunch yet?"

"As a matter of fact," I announced, "I brought ham and cheese sandwiches in our cooler, I thought you might feel like going to the beach."

Charlie and Ruth looked at each other. "The girls should be back soon," Ruth said. "I bet they'd like that a lot. I can make sandwiches too."

"I think I have plenty for all of us and I brought some chips too," I said.

"I should make a couple of peanut butter and jelly sandwiches," she suggested. "You know how kids are. And I have potato salad; how about that?"

"Sounds like a beach picnic in the making…"

"Oh Mom," Pam said as the girls came back from their walk. "This dog is so cute, couldn't we get a puppy too."

249

"Here we go again," Ruth laughed, "I'm not saying no, but we can talk about that later. Would you like to go to the beach?"

"Yeah, yeah," both girls said in chorus, "can the puppy come too?"

"Of course," Ruth replied. "Now get your suits on while I make the sandwiches."

"Are you making peanut butter and Jelly?" Amy asked.

"Yes!" Ruth nodded toward me. "See what I mean?"

"You know your girls very well," I laughed.

The girls were back with their swim suits on in hardly any time at all.

"It looks like the girls have everything under control; "Charlie said. "It's going to be a wonderful beach day. We don't make the time to do this often enough. I'll get the beach ball out of the garage."

We decided to take both cars. We followed them to their favorite spot on the beach. We were surprised that it wasn't very crowded. We carried out blankets and coolers from the parking lot to the sandy beach. It was a gorgeous day; the blue ocean waves washed the lacey aqua foam gently over the sand on the shore. We attached Torrey's leash to one of the folding chairs. I think the girls had tired him out on their walk because he looked for a shady spot to lie down under Eddie's chair and take a nap. We all went in and enjoyed the coolness of the water and the warmth of the sun. Ruth and I chose to stretch out on our blankets after we ate lunch while Eddie and Charlie played dodge ball with the girls. The afternoon went by too quickly.

"I don't know if we'll get a chance to go to the beach again before we go back home," Eddie said, "the days seem to be running into one another and there's still so much to do."

"We're going to miss you," Charlie extended his hand to Eddie; "I wish it could have worked out for you to settle down here."

"Who knows?" I hugged Ruth, "we might end up back here some day; this war won't last forever."

"May I put Torrey in his box?" Amy asked.

"Of course you can," I handed her the leash. "Maybe Pam can help you, Torrey looks like he needs a couple of extra hugs; he really likes you two."

It was a short walk to the parking lot, Eddie and Charlie organized the blankets and coolers in the trunk of the cars. The girls giggled as they discussed which of them would actually settle the dog in the box and which one would untie his leash. Torrey seemed to be happy with all the attention. Ruth and I hugged once more while the men took their place behind the wheel of our respective cars. I gave the girls a quick hug and thanked them for helping with Torrey.

"Are you coming back to the house?" Charlie asked.

"No," Eddie replied. "It's been a great afternoon but it's time for us to get back home."

"You'd better keep in touch," Ruth called out.

"I will," I assured her, "that's a promise."

We drove out of the parking lot behind our friends and followed them for a while until they took the turn toward their home and we continued down the highway toward Torrance.

"Every time I see Charlie and Ruth I remember Yellowstone Park and how cold it was up there in July," I reminded Eddie.

"Yeah, I never expected to see snow anywhere at that time of the year," he said.

"It was so cute to see those two little girls snuggled up in the makeshift bed in our breakfast nook," I remembered, "I could only imagine how it could be for us if we had kids of our own."

"That thought doesn't ever go away for you," he said, "does it?"

"I guess not," I thought a little. "I know you want kids too and sometimes I feel like I'm letting you down."

"Okay," he said firmly, "yes, I'd like to have a family; get it out of your head that you're letting me down. It'll happen when it's supposed to happen, in God's good time, and we can't change that; so, no more of that kind of talk."

That was the signal for the end of that conversation, and just in time. We turned into the entrance of the trailer park. We were home. I took Torrey for a walk while Eddie unloaded the trunk of the car. I set food out for the dog and he ate while I put everything away.

"Rhubarb's playing at the movies," Eddie announced, "do you feel like going?"

"To tell you the truth," I said, "all that fresh air today made me sleepy and I'm afraid I'd fall asleep during the show."

"It's playing tomorrow too," he told me, "we don't have any plans with anyone do we?"

"As a matter of fact no," I replied.

"Good, then let's have those left over sandwiches from the picnic, we'll play cards and then maybe we can work on that family you're so worried about," he laughed, "Rhubarb can wait until tomorrow."

251

It's funny how our body gets accustomed to a certain time to wake up and it doesn't keep track of the day of the week. 'It's Sunday today, Body, you can sleep a little longer,' I'd like to say but it doesn't work that way. Eddie and Torrey were gone out for their walk and had already made enough noise for me to be aware it was time to get up and get ready for Mass. I rolled off the bed and put my robe on before I folded the blankets and stored them and the pillows under the sofa. In an attempt to wake up a little more, I fixed the coffee pot and put it on the hot plate but didn't turn it on. I picked out a gray skirt and a pink blouse to wear for church and prepared to go to the Community House.

"I'll get the dog settled and then go on up to take a shower," Eddie said when he came in. "We should be able to make the 8 o'clock Mass." He put the newspaper on the table.

"Okay, I'll be ready when you get back." I headed out the door with my grooming paraphernalia and clean clothes.

The Community House was well maintained. There were several private shower stalls and a dressing room for each. We had separate entrances and accommodations for men and women. The toilets were against the wall closest to the entrances. Some mobile homes had their own toilet and shower facilities within their own trailer and they were stationed in a different area of the park; but there were many, like ours, which did not. I guess one could say this was a more modern version of an outhouse with the convenience of a shower included. It wasn't exactly the 'Ritz' and we didn't have the luxury of a granite bathtub but it served the purpose and we managed our personal care very well.

Eddie returned to our trailer shortly after I did. We checked the puppy and then left for Mass right on schedule. Again the church was full and again the Mass lasted only about forty minutes.

"One thing we can say," Eddie sat behind the wheel, "the Mass here doesn't last any longer than it does back home."

"That's true," I closed the passenger side door. "But I think the people are friendlier here than they are back in Fall River."

"Maybe that's because there's no parking lot at Saint Anne's church," he reasoned. "Everybody parks on the street and everyone just rushes out not paying much attention to anything or anyone else."

"I'm going to miss this place," I said.

"Not to change the subject," Eddie remarked. "Do you have Joan and Jessie's address?"

"As a matter of fact, I do." I answered. "I got it just before they moved. Why?"

252

"I thought we'd stop by to see them after the movie," he quickly added, "I don't want to stay long, I just think we should let them know we're leaving."

"That's a good idea," I agreed, "I'd really like to see their house too."

"Yeah," he drove into the trailer park. "We've had some good times together; we need to tell them good-bye."

"I agree," I entered the trailer first. "Besides, it will be good to see them again."

As soon as I put my hat and my purse away I donned my apron and began to fix breakfast. I turned on the burner under the coffee pot and got busy with the scrambled eggs, beans and ham and toast. Eddie spread the paper out on the table while I was getting everything ready. Torrey was happy on the floor with his chin resting on Eddie's shoe.

"What time is the movie this afternoon?" I asked.

"'Rhubarb' is the only film playing today," he looked for the movies section in the paper. "Here it is; 'Rhubarb' is the main movie. It starts at one, there are short subjects in between and then 'Rhubarb' runs again."

"I hope they're not going to show 'The Three Stooges'," I complained, "I really don't like those guys."

I put our filled breakfast plates on the table and poured the coffee.

"Somebody must like them," Eddie folded the paper. "They sure make a lot of movies. Anyway, we'll find out when we get there; I figure we should leave around twelve-thirty."

"Good, that'll give me time to read the funnies before we go." I took a bite of scrambled eggs and ham.

"Ah yes," he teased, "the educational section."

We were getting more confident about leaving Torrey for a couple of hours; he still had ample room in his box and seemed content to nap while we were away. Apparently 'Rhubarb' was a popular movie; the parking lot was full when we reached the theater. The stars were Ray Milland and Jan Sterling and also featured Gene Lockhart. The story was about the owner of a baseball team that isn't doing very until his Press Agent gives him an orange cat. He names the cat Rhubarb and the feline becomes a sort of lucky charm for the players. When the owner dies he leaves the bulk of his multi-million dollar estate, including the baseball team, to the cat with the faithful Press Agent in charge. The owner's daughter is not happy about her meager million or two and sets out to cause trouble for the Press Agent and his girlfriend and especially the cat. The movie ended well in spite of the daughter's antics and lawsuits. The Press Agent and his girlfriend get married and have a child and Rhubarb becomes a father and has his own little family of kittens.

"I think that's the funniest movie I ever saw," I said to Eddie as we left the theater.

"Me too," he held my hand as we walked to the car. "I don't know how the trainers were able to get the cat to do such crazy things like chasing golf balls in the beginning and running after the opposing team's dog later on in the movie."

"I liked the romantic scene when Rhubarb saw a picture of the pretty female cat and went chasing after her," we reached the car; I opened the passenger side door and got in.

"And you got your wish, no Three Stooges," he started the engine.

"I always enjoy Crazy Cat," I settled in my seat. "It seemed appropriate to have a cat cartoon today. And of course I always enjoy the Movietone News."

"Do you have the directions to Joan and Jess?" Eddie asked.

"Joan said their house was just off the highway," I pulled the note out from my purse and directed him down the road.

"Okay, so far, so good, just tell me where to turn."

"There's the house with a wishing well," I pointed, "that's where you turn right. That should be their street."

It was easy to distinguish their house from the others on their street because we recognized their trailer parked between the garage and the property fence. Eddie pulled in the driveway. They didn't wait for us to ring the front doorbell they came out to meet us as we stood by our car.

"We're so glad to see you," Joan opened her arms to hug me.

"Did you have any trouble finding the place?" Jessie extended his hand to Eddie.

"Joan gave the wife good directions," Eddie shook Jessie's hand. "We came right from the Stadium to here."

"Come on in," Joan invited, "let me show you around."

"Yeah," Jessie opened the door. "We have a lot more room here than we did at Shady Grove Trailer Park."

We got a quick tour of a beautiful roomy home decorated in subdued colors. The master bedroom was in blue and the guest room in pale lavender. The moderately sized kitchen was predominantly yellow with pretty daisy wall decorations and the tiled bathroom was green. The large living room's walls were off white and the furniture was upholstered in beige.

"This is really lovely," I said. "I know you're going to be happy here."

"We are already," Jess remarked. "It's not too far for either of us to travel to work and it's nice and quiet when we get home."

"What's going on with you two?" Joan asked.

"Quite a lot, actually," Eddie explained. "I got my draft notice and we have to head back to Massachusetts."

"Oh, no!" Jessie looked stunned. "You guys talked about settling down here." He ran his fingers through his hair. "That stupid war! I served in the last one and it wasn't funny; I know one thing for certain: I don't want to go there again."

"We didn't want to leave without telling you," Eddie said. "We've had some really good times together."

"Yes we did," Joan headed for the kitchen. "How would you like some crackers and cheese and soda?"

"We hadn't planned to stay very long," I said, "we have a new little puppy and we don't want to leave him for too long."

"Nonsense," Jessie said, "puppies are always fine. There's always enough time for a couple games of Hi-Lo-Jack. Get the crackers, Joan, I'll get the cards."

It was good to be with our friends again, even though we had no idea if or when we would ever see them again. There's an old saying: 'Enjoy today and let tomorrow take care of itself'.

The afternoon ended with the girls winning one game and the guys winning the other. We decided to call the games a draw rather than to play a rubber match. Joan and I hugged each other tearfully and the men gave firm handshakes all around with a promise that we would keep in touch.

Torrey's tail was wagging frantically when we came home. His tail had been clipped soon after birth, which is customary for Doberman Pinschers. I always found it comical to see this little stump of a tail moving as fast as it did and it seemed like his whole rear end was trying to overcompensate for the missing part of the tail. I picked him up and placed him on the floor where he danced around in circles.

"I guess that's our signal that he wants to go out," Eddie picked up the leash and tied it on the dog's collar. "Come on, Pup, you've been cooped up long enough."

They went out the door and that was my signal to look in the ice box to see what leftovers could be prepared into supper. Julie popped in as I opened a loaf of bread.

"Where have you guys been?" She sat at the table. "We haven't seen you for a couple of days."

"We just came back from visiting Joan and Jessie," I explained. "They're doing really well and their house is beautiful."

"We haven't been over there yet," she leaned on her elbows. "Darryl said we should get over there one of these days."

"We went to see 'Rhubarb' at the Stadium and decided to go over there after the movie," I put mayo on the bread and added baloney. "We're having sandwiches for supper; do you want to join us?"

"That sounds great to me," she got up and went to the door. "I'll go check with Darryl; I'll be right back."

Eddie returned with Torrey and filled his bowl with dog food before putting it on the floor. "Did I just see Julie leaving here?" he asked.

"Yes, I invited her and Darryl to join us for supper," I said. "I think it's time for us to tell them about us leaving."

"You're right," he agreed. "We don't want them to hear about it from anyone else."

"Here I am," Julie called from outside the door. "Darryl said to give him about ten minutes and he'll be right over." She came in carrying half of a pineapple upside down cake. "I thought you could help us get rid of this dessert I made yesterday."

"You know us," Eddie laughed, "there's always room for dessert."

"Is baloney okay or do you prefer peanut butter?" I asked. "Yes, baloney is fine; do you have any mustard?"

Sure," I pulled out the jar from the icebox. "I'll put it on the table, use as much as you want."

"Oh," She added, "and Darryl said he'd like to play cards after we eat if you guys don't have other plans."

Julie helped me set the table and poured the lemonade while I put out the sandwiches and the potato salad and chips. Darryl came in just as we were ready to sit down.

"So, is there anything new around here?" he asked.

"Well," Eddie hesitated, "we were going to tell you later but since you asked; yes there is something new."

"Whoa," he suddenly looked serious, "what's going on?"

"I received my notice a couple of days ago and I have to report to the draft board in Massachusetts in about a month," Eddie said.

"That sort of blows your plans for staying in California," Julie reached for my hand, "doesn't it?"

"I guess it does," I shrugged, "but we're not gone yet. Let's enjoy this supper and see if these guys can beat us at cards tonight."

"Oh yeah, right," Darryl said, "like you have a chance. Pass the platter of sandwiches."

No one talked about either the draft or the Korean War or about us leaving; it was like our lives were being put on hold for this evening and we would be able to hang on to this moment forever. Without saying a word we held our hugs a little longer as our friends were leaving and substituted the verbal 'good-byes' with 'See ya tomorrow'. Eddie and I walked the dog together before we settled in for the night.

"It was a nice evening," I looked up at the sky, "It's good we told Julie and Darryl about us having to leave."

"Yes it is," he held my hand; "it wouldn't have been right just to spring the news on them at the last minute."

Torrey ran back and forth between us as we proceeded on our evening visit to the Community House and back. Eddie opened the sofa while I gave our puppy his water and then put him in his box for the night.

"Good night, Hon," I slipped into bed.

"Good night, Sweetheart," he crawled in beside me; "don't worry, kid, everything will work out all right." He kissed me.

# HOUSE ON WHEELS

## CHAPTER 19

Making Eddie's lunch was easier this morning, I had wrapped up the left-over sandwiches individually in wax paper after supper last night, so it was just a matter of packing two of them in his lunch pail and filling his thermos with coffee. I added two Twinkies and...Voila: lunch. Mine would be the same.

"I'm glad Julie and Darryl came over last night," Eddie said, "it was almost like having a party."

"I know," I agreed, "I'm going to miss them."

"We're both going to miss a lot of things," Eddie bit into his toast, "for one thing we're not going to have this kind of weather in Massachusetts."

"You're right, especially with the winter months ahead," I took a sip of coffee. "I'm not looking forward to the snow."

"I don't think we need to worry about snow for now," he got up from the table and picked up his lunch pail. "The weather may not be as warm as here but it should be pretty good all across the country at this time of the year."

"When do you think we'll actually be leaving?" I picked up the dishes from the table and put them in the sink.

"The job should be done today or tomorrow," he thought a little, "and I think we could probably be ready to go by Sunday."

"That's less than a week," I turned on the heat under the kettle of water. "I'd better start checking things off our 'to do' list today."

"That's a good idea;" he kissed me, "I'll see you after work."

Torrey had become accustomed to being tied to the fence. He seemed to like being outside and had found a shady place under the trailer where I placed a dish of water and an old carpet for him to lie down. This worked out well for me to go over to the Community House to get my laundry done. After I put the clothes in the washer I went looking for the manager.

"Hi, Jim," I said when I located him near the storage room. "I was wondering if you could find me another box for our dog."

"Did he bust up the old one?" Jim asked.

"No, not really," I stretched my neck to peek into the storage area. "He's growing and we need a bigger box."

"How is he getting along with the fish?" he wanted to know.

"He doesn't bother much with them," I said, "I keep him tied close to the fence and he likes to sleep under the trailer."

"I got a few boxes back there," he headed for the storage closet, "come take a look and see if there's something you can use."

We looked around and I found a good sturdy box that would fit in the back seat of the car, "I'll take this one, if it's okay."

"Sure," he pulled the box out from the back of the room. "Is there anything else I can do for you?'

"Well," I hesitated, "Eddie and I are going to be leaving in about a week."

"I'm sorry to hear that," he lifted up his cap and scratched his head. "You've been good tenants; is there anything wrong?"

"Oh no," I answered quickly, "We really like it here. It's just that…Eddie got a letter from Massachusetts that he's being called up. He has to report to the draft board in a couple of weeks."

"I thought we'd be all done with wars after WWII," he shook his head, "but now we're looking at that mess in Korea. It never seems to end." He picked up the box, "here let me take this down to the trailer for you."

"Thank you," I started back to the laundry room to put my clothes in the dryer, "just leave it near the fish pond, the dog can't reach it there."

Torrey was still sleeping under the trailer when I got back with the laundry. He definitely was making progress. He was eating better and was beginning to get a little meat on his bony frame. He came to greet me at the trellis but showed no interest in following me into the trailer. "Okay, stay out here if you want," I said out loud, "that'll give me a chance to get something done without having to put you in the box." He looked at me sort of funny. I proceeded to get the ironing done and was able to wash the floor before Eddie came home.

259

"Well, Sweetheart," Eddie said when he came in, "tomorrow's my last day at work, and it looks like we may be able to leave early next week."

"I think we can be ready," I put a pot of water on the hot plate to cook the pasta for American Chop Suey. "Tomorrow I'll check the cupboards and see what we'll need for the trip. I'd rather not have to stop at a market if we don't have to."

"I figure it will take us about ten or twelve days to go back," he picked up his clean clothes from the sofa, "that's counting the time to visit the parks we want to see on our way." He started out the door to go up to the Community House.

"Oh, Honey," I called, "would you mind putting the big box that's next to the fish pond in the back seat of the car?"

"Okay, I got it!"

I set the plates on the table and finished putting supper together while he was gone. He put his work clothes in the laundry basket and then sat down. "I was thinking while I was taking a shower," he filled his plate from the serving bowl. "I'll stop at the gas station tomorrow and see if I can pick up some maps."

"That's good thinking," I poured milk in both our glasses. "Do you have an idea of the places you want to visit?"

"Grand Canyon is right up there on top of the list," he took a second helping of Chop Suey and a few green beans. "I also want to see the Petrified Forest and the Carlsbad Caverns."

"Are those places close together?" I stood up to get the bowl of tapioca pudding from the ice box and scooped some out into two dessert dishes.

"See?" he took a sip of milk. "That's what we need to find out," he took a spoonful of pudding, "...and why we need the maps."

I was beginning to get excited about our upcoming adventure. Our sojourn in California was nearly over, at least for the time being, there was still more to see in this wonderful country and we were about to set out and complete Eddie's life time dream of seeing the Wonders of the United States. We cleared the table together and chatted about how good it will be to see the family again. He fed the dog while I did the dishes and then we played a few games of rummy.

"Let's walk Torrey together," Eddie clipped on the leash. "It's going to be a long ride for him too, I'm glad you got him the bigger box today, he's going to need it."

"He's growing fast now that he's eating better," we walked hand in hand. "I didn't want him to feel all cramped up during the ride."

It was a beautiful starry night, the moon was high in the sky and there was a slight breeze, "there aren't going to be many of these nights once we get back to Fall River," he said.

"Well there may be," I contradicted, "but somehow, over there, we don't make time to take advantage of them."

"I guess you're right," he handed me the leash; "we just get too busy to go out and enjoy these simple things."

I waited for Eddie to come out of the Community House and then he held Torrey's leash and waited for me. We walked back silently, hand in hand, connected, and yet each of us deep in our own thoughts. We put Torrey in his box when we got home. I thought about the uncertainties which lay ahead and about the joy of this special time together; and this moment in our snug, homey little house on wheels, became all the sweeter.

"Shall I pack you a lunch?" Eddie was just returning from his walk with the dog.

"Yes, I think I'll be working all day," he put the leash away. "Even if the job is done early, I still have to go to the union hall to let them know I'm leaving the area and then I'll get my journeyman's book back."

"So, you expect to get home at the regular time?" I asked.

"Probably," he buttered two pieces of toast with peanut butter. "I'll also stop to get those maps I was telling you about. If they don't have all the ones I'm looking for at the first one I'll try another one or a couple more if I have to."

"That's what I like: tenacity," I quoted: "If at first you don't succeed…try, try, try again!"

"Don't laugh," he persisted, "this is how we're going to save ourselves a lot of unnecessary miles and aggravation."

"I know," I kissed him on the cheek, "that's how you've gotten us this far."

It wasn't the usual hearty ham and eggs breakfast but it filled our tummies and Eddie left for work. As a result of this easy morning meal the cleanup was a cinch and I was ready to tackle the inventory chores. First, I tied Torrey to the fence; I really didn't need for him to be sniffing around the contents of everything that came out of the cupboards. And then, armed with a pad and pencil, I began to make a list of the things we would need to buy in order to replenish our supplies for travel. We couldn't always be able to plug in to electricity when we were in the National Parks and so we had to stock up on foods we could either prepare on our small Coleman burner or foods we could eat cold.

I heard a knock on the door, and opened it. Julie stepped in. "What are you do-ing?" She looked around, "this place is a mess!"

"Eddie's finishing up his job today and so I'm checking out what we're going to need for our trip back east." I pushed some stuff over on the seat near the table and sat down. "Push the containers over on your side and sit."

"That's sooner than you expected," Julie looked surprised, "isn't it?"

"There are some parks we want to visit on our way back," I explained. "And of course there may be a few loose ends we'll need to tie up back in Fall River before Eddie leaves for the service."

"Yeah, there's always unexpected stuff," she looked up at me. "I've decided to go to business school in January."

"I'm glad for you, Julie," I put my hand over hers, "we've talked about this be-fore, you'll do very well. I'm sure of it." I stood up and reached in the cupboard for two glasses. "Let's celebrate with a glass of lemonade."

"I don't want to interrupt!" She said quickly, "but hey, why not?"

She stayed for about a half hour and we talked about her plans for after school and the possibility of a career in business.

"I'm a little nervous about going back to school," she said.

"Hey," I encouraged her, "It's always scary when we set out to do something we've never done before. But I'm sure you're going to do very well."

"What makes you so sure?" she sipped her lemonade.

"Look at yourself," I smiled at her, "you're pretty, you've got a great personali-ty, and you're smart. All you need is confidence."

"Confidence, that's a big one," she looked more than a little apprehensive.

"Well that's the point about going back to school, isn't it? When you acquire the skills you need in school, confidence will follow. You'll see."

"I guess you're right," she finished her lemonade. "I should go, if I keep hang-ing around here you'll never get anything done; thanks for the pep talk."

"I'm going to miss you a lot," I hugged her; "we'll see you before we leave."

I resumed my inventory and began returning the stock to the shelves and making note of the items we would need to replenish. By the time Eddie returned it was as if nothing had been done.

"What did you do all day?" he asked as he came in. "It looks the same as when I left."

I suppressed a growl and pulled out a long piece of paper from the drawer, "I took everything off the shelves and made this list of things we need to pick up before we leave. How did you make out? Were you able to get all the maps you wanted?"

"As a matter of fact, yes," he held up a handful of brochures, "I even got one for southern California and Mount Palomar."

"When are we going to be able to go there?" I asked.

"Maybe the day after tomorrow," he said. "Do you think Julie could watch the dog for a day while we take a trip to the San Diego Zoo and Tijuana; and on our way back we can go to see the observatory at Mount Palomar; look, I have it right here."

"We can ask her, I guess." There wasn't a lot of information on the brochure, "this might be interesting. But, even if it's not we know the zoo and Tijuana will be good to see."

"We'll look at these maps tonight after supper," Eddie placed the little pile on the counter, "we'll be able to see where we should go first and plan our trip accordingly."

I warmed up the leftover chop suey while he went up to the Community House and he brought Torrey in from outside when he came back. "Has he been out all day?"

"I didn't want him jumping on the stuff I was taking down from the shelves," I told him, "so I tied him outside. He seems happy there."

"I hope that's not going to cause a problem for us when we have to confine him to the box in the car."Eddie sat at the table.

"I hadn't thought about that," I set the platter of chop suey in the center of the table before I sat down. "But then again, while we're in the car he won't have much choice, will he?"

"I guess not," he reached for another spoonful of peas. "I had to go to three different gas stations to get all the maps I wanted."

"Did you find all the places you were looking for?" I took a swallow of milk.

"Yes, I did," he looked toward the maps on the counter; "we can work on them tonight and put them in the order we plan to travel."

"You know more about that stuff than I do," I picked up the plates to put them in the sink. "Do you want some cookies for dessert?"

"If there's some tapioca pudding left," he said, "I'll have that."

I scooped the last of the pudding into a dish and handed it to him before I finished clearing the table. "I'm anxious to see what places you want to see."

"Get a pad and pencil so you can make notes as we go through the maps and we'll have an idea of what routes we're looking for." He finished his dessert.

He spread the maps and brochures on the table and began arranging them as if he were working on a jigsaw puzzle. "This state is before this one, and that one comes after that, and we'll have to go a little further south to take this one in," he mumbled aloud as he moved the maps and brochures around.

Finally I was done with the clean-up and brought the pad and pencil to the table as he dictated our tentative itinerary.

"But, you know," he held one more brochure in his hand, "I think we really should spend one more day in southern California and a few hours in Tijuana."

"You mentioned this before," I thought about all the things we had to do before we planned to leave. "I don't know if Julie can watch Torrey on such short notice."

"I think Julie will be happy to watch him while we're gone," he opened the brochure about Mount Palomar. "He knows her and she likes him, she'll take good care of him, I'm sure."

"Do you still think Thursday is good?" I sat closer to him to look at the pamphlet.

"I think Thursday is the only day we can go," he looked at the pictures and the information regarding the observatory. "We'll ask her tomorrow and if she agrees, then we can go out to shop for the canned goods and cereal we're going to need for the trip. That will leave the milk and stuff for the icebox for us to pick up on Saturday. That should work out all right."

"You've got it all figured out, haven't you?" I waited for the announcement of his further plans.

"Look at this map," he pointed. "We can go straight down to the San Diego Zoo first, that's not far from Tijuana and then we can come up this other route and that will take us right to Mount Palomar. It's like a big circle." He looked at me, "it would be a shame to be so close to this place without going to see it."

"I'm always amazed at how you know about these places," I gathered the maps in the order he had set them up along with the pad and proposed itinerary and wrapped a rubber band around them. "How do you even know about this place?"

"There was an article in National Geographic about it when it opened up a couple of years ago," he said, "and I've been curious about it ever since."

"Well, I guess your curiosity will be satisfied on Thursday," I replied, "now it's time to take Torrey for a walk before we get to bed."

I knocked on Julie's door around ten o'clock. She was still in her bathrobe, sitting at the table with a cup of coffee. "Come on in," she invited. "I'll get you a cup of coffee."

"I'm sorry," I apologized, "did I wake you up?"

"Oh no," she poured the coffee, "I just like to lounge a little in the morning, you know, read the paper and all that."

"I came to ask you a favor," I took a sip of coffee.

"Sure," she sat at the table, "anything, what is it?"

"Eddie and I would like to take a trip to San Diego and Tijuana tomorrow," I hesitated. "And we wondered if you could watch Torrey for the day."

"Are you kidding?" she smiled. "I'd love to, just leave his food and his leash and we'll get along just fine."

"Oh, wow! Thanks," I answered, "that's such a relief."

"Hey, it's no problem," she smiled again, "I love that dog."

"We want to leave early," I said. "Will that be a problem?"

"Of course not," she assured me. "I need something to get me going in the morning; I'm looking forward to it."

"We'll be going out for awhile today to get supplies for the trip," I finished my coffee. "We'll leave Torrey in his box; he'll be alright while we're gone."

"No, no bring him over now," she insisted. "Bring his leash; we can start to get acquainted today."

"Okay," I got up from the table, "but I'll tell you what; I'll wait 'til you get dressed and you can come over when you're ready."

"It'll only be about a half hour," she picked up the coffee cups. "I won't take long."

True to her word, Julie arrived less than a half hour later. Eddie and I were ready to go on our errands and Julie came to pick up the dog. "Take your time, you two," she called back, "We are going to be just fine."

We went to the supermarket in San Pedro where the prices were slightly cheaper than our neighborhood market. We picked up Campbell's soups, beans, pasta, dog food, paper supplies and the like. When we returned, we worked together to place our purchases securely on the shelves and ready for travel. Our previous experiences had taught us that everything needed to be in its place and packed well enough and not likely to land on the floor if we should encounter bumpy roads. This took up a good part of the day.

"I've had a great day with this little guy," Julie came over with the dog on the leash. "I can't wait until tomorrow."

"It looks like he had fun too," I said, "where did you guys go?"

"Oh, not far," she put Torrey on the floor and untied his leash. "We walked all around the trailer park and we had to stop every once in a while for people to pet him." She rubbed him behind his ears, "he's a really friendly dog."

"I know," Eddie put the leash away, "thanks for agreeing to take care of him tomorrow."

"I'm looking forward to it," she started for home, "see you tomorrow Torrey."

"Is between 8:00 and 8:30 still okay?" I asked.

"Oh yes," she assured me, "I'll be up and ready for him; Darryl usually leaves around that time."

"It looks like our dog has a new friend," I looked at Eddie. "Okay, what were we going to do?"

"You said you wanted to make a list of the stuff you wanted to get for the icebox on Saturday," he reminded me.

"Right," I reached for my pad and pencil, "and with your help it'll be a lot easier because you can tell me what your preferences are."

"Okay," he stated firmly, "baloney is on the top of the list…write it down."

"Why am I not surprised?" I wrote down another few things like cheese and tomatoes and lettuce." I looked the list over. "I think if we shop for the icebox stuff later in the day on Saturday it would be better. "

"We should probably pick up some ice at the same time," Eddie suggested. "That way we can pack the food right around it and it'll stay cold longer."

""It'll also be easier if we gas up the car before we hitch up," I said, "that'll be one less thing to do in the morning."

"That's enough for today," Eddie opened the icebox. "Put that pad and stuff away; just leave the map and stuff for tomorrow on the counter; I'm getting hungry." He moved the containers around in the icebox and picked out a few leftovers and put them on the counter. "Here, let's have an 'icebox clean-up meal' and make room for the stuff we'll be buying on Saturday."

"I like that idea, and," I reached for the warming pots, "it'll take a lot less time than making something new."

"I didn't get a chance to read the paper this morning," Eddie said during supper. "I'll read the news while you clean up the kitchen and then we can take the dog for his walk a little earlier."

"Did you hear me tell Julie we'd bring Torrey over between 8 o'clock and 8:30?" I asked. "That sounds about right and we should get to San Diego close to ten." He picked up the paper from the seat next to him and opened it up. "There's a few pictures here about the Korean War, but not a lot of news about it."

"I guess that's good," I tipped my head, "that must mean things aren't getting worse."

"Here's a bit of news," he turned the sports page for me to see. "The New York Giants won the World Series Pennant over the Brooklyn Dodgers; I bet there's a lot of celebrating going on over there."

"That's one thing I've noticed around here," I looked over Ed's shoulder, "people don't get as excited about baseball as they do back east."

"That's because there aren't any major league teams around here." He looked at me, "at least none that I know of."

"Come to think of it, I think the teams farthest west are the Cubs and White Sox from Chicago, and maybe Saint Louis, I'm not sure." I thought a minute, "I guess if the teams were more spread out, they would be spending more time traveling across the country than playing baseball."

"You've got a point there," he folded the paper. "I guess we've got time to play cards before we go to bed."

"Okay," I pulled the cards and pad out of the drawer, "here you shuffle while I get a pencil."

After a couple of games of Rummy, we were ready to proceed with our evening routine and our evening walk with Torrey before calling it a day.

"I'd better set the alarm for tomorrow," Eddie said, "I do want to get an early start."

"You'll probably be up before it rings anyway," I replied.

"Probably," he laughed, "but that little jingle might just be helpful for you, you know what a sleepyhead you are."

"Touché", I proceeded to fix the sofa, "and in that case I should get into bed right now."

He put out the lights and crawled in beside me.

267

The alarm roused me out of my sound sleep. Eddie and Torrey were gone for their morning walk. I picked up the brown plaid dress with the wide white collar and other paraphernalia I had set out the night before and headed for the Community House. I met Eddie on the way.

"Are you going to want a big breakfast before we leave?" I wanted to know.

"No, I think Rice Krispies and milk will be fine," he answered. "I'll just take Torrey home and then I'll come back to take my shower; I'll meet you back at the trailer."

By the time he returned I had the bowls and the cereal on the table and we sat down to eat. "We're running good on time," he said. "By the time we clean up in here, it'll be time to bring the dog over to Julie's."

"Yeah," I looked at the clock. "This is about the time Darryl usually leaves for work."

It didn't take long for the cleaning up, I picked up the leash and walked Torrey over to Julie's trailer; she was up and dressed in blue shorts and a white shirt.

"Shall I leave the box for you?" I asked.

"Oh no, he'll be fine," she said. "He'll be okay on the floor while he's in here and I'll use the leash when we go out."

I handed her the dog food and the water dish. "He usually eats around five and I just keep the water dish full and he drinks whenever he's thirsty."

"Stop fussing," she laughed. "You sound like a mother hen, we're going to be just fine; you guys have fun."

"Look who's talking," Darryl said as he came out of the bedroom dressed in a suit and tie. "All she's talked about the last couple of days is about having a day with the dog."

"Oh you!" She kissed him. "Get going, I'll see you tonight."

I walked out with Darryl and we got into our respective cars.

"See you tonight," Eddie waved, he was already behind the wheel.

I got settled in the passenger seat and we were on our way. We drove through the now familiar streets of Torrance and headed straight for the highway going south. Although we had driven in this direction before, the scenery continued to amaze us. It was another beautiful day.

"Turn on the radio to a music station," Eddie suggested, "see if you can find some Country Music."

I fiddled around with the dial and Hank Williams' voice came blaring out:

"Hey, good lookin' what-ya got cookin',

how's about cookin' something up with me"...

We both laughed and joined in:

"Hey, sweet baby, don't ya think maybe,

We could find us a brand new recipe"...

Singing made the time go by faster as we drove past the scenic countryside; at once getting a glimpse of the beautiful blue ocean and then seeing towering mountains in the distance. I wanted to hold the picture in my memory forever. We arrived in San Diego in mid morning and Eddie drove directly to the zoo. The first animal we saw was a white, Salmon-crested Cockatoo. He was at the entrance making loud hard sounds. We found out his name was King Tut and had come to the zoo through the efforts of Frank Buck, the wild animal hunter. He was acting as a greeter for the visitors of the zoo. He was amazingly agile; now on his perch and now on the ground, he seemed to have free run of the area. King Tut was a crowd pleaser and held our attention for quite some time. When we finally progressed into the grounds of the zoo, we saw beautiful peacocks roaming around free. Most of them dragged their long tails behind them. We walked from one display to another and then we finally did see one who strutted around majestically with its fan of a hundred eyes spread proudly behind him as if to say: 'Look at me!'. He was beautiful.

This was a zoo in progress. One of the most recent acquisitions had been a Snow Leopard, unfortunately for us the animal had died about a month before we visited there. The large concrete formations which had been its home were still there but unoccupied. All that remained was a photograph. There were signs around the park indicating some of the animals we visited were newcomers to the zoo. There was a threesome of young Gorillas who had been there for only about two years. They had been named Albert, Bouba and Bata by some school children in California. I could only imagine what they might look like when they would be full grown.

"Did you notice something different about this zoo?" I asked Eddie.

"What do you mean?" he stopped to look around.

"There aren't many cages," I remarked, "each group of animals is kept in enclosures similar to what they'd be living in if they were in the wild."

"I see what you mean," Eddie pointed to the large rocks and trees and water holes in the Gorilla area. "It's fixed up like they might be living in an African Jungle."

"Right," I noticed an oversized pond with raised uneven borders. "Look over there! What's that big animal? Can you see what the sign says?"

"It's a Walrus," he moved closer to the sign. "It says here his name is Bosco and he's a newcomer to the zoo as of this year."

He was much larger than the pinnipeds we had seen before. He had whiskers but no tusks and made loud barking and whistling sounds.

"Every turn of the road is a new adventure," I said. "Look at those monkeys over there, they look like they're people watching from those high tree branches."

A little farther down the path we saw brown bears content to lie in the sun within their own large enclosures; and still further along there was a large pool of icy water for three young beautiful white Polar bears named Olaf, Frieda and Hilda who had recently come from Norway as cubs. We couldn't help but notice their enormous paws, I wondered if the paws would grow even larger of if the Polar Bear would grow larger in proportion to the paws.

"Well, what do you think?" Eddie asked as we came out of the Polar bear exhibit. "Are you getting hungry?"

"Yes, I am a little," I replied. "But I don't really want to eat here. I thought maybe we could get a taco or something in Tijuana."

"That's what I was thinking," he took my hand and we walked toward the exit. "We're not that far from Mexico."

"Okay, then let's do it." We passed King Tut on the way out of the zoo. He was still charming the visitors. "I'm glad we didn't miss this place, it's pretty interesting."

Eddie was right; we reached the Mexican border in about thirty minutes and drove into Tijuana without incident. We looked for a place to park and found one in front of the leather shop where we had stopped the last time we were there. Our first order of business was to locate a taco stand.

"I love these things," I said as I bit into my fried tortilla loaded with ground beef and salad vegetables and cheese. "Now this is something I AM going to miss. I've never seen any tortillas for sale at the Stop and Shop back home."

"Well," he thought for a minute, "I guess you could make them on flat toasted bread."

"I suppose so," I looked at him, "but it wouldn't be quite the same."

We ate with relish, drank our containers of lemonade and walked around leisurely. We saw a mule attached to a cart. The entrepreneur had dyed zebra-like stripes on the mule and offered to take our pictures wearing large Mexican sombreros. How could we resist? We climbed on the seat, the senor handed Eddie the reins and we put on our best smiles for the camera.

We visited the little shops and bought little statues, toys, and souvenirs to bring back to our family back home and a dress and a leather purse for me as a remembrance

270

our time in this quaint little town. Again, this time, the bull fights were scheduled for later in the evening so we opted to leave Mexico and head toward Mount Palomar.

When we reached the border again, the customs officer examined our purchases, looked at our birth certificates and waved us on our way. It was late afternoon when we reached the planetarium. It had taken us more than two and a half hours to reach Mount Palomar. It was an uphill ride along a winding road with incredible views at every turn. We saw the dome which housed the Hale telescope from a long distance away but it was not constantly in our vision. When we reached the summit it was more than a little disappointing to find out it was closed to visitors. There were guards around the perimeter of the facility but no access to the inside.

"I'm sorry," the uniformed guard apologized. "You are not allowed inside; actually there would be nothing you would be able to see because it's still too early to observe the night sky."

"Of course I realize that," Eddie said, "but isn't there a planetarium in there where we could see a simulation and also see how the telescope works?"

"No, Sir," the guard replied, "this is the real thing, no simulations here; you can only observe when it's dark. Sorry."

"Well," Eddie looked very disappointed, "at least we saw the place. Maybe someday we'll be able to come back. Who knows?"

"If we ever do," I suggested, "maybe we can check first and see when it's open for viewing."

"Okay, Smarty Pants," he took my hand, "maybe we should. In the meanwhile, let's head down the mountain."

When we reached Rincon Valley, we saw a nice restaurant. "Hey, kid," Eddie said, "how about we splurge?"

"Do you mean eat here; really?" I got excited. "Are you sure we can do this?"

"Who knows if or when we'll ever get back here," he drove into the parking lot. "Let's just do it."

We walked into the foyer from which crystal-like chandeliers hung from the ceiling.. The tuxedoed maitre d' greeted us at the door and led us to the gracious dining room and seated us at a small rectangular table covered with a white tablecloth and two place settings with white cloth napkins and silverware. I felt so elegant. He handed us each a huge menu and took our orders. I chose a petite filet mignon and Eddie ordered a cattleman's steak. We were served hot coffee while we waited for our dinners. When our steaks arrived they were perfectly done (medium rare) and were served with stuffed baked potatoes and haricots verts (string beans). The dessert was included and consisted of puff pastry with strawberries and cream. We ate heartily and chatted about our wonderful day. The waiter brought the check on a small brown tray.

"This isn't bad," Eddie said, "the bill comes to nine dollars. I'm going to leave a dollar tip."

"Are you saying the meal cost ten dollars?" I was flabbergasted. "No wonder we don't go out to eat often."

"Don't worry about it, Sweetheart," he put the money on the tray, "it's okay, you only live once."

We walked out to the parking lot together. "We still have another couple of hours before we get back to Torrance," Eddie announced.

"It'll be dark by the time we get home," I said. "I hope it won't be too late for Julie and Darryl."

"You know," Eddie got in the car, "I didn't even think about the dog all day, until now."

"Come to think of it," I sat next to him, "neither did I; I hope they didn't have too much trouble with the dog."

"I doubt it," he backed out of the parking space, "every time I see them together they all seem to be having fun."

"That's true," I turned on the radio. "Look toward that field over there, the sun is starting to go down; isn't the sky beautiful?"

"Yeah, it'll be dark soon," he drove onto the highway. "See if you can find some news on the radio."

I moved the dial to a CBS station, Edward R. Murrow was already broadcasting from New York. He reported heavy fighting in Korea at Heartbreak Ridge since mid September where North Korea was fighting against American and French forces for control of Mundung-ni Valley.

"It doesn't look like the fighting is getting any better over there, "Eddie remarked. "I think it's going to get worse before it gets better."

"You're probably right," I replied, "otherwise the government would have ended the draft and we wouldn't have to be heading back east quite so soon."

The news ended with Mr. Murrow's famous words, "Good night and good luck."

"See if you can find some music," Eddie suggested.

"You know," I turned the dial, "there used to be a lot of shows on radio on Thursday nights; but a lot of them like the Kate Smith Hour and The Hit Parade have gone on TV."

"Yeah, I know," he replied, "but maybe there's a disc jockey on who plays popular songs, or even cowboy stuff."

272

We were driving on a country highway and the reception was not that great. I turned the dial slowly: '...too young to really be in love...' "Hey," I said, "That's Nat King Cole!"

"It sure is," Eddie started to sing along...

"They say that's love's a word, a word we've only heard..."

"And can't begin to know the meaning of..." I chimed in.

The course was set for the rest of the way home. Tony Bennett sang his rendition of Hank William's 'Cold Cold Heart', Mario Lanza sang 'Be My Love' and we sang along with them all. The time and the miles melted away.

"Come on in," Julie called out when we knocked on their trailer door. "How was your day?"

"It was unbelievable," I was delighted to see our little puppy jumping around and happy to see us. "I hope Torrey didn't give you too much trouble."

"We had a good day too," she nudged Darryl, "I even got this guy to come walk with us tonight after supper."

"We brought this for you," I handed her a little statuette made of adobe clay and yarn. "It's not much but we want you to know we appreciate you watching the dog for us."

"I love it," she said, "but you know you didn't have to do that."

"It's just a little remembrance of us," Eddie picked up the puppy, "we'd better get going, thanks a lot."

Julie handed me the leash and Torrey's bowls, "there's no need to rush off."

"I'm sure you're ready to call it a day too," I hugged her, "thanks again."

Eddie carried Torrey home and settled him down. He then retrieved our purchases from the car and we put them away before we took our pre-bedtime trip to the Community House. We were still exhilarated about our wonderful adventure as we prepared the sofa and tucked Torrey into his box for the night.

"I'm going to remember this day for a long time," I said as I slid under the covers."

"I am too," Eddie turned off the lights. "It's too bad we didn't get to see the Hale Telescope and see how it works."

"Our timing was off this time," I lifted the covers for him; "maybe we'll get a chance to come back someday." We kissed good-night.

Both Eddie and I slept past seven this morning. We didn't have any particular place to go today except to Aunt Bina's this evening.

"Are you planning to do laundry this morning?" Eddie poured cereal into two bowls and added milk.

"I thought I'd wait until tomorrow," I collected the spoons and napkins from the drawer, "I'll strip the bed first thing and we'll be all set for our trip home."

"I'm going to take the wheels off the trailer and have them checked," Eddie got up from the table to reach for the coffee pot on the hot plate. "Do you want a cup?"

"Yes, thanks," I moved the cups next to each other. "That's a good idea to check out the wheels."

"Well we don't want to have a problem like we had when we left Fall River," he sat down at the table. "It shouldn't take me too long to do that."

"And while you do that, I'll double check the list we put together to make sure we're not forgetting anything." I took a sip of coffee. "Did you take the dog for a walk yet?"

"I'm going to do that as soon as I finish my coffee," he finished his cereal and put his bowl in the sink. "While I'm at the Community House I'm going to inquire about checking out."

"That's a good idea," It was my turn to put my dish in the sink. "While you're up there you might want to pick up a newspaper."

"You're a mind reader!" he drank his coffee. "That's just what I planned to do; and while I'm up there I'm going to ask Jim if I can borrow some blocks for the trailer while I get the wheels checked out."

"It looks like we both have a busy day ahead of us," I picked up Eddie's cup and he headed out the door.

Except for a short break for lunch, we hardly saw each other all day. He replaced the trailer wheels after lunch and returned the blocks to the Community House.

"We've got six good wheels and six good tires," he announced, "the tires on the trailer were a little low but the attendant at the gas station said it was probably because they were not used for a couple of months."

"Did he check for leaks?" I wanted to know.

"Oh yeah," he nodded his head, "he put them in water and there were no bubbles indicating any problems."

"That's good," I said, "I'm assuming it was the same with the car tires."

"Yep," he sat at the table. "What time are we supposed to be at Auntie's?"

"She said around five," I sat across from him. "I baked a cake to bring over there tonight."

"They'll like that," he spread the paper on the table. "I'll read the paper while you get ready and then I'll go up for a shower."

Torrey was settled comfortably with his chin on Eddie's foot while I went up to the Community House with my clothes over my arm. The paper was folded neatly on the table when I returned. I set out Torrey's food and we were ready to leave when Eddie came back.

Albert and Bonnie were already at Aunt Bina's when we got there. Bonnie had taken over the kitchen and Eva and Loretta were in charge of the dining room. Uncle Victor and Albert were delegated to the living room and Auntie invited us to join them.

"When Bonnie's in charge I just stay out of the way," she said. "Jeanne will you help me carry these lemonade glasses in to the men?"

Loretta was not far behind us, "where's the dog?"

"I thought you were helping out in the dining room," Aunt Bina questioned.

"My mother said she's all set in there and I can go walk the dog if I want to," she announced. "Where's his leash?"

"Don't be long," Eva called out, "dinner will be on the table in about fifteen minutes."

It was too early for the wrestling matches, so we watched the news on TV until dinner was served. Bonnie had outdone herself again with a feast starting with tossed salad, followed by roast chicken and prime rib beef (done medium rare). There was a choice of mashed or baked potatoes and mixed vegetables in a buttery sauce. She had baked apple and blueberry pie (with ice cream of course). My poor little cake paled by comparison but she graciously served it with her gourmet fare on an elegant platter.

"I hope someday I'll be able to cook like you, Bonnie," I said as she served the coffee.

"Of course you will," she answered, "you just have to keep trying new things and don't be afraid to make mistakes," she pinched my cheek, "that's how you learn."

"We're going to miss all of you," I said.

"When are you actually leaving?" Auntie asked.

"We've decided to leave on Sunday," Eddie stirred his coffee. "We figure there will be less traffic on the road for the first leg of our trip."

"Eddie got the tires checked out for the trailer and the car today," I said, "that's one thing less to worry about."

"I sure hope you guys make it back here again sometime soon," said Bonnie. "I can tell you for sure, I'm going to miss you too."

"Right now everything is up in the air for us." Eddie reminded everyone, "I'll be going in the service. Where? I don't know, and whether the wife will be able to come with me, I don't know that either."

"Hey," Auntie stood up. "Enough of this 'missing' and 'maybe' there's going to be time enough for that later. Let's enjoy tonight while we're here, all together. Let's watch those crazy wrestlers."

I started to help clear the table but Bonnie would have none of it. "You git in there and enjoy the time you have with the folks."

"Come on over here," Uncle called to me. "There's a place for you between me and Albert on the couch."

"You come with me, Eddie," Aunt patted the seat of a stuffed chair. "Sit right here."

"Hey, p'tite fille," Uncle looked at Auntie, "it looks like your favorite Baron Leone is not wrestling tonight."

"I guess he got the night off," she settled herself down in the other stuffed chair. "Did they announce who's on?"

"Somebody named Billy Varga and a guy called John Cretoria," he said.

"I've heard of them," she nodded, "did they mention Johnny Swenski or Dave Levin?"

"I really didn't pay much attention," he admitted, "but we'll find out as the matches go on."

Auntie was not as enthusiastic as she was when her favorite Baron was in the ring, but she still got angry at some of the referee's calls and yelled when she thought he was counting too slowly.

'I am going to miss this' I thought to myself. This was a perfect way to remember this wonderful family. Bonnie and Eva had joined us in the living room, Loretta played on the floor with Torrey. We were reluctant to say our good-byes. Eddie stood up first and stood in front of Auntie, he kissed her on both cheeks. She hugged him tightly.

"Don't say good-bye," she said, "I'm sure we're going to see each other again."

"I hope so," I replied tearfully, "you're all very special to both of us."

Loretta walked the dog out and put him in his box. There were many words left unsaid but our hugs and our tears spoke loud and clear. Uncle opened the car door for me and hugged me before I sat next to Eddie. "Thank you for everything," was all I could say.

Our little circle of family stood by the driveway waving as Eddie backed out, "seeing these great people tonight makes leaving here all the harder," he turned into the street, "doesn't it?"

"I agree," I wiped away another tear, "I never knew your aunt and uncle before we came here, but I can tell you for sure that I'll never ever forget them."

Neither of us had much to say on the way home. It was a lovely night. The same stars filled the sky back in New England and yet everything seemed different here. The traffic was light and there was not a sound coming from Torrey's box. I guess Loretta had tired him out. Eddie picked him up when we got back to the trailer. We all walked up to the Community House together and we both took turns using the facility. It was too late to play cards. We settled in each other's arms under the counterpane. Tomorrow would be our last day at Shady Grove Trailer Park.

"Achoo!" I reached for a Kleenex and blew my nose.

"Are you catching a cold?" Eddie asked. "I heard you coughing during the night."

"I hope not," I rolled out of bed. "This would not be an ideal time to be sick."

"Maybe you should think about taking it easy today," he was getting ready to go out with Torrey.

"I'll be fine... achoo," I put on my bathrobe. "I don't have a fever or anything; go on out with the dog, I'll have the coffee made when you get back."

I stripped the bedding and closed the sofa and put the sheets in the laundry basket. I got dressed into dungarees and a checkered blouse; I put on my penny loafers and then fixed the coffee pot but didn't turn on the burner. Instead I walked up to the Community House to freshen up. I really didn't feel so hot. This malaise was not in my plan. I took a hot shower, toweled off and got dressed again before returning to the trailer.

"I hate to say this, but you don't look so good," he had already turned on the burner under the coffee pot. "Maybe you should lie down on the sofa for a while longer."

"I'll be okay," I sniffled, "do you want some eggs?"

"No, I don't want any eggs," he pulled the toaster out from under the counter. "We'll have toast and that'll be enough. Sit down; I'll fix 'em."

277

"There wasn't anyone in the laundry room while I was up there," I took the butter dish and jar of strawberry jam out of the ice box., "I'm going to go up after breakfast and get the wash done."

"I don't call that resting," he put two slices of toast on my plate.

"Well, I've already stripped the bed, and I have enough clothes piled up for a load," I buttered the toast. "I have to get it done today, we don't know what the facilities will be like at the trailer parks on the way home; I don't mind piling up dirty clothes for a week, but a week plus what's already in the basket would be too much."

"Okay," he agreed, "You stay up there until you're finished and I'll wash the floor while you're gone; and then I'll help you make up the sofa when you come back."

"That sounds good," we finished breakfast and I headed up to the Community House. When I returned the dishes were done and the floor was clean. Torrey was tied to the fence in the front yard. "Okay," I announced, "after the bed is made, I'll do the little bit of ironing and put it away while Torrey is outside."

"Is the list ready for the stuff we need at the store?" he asked.

"Yes," I pulled it out from the drawer. "If you don't mind, maybe you can pick up some cough syrup and some Vicks VapoRub so this cold doesn't get any worse."

"Of course, I don't mind," he reached in the drawer for a pencil. "I'll add it to the list."

"We'll have tomato soup and a sandwich when you get back," I suggested.

"I'll be ready for that, I'm sure," he pulled the sofa open, "okay let's get this thing put together and I'll be off."

I set up the ironing board and got the few pieces of clothing pressed and put away before he came back with the ice and groceries. As soon as the ice box was set up with the most perishable items placed nearest the ice, I proceeded to fix our late lunch. I wasn't very hungry but the soup was very soothing to my scratchy throat.

"I hope you feel better tomorrow, Sweetheart," he bit into his baloney sandwich.

"So do I," I munched on a few saltines. "I'll rub some Vicks on my chest tonight, I should be much better in the morning."

We decided to play cards for a while when Julie and Darryl knocked on the door.

"Come on in," Eddie said, "I'm glad you stopped by."

"Do you feel like playing Hi Lo Jack?" I asked.

"Of course," Darryl said, "I'm always ready to play cards."

We sat at the table; Eddie won the cut to deal.

278

"We'll be leaving in the morning," he dealt out the cards three at a time.

"I thought you were going to wait until Monday," Julie said.

"We were," I picked up my cards, "but we figured we'd go to an early Mass tomorrow and just keep going after that."

"I already made arrangements with Jim to help us hitch up around seven," Eddie told them.

"Okay," Julie announced, "this is party time!"

"Good idea," I agreed, "I'll get the lemonade and the girls are definitely going to beat the guys." I tried to keep my sniffles stifled and hid the tissues out of sight. This was a night to celebrate, friendship, love and new beginnings for all of us.


HOUSE ON WHEELS

CHAPTER 20


It was still dark when the alarm went off. Our clothes were laid out in the breakfast nook. Eddie was up first and turned on the light. He got dressed and took Torrey out for a walk while I got dressed and then stored the pillows under the sofa before closing it. I coughed and sneezed a few times; I grabbed a few tissues to put in the pocket of my blue waffle pique dress. "It doesn't sound like your cold is much better," Eddie said when he came back with the dog. "Are you going to be all right to travel?"

"The way I see it," I blew my nose, "it doesn't make much sense to sit around here because of a cold; I'm not going to do anything here anyway so we may as well go ahead with our plans."

"You could rub your chest with Vicks and rest," he suggested as we walked up to the Community house together.

"So, I can rub my chest and ride," I reasoned. "It doesn't make much difference."

"I suppose you've got a point," he shrugged and went in to the men's side of the facility.

The Mass was at 6:00 a.m. We left Torrey in his box in the trailer and were back within an hour. The sun was up before we came out of church.

"It looks like it's going to be another beautiful day," Eddie observed.

"I'm surprised there were so many people in church at this early hour," I said.

"Me too, but it's a great way to get started in the day," he remarked, "as a matter of fact, for us today, it's ideal; there shouldn't be much traffic at all."

We had a quick breakfast of cereal and milk and I cleaned up the kitchen before Jim arrived to disconnect the water and electricity. Eddie pulled up the section of fence in front of the trailer and leaned it against the trellis. Jim directed him as he backed the car in and then helped him hitch up.

The men shook hands, Jim hugged me. "We're going to miss you guys around here."

"We're going to miss being here too," I had a lump in my throat, "take good care of the fish."

I held Torrey on the leash while Jim and Eddie secured the car and trailer and then Eddie put Torrey in his box on the back seat. He could see over the top of the box when he sat down and there was ample room for him to lie down or play with his squeaky toys.

Jim opened the door for me and I got in the car. Eddie sat behind the wheel and started the engine; he drove out slowly into the driveway and then turned out of the trailer park onto Main Street heading east.

"I put the maps in the glove compartment, the one we need now is on top," Eddie said. "Pull the top one out and put the rest back," he directed.

I slid the map out of the rubber band before replacing the others and closing the glove compartment. I unfolded it, spread it in my lap and looked for Torrance and Las Vegas.

"Okay," I followed the line with my finger, "Las Vegas is northeast of here," I announced. "We need to follow route 66 for a while toward the Mojave Desert."

"If I remember right," he glanced over at the map, "route 66 goes farther north than Vegas."

"You're right;" I traced the route more closely, "route 66 doesn't seem to go into Nevada at all."

"Mojave Desert has to be huge," he said, "we passed a part of it when we came down from Yosemite to Redondo Beach."

"Yeah, I remember how hot it was." I thought for a minute. "I wonder if we'll see any of those Juniper trees."

"I wouldn't be surprised," he had his sunglasses on as he drove facing the sun on the long straight road, "watch for the turn off for route 66; I don't want to miss it."

We passed several more miles of sand dunes and scattered desert flowers before I saw the sign, "There it is," I pointed ahead, "the sign says to take a left at the fork."

"It's a good thing we left early," he slowed down to make the turn, "there's not a lot of traffic and I bet this area will be a lot hotter by this afternoon."

"This sure is a barren place," I observed, "I can see why there aren't any homes around here; the terrain is so dry."

"How are you feeling?" he looked concerned, "I haven't heard you sneeze for a while."

"I'm okay," I smoothed out the map in my lap. "I'm still sniffling but the Smith Brothers cough drops seem to be keeping the cough in check."

"See if you can find some music on the radio," he suggested, "we're a pretty good distance from L.A. but there must be a station out there we can get."

I turned the dial but most of what we heard was static. "I guess we won't get much reception until we get closer to a city," I said.

"You're probably right," he kept a steady speed. "There's a lot of sand out there; how far did you say the Mojave Desert is from L.A.?"

"According to the scale, down here in the corner," I set my fingers to about an inch and a half apart to measure. "It looks like it's about 100 miles."

"I figure we should get there around 10 o'clock," he nodded his head. "That's not bad."

It was an interesting highway. Now and then we came upon evidence of a past settlement where small wooden homes were collapsed and broken equipment lay in the sand.

"It's kind of sad to see these abandoned homes, I wonder what these people did for a living," I looked around, "I'm sure they couldn't raise crops in this dry soil."

"I think they might have done some mining," Eddie said. "Do you see the mountains over there?"

"Yeah," I looked where he was pointing, "but that seems like a long way off for somebody to have to go to work every day riding on a horse drawn wagon."

"I guess when you expect to find gold," he reasoned, "you're ready to do anything."

"I suppose; Hey!" I sat up higher. "I think I see a town coming up. Look at that tall sign: Amboy."

"And just past it there's an even higher sign: Roy Hamburgers; are you hungry?"

281

"No," I said quickly, "not really. I didn't see any signs telling us we are in the Mojave; did you?"

"As a matter of fact, no; but there's a big red star over there," he nodded straight ahead; "That has to be a Texaco Station; I'm going to stop and ask if we're headed in the right direction; and maybe I'll take Torrey for a little walk."

It was a nice break for both of us. Eddie bought us each a bottle of Coca Cola from the five cent vending machine. "Here, this should go down easy."

"I don't usually like soda," I took a long sip, "but this does feel good going down my throat. "

There were fans inside the store. It wasn't noon yet but the day was already getting a lot hotter.

"It's a good thing you have these fans going," Eddie remarked to the attendant.

"Oh yes," he answered, "It gets pretty hot out here and we couldn't get along without 'em." He hesitated a moment, "where are you folks headed?"

"We're going to Las Vegas," Eddie answered, "and then to Grand Canyon."

"You'll have to turn off of 66 up yonder," he reached out to Torrey with an open palm and the dog licked his hand. "Vegas is still a couple hunnerd miles away but you should be able to make it afore the end of the day."

"This area is pretty much the same as it was when we left L.A. early this morning," Eddie remarked.

"You're in the desert," the attendant said as if we should have already known that, "it's gonna be pretty much the same until you get past Vegas; except for them low lyin' mountains way over there, you're gonna see a lot of sand."

"I was curious about those mountains," I said, "did anybody ever try mining for gold over there?"

"Oh, mebbe years ago," he pulled out a chair and sat down, "that's why you see some old ghost towns once in a while. The folks tried their luck in the hills and when it didn't pan out they pulled up stakes and moved on."

"You're still here," Eddie drank the last of his soda.

"Well," he leaned his chair against the wall, "there's water in this spot, my daddy found this place years ago, and we can make a livin' taking care of travelers; it works out good for our family."

Our gas gauge read about half, but Eddie decided to fill up just to make sure we had enough fuel to make it past Vegas. He shook hands with the attendant as we left and then put Torrey back in his box.

The desert has a beauty of its own. We saw cactus plants in various shapes and heights, some had blossoms; and in other areas we saw colorful flowers bravely growing in the shade of a decaying porch attached to a collapsed wooden house.

"Remember the poem: Water, water everywhere and nary a drop to drink?" I asked.

"All I can think of out here is: Sand, sand everywhere and nary a beach in sight."

"Aw, that's pretty corny," he said. "Not to change the subject, but, I think we should be coming close to that turn-off      we need to make to get off 66."

Sure enough; "How do you do that? It's like you have a sixth sense," I sat up a little higher, "there's the sign, it shows a fork where route 66 goes left toward the northeast and the right  points east to Las Vegas."

"It's not much of a scenery change," he said, "but at least we know we're on the right road."

"You must be getting hungry," I looked at my watch. "It's after noon; see if you can find a wide part of the road where we can stop to have lunch."

"That's not hard to do on this road," he started to slow down. "There's no time like the present."

He stopped on the rough gravel. Eddie put Torrey's leash on and walked along the outside shoulder. I went in the trailer, it was hot. I made sandwiches and poured two glasses of lemonade for us and water for the dog. We didn't hang out for very long in the hot sun. I had another coughing spell.

"That doesn't sound very good," Eddie said, "maybe you should lie down for a while."

"I thought about resting on the sofa," I closed the trailer door, "but it's much too hot in there."

"Yeah, I noticed that too," he settled Torrey in his box, "at least in the car we can have all the windows open and there's a breeze."

"A warm breeze, but it's a breeze." I took my place on the passenger side. "If you need a break, I'll drive."

"No, it's okay," he started the engine, "maybe you'll be able to sleep for a few miles and you'll feel better."

I must have nodded off at some point or other because the next words I heard were:

"Sweetheart, look at that!" we were driving down Fremont Street in Las Vegas and Eddie was pointing at this huge neon-lit animated cowboy wearing a yellow shirt, blue pants, a red bandana and of course, a big black cowboy hat. He was waving his arms around and blowing smoke rings over another set of neon lights identifying the Pioneer's Club. It looked like a popular place because we saw many pedestrians on the sidewalk, some entered the Pioneer Club and some walked to the corner where the large neon lights of the Golden Nugget beckoned the gamblers. We didn't stop; it would have been awkward to try to park our trailer at the curb. A little farther down the street, on our way out of the city, we stopped at a small store to pick up a loaf of bread. We tried our luck at gambling on one of the four 'one-armed-bandit' machines. We each played five dimes and didn't win. That was it! We were not going to feed any of those monsters again.

Eddie put the bread in the trailer, and then we drove the thirty or so miles to Boulder Dam where we saw the spectacular view of the Colorado River as it tumbled over the dam creating a thunderous waterfall.

"Did you know that this dam creates enough power to provide electricity as far as California?" he informed me.

"As a matter of fact I didn't," I sat up straight to see as far as I could. "But I'm not surprised you do."

"I read a lot," he said simply. "Take a look over there; that's Lake Mead, it's twice as big as the state of Rhode Island."

He was pointing to a huge body of clear, teal water, the view was incredible. It was a total contrast to the dry sand we had seen for hundreds of miles on our way over here. The breeze was cooler and the surroundings were amazingly refreshing. We saw mountains and valleys and red rock formations as we drove over the picturesque highway into Kingman, Arizona. We stopped at a trailer park just off the highway where we hooked up for the night.

"What do you want for supper?" I pulled out the hot plate from under the counter.

"You know what?" he sat at the table. "A can of Campbell's beans and fried baloney would suit me fine.

"Okay," I took out a saucepan, "and I'll have a can of chicken noodle soup."

"That's all?"

"I'm not very hungry," I coughed again.

"You'd better rub your chest with Vicks again before going to bed," he suggested.

"You sound like a broken record," I opened the cans, "I think tomorrow will be easier driving. I sure hate feeling lousy."

"I know," he put the plates on the table. "You don't get sick very often, but this cold is really getting the best of you."

"No it's not," I stated firmly, "I'll be rid of it in a day or so; I don't want to be sniffling all the way home." I reached for his plate; "here, let me put the beans on your plate; the baloney's almost ready."

"I'll feed the dog while you get your soup ready," he said.

I rinsed out the pan and then poured the soup and water inside. "There, this will be hot in a jiffy." I reached in the cupboard for the saltine crackers and we were ready to sit and eat in no time. After supper we walked up to the Rustic log cabin which was the Community House. We brought Torrey and took turns holding his leash. The trailer park was in a wooded area and the view was lovely. There were mountains in the distance and a lush green valley below. The last glow of sunset gave a purple tinge to the mountain peaks and little gold nuggets blinked among the trees in the last breath of the day. Eddie put his arm around me as we stood mesmerized in the beauty that surrounded us. Torrey sat at Eddie's feet; it seemed that even he didn't want to break the spell that enveloped us.

There was no card playing tonight, we laid out our clothes for the morning, and I went to bed while Eddie studied the map he had brought in from the car. I don't know how long he was up after I went to sleep; or, for that matter, if he went to sleep at all. The next thing I knew he was saying:

"Stay in bed, Sweetheart, I'm going to get an early start." He held Torrey in his arms and closed the door of the trailer.

I felt the movement of the trailer as he hooked up and the hum of the vehicles moving on the pavement lulled me back to sleep. I didn't wake up until several hours later.

"Hey!" he poked his head in the trailer, "we're here. I just wanted to warn you that I'm going to unhitch the trailer."

"Here?" I sat up in bed. "Where's here?" I moved the curtain to see outside.

"This is it!" he announced, "We're at the Grand Canyon. I have to unhitch the trailer so we can use the car to drive around the park."

"Wow! That was fast. Okay, give me a couple of minutes," I reached for my clothes on the seat of the breakfast nook, "is there a bathroom facility nearby?"

"Yep, right up the hill there," he stepped out of the door. "I'll go get the jack ready."

I didn't take the time to fix the sofa; I got dressed and picked up my little 'freshen-up' bag before heading for the washroom. It was mid-morning, the sun was bright and the air was clear. Eddie had already positioned the trailer in our spot; and, as it was in all the other parks we had been in so far, we didn't need to hook up to water or electricity. There was a common water faucet in the area and that was it. By the time I got back from the Lodge our car was parked alongside the trailer.

"How are you feeling?" he asked. "Was the ride too bumpy?"

"I'm feeling a little better," I opened the trailer door, "I didn't notice any bumps; I slept the whole time. Did you eat breakfast?"

"No," he followed me inside the trailer, "I gave Torrey some water but I thought we could have some cereal before we head out to view the canyon."

"That's a good idea, I'm getting a little hungry." I pulled the Cheerios from the cupboard and poured some into two bowls.

"Do you think we should leave Torrey in the trailer while we drive around the park?" he asked.

"I think he'll be okay if we leave the windows open," I suggested. "It's pretty cool in here right now; and he's used to being in his box." I smoothed the blankets on the bed and left the sofa open.

"When we get back, we can tie him to the trailer hitch so he can run around," he finished up his Cheerios.

I picked up the two bowls and spoons and walked over to the spigot to wash them before we left to go sightseeing. Eddie settled the dog in the trailer and then we got in the car.

"What was the scenery like on the way over here," I coughed a little.

"You know me," he shrugged, "I'm not good at describing things. There were nice mountains and pretty flowers and every once in a while I saw a river flowing down in the valley. I can't tell you what kind of trees or flowers they were but they were nice."

"Nice?" I looked over at him, "we've seen a lot of that. I can just picture what you mean."

"I see some cars parked close to that railing," he slowed down. "I'm going to pull in; maybe we'll see some more 'nice' over there."

There were several people standing by the edge of the canyon. There was hardly any chatter; it was more like the whispering one hears when standing in a holy place. No one paid any attention to anyone else coming or going. 'Nice' is not a word I would have used to describe the view before us. We stood there entranced and silenced like everyone else.

The canyon was a mile deep and from our vantage point we could see the Colorado River winding throughout the lower canyon like a long, uneven green ribbon threading its way among the rock formations. As far as our eyes allowed we saw layered, multi-colored rocks in a multitude of shapes, some with a pointed top and others a flat plateau. All of them rose from the bottom of the canyon up to heights of a mile or more, although some were smaller. It was impossible to view the entire canyon from one location so we moved from one viewing spot to the next. Each one different from the other and yet there were similarities in color or striated layers. In one area we saw a waterfall which seemed to come out from the middle of the mountain. I say mountain because

286

that's what the shapes looked like, mini-mountains dispersed throughout the eighteen mile wide canyon. In one location the formations were all orangey-red in color and in another they were like the color of sand. Another few seemed to be made up of huge cut brownish stones stacked one layer of blocks over the other. One can only wonder how mother nature achieved this. We stood in awe as we looked upon the rocky hills which rose up in multiple layers of different colors as though they were designed by a master painter; beginning with lava-like grayish black at the bottom and tiers of orange and yellow and brown and red alternating to the reddish yellow peak.

"Oh, Honey," I started to cough again, "I hate to leave this place, but, I'm really feeling lousy."

"Do you want to go back to the trailer?" he put his arm around me.

"You can come back and look at some of the other look-out points if you want," I blew my nose again. "I just need to lie down."

"Come on," he led me back to the car, "Torrey is probably ready for a walk right about now anyway."

Our campsite was in a forest area and the trailer was cool. Torrey peeked over the side of the box as we came in and I headed for the bed and lay down fully dressed on top of the blanket.

"I'll get a long cord and let the dog run around awhile," Eddie said, "try to get some sleep."

I must have conked out, because the next thing I knew, the trailer was leaning over. I was still on the bed but my head was down and my feet were up. Eddie was looking in the icebox with his back to the door. He barely had time to slam the icebox shut and grab on to the table.

"Honey," I screamed, "there's a deer in the trailer."

"Yeah, I can see that," he said calmly. "I guess he's hungry."

I held onto the side of the cabinet and pulled myself up from the tilting sofa. I sat upright staring at the young deer. His short antlers looked velvety and much smaller than those of a full grown animal and it had been easy for him to get most of himself inside.

"How are you going to get him out?" I screamed; I was afraid the whole trailer was going to topple over. "All I need is for him to poop in here."

"Don't worry about that, his rear end is still outside," he patted the deer's neck gently. "If he gets his back hooves in here, he'll tip the whole trailer over." Frantic is a feeling I entertained.

"He likes celery," he continued to pat the animal; "I'll start pushing him outside while you get the celery out of the icebox and hand it to me."

287

The trailer resumed its normal position as soon as our guest left. Eddie took the handful of celery and walked closer to the trees. I closed the door and then sat at the table. I decided this was a good time to pour myself a glass of lemonade. I coughed some more.

"Sweetheart," Eddie called from outside, "come on out; you have to see this!"

I opened the door and stepped outside. Eddie was holding Torrey up to the deer's face and the animals were staring at each other.

"Don't move," I went back in the trailer. "I'm going in to get the camera."

"I never expected deer would be so friendly," Eddie held the pose as I aimed with my Brownie Box camera.

"Wait, as soon as I snap this picture I'll get some more celery?" Somehow, watching Torrey nosing up to the deer, made it appear more beautiful and far less threatening.

"That's a good idea," there was a wonderful grin on Ed's face; "you can feed it to him this time."

I can't say that I jumped at the offer, but, I did bring out the stalks and offer them one at a time to our new friend. He nibbled gently until all the celery was gone and then he walked back into the woods.

"How did all that happen?" I watched the deer disappear among the trees.

"I was sitting with Torrey, munching on a stalk of celery and the deer just came up to me," he explained. "I offered him a bite and he ate it; and then he just hung around."

"So when you came in to get more celery he just followed you?"

"That's what happened," he laughed, "you should have seen your face when you saw him."

"Whoever expects to be awakened out of a sound sleep by a deer in the house?" I coughed a few times.

"Are you feeling better?" Eddie walked back to the trailer with me.

"Yes, I guess that little nap helped," I went in and grabbed the pitcher of lemonade from the icebox. "I'm thirsty more than anything else. Shall I pour some for you?"

"Yes, I'll get a glass." He sat at the table. "Maybe you should lie down again until it's suppertime."

"That's not a bad idea," I finished my lemonade. "Do they sell hot coffee or tea up there at the Lodge?"

"I think they do," he put our glasses in the sink. "Do you want some now?"

"No," I walked toward the sofa to lie down. "But, I thought a cup of tea would go well with a sandwich later on."

"I'm going to go for a walk with Torrey while you rest," he picked up the dog. "I'll shut the door so you don't get any more unexpected visitors."

I dozed and coughed and sniffled while they were gone. When I got up I went to the spigot to wash out our glasses and then went up to the Lodge before I made the sandwiches for supper. Eddie came in shortly afterwards and settled Torrey in the trailer before he went up to the Lodge to get the hot tea. I fed the dog and then we ate. It started to get dark around seven o'clock, Eddie took out the Coleman lamp and we played Rummy for awhile. I rubbed my chest with Vicks before we went to bed; by this time I was smelling like a cough drop.


There was not a lot to do before we left Grand Canyon. We were not hooked up to anything so it was only a matter of hitching up the trailer to the car before leaving. We made an early visit to the Lodge, I washed our cereal bowls at the spigot, Torrey and Eddie went for a walk and by the time we were ready to leave the campground it was around 5:45 a.m. It was a little chilly so I dressed in dungarees, a warm shirt and a jacket. I was feeling a little better but, at Eddie's suggestion, I rubbed Vicks on my chest again before leaving the trailer.

"We've got a long ride ahead of us," he said. "I think that stuff will help you breathe easier."

I couldn't argue that point because I didn't seem to cough as much during the night as I had during the day. He sat behind the wheel and I took my place beside him.

"I was checking out the map," Eddie said. "We have to connect with Route 66 again to get to the Painted Desert."

"I suppose we'll see some signs along the way," I remarked. "This road is incredibly straight for as far as we can see."

The terrain was pretty flat but we could see mountains in the distance. We were headed east when we passed a large sign that said: 'Navajo Reservation'.

"There doesn't seem to be much activity going on at this place," I commented. "I wonder if the living area is farther in from the road."

"That would make sense," Eddie nodded his head. "It would be one way to make sure the people here won't be bothered by nosey tourists trying to see how they live."

"Except for that big sign we saw back there," I observed, "I don't see any evidence of anyone living out here at all."

"It's also pretty early in the morning; there's not a lot of traffic on the road either."

The road was so straight we could foresee even a slight curve from a long distance away. We came up on a town called Cameron and the road headed slightly north but it was still straight. We began seeing the medallion-like signs of Route 66 and continued northeast until we saw another curve as we approached Tuba City. We stopped at a gas station to fill up. Eddie took Torrey for a short walk before we resumed our drive now heading southeast still on Route 66.

"Hey," I pointed ahead. "There's another sign."

I read out loud: 'Hopi Reservation'. "This place looks different."

Eddie slowed down, "There's a little parking lot over there; do you want to stop?"

"Yeah," I sat up higher on the seat, "I want to be a nosey tourist."

We didn't take Torrey out of his box but we got out of the car to look around. There were lots of handmade souvenirs for sale made out of red clay or adobe as well as leather vests and jackets. We could see teepees in a village setting and families in native attire within walking distance of the gift-shop. That area was off limits to the tourists. I bought a set of red clay salt and pepper shakers.

"Is that all you're going to get?" Eddie asked.

"Yes," I paid the girl at the counter, "I don't need anything else; besides, we don't really have a lot of room to put a ton of stuff."

I put my little bag on the rear seat and Eddie and I got back in the car. It wasn't long before we began to see vast plains reminiscent of the desert we had seen before. Except this place wasn't all sand. Where we would have expected to see dunes, we saw what looked like stratified smooth stone in different colored layers. There were several more miles of similar scenery before we came upon the entrance to the Painted Desert around 10:30. When we entered the park we were surrounded with color. In some ways it was reminiscent of the Badlands we had seen in South Dakota; not so much in color but in the way some of the hills before us were flat on top like those we had seen before. Most of the hills here were gently sloped and some had grown vegetation which could have been moss or low vines. These created a graceful green incline down into a moderately deep crevice. Some hills were rusty red such as we had seen in the Grand Canyon, except these hills were more spread out; others were made up of layers of siltstone, mudstone and shale and fine grains of sand. Some of these containing iron or manganese produced a variety of different colors like sand and gray and black with hints of red and maroon and yellow; and still other rocks were light purple. There was no particular viewing area but there were also no restrictions regarding parking along the side of the road in order to walk around to get a closer view. One of the places we stopped to look at was the Painted Desert Inn. This was a rectangular earth colored building within the park. It had several levels of interesting looking flat roofs and it was made of Ponderosa Pine as well as stucco and there were pale colored wooden poles near the entrance. The outside terrace floors were made of flagstone and the openings were shaped like ordinary upright rectangular windows. It looked like it might have been a facility to accommodate tourists but we didn't go inside to check it out. We continued on Route 66. There were tall electric poles along one side of the road with wires held in place in glass conduits on narrow wooden crossbars at the top. We hadn't driven far when we saw the sign: Entering Petrified Forest National Monument. We stopped at the small wooden stand at the entrance, staffed by a Ranger, and paid our fifty cent fee which entitled us to visit as many times as we liked for a whole year.

"I didn't realize The Petrified Forest wasn't a National Park," I said as we drove into the park. "I wonder what the difference is."

"I think I read about that in one of those brochures in the glove compartment," Eddie pointed, "check it out."

Of course it was on top; Mr. Efficient had put everything in order. I scanned through the information. "Here it is," I read out loud, "President Theodore Roosevelt declared the Petrified Forest a National Monument in 1906."

"Does it say why?" he asked.

"Wait," I read a little more, "President Roosevelt saw its historic and prehistoric value and set it aside as a monument to protect the wilderness for future generations."

"I wonder if it will ever become a National Park," he parked by the roadside for us to look around. "Can I look at that?"

I handed him the pamphlet and then I opened the door of the car and stepped out. For as far as I could see there were colorful stone trees scattered everywhere. There were stumps coming out of the ground like someone had just hewn some glass trees, and in other places there were large logs lying around hap-hazardly.

Eddie was still holding on to the pamphlet, "It doesn't say so in here but I think I read somewhere that it takes an act of Congress for an area to be declared a National Park;" he shoved the booklet in his back pocket and came to stand next to me. "Will you look at that?"

In the distance there were areas of green fields and an occasional dried tree as well as short, spindly bushes looking very much like tumbleweeds. There were mountains in tiered shades of light and dark gray and white.

"I'm always amazed at how there are not two mountains that are the same," I observed. "The mountains in the Painted Desert were about the same height as these but the layers were much more colorful. Over here it's less hilly and there are a few red mountains but most of them are grayish."

"Will you look at these trees?" He was crouching at the end of a long log. "It's about a foot and a half in diameter and I can count the rings."

Eddie went back to the car to get Torrey and we walked amid the scattered fossils. The colors were breathtaking; it was like someone had collected a treasure of precious stones and arranged them in circles to form the rings in a garden of fallen trees.

"I'm trying to picture this place more than a million years ago when dinosaurs roamed the land and these very trees were tall and part of a huge forest," I imagined out loud.

"According to the pamphlet there are supposed to be some dinosaur fossils lying among the petrified logs," Eddie remarked, "but I have no idea what to look for."

"I don't know either but I would guess dinosaur fossils would probably be in the form of bones," I said.

"I guess you're right," he looked around, "and, by now, if someone had found them they'd be stored in a museum somewhere."

I nodded in agreement. "Look at these trees," I observed, "they don't look like they're the same kind of tree." I touched the hardened bark on a few logs, "but I don't know enough about trees to be able to tell the difference between a pine, a maple an aspen or anything else."

"Neither do I." He held on tightly to Torrey's leash, "whoa, don't roam too far away; I don't want you to fall into one of those crevices," he patted the dog's head. "All I do know is it must have taken a heck of a force of nature to first knock down and bury these trees and then, thousands of years later, here comes another jolt and they're back up to the surface in this petrified condition."

"Turn around and look back," I pointed to the car and trailer in the distance by the side of the road; "we've walked a lot farther than I thought. Are you getting hungry?"

"Yeah," he looked toward the road. "This is as good a time as any to have lunch. We should turn back; it would be easy to get lost out here."

We circled back to the trailer and I went inside to make sandwiches and pour our glasses of lemonade. It was a cool afternoon and we sat comfortably at the table with the door open while Torrey was content to sit at Eddie's feet after he drank from his bowl of water.

"I think we still have a few more miles to drive through the park before we reach the next town." Eddie said. "And then I believe we leave route 66 again to drive toward New Mexico."

"There must be a Ranger Station close to the the exit," I sipped a little lemonade, "we can stop there and see if we can buy a small piece of petrified wood."

"We'll need gas too," Eddie anticipated, "but I think we'll have to fill up when we come to a town."

I put our disposable containers in the rubbish container and we got back in the car. We stopped a few more times; once we stopped to observe a full sized tree lying horizontally on the ground.

"Look at that thing," Eddie stood by the long trunk. "It looks like it's been cut in sections with a saw."

"That's how it looks all right," I touched the edge of one of the pieces, "but what kind of saw would be able to cut into that stone?"

"None that I know of, and yet it's hard to imagine what kind of force could have made these cuts so deep while still keeping the tree in line and close together," he tried to see into the narrow cracks.

"We could look around this place for another two weeks and still never see everything there is to see," he opened the door for me to get in the car.

We drove a couple of miles farther, we saw many odd looking formations in the distance and strewn logs everywhere.

"Hey," Eddie slowed down, "that tree over there is still in the ground and it's standing up about four feet."

"Wow!" I got out of the car when Eddie stopped. "It has to be about five feet in diameter."

"It's a big tree all right," he walked around it, "I wonder if it was some kind of an evergreen, like those redwoods we saw in California?"

"I don't know," I had to stand on tip-toes to see the top and center. "Look at the rings from the center to the outside perimeter, the stones look like agates and they're all intertwined in wavy and curved lines in all the colors of the spectrum."

"It would be hard to figure how old this tree was," he ran his hand over the rough top, "the rings kind of weave into one another; some spaces between are wide and others almost on top of each other."

"Don't you wonder at how nature could have achieved these phenomena? We're standing here, right now, in the present; and we're touching trees that were alive a million years ago and shared their history with creatures who no longer exist as living matter; and yet all of them were and are part of who we are right now," I looked around in awe.

"Hey, Kid," he reached for my hand, "that's a lot of deep thinking; you're right, though, this place is something else; but we need to get going." He led me back to the car.

We didn't make any more stops until we reached a Texaco gas station soon after we left the park. We stopped to fill up the gas tank and pick up a piece of ice and then Eddie took the dog for a short walk. Route 66 was an interesting road. There were stores and gift shops all lit up with neon signs. Eddie picked up a map of New Mexico to compare it to the one he already had. He spread it on the hood of the car.

"According to this map we're definitely going to have to leave 66 and head southeast to Socorro, New Mexico. We still have about two hundred miles before we reach there." He traced the road to the Carlsbad Caverns with his finger, "and then there are another couple of hundred or so miles before we get to the caves."

"You talk about a hundred miles like it's around the corner," I said.

"On these straight roads the miles go by pretty fast," he settled Torrey in his box and took his seat behind the wheel. "We should be able to find a trailer park close to Socorro to hunker down for the night."

"That'll be good," I settled onto my seat, "I think I'll sleep well tonight, I haven't been coughing as much today and I'm beginning to feel much better."

"See? My old Vicks treatment does work, doesn't it?" he was taking complete credit for my getting better.

"Okay, Doctor," I smiled at him, "I hope your fee isn't too excessive."

"Now that you mention it," he grinned. "I'm sure I can come up with something".

"I bet you can." I tried to find a music station on the radio but we were still pretty much in the wilderness. The scenery was lovely but the reception was terrible. "I'll tell you what," I thought my idea was brilliant. "Let's see how many holiday songs we can come up with starting with Valentine 's Day in February."

"Okay," he started to sing, "Let me call you Sweetheart, I'm in love with you."

"Let me hear you whisper," I chimed in, "that you love me too…"

"I can't think of an Easter song for March," he said, "how about April Showers for April?"

"Though April Showers may come your way," we sang together, "they bring the flowers that bloom in May…"

"May, that's the month for Mother's Day," I started to sing,

"M is for the million things she gave me,

O means only that she's growing old.

T is for the tears she shed to raise me,

H is for her heart as pure as gold.

E is for her eyes with love light shining,

R means right and right she'll always be.

294

Put them all together they spell Mother,

A word that means the world to me."

"You know all the words," he looked surprised, "I could only remember some of them."

"I don't know if I got them exactly right either," I shrugged, "but they seem to work. Now how about June? Do you know any Father's day songs?"

"I can only think of one song," he said, "but I don't remember all the words. It's an old cowboy song called 'That Silver Haired Daddy of Mine."

"Oh yeah," I thought about it, "I remember that. I think it was Gene Autry who sang it quite a few years ago. I think he might even have written it but I'm not sure."

"I sort of remember the tune but I can't recall all the words," he shook his head and started to sing:

"If God would but grant me the power

Just to turn back the pages of time,

I'd give all I own, if I could but atone

To that Silver Haired Daddy of Mine."

"Yes, that's it!" I nodded my head. "You remembered more than I did."

It was easy to find songs for July; George M. Cohan had provided a slew of patriotic songs which kept us singing for a good part of our journey: 'You're a grand ole flag'; 'I'm a Yankee Doodle Dandy'; 'Over there'; we were on a roll. We bellowed out Irving Berlin's 'God Bless America' and felt we had given a wonderful tribute to our beautiful country.

We arrived at the trailer court just outside of Socorro in the late afternoon. The main office was a rustic log cabin and the Community House was a large wooden building set up on cinder blocks and it had all the amenities we needed. I walked around while Eddie and the manager set the trailer in its spot and made the necessary connections. It would be good to hook up to water and electricity so I could prepare something hot for supper. I was looking forward to a cup of hot tea.

"How would you like corned beef hash for supper?" I asked after Eddie had secured the trailer.

"That sounds fine," he called back, "if you have beets, you know that's always okay with me."

We sat at the table and ate leisurely and then lingered over our cup of hot tea and Lorna Doone cookies. "Do you feel like playing cards?" Eddie asked.

"We've been sitting for a long time," I took a sip of tea; "I'd really like to take a little walk around the trailer park."

"That's a good idea," Eddie agreed. "This place is really well lit; I think the dog will like that too."

We walked up the flagstone walk to the main office, where Eddie picked up a copy of the El Defensor Chieftain.

"I'll read this when we get back to the trailer," he folded the newspaper.

"You haven't picked up a paper for awhile," I said, "it'll be good to find out what's going on in the world."

The flagstone path joined all the trailer sites to the Community House, where the showers, toilets and the laundry facility were housed. It was dusk when we started out and even though it was dark when we returned to our trailer, it was easy to see the neatly proportioned trailer sites separated by log fences and a numbered light pole at the entrance of each one. Our car was parked on the road in front of our site. Eddie untied Torrey's leash as he entered the trailer and settled himself at the table with his newspaper while the dog lapped up some water from his dish on the floor. I heated some water to wash the dishes and set out two cups for hot tea.

"There's not much news about the war," he said. "There is a picture here of some soldiers in the snow; I guess it's much colder in Korea than it is here."

"I hope you won't have to find out what it's like in that part of the world," I poured some hot water over the tea bags in our cups and then poured the rest in the sink and added detergent. "I know you like to travel but Korea doesn't seem like a very fun place."

"You're right," he dunked the tea bag in his cup. "And nobody seems to know what this war is all about."

"Our whole life is about to change and we have no idea why they're fighting over there," I put the rinsed dishes in the drainer on the counter.

"Here's something interesting," he turned the page. "There's a School of Mines in the city of Socorro that's having its name changed."

"What's a School of Mines?" I frowned. "I've never heard of such a thing."

"There's a little history about it in this article," he continued. "It says here there used to be silver and lead mining in the Magdalena Mountains in the mid 1800's."

"All the mountains seem to run into one another and it's hard to tell where one ends and the other begins," I sat down across from him at the table. "Magdalena, those must be the ones we saw in the distance on our right as we were coming toward Socorro."

"Yeah, I remember seeing them too," he nodded and then continued reading. "It says here the school was started in 1889 to teach the techniques of mining at the college level," he looked up from the paper. "New Mexico was only a Territory back then."

"It's amazing that somebody had the foresight to establish such a school," I put my elbow on the table and cupped my chin with my hand. "When I think of mining, I think of prospectors in the old west, hauling a lantern, and digging with a pick and shovel."

"Me too, I never really thought about mining as a science," he said. "I guess the school worked out well because it says here that in the 1930's they expanded the courses to include petroleum science and engineering." He followed the text of the article with his finger: "The new name will be the New Mexico Institute of Mining and Technology."

"That's impressive," I nodded my head. "Someday when we have kids, if we ever do, and they want to become miners or dig oil wells, we'll know where to direct them; in the meanwhile, I'm going to bed."

"Okay, I'll finish reading the paper and walk the dog before I join you," he went back to reading.

"Hey, sleepyhead," Eddie was putting Torrey's leash away in its drawer. "It's already 6:30; if you want to get an early start, you'd better get up."

"What time did you get to bed?" I sat up and put on my slippers. "I didn't even notice when you turned off the lights."

"I noticed you were sleeping pretty good," he put Torrey's dish of water on the floor. "I was up at 5:30 as usual; it was still dark when Torrey and I went out."

I stood up and tucked the blankets in before I closed the sofa. "Give me a few minutes while I go to the showers and get dressed," I grabbed some clothes from the closet and the drawer, "I'll make breakfast when I get back."

"I'll make the coffee while you're gone, and I'll take my shower while you cook the bacon and eggs," he reached for the pot and was filling it with water as I was leaving.

We didn't ever leave the hot plate unattended when it was on. Eddie waited patiently for my return and then he headed for the Community House. I set the coffee pot aside and fried the bacon first, before I prepared the eggs and toast, those would only take a few minutes once he came back.

"What time do you want to leave?" I buttered the toast.

"Do you think we can be ready around 8 o'clock?" He asked.

"If not, it won't be much after that," I sat at the table. "There isn't much to clean up."

"Okay," he took a sip of coffee, "I'll go up to the office after breakfast and make arrangements for the manager to unhook us and then we can hitch up to the car."

We were into a new routine; we spent only one night at a trailer park and moved on to another destination the next day. We didn't have to wait long before the manager came to unhook our utilities, and for Eddie to hitch up. As usual, we stopped at a gas station at the beginning of the day to fill up and pick up a block of ice whenever it was available. It was lucky for us today. We needed ice and it was available.

"We're going to have to pick up eggs and milk at our next stop," I said as I made room in the ice box.

"We should be able to find a grocery store when we stop at the next trailer park," Eddie got back in the car.

Our next destination was southwest of Socorro. The scenery was varied. In some places we saw mountains and in other areas the land was flat. It was always interesting.

"There's another Indian village over there," I pointed to a square-shaped red stucco structures ahead of us. "I don't see any teepees anywhere."

"I think these are Pueblos," Eddie informed me. "They don't move around very much; I think there are Navajo's around here too."

"Whenever we hear about Indian lodgings we always think teepees," I said, "but the structures we've seen around here are stucco or stone."

"That's because they don't roam around," he said. "They don't go out hunting so they don't need to bring their homes with them. The Crow, who are farther up north, are hunters and they bring their teepees with them."

He amazed me again with his knowledge. The villages were not close to each other and when we could see the people occasionally, we noticed they wore rustic clothing. We saw quite a few cotton fields and open acreage too.

We had driven along for several hours when I saw the sign: "Roswell, 25 miles," I read. "Hey, wasn't that city in the headlines a while ago?"

"Yes it was," Eddie looked around. "That's the town where some people said they spotted some flying saucers."

"It's only a few miles down the road," I sat up straight. "Do you want to stop?"

"What for?" He shrugged. "I don't think there's much over there for us to see," he laughed. "The saucers are gone and I don't expect we're going to find any Martians over there."

I relaxed in my seat, "I guess you're right," I looked over at him. "I still wonder if there was any truth to any of that."

'Who knows," he reflected, "lots of people write stories about space travel, who are we to say it will never happen?"

I turned on the radio and found a country music station. We sang along for another few miles before we saw the Guadalupe Mountains in the distance and signs announcing accommodations at White's City.

"Keep your eyes open for a trailer park," Eddie said. "White's City is supposed to be pretty close to the Caverns."

The mountains dominated the scene and we saw cactus plants and yellow flowers growing here and there along the road. "There seems to be some signs of life up ahead," I pointed. "I see a sign 'White's City Trailer Park' just ahead on Carlsbad Cavern Road."

"We made good time," Eddie remarked. "We'll have time to hook up and unhitch, and have lunch before we go up to the caverns."

"That sounds fine with me and we'll still have time to go to the market before it gets dark," I figured.

Eddie hauled our little house in front of the main office. I waited in the car as he went in to fill out the papers and make the payment of one dollar to the manager who came out to direct us to our spot and helped us settle in.

"I've got enough cheese for grilled sandwiches," I looked in the icebox. "How about grilled cheese with tomato soup?" I asked.

"That's okay with me," he reached for Torrey's leash. "I'll take the dog for a walk while you're getting that stuff ready."

It was early afternoon by the time we finished lunch and headed out to the Caverns. The temperature was around 75 and we opened all the windows in the trailer to make sure Torrey would be comfortable while we were gone. The trailer park was only a few miles from the Carlsbad Caverns National Park.

"There's plenty of room to park," Eddie observed as he parked in a space a short distance from the entrance of the Cavern.

"I guess that's because it's a weekday," I got out of the car. "I bet it's a lot more crowded on weekends and during the summer when the kids are out of school."

We picked up a brochure at the visitor's office and learned there were two entrances: a natural entrance and an elevator entrance. The natural entrance consisted of a walk down a narrow path for about a mile and a half on uneven ground down into the cavern. The elevator was a flat platform as wide as a factory freight elevator and it was maneuvered mechanically by ropes and took a lot less time to get down the quarter of a mile descent into the caves. We opted for the elevator.

"Oh my God!" were the first words out of my mouth as I stepped into the enormous cavern. "I've seen icicles hanging from wires and eaves during the winter but they don't even begin to compare with this."

Wherever we looked we saw long spikes of limestone, called stalactites hanging from the nearly three hundred foot high ceiling. They hung down in points and in various lengths. Reaching up from the floor, almost directly beneath them, were the stalagmites. In some places the stalactites joined together with the stalagmites to form columns from floor to ceiling; some of them were a foot in diameter and looked like a hundred pies had been crushed one on top of another up to the top of the cavern. There were no two shapes alike. We followed a narrow path through the Big Chamber. In some areas the stalactites and stalagmites joined together in narrow perpendicular formations, only about three inches in diameter; they were side by side and reminded me of the pipes in a church organ. Some formations were rounded and as wide as an elephant's backside and connected to different shapes coming from the ceiling.

"Look at that group of stalactites on the ceiling," Eddie pointed to a roundish group of 'icicles" of a shorter length, "it looks like a fancy light fixture."

"It does." It was about the size of a ballroom chandelier. "Did you notice a funny smell in here?" I wrinkled my nose.

"Yes, I think it's the smell from the bats that live in these caves," he looked around. "I don't think anyone can see them during the day but they let go this stuff called guano. Some people used to collect it and sell it to use for fertilizer."

"That's interesting; I wouldn't even know what to look for." I sniffed. "It sort of smells like something hung around too long and got stale." I stopped. "Look over there between those two fat columns, is that a small cave?"

"I've noticed a couple of those around," he moved toward the formation. "I was wondering if there's anything inside."

"Be careful," I warned. I watched as he got on his knees to look into the hollow on the ground. He crept into the hole and disappeared inside for a minute that seemed like an hour. "Come on out of there!" I called to him.

"There's nothing in there," he crawled out, "but it's pretty dark."

"Suppose there was a crevice in there," I feared the worse, "you could have disappeared to who knows where!"

"You worry too much," he grinned as he stood up, "I'm fine."

We continued on the path and Eddie observed, "Did you notice most of this place is kind of a gray color but every once in a while there are wide spaces of green."

"I did see that," I agreed, "and every once in a while we see some columns that look pinkish-purple."

"Something else I noticed is there's no water in here," he said. "There had to be liquid to create these formations but there's no river in here."

"That is strange, especially since we saw a place that looked like a frozen waterfall; it makes you wonder how all that happened." I was in awe.

"That's nature for you," he took my hand. "At times like this I wish I knew more about science. I'm glad we didn't miss seeing this place."

"Me too," we were nearing the end of our tour, "it's like an underground fairyland down here."

We waited for the elevator with other visitors. We had been walking around for more than an hour and a half and it seemed like it had been only fifteen minutes. We were still holding hands when the elevator reached the parking level.

"Is this the last place you wanted to visit before heading for home?" I asked as we walked toward the car.

"I would have liked to see the 'Alamo'," he said, "but when I looked at the map of Texas last night, I realized it would take us an extra two days to go the nearly 500 miles down there and back. I guess we'll have to leave that for another time."

"We still have to find a Vet to give Torrey his puppy shot," I reminded him.

"Tomorrow's another day," he said. "Let's get what we need at the store before we go back to the trailer and we can figure out what we're going to do after that."

Torrey looked up from his cushion on the floor when we came in. His little stumpy tail was wagging and I bent down to stroke his floppy ears. Eddie put the groceries on the table.

"Are you going to need help to put this stuff away?" he asked. "I figured this would be a good time to take the dog out."

"That's a good idea, there's not much to put away," I started to sort out our purchases. "I'll make a salad and American Chop Suey while you're gone and we can eat when you get back."

"Make enough for leftovers," he suggested, "it'll be easier for you than cooking something up fresh for the next day or two."

"You just read my mind." I pulled out the cutting board and the salad bowl as he went out the door and proceeded to line up what I needed to make supper and put the rest away.

I was putting the dog's food dish on the floor as Eddie came in, "that was good timing, everything's ready." I put the salad on the table.

Torrey went directly to his dish and Eddie washed his hands at the sink before he sat down. "It smells good in here.

301

"Do you have an idea of what you want to do tomorrow?" I handed him the salad bowl.

"If we get an early start, I think we might be able to make it to Fort Worth, Texas," he said.

"How far is that?" I wanted to know.

"I checked the map and it looks like it's around five hundred miles east of here," he took a second helping of salad."

"We should think about looking for a Vet for Torrey sometime soon," I reminded him.

"I figured we could get across Texas tomorrow and look for a Vet on the day after that," he said.

"Can we do that?" I wondered. "Texas is a pretty big state."

"We won't be going through the widest part," he sounded sure of what he was saying. "We'll be crossing close to the panhandle; I'll show you the map after we eat."

"We'll want to get an early start in the morning," I pulled out a container of tapioca pudding from the icebox for dessert.

"Yeah, but after we look at the map, we'll have time for a couple games of cards," he took a large spoonful of pudding.

"What'll it be, Hi-Lo-Jack or Rummy?" I put the dishes in the sink.

"Hi-Lo-Jack is more fun when we play partners," he said. "I'm up for beating you again at Rummy."

I wiped the table before he spread out the map. "We'll see about that."

"Look over here," he pointed with his finger. "From here we head east and pick up route 81 into Fort Worth. It looks like a pretty straight line just below the panhandle of Texas."

"What would we do without these maps?" I wondered out loud.

"They're handy, all right," he folded the map. "Let's get these dishes done so we can play cards."

We settled ourselves comfortably at the table, across from each other and Torrey rested on the floor near Eddie's feet as we played 500 Rummy. We played two games and we were tied.

"Okay, I quit," I announced. "We don't have to play a rubber, it's getting late."

"Are you afraid I'll win?" he laughed.

"No," I put the cards back in the box. "It's time for our nightly trip to the Community House before bedtime. I'll get Torrey's leash."

"You'd better get a sweater, it's getting a little cool out here," he took the leash and tied it on the dog. "She thinks she won," he looked at Torrey, "well, I might have something to say about that later…right?"

We didn't set the alarm. Eddie was up first, as usual, and had been out for a walk before I was awake. "Okay, Sleeping Beauty," he put the leash away. "What's for breakfast?"

"Breakfast! What time is it, anyway?" I sat on the edge of the bed and slipped on my bathrobe.

"It's six-thirty," he announced. "We've got a long drive ahead of us and I'd like to get an early start."

"Okay," I picked up a brown plaid dress and shower paraphernalia and headed out the door. "How about making the coffee while I'm in the shower? I'll make breakfast when I get back."

"Sounds good to me," he reached for the coffee pot as I was leaving.

It wasn't unusual to see people in their bathrobes at the trailer parks. Many of the smaller trailers, like ours, didn't have bathroom facilities and the residents got dressed in the small dressing rooms provided next to the showers. My hair was short and I didn't have to fuss with it so I was back to our house within a half hour. Eddie was already having his coffee.

"How about a bologna and egg sandwich," he suggested as I came in the door.

"Sure," I put my dirty laundry in the basket and hung up my robe. "That won't take long."

Torrey had his breakfast while we ate and Eddie checked with the manager while I cleaned up the kitchen in readiness to unhook the lines and hitching up before leaving. We bid good-bye to White's City by 8:30 a.m. and stopped at the gas station, as usual, for a final check. It was around mid-morning when we crossed into the 'sovereign state' of Texas. Although most of the state was level, we did see some mountainous areas. There were cacti and cotton fields and cows. It was a beautiful sunny day and we could see for miles around us as we traveled the mostly straight roads.

"The scenery really looks like we see it in the movies, doesn't it?" I commented.

"Yeah," Eddie looked around, "you can almost expect to see Randolph Scott or John Wayne heading a posse coming yonder around any one of the ranches."

"It's really beautiful country, isn't it?" I nodded as we passed a field of cactus in bloom.

"It sure is," he agreed. "We're getting low on gas; keep your eyes open for a gas station."

It wasn't long before we saw the Socony sign near Amarillo. It was around one o'clock. We stopped to fill up and use the facility. It was a good time to walk the dog. I put out a dish of water for him.

"We may as well have a sandwich while we're stopped," Eddie suggested. "I'll get a couple of cokes from the machine."

"That's a good idea," I agreed, "as a matter of fact I made a couple of sandwiches this morning and put them in the ice box; I'll go get them."

We sat at a small round table outside the office and Torrey was content to sit near to us, tied to his leash.

"We've been pretty lucky," Eddie said. "The weather's been very good."

"Yes, it's been nice and sunny and not too hot," I picked up the wax paper from the sandwiches. "I hope our luck holds out until we get back home."

I found a trash barrel to dispose of our rubbish and then we got settled in the car. We drove on for a few more hours until we reached a trailer park just outside of Fort Worth in the late afternoon. Here it was: the wild, Wild West but there was nary a gun-totin' cowpoke in sight; there were cowboys wearing ten-gallon hats but none of them looked threatening. Eddie got us registered at the desk and settled in our site while I took the dog for a short walk around to acquaint myself with the campgrounds. The main office was a generously sized log cabin attached to the larger Community House which was also built with logs. Each trailer space was separated from the next by a log fence propped up on Y posts; the front was grassy and had a wooden lawn swing in the yard next to the trailer; the rest was open on the street side.

"This is a pretty nice place," I said. "There are about 30 trailers in here, most of them with a Texas registration."

"It's too bad we're only staying one night," Eddie was sitting on the swing. "I bet there's a lot to see around here."

"I know," I handed the leash to Eddie. "But we do have a deadline to get back home."

"Don't I know it!" he stepped off the swing. "I'll walk around a little while you fix supper."

It had been a great idea to fix 'planned-over's': there was less cooking and less cleaning up and more time for relaxing before bedtime. It was getting dark a little earlier than when we were in California, and the nights were less balmy, but the Texas sky was beautiful and after having been sitting down in the car all day it was pleasant to walk on this moonlit evening.

"We've got a busy day tomorrow," Eddie informed me.

"I know we should look for a Vet," I slipped my hand into his. "Did you have something else in mind?"

"I want to check the tires and switch them around first thing in the morning," he said. "I don't want to take a chance on having a flat for the rest of the trip; I spoke to the manager and he told me about a garage between here and Dallas who does that kind of thing."

"Is Dallas far from here?"

"It's about thirty five miles from Fort Worth, and the garage is on the highway before we get there," he sounded confident.

"So, wherever we are in the early afternoon," I reasoned, "we can stop to look for a Vet who can give Torrey his shot."

"That's what I thought too," he stopped for a minute and tugged at the dog's leash. "Let's head back to the trailer. We can stop at the Community House and take turns staying with Torrey."

"I'm okay with that," I followed his lead. "Maybe we can play a little 500 Rummy if you want."

"We'll see," he looked at Torrey, "she wants to get beat again."

As it turned out, Eddie won both games. We laid out our clothes in the breakfast nook for easy access in the morning. Torrey had graduated to a cushion on the floor while we were in the trailer, although he still stayed in the box while riding in the car or if we left him alone. He watched as we prepared the sofa and headed for his cushion as I climbed into bed. Eddie turned off the light and joined me.

I prepared the batter to make pancakes for breakfast and put it aside. Eddie and Torrey were already out when I got up and dressed. I opened a can of 'Pard' dog food and put about one third of it in Torrey's dish for when they returned. I then proceeded to go up to the Community House while they were still out. When I came in Torrey had found his dish and was eating heartily. Eddie had picked up a Fort Worth Star Telegram at the office and was reading at the table.

He lifted the paper so I could see, "There's a picture in here of the 936th Field Artillery Battalion, in Korea. They're a part of the 8th Army over there. It shows them firing shells at the Chinese Communists near Choriwon. Look at that, one of the men is blocking his ears, the sound must be awfully loud."

"I've never even heard of Choriwon, Korea," I looked at the picture. "It sure looks like that is not a fun place to be. I hate the thought that you might have to go there."

"I'm not exactly looking forward to it either," he folded the paper. "Will breakfast be ready soon?"

"I'll get the bacon started," I took out both frying pans. "The pancake batter is ready."

"Shall I pour you a cup of coffee?" he held out a cup.

"Sure, I can sip on it every once in a while," I arranged the bacon to get it started.

"I told the manager we should be ready to leave around 8:30," he set the plates and utensils on the table. "Does that sound about right?"

"Oh yes," I flipped the bacon, lowered the heat on that burner and then started cooking the pancakes on the other. "That'll give us plenty of time."

We didn't talk about Korea any more. We ate breakfast and I had just finished cleaning up when the manager arrived to disconnect the electricity and water.

"Are you going to need any help hitching up?" he asked Eddie.

"It would be a help," Eddie answered, "If you don't mind."

"Not at all," he stood in front of the trailer and guided Eddie as he backed the car up to the hitch. "That garage I told you about is not far from here, they'll take good care of you."

The men shook hands while I held Torrey on the leash; then we took our places in the car and we were on our way. We hadn't gone more than a mile before we came upon the garage. I was amazed at the short time it took to get the tires checked and switched. The garage also had a gasoline pump so we filled up before leaving there and we were on the road again about an hour and a half later.

"What time do you think we'll get to Texarkana?" I asked.

"If I read the map right, it's about 180 miles from here," he estimated, "it looks like the roads are pretty straight so I think we should get there in the early afternoon."

Our direction was northeast, we continued past cotton fields and ranches similar to what we had seen in Texas on our way to Fort Worth.

"See if you can pick up some music on the radio," Eddie nodded toward the dashboard.

"I don't know, Honey, the towns are still pretty far apart from one another," I turned the dial very slowly and suddenly I picked up some country music. "Hey, this is a little scratchy but it's not too bad."

The sound grew clearer as we drove closer to the towns and then it faded as we entered the wide open spaces at which point I tried again to find another station. We went through Greenville and then Mount Pleasant with the radio fading in and out. We sang along as well as we could and continued on until we reached Texarkana around 1:30 in the afternoon.

"Did you bring Torrey's papers with you?" Eddie asked as we entered the city.

"Yes," I reached for the cloth bag on the floor in front of me. "They're right in here."

"Let's look for a phone booth so we can look through the yellow pages," he suggested.

"That's a good idea," I sat up and looked around. "It'll be easier to ask for an appointment over the phone rather than drive from place to place."

He saw the phone booth at the same time as I did and drove in the parking space just in front of it. I got out of the car to make the call. I had to call three vets before I was able to make an appointment for today. I got the directions and we headed for the Veterinary Clinic on the other side of the city. We decided to go directly to the parking lot over there and had time to walk Torrey a bit and have a sandwich before our appointment time.

"Well, look who we have here," Dr. Wolfe said. "You're only a little guy."

"Yeah," Eddie said, "he was the runt of the litter and pretty sick when we got him."

"Well he doesn't look sick anymore," the Vet felt his stomach.

"I have his papers here from the doctor he saw in California," I offered him the folder.

"Oh yes, I see he needs another puppy shot," he rubbed behind the dog's ears.

"We're on our way back home to Massachusetts and the Vet in California said the dog should get a shot before we get back there," I informed him.

"I see that in his record," the doctor said, "here, hold him while I get the syringe and he'll be all set to go."

307

The doctor administered the shot, filled out the record and handed it back to me. "Hold on to these records, and take him to see a Vet in about four more weeks, bring this file with you and the Vet will know what the puppy is going to need."

Eddie attached the leash to Torrey and extended his hand to the doctor. "Thank you very much; how much will that be?"

"You're welcome," he said, "it's five dollars and you can pay the receptionist on the way out."

We left the office and headed back to the car. "It's a little early to stop for the night, Sweetheart," Eddie settled Torrey in his box on the back seat. "I think we should drive a little farther north before we call it a day."

"That's okay with me," I agreed, "Torrey will probably sleep for awhile and we've already had lunch so we can go for awhile longer."

We continued on in Arkansas for three or more hours passing busy cotton fields and ranches.

"The radio reception is better around here," Eddie noted. "There's a lot less fading out."

"I noticed that too," I checked in the back seat to see if Torrey was okay. "I guess we must be getting closer to some bigger cities."

"I saw a sign a while back that said Little Rock was not far from here," he said. "I think there's a turn-off up ahead."

"Are you planning to stop there for the night?" I wanted to know.

"No, I don't think so," he glanced quickly in my direction, "not unless you do."

"It's getting late in the afternoon," I reasoned, "We wouldn't be able to explore much of the city before it gets dark. I think we should just keep on driving until we find a trailer park on this road and stay there for the night."

"I was thinking the same thing," Eddie said.

It was another sixty some miles before we saw a billboard advertising a trailer court on the outskirts of Malvern. It was an easy access. Eddie drove off the highway and turned into the park about a quarter mile down the road. The main office was a large white clapboard house attached to a brick Community house that included showers as well as laundry facilities. Once we were settled in, I gathered our few days' accumulation of laundry and got acquainted with the Community House for a couple of hours. Our leftovers worked out well again since I could work in our suppertime between the washing and drying cycles. Eddie took Torrey for a walk and then watched a cowboy show on a newly installed TV in the Lounge of the Community House while I was busy.

"How was the TV?" I asked. "I noticed some horses on the screen when I went by."

"The picture wasn't as big as Aunt Bina's TV and it was a little snowy," he said. "But it passed the time okay."

Eddie picked up the basket and carried it back to the trailer. By the time I was done with folding, ironing and putting everything away, there wasn't much time left for card playing tonight.

"This is a good job done," I said. "I figure I won't have to do this chore again until we get back to Fall River.

"Do you want to set the alarm for tomorrow?" Eddie asked.

"I don't think so," I fixed a snack of buttered graham crackers and cocoa. "You're always up before it rings anyway; and we don't have any deadlines."

It was a good way to end the day. Torrey wasn't any the worse after his ordeal at the Vet's and for us, the thoughts about getting home had now become a priority.



We were up early the next morning. Eddie had made arrangements with the manager for us to be disconnected by 7:30 a.m. He was hoping we would reach Saint Louis, Missouri before stopping for the night. It was a cool morning and the bright sun was already promising a great day. Two hours after we left we were still in Arkansas, heading north, when we came upon some highway construction. It caused a little slow-down for several miles because only one lane was allowed to travel at a time.

"When we finally get moving again we'll stop at a gas station," Eddie said. "It'll be a good time for all of us to stretch our legs and gas up at the same time."

"It's a good idea to stop every couple of hours," I agreed, "When we stop around noontime we can have lunch."

We continued on our northern trek, and about five miles past the end of the construction area we stopped as planned. We were still in Arkansas.

"How much farther is it to Missouri?" Eddie asked the attendant.

"Oh, maybe an hour and a half," he wiped his hands on a cloth. "Where are you headed?"

"Massachusetts," Eddie said, "we figure it'll take us another couple of days of steady driving."

"That'd be about right," he lifted his peaked cap, "if you're not planning to drive right through."

"No," Eddie gave him three dollars, "we try to stop for the night and get a good night's sleep before traveling the next day," he followed the attendant to the register for his change; "there's not much to see when you drive at night."

By the time the gas tank was filled and the windshield had been washed, Torrey was back in the car; we made our visit to the facility and then we were on the road again enjoying the open farm lands interspersed with trees and various styles of homes. Many of the houses we passed had different types of antennae on the roofs for TV reception. We went by small rural towns with rustic buildings and some more modern ones. We were also enjoying a more varied style of music on the radio since we were driving through more populated areas. We crossed into Missouri and stopped shortly after noontime. We took time to walk Torrey and have a leisurely lunch.

"We're going to need more ice," I checked the ice box. "If you see a market, it might be a good idea to stop and pick some up and maybe something different for supper."

"I noticed we still had some potatoes," he said, "I was thinking maybe we could pick up some steak and have that with mashed potatoes."

"Why not?" I nodded, "we haven't had steak for awhile."

We found a market just before we reached Saint Louis and stopped. We picked up a few vegetables as well as the meat and put our groceries away.

"Let's see if we can find a trailer park," Eddie said, "I'm ready to stop for the night."

"Me too," I looked around, "I just saw a sign saying we're coming into Illinois; I didn't realize Saint Louis was so close to Illinois."

"Hey," Eddie pointed ahead, "there's a park in Vandalia up ahead."

"I never heard of Vandalia," I remarked, "but if it has a trailer court it will be a welcome sight."

We followed the signs and turned off the highway. Within a half hour of checking in at the office, Eddie had unhitched the trailer and we were hooked up to the water and electric. We were settled in for the night.

"We've been traveling for a week already," I was peeling potatoes. "Tomorrow is Sunday."

"I know," Eddie put the dog's leash away. "If you're not quite ready for supper, I'll go check at the desk to see about a church and the Mass schedule."

"That's a good idea," I put the pot on the burner. "Supper will be ready soon."

I peeled and sliced carrots and put them on the other burner and set the table before he came back.

"The Mass at the church in town here is at 8 o'clock," Eddie announced when he came in. "But Sacred Heart Church in Effingham, which is about 34 miles from here, has a Mass at 7 o'clock."

"We'd have to get hitched up by six," I said, "is the manager okay with that?"

"Oh yes, I already asked him," he sat at the table. "We can gas up after Mass and have a sandwich later on when we're on our way."

I mashed the potatoes and put the lid on the pot before I fixed the steak; "Honey would you mind feeding the dog?" I pulled out the frying pan, "how far do you think we'll drive to tomorrow?"

"I'm hoping we can get close to the east side of Ohio," he got up from the table and fixed a bowl of food for Torrey and put it on the floor before he sat down again.

"Pass me your plate," I picked up a piece of steak from the frying pan and put it on the plate before I handed it back. "We've been doing about 400 miles every day, that isn't bad." I picked up my plate and did the same and then put two pot holders on the table where I placed the carrots and potatoes. "The kettle is on the burner for hot tea later."

Torrey finished his meal before we did and pushed his pillow next to Eddie's feet with his snout and lay down while we finished our supper. I made a pot of tea and we ate fig newtons for dessert as we talked about the events of the day.

"What do you say," Eddie suggested, "shall we go for a walk around the park tonight?"

"Sure," I poured the rest of the hot water into the sink, "it'll feel good after sitting all day; here's a dish towel, you can help me with the clean-up before we go."

It was a lovely starry night but a little cool. We wore light sweaters and walked twice around the perimeter of the park before visiting the Community House on our way home. We fixed the sofa. Eddie set the alarm and we laid out our clothes for the next day before going to bed.

It was still dark when we got up. I fixed cheese sandwiches, wrapped them and put them in the ice box while Eddie went up to the Community House. I fed the dog and walked up to meet Eddie and continued on to take my shower. Eddie brought the dog back with him and waited for the manager to arrive. We were already unhooked when I got back and Eddie was in the process of hitching us up to the car. We pulled out of the trailer court and headed for the highway a little after 6 o'clock.

"We're right on time," Eddie said, "It shouldn't take us more than 50 minutes to get to Effingham."

He was right, of course, and we parked our trailer on the street several feet away from the old church which had been built in 1862. It looked to be an active parish because even at 7 a.m. the church was nearly full. The Mass lasted about 30 minutes and there was no music. As we approached our car there was a couple, with two small children, standing by the trailer. A little blond boy, who looked to be about 8 years old, pointed to the trailer and asked, "What's in there?"

"It's where we live while we're traveling," Eddie answered.

"You're a long way from home," the father in a gray suit, white shirt and red and white striped tie pointed to the license plate on the car.

"Yeah," Eddie answered, "I guess we are."

"Will you be staying in town long?" the man asked.

"No," Eddie said, "we're just passing through; we hope to be back to Massachusetts by next Tuesday or Wednesday."

"Welcome to Effingham, I'm Jim and this is my wife Ellen," he extended his hand, "and this is little Jimmy and his sister, Laura."

"Nice to meet you," Eddie shook his hand, "this is the wife; you've got some good looking children there."

"I'm in third grade," little Jimmy extended his hand to Eddie and nodded toward Laura, "she's only in kindergarten."

"My name is Jeanne, I'm very glad to meet both of you," I nodded to the parents and shook hands with both children, "I'm sure your parents are very proud of both of you."

Torrey was peeking from the backseat window of the car.

"Mom," Jimmy put his hand on the glass, "look at the puppy."

Eddie opened the car door and picked up the dog. "Do you want to pet him?"

Both children came up to the dog and patted his head, "Oh wow!" Jimmy exclaimed.

Torrey licked their grinning faces. "Mommy, we should get a dog, isn't he cute?" Laura hugged him like a dear friend.

"We've heard that plea before," Jim said, "okay kids, we've got to get home, say good bye to the puppy."

"Have a safe trip home," Ellen said.

Eddie put Torrey back in the car and took his place behind the wheel. "Thanks, you've got great kids there."

I nodded in agreement and settled in beside him. The little family waved as we pulled away from the curb.

"I love seeing happy families," I said, "I get a little jealous, though, and wonder if we'll ever have any kids."

"If we're meant to have kids I'm sure it'll happen," he assured me. "Not to change the subject but I see a gas station ahead."

He stopped at the Esso station. The attendant, wearing a blue one piece uniform and a peaked cap filled the tank and washed the windshield.

"If you pull over by the air pump, I'll check the tires," he offered.

"That's a good idea," Eddie answered.

While they were checking over the car and tires I walked the dog around the station away from the office and pumps. I wanted us both to get in a little of exercise because knew it would be a couple of hours before we would stop again.

"That'll be $3.25," the attendant was saying as I put the dog back in the car.

"Here you go," Eddie paid him and took his seat behind the wheel.

"Thanks," he waved as he walked toward the office. "Have a safe trip!"

I took my place on the front seat and turned on the radio. "Are we close to the highway?"

"The attendant said we should take a right at the next light and that will take us back to Route 40 where we can turn east on the highway," he put on his sunglasses.

"Oh my gosh!" I exclaimed as I turned the radio dial, "It's Milton Cross, nobody can mistake that voice."

"Doesn't he usually do that opera thing on Saturdays?" he asked.

"Yes but he also does this kids program on NBC on Sunday mornings too," I adjusted the dial. "Coast to Coast on a Bus is what it's called; I haven't heard this in a very long time."

"I never heard of it," Eddie shook his head.

"We used to listen to this at home, every Sunday morning," I was excited.

"Okay, so what's so great about it?"

"Milton Cross is the conductor and he says, 'the White Rabbit Bus goes any place any time!' They usually start out with a hymn, and then the bus goes on to pick up kids who always have a song or a poem to perform; or they play an instrument; and sometimes they do a little skit too. Some of the kids who start out on this show turn out to be famous like Ann Blyth and Skippy Homeier; just wait." I sat back and listened.

Eddie wasn't impressed at first, but when he heard a six year old girl sing: 'A Bicycle Built for Two' he was impressed. A group of children sang the children's marching chorus from the opera 'Carmen' and then an eight year old boy played 'The Beer Barrel Polka' on the accordion.

One of the children asked Mr. Conductor (Milton Cross) to sing and he sang an operatic song I wasn't familiar with.

"He sort of sounds like that guy you like who sings 'Bluebird of Happiness," I remarked.

"You mean Jan Pierce?" he asked. "I guess he does a little, in the way he pronounces his words; like rolling his r's."

The hour went by fast and then I fiddled around with the radio some more (I had taken on a new job: to try and find another music station); and when I did we sang along.

"I like how listening to the radio seems to make the time go by faster," he said.

"You're right," I agreed, "and there are more stations to choose from in this part of the country."

The area was more populated as we drove farther east through Illinois, Indiana and Ohio. There were fewer and smaller farmlands compared to Texas and Arkansas, and the cities seemed to be closer together. We saw more and more homes with antennae on the rooftops. We stopped a couple of times for lunch and gas and to walk the dog but the day went by quickly. When we arrived at a trailer park just off the highway on the outskirts of Saint Clairsville, Ohio we decided to stop for the night.

"The Community House is a little smaller than we've seen at other parks," I said as we set out for a walk around the park.

"Yeah, but it has everything we need," Eddie held on to Torrey's leash. "And there's plenty of room to stretch our legs around the court before we settle down."

"Did you notice the leaves are beginning to change color?" I remarked. "I bet the trees will be a lot more colorful as we get closer to home."

"I wouldn't be surprised," he looked around. "I don't see any maple trees around here and they usually are the most colorful."

"I think autumn is the prettiest time of the year in New England," I said.

"But we're not in New England yet," he informed me. "We'll be heading a little further north tomorrow after we leave New York; then it should start getting a lot prettier."

"What do you want for supper?" I asked.

314

"How about grilled ham and cheese sandwiches and tomato soup?" He suggested.

"Yeah," I nodded my head, "we can do that. And maybe tonight we can play cards, before we go to bed."

"I'll feed the dog while you get supper ready," he offered.

"Great!" I replied, "It won't take long; oh, by the way, we're going to need ice tomorrow."

"Remind me when we're at the gas station," he put the dog's dish on the floor. "That'll probably be the last we'll need ice before we get home."

"That's what I was thinking too," I put two sandwiches on Eddie's plate and one on mine. "Will you get the soupspoons out of the drawer before you sit down?"

I put the hot bowls of soup on the table; we said grace and proceeded to eat dinner and clean up the kitchen before we played three games of 500 Rummy. He won all three games.

"Okay," I collected the cards and the score pad to put them away, "I guess this is not my night to win."

"That depends on your point of view," he opened the sofa. "Après vous!"

The alarm woke me up at six. Eddie had already been out with Torrey. I fixed breakfast and cleared the kitchen before I went to the Community House and Eddie was ready to leave by the time I got back. We were on our way before 7:30 a.m. and, as usual, our first stop was at a gas station.

"How far are we from Pennsylvania," Eddie asked the attendant.

"Maybe about 40 some miles," he said. "What city are you headed for?"

"We're actually headed for New York City," Eddie replied.

"Now there's some distance," he whistled. "You're talking a good three hundred miles across Pennsylvania before you reach the New York state line."

"I figured as much," Eddie got in the car to drive to the air pump. "Let me check the tires before we leave, and yeah, we need a block of ice for our icebox."

The attendant walked next to the car and they both checked the pressure and whatever else they needed to do. I opened the trailer door and when Eddie had paid the

315

attendant he brought in the ice, put it in the icebox and then he secured the trailer door. Torrey and I were in the car and as soon as Eddie was settled in the driver's seat we headed for the highway. We were blessed with another beautiful day. It was a little chilly but we were comfortable wearing a light sweater.

"Do you think we'll be able to make it to Claire and Bob's house in Merrick today?" I asked.

"It depends on the traffic and the roads through Pennsylvania," he put on his sunglasses. "Like the attendant said, we still have at least three hundred miles before we get to the state of New York, and then we can figure another hundred miles or more to get to New York City before we get to Long Island."

"It's a work day so we may find a little more traffic on the road than we did over the weekend," I said.

"That's right, but it shouldn't be too bad on the highway," he looked around. "We've gotten an early start so we should make good time."

We passed farmlands and farmhouses and small towns and stopped every two or three hours, as we needed, for gas or food or for just stretching our legs. Torrey was an excellent traveler. He was still happy in his large box, set next to the window; he slept part of the time and sat up to look out the window every once in a while, played with his squeak toys every now and then and slept some more.

"Now that we're getting closer to home I'm looking forward to seeing everyone from our family again," I remarked. "All of a sudden I'm realizing how much I miss my mother and father and sister; Lucille turned fifteen last month."

"I know what you mean," Eddie agreed. "I think they'll be surprised when we pop in. I guess there's something to that old saying 'there's no place like home'."

"I think they'll be surprised too because I wrote just before we left California," I reminded him, "but I didn't tell them we were coming home."

"It's just as well," he assured me, "it's better to surprise them than to have them worry about us being on the road."

Pennsylvania was a wide state and the roads were not quite as straight as we had seen out west, but we made good time. The largest city we passed was Harrisburg. We encountered a little traffic there but it was a good place to gas up and have a snack and to take Torrey for a walk. We were lucky that at most of the gas stations where we stopped there was always an area where we could park the trailer out of the way and stretch our legs for about a half hour or so, and of course, there was always a bathroom facility. We stopped once more after crossing the New York State line and continued on to New York City. Our timing wasn't great. We found ourselves on Broadway at 5:00 p.m., the rush hour. We tried to follow the traffic as much as we could, I don't know how we ended up on Fifth Avenue, but there we were. We drove some more and we were back on Broadway. It was difficult to change lanes hauling the trailer behind us and because of the heavy traffic. We were trying to find a way to get to Long Island and ultimately to Merrick, where my sister lived but, after three hours of driving around New York Eddie saw a sign showing an arrow pointing to Route 1 East.

"I'm sorry, Sweetheart," he said, "we'll have to go to see your sister in Merrick another time; I know Route 1 is the Boston Post Road and I know where it goes, so when I see the turn that's where I'm heading."

"It's okay," I said, "and we'll probably need to stop for gas too; we've been driving around for quite a while."

"I'll feel better when we're on more familiar ground. Ah there it is!" He made the turn on to Route 1.

We crossed into Connecticut soon afterward and found an open gas station. We took our usual half hour rest before continuing on and began looking for a trailer court where we could spend the night. It was getting to be late and we had been on the road since early morning.

"I don't know, Honey," I said. "You must be pretty tired, maybe we should just stop somewhere on the side of the road."

"We may have to do just that," he agreed. "This area seems to have a lot of nice homes; I don't imagine there are many trailer parks around here."

"There's an 'All night diner' up ahead," I pointed up front. "Do you think they'll let us stop there for the night?"

"All we can do is ask," he began to slow down.

"It's a pretty big parking lot," I observed, "maybe you can park in the farthest spot away from the entrance."

"I'll do my best." He pulled up next to the fence at the rear of the lot. We got out of the car and went into the diner and sat at counter. "Two coffees with cream," Eddie said.

"Coming right up," the waiter said. "Can I interest you in anything else? A muffin? A grilled cheese?

"No thanks," Eddie looked at me, "how about you?

"No, I'm not hungry," I looked at the waiter, "I'm pretty tired, the coffee will be fine."

"We left Saint Clairsville, Ohio early this morning hoping to make it to Merrick, Long Island," Eddie told the waiter. "We couldn't find the turnoff in New York so we decided to take Route 1 and head home."

"Wow!" The waiter scratched his head, "that's a long way to travel."

"Yeah," Eddie said, "we were hoping we could park our trailer in the parking lot for a couple of hours, we'll be out of here before your morning crowd."

"We'd be glad to pay you," I added.

"Nah, there's no need," he said. "Just come in for breakfast before you go and we'll call it square."

"You've got a deal, thanks," Eddie extended his hand. "We'll be out of here before 5:00 a.m."

We finished our coffee and walked Torrey around the parking lot before settling down for the night. It was around 10:30 p.m. by the time we returned from the walk and fed the dog, Eddie set the alarm for 4:00 a.m. and it was probably 10:33 by the time we were asleep.

We got up and dressed, fed Torrey and then went into the diner for pancakes and bacon with Sunnyside eggs on the side.

"This is a really a great breakfast," Eddie told the waiter, "and thanks for letting us stay the night."

"Hey, it was my pleasure," he poured more coffee in our cups, "if you're ever out this way again maybe you'll stop by."

"You can count on it," Eddie paid the $6.00 bill and gave a $2:00 tip (it would have cost us a dollar if we had found a trailer court) we figured we got a bargain.

We were on our way a little after 4:30. We continued down Route 1 heading ENE toward Rhode Island. We were greeted by the early morning sun and we began to see the beautiful autumn scenery. The foliage was not quite at its peak but certainly more colorful than what we had seen farther west. I turned on the radio and as we approached Rhode Island the stations were more familiar. We listened to Salty Brine on WPRO. He had a wonderful mix of popular music and local news.

"Did you hear that?" I said.

"Ssh, listen!" Eddie turned his ear toward the radio. "He said an Ironworker was electrocuted."

"They didn't give the name!" I listened more closely.

"Ssh! Turn it up louder." Eddie slowed down.

"The injured man is from Fall River, Massachusetts. He's in the hospital in critical condition," the announcer said.

"Who is it? If he's from Fall River I must know him, I hope it's not one of my brothers," he said softly.

318

"The worker has been identified as Gerard Dupéré of Fall River," the announcer continued, "we'll have more news for you as it comes in."

"Gerry!" he said out loud. "That's my brother-in-law, that's Dora's husband."

"They said he was electrocuted," I remarked, "how can that happen?"

"If the crane that's holding the beam an Ironworker is on accidently goes too close to a live wire, the current can cause an arc, even if the crane doesn't touch the wire. Sometimes it can be fatal," Eddie explained.

"But the announcer said Gerry is in the hospital," I was trying to be hopeful.

"That's a good sign," he acknowledged, "but it could be a long recovery."

"It's going to be tough for Dora and their four children," I remarked.

"My sister is a fighter; she'll keep that family together no matter what," Eddie assured me.

"I love your sister," I said, "we'll get in touch with her today as soon as we can."

We missed the commuter traffic through the busy cities of Connecticut and Rhode Island and arrived at the Brightman Street Bridge, between Somerset and Fall River, Massachusetts around 10:30 a.m. From there we could see the spire of Saint Mary's Cathedral and the beautiful double domed spires of Saint Anne's Church. We were home within fifteen minutes. We parked our trailer by the curb in front of our apartment and introduced Torrey to his new permanent home. I pulled out some towels and some clean clothes from the trailer and prepared to take a well needed bath.

"Me first," I announced. "Please bring in the perishables from the ice box and put them in the refrigerator; I'll fix lunch while you have your turn."

319

EPILOGUE

At mid October; the trees were dressed in the beautiful colors of autumn. We spent the first few days unpacking the trailer and settling it down in Eddie's mother's yard for the winter, and visiting our parents. I still wasn't feeling great.

"Why don't you call the doctor," Eddie suggested.

"I'll be okay," I said. "I think I'm just a little tired from all that driving we did during the last couple of weeks. I'll be fine."

Eddie checked in at the Draft Board as per the directives on his notice. His orders were to report for duty on January 10th 1952. There was a lot to do before his departure date. We both went back to work. We looked for and found a Vet. He recommended for us to schedule Torrey to have his ears clipped before his next puppy shot, which we did. When he healed, although he was still a puppy, he was beginning to look more like a handsome Doberman with his sleek coat and his pointy ears. He lived to be more than 10 years old.

Eddie's brother-in-law had a long, slow recovery which involved the amputation of one leg, below the knee and the loss of three fingers. In spite of his disability, he and Dora managed to raise a beautiful family.

Just before Christmas, a few weeks before Eddie was due to leave, he insisted I visit my doctor for a check-up. The nausea and loss of appetite just weren't going away since we had returned from our adventure. I made an appointment with the Gynecologist for late afternoon, after work, and was totally surprised with his diagnosis.

"You're pregnant," he said. "You should be having your baby around July."

I was going to be a mother! I couldn't wait to get home and tell Eddie.

"Shnaitoy!" he said. "That's great." He kissed me.

"July?" He thought for a few minutes. "That kind of explains why you haven't been feeling so good."

"Yes it does," I agreed, "but the doctor said I should start feeling better soon."

It was wonderful news, but as it happens sometimes, even good news has unforeseen challenges. On the day before Eddie was scheduled to leave, I experienced complications. I called the doctor.

"The doctor said I need to have complete bed rest," I said as I hung up the phone

"You need to call your mother," Eddie said. "No, I'll call your mother. You get to bed."

I could only hear what Eddie was saying from our end of the line. "Okay, I'll get her clothes ready and take her down there tonight."

He hung up the phone. "Your mother said you can't stay alone, she insists you have to move in with her and Pop and your sister."

"Okay, but can't I wait until morning?" I pleaded, "I want to be here when your brother picks you up in the morning."

Eddie called my mother back and he made arrangements for my Dad to pick me up in the morning. I had my orders to stay in bed until my parents arrived to bring me to their house. Eddie reported for duty without knowing whether our little bundle of joy would ever be and I had no idea where he was being sent for basic training. It would be several weeks before I learned he had been drafted into the U.S. Marine Corps and he found out that our little one had passed her first challenge. We saw each other in April, and then in June, right after Dianne was born. Another separation ensued until October when I flew to California with our new little girl in tow. Dianne's brother David was born less than a year later in the hospital at Camp Pendleton. This was the beginning of our family which grew to include Paul, Edward, Jr., Anne-Louise, Russell and Joanne.

Eddie bought an old ark of a boat in 1962 which served as our summer weekend family vacation locale and Eddie's fishing vessel with his boys (and occasionally the girls). The winters dry-dock for the 'West Wind' was our back yard where she got her TLC in preparation for the following summer's adventures.

In 1982 we relocated to Hawai'i. Eddie had sustained a serious injury at work which made it difficult for him to endure the cold New England winters. Our youngest daughter came with us. Our two other daughters followed us there with their families and are still enjoying the Aloha lifestyle.

Eddie's illness had brought us to Hawai'i and Eddie's illness brought us back to New England. He passed away in 2006 leaving 21 grandchildren and a growing number of great-grandchildren.

We often reminisced about our romantic adventure and the wonderful places we had visited together. This book is the fulfillment of a promise I made to my 'Honey' that I would write this story to share with our family how our life and theirs began on our wonderful journey in our 'House on Wheels'.

Made in the USA
Middletown, DE
03 August 2018